VALUE AND CRISIS

Studies in Critical Social Sciences Book Series

Haymarket Books is proud to be working with Brill Academic Publishers (www.brill.nl) to republish the *Studies in Critical Social Sciences* book series in paperback editions. This peer-reviewed book series offers insights into our current reality by exploring the content and consequences of power relationships under capitalism, and by considering the spaces of opposition and resistance to these changes that have been defining our new age. Our full catalog of *SCSS* volumes can be viewed at https://www.haymarketbooks .org/series_collections/4-studies-in-critical-social-sciences.

VALUE AND CRISIS

Essays on Labour, Money and Contemporary Capitalism

ALFREDO SAAD-FILHO

Haymarket Books
Chicago, IL

First published in 2018 by Brill Academic Publishers, The Netherlands.
© 2018 Koninklijke Brill NV, Leiden, The Netherlands

Published in paperback in 2020 by
Haymarket Books
P.O. Box 180165
Chicago, IL 60618
773-583-7884
www.haymarketbooks.org

ISBN: 978-1-64259-190-3

Distributed to the trade in the US through Consortium Book Sales and
Distribution (www.cbsd.com) and internationally through Ingram Publisher
Services International (www.ingramcontent.com).

This book was published with the generous support of Lannan Foundation and
Wallace Action Fund.

Special discounts are available for bulk purchases by organizations and
institutions. Please call 773-583-7884 or email info@haymarketbooks.org for
more information.

Cover design by Jamie Kerry and Ragina Johnson.

Printed in United States.

10 9 8 7 6 5 4 3 2 1

Library of Congress Cataloging-in-Publication Data is available.

Contents

PART 2
Essays on Contemporary Capitalism

Acknowledgements

I am grateful to Marco di Tommaso and his colleagues at the University of Ferrara, who welcomed me generously during the final stages of preparation of this book. I am especially thankful to David Fasenfest for his friendship and continuing support. This book would not have been possible without him.

This book is for Lucas and Julia, with love.

Introduction

I shivered with anticipation when I first started reading *Capital*.[1] Not many of my comrades had ever opened 'The Big Book'. It was expensive, and said to be forbiddingly complicated. It was appropriate reading only for *really old* academics and for members of the Central Committee, and we – lower life forms, useful primarily for selling the Party newspaper – could not hope to make sense of its mysteries. It was dangerous even to try, as countless heads had been turned by their misreading of the Classics, often with disastrous consequences. More persistent comrades would eventually be told, in a quiet corner, that The Great Althusser had said that the first three chapters of *Capital 1* were both incomprehensible and unnecessary, and that readers should start from Chapter 4 instead. This was a bombshell. There was an unbearable tension between the alleged words of the great French scholar (whose writings none of us had actually read) and the revelations that must be contained in the Bible of Communism. How could Althusser have said *that*? Changing the order of the chapters implied that Marx had got it wrong – or, maybe, that Althusser thought that he was better than Marx. Who could we trust? And how to make a decision? We were used to clarity, and to simple texts. Stalin's style was especially acclaimed; Lenin was good too, but his works were more difficult. As for The Big Book, and intellectual endeavour more generally, well, kid, the District Secretary told me, you should leave this to Comrade x in São Paulo. He is in charge of research. And please do not forget to pick up your quota of newspapers on the way out and, this time, *do* make sure you sell all of them.

But read *Capital* I would, because I was certain that value theory could unlock the secrets of capitalism and show me things that I could barely imagine. Surprising revelations would spring out from the page fully formed, and beautifully constructed chains of reasoning would demonstrate logically that capitalism was doomed, why and – perhaps! – how and, even, when. But there was more, and just as important: The Big Book would surely prove that our Party was the *only* legitimate heir to the Marxist tradition in Brazil. *Capital* would demolish all arguments for capitalism, social democracy, reformism and Trotskyism, and the understanding of reality that would emerge from it would give us confidence in the future, making a little more bearable our gnawing

---

1 This book includes 15 essays written between 1993 and 2017, both published and unpublished; those that were published previously (and, especially, the single-authored pieces) have been revised to a greater or lesser extent, giving them independent value. Where appropriate, the original publication details are listed in a footnote on the first page of each essay.

fear of police dogs, truncheons, armed thugs, infiltrators, military officers bark-
ing orders, beatings in a dark cell and, ultimately, 'disappearance'.

Capital 1 turned out to be a very good book but, to my complete surprise and
slight annoyance, it was not forbidding at all. The analysis of the forms of value
in the first chapters was especially attractive, because it was both intellectually
cogent and aesthetically pleasing. The historical chapters were truly gripping,
and they offered a model for empirical work in current times. I finished the
first Volume not quite understanding what the fuss was about. That was a book
that anyone could read, and that everyone should try. I did, however, find it
a little troubling that there were no *revelations* in there. The book contained
clear analysis but it proffered no secrets; it talked about things that I could see,
but they were also quite general. It contained no specific insights about the
troubles of capitalism in the early 1980s. What now?

1   Method

It is easy to chuckle at my entire approach, but it was a product of the times
and of my youthful enthusiasm. For, Marxian political economy does not un-
veil 'secrets' to the initiated: there are none to share. Instead of spewing out
mystical revelations, Marx's analysis can help the reader identify *connections*
between aspects of reality that other theories tend to analyse separately. Using
value theory, it becomes easier to see systemic relationships across history and
between and within societies, allowing us to explain such social phenomena as
class, exploitation, imperialism, unemployment, crises and related structures
and processes that are not always immediately obvious. In contrast, mainstream economic theory deploys discrete models built with interchangeable
concepts, like Lego blocks, ultimately seeking to validate claims about the op-
timality of capitalism. The mainstream approach is flawed at two levels: it presumes that reality is an agglomeration of elements linked only externally and
more or less contingently, which is philosophically doubtful; and it subsumes
scientific enquiry underneath apologia, which is intellectually dishonest.

For Marx, reality is a concrete whole that determines its moments, rather
than being determined by them through some process of 'aggregation' of independent elements. In order to understand reality, we have to reconstruct in
thought the *real* structures of determination that link the whole and its parts.
This must be done in an orderly manner, starting from the most abstract and
fundamental structures and processes and their contradictory dynamics. This
should help us to understand real processes in historical time, which is what
shapes our lived experience. This systematic analysis, operating at increasingly

complex and concrete levels, can illuminate from different angles the links between distinct aspects of reality; it also allows the orderly introduction of concepts expressing these relations. In this sense, Marx's materialist dialectics is about bypassing artificial oppositions, finding the unity underpinning the moments of reality, drawing structured and historically specific connections where none may be apparent, and identifying the sources of dynamics and the tensions in the fabric of the present. This is very useful, and it can inform both scientific analysis and political activity – but it is not a magic key to the universe.

Although dialectics is centrally important for Marxian political economy, Marx never wrote in detail about his own method of analysis, or even about his method of presentation (which should be even easier to do). I believe that E.P. Thompson (1978, p. 306) was right, when he argued that:

> We have often been told that Marx had a 'method' … and that this constitutes the *essence* of Marxism. It is therefore strange that … Marx never wrote this essence down. Marx left many notebooks. Marx was nothing if not a self-conscious and responsible intellectual worker. If he had found the clue to the universe, he would have set a day or two aside to put it down. We may conclude from this that it was not written because *it could not be written*, any more than Shakespeare or Stendhal could have reduced their art to a clue. For it was not a method but a practice, and a practice learned through practising. So that, in this sense, dialectics can never be set down, nor learned by rote.

In other words, Marx's method is critically important for the achievement of his intellectual goals, but it does not exist in the abstract, as a disembodied set of rules of thought or presentation. Marx's method exists only concretely, through the analysis of specific problems. One can certainly extract regularities from a study of Marx's work, but this is not the same as deriving a set of philosophical principles that can be summarised into a couple of pages. Even a cursory reading of Marx's works suggests that he was far more flexible with respect to his methods of investigation and exposition than some of his Hegelian interpreters would wish.

2   The Theory of Value

The methodological flexibility outlined above does not imply that Marxian political economy is unstructured. Instead, it is articulated quite tightly and rigorously by *value* categories. The theory of value plays an essential role bringing out the connections between different aspects of capitalism; in this sense, it underpins the entire theoretical edifice of Marxist political economy. It follows that one cannot *do* Marxian political economy at any level of complexity except starting from value theory, and constantly checking the work against value categories, even if this is done only implicitly, or in the background. This is what gives Marx's political economy its analytical integrity and power, and the potential to explain systemic features of capitalism that other schools of thought have difficulty analysing. For example, the necessity and origin of money, the nature of technical progress, conflicts over the intensity of labour and the length of the working-day, the growth of the wage-earning class, uneven development, cycles, crises, and the impoverishment of the workers – not through the relentless decline in their living standards across all time (which is obviously untrue) but, instead, because of the shifting tensions between their socially constructed needs and what they can afford to buy, often leading to social divisions, marginalisation, debt, or overwork.

Marxian political economy is, then, the study of the production of the material conditions of reproduction of society. In this sense, value theory is a theory of *class* and *class relations*. When it is deployed to capitalism, Marxist analysis can explain the relations of exploitation and conflict that are intrinsic to this mode of production, despite the predominance of seemingly voluntary market exchanges; it can also explain the dynamics and the limits of this economic system.

From this angle, the theory of value is a theory of class, class relations, and exploitation in capitalism, with capitalism being understood as a mode of production, social reproduction and exploitation, distinguished by five interrelated elements. They are, first, the social form of the property relations, that is structured by the capitalist class monopoly of the means of production, and, therefore, the separation between the workers and the means of production. Second, the social form of labour, which is wage labour, imposed through the dispossession of the working class, the commodification of labour power and the generalisation of the wage relation. Third, the mode of labour control, that is based on the capitalist right to manage the performance of work. Fourth, the social form of the products of labour, as commodities, and, fifth, the goal of social production, which is profit.

It follows that *capital* can be approached – correctly – in three ways. First, capital is a totality engaged in self-expansion through the employment of wage labour for the production of commodities for profit. This implies that capital exists primarily at the level of society as a whole, that is, at the level of class, and its expanded reproduction is mediated by the market-led distribution of labour and its products. Second, capital is a relationship of social reproduction in which labour power, the products of labour, and goods and services more generally, are commodities. Third, capital is a class relation of exploitation defined by the ability of the capitalist class to compel the working class to produce more than it consumes or controls, and the capitalist command of the surplus, which includes the investment funds. In these circumstances, the products of labour generally take the value form, and economic exploitation is based on the extraction of surplus value.

The class interpretation of Marx's value theory that is being outlined here starts from these categories as historically determined modes of existence of capitalist social relations, in order, then, to explain systematically the process of production of the material conditions of social reproduction in this type of society. This value theory is, necessarily, dynamic, and it is incompatible with the organising concept of 'equilibrium' that is central to neoclassical economics. Instead, the focus is on the identification of forces and tendencies, and their interaction with the inevitable counter-tendencies, leading to complex outcomes in historical time. Finally, this approach recognises the limits of abstract analysis, and the need to incorporate historically-specific material, whether reflecting broad outcomes, such as the stages of capitalism, or more concrete aspects such as country-specific relations between industry and finance or the balance of class or other forces.

In doing this, Marx's value theory can help us to overcome the fragmentation of the experience of exploitation, and it can show that capitalist production necessarily involves social conflicts in production and in distribution. It can also inform action to end this system of production, not only as the implication of consistent theoretical work but, especially, and much more urgently, in order to articulate the possibility of human freedom, and even of biological survival given the rapid environmental degradation promoted by modern capitalism.

The interpretation of Marx's work outlined above is orthodox in the sense of Lukács, that is, it seeks to follow Marx's method closely, but it does not assume that Marx's every scribble was right, or that every silence implies his disapproval. As Agnes Heller (1976, p. 22) rightly put it,

> there is no such thing as an interpretation of Marx which is proof against being 'contradicted' by means of quotations ... What interests me is the main tendency (or tendencies) of his thought.

That seems right to me.

3   Systems of Accumulation

The theory of value provides a grand theoretical framework for detailed studies of capitalist realities.[2] This is necessary for reasons of internal consistency;
it also helps to avoid the twin risks of inconsistency ('anything goes if I happen to fancy it') and excessive focus on short-term description at the expense
of insight (low-level 'journalism' instead of analysis). Only grand theories can
illuminate long-term patterns, structures, systemic contradictions and historical shifts that may be difficult to discern, hard to understand, or obscured by
countless events of fleeting relevance. Those patterns and structures frame the
progression of the concrete over time; that is, the making of history.

The system of accumulation (SoA) is the instantiation, configuration, phase,
form, or mode of existence (these terms are used interchangeably in what follows) of capitalism in a given conjuncture. The SoA is determined by the class
relations encapsulated in the mode of extraction, accumulation and distribution of (surplus) value, and the institutional structures and processes through
which those relations reproduce themselves, including the political forms of
representation of interests and the patterns of social metabolism.[3] Since the
SoAs express the form of the capital relation relatively concretely, at a specific
time and place, they are intrinsically variegated.

Examination of the SoA should include, first, the forms of the state, property, law, labour, exploitation, markets, technology, credit, money, distribution and competition, and the relationships between capital accumulation,
social structure, the natural environment, and the rest of the world. Second,
the forms of political representation and the hegemonic ideology legitimising the SoA and stabilising incompatible interests. These historically constituted structures and processes can be examined only concretely, through the
political regimes, policy choices and institutional histories in which they are
embedded.

Accumulation within each SoA is limited by *constraints* expressing the contradictions of capital in specific contexts and setting limits to economic and
social reproduction. The constraints are contingent and historically specific,
rather than permanent or logically necessary. They must be identified empirically, and they are usually addressed by public policy. While the existence
of constraints to accumulation is widely recognised in the literature, each

---

2   'Grand' theory is used here in the sense of Gallie (1956) and Merton (1968); see also Saad-
    Filho (2000b).
3   The SoA is obviously a more concrete form of the mode of production. For the latter, see
    Banaji (2010), Byres (1995), Lenin (1899) and Ste. Croix (1984).

constraint is usually examined in isolation, as if they were unrelated elements blocking an otherwise undifferentiated process of 'growth'. This is misguided. The constraints are embedded within the SoA, and they help to define it. Since the SoA and the constraints are inseparable in reality, they must be analysed together.

Identification of the constraints to accumulation can usefully start from the circuit of industrial capital as outlined in *Capital* Volume 1, that is, $M - C < {}^{MP}_{LP} \ldots P \ldots C' - M'$, where M is money, MP is means of production (land, buildings, machines, material inputs, and so on), LP is labour power, ...P... is production, C is commodities, and M' is greater than M. This suggests that typical constraints include (but are not limited to) labour, finance and resource allocation, the balance of payments, and the institutional setting (the property structure, mode of competition, role of the state, and so on).

At a further level of concreteness, the *accumulation strategy* includes the spectrum of economic, social and other policies securing the reproduction of the SoA, managing, dislocating or transforming the constraints, and shaping the restructuring of capital in a specific conjuncture.

4 Neoliberalism

Recognition that capitalism exists in historical time in the form of specific systems of accumulation is key for the identification of its phases, for example, Keynesianism in the post-war 'golden age', different forms of developmentalism (e.g., Latin American import-substituting industrialisation in the 1930s–70s or East Asian export-oriented industrialisation in the 1960s–80s), and, currently, neoliberalism in most of the world. The transition from various systems of accumulation to a more-or-less homogeneous global neoliberalism is one of the defining events of contemporary international political economy.[4]

In contrast with much of the literature, then, neoliberalism is not simply a set of economic and social policies (privatisation, the 'rollback' of the welfare state, and so on). It is that, and much more; neoliberalism includes an accumulation strategy, a form of regulation of social and economic reproduction, and a mode of exploitation and social domination. They are based on the systematic use of state power to impose, under the ideological veil of non-intervention, a hegemonic project of recomposition of the rule of capital in each area of social

---

4 For an overview of Keynesian policies and experiences, see Clarke (1988). Neoliberalism is critically scrutinised by the contributions in Saad-Filho and Johnston (2005); see also the essays in Part 2 of this book.

life. This project is guided by the imperatives of the international reproduction of capital, represented by the financial markets and the interests of US capital.

The rise of neoliberalism was closely related to the perceived failure of Keynesianism, developmentalism and Soviet-style socialism in the 1980s, the evolution of economic theory after the exhaustion of the so-called neoclassical synthesis and monetarism, the rise of conservative political forces in the US and the UK, and the recomposition of class relations in these countries. These social, economic, ideological and political shifts spread across the global periphery through persuasion (including the images of success beamed by the media, the slanted development of economic and political theory, and the deliberate promotion of useful intellectual fashions), and coercion.

Neoliberalism institutionalises the pre-eminence of financial market imperatives on key aspects of macroeconomic policy-making. In this system of accumulation, finance is *not* an independent sector 'competing' against industrial capital. In advanced neoliberal economies with developed financial systems, finance is the pool of liquid capital held by the financial *and* industrial sectors and, at a more abstract level, it is the mode of existence of capital in general. The liberalisation of domestic finance and international capital flows, which is an essential aspect of every transition to neoliberalism, promotes the integration between industrial and interest-bearing capital and between domestic and international capital. In this sense, the frequently noticed inability of the neoliberal reforms to foster higher levels of investment or rapid GDP growth is irrelevant. Similarly, the common critique that the neoliberal reforms increase the returns of financial capital at the expense of industry is a red herring. For the primary purpose of the neoliberal reforms is *not* to promote economic growth, reduce inflation or, even, expand the portfolio choices of the financial institutions. The reforms are meant, instead, to subordinate domestic accumulation to international imperatives, promote the microeconomic (firm-level) integration between competing capitals, mediated by finance, and expand the scope for financial system intermediation of the financing of the state. The consequences of these shifts for macroeconomic performance, welfare, political democracy, and so on are entirely secondary.

The transfer of the main levers of accumulation to (international) capital, mediated by (US-led) financial institutions, and regulated by (US-controlled) international organisations established the material basis of neoliberalism. In this system of accumulation, stable capital flows are essential not only to close the balance of payments, but also to finance domestic activity and the public sector. In turn, the stability of these flows is conditional upon compliance with the neoliberal policy prescriptions. Internationalised finance is the main instrument for the imposition, around the world, of this project of accumulation and social domination in which production and finance are inseparably linked. At a further remove, the prominence of finance is symptomatic of the subsumption of sectional interests by the demands of capital as a whole.

It follows that there can be no presumption that there is an antagonistic relationship between production and finance under neoliberalism; similarly, there should be no expectation that industrial capital might change its mind, 'rebel' against finance and push – for the sake of argument – for the restoration of Keynesianism. Under neoliberalism, industrial capital is *subsumed* to finance; it has a stake in the neoliberal model, and is committed to the reproduction of the system of accumulation. It benefits from the suppression of the demands of the working class, the enhanced international connections established under neoliberalism, the flows of labour, technology, culture, law and patterns of consumption, and so on.

Once the material basis of neoliberalism has been identified, above, two things become clear. First, it is often argued that the increasing frequency of crises under neoliberalism, including the spectacular Great Financial Crisis starting in 2007, show that this system of accumulation is flawed. This is true in the same sense that, in the abstract, economic crises show that capitalism is a flawed mode of production. However, just as crises offer the opportunity to restore balance in capitalist accumulation, crises also play a constructive – or, perhaps, constitutive – role under neoliberalism, because they help to impose policy discipline on governments, and they compel both capitalists and workers to behave in ways that support the reproduction of neoliberalism. In this sense, crises can help to fine-tune the system of accumulation, instead of merely corroding it from within.

Second, deteriorating economic performance, worsening distribution of income and wealth and repeated crises have robbed neoliberalism of political legitimacy, and contributed to the election of several governments advocating alternative policies. However, they have often failed, and spectacularly so in the recent (at the time of writing) cases of Syriza, in Greece, and the Workers' Party, in Brazil. These setbacks show that transcending neoliberalism is both complex and costly. Beyond these practical difficulties, those failures also show that moving away from neoliberalism, or transcending it, is not primarily a subjective problem of identifying 'better' industrial, financial or monetary policies, even if they 'ought' to be in the interests of industrial capital or any other powerful constituency.

Neoliberalism is a stable system of accumulation. The neoliberal transitions have restructured the process of production of the conditions of material reproduction of society, and transformed both social structures and the institutions, leading to the fragmentation of the working class at the national and international levels, the transnational integration of the circuits of capital accumulation, a whole range of institutional and economic policy reforms, for example privatisations and changes in Central Bank policy, and the transfer of control over resource allocation from governments to finance. Since neoliberalism is not merely limited to ideology or policy choice, but has developed its own material basis, it cannot be rejected simply by voting for something else.

Having emphasised the strengths of neoliberalism, above, it is also important to point out six of its limitations. First, neoliberal policies are guided by the imperative of 'business confidence', meaning, in practice, the short-term interests of finance. This is unsatisfactory, because confidence is intangible, elusive and self-referential, and subject to sudden and arbitrary changes. Neoliberal governments and their mouthpieces invariably overestimate the levels of investment that can be generated by adhering to the neoliberal project. Second, neoliberal policies systematically favour finance and large capitals at the expense of smaller capitals and the workers. The ensuing transfer of resources to the rich, the global growth slowdown associated with this system of accumulation, and the mounting environmental disasters unfolding under neoliberalism, have led to adverse consequences that are, increasingly, rejected politically. Third, economic 'deregulation' disintegrates the established systems of provision, undermines the co-ordination of economic activity, reduces state policy-making capacity, creates undesirable employment patterns and precludes the use of policy instruments for the implementation of socially determined priorities. 'Market freedom' increases economic uncertainty, volatility and vulnerability to crisis. Fourth, the neoliberal reforms introduce mutually reinforcing policies that destroy jobs and traditional industries that are defined, often *ex post*, as being inefficient. The depressive impact of their elimination is rarely compensated by the rapid development of new industries, leading to structural unemployment, greater poverty and marginalisation and a more fragile balance of payments. Fifth, the neoliberal policies are not self-correcting. Failure to achieve their stated aims generally leads to the extension and intensification of the 'reforms', with the excuse of ensuring implementation and the promise of 'imminent' success this time around. Finally, neoliberalism is inimical to economic democracy, and it hollows out political democracy, making this system of accumulation vulnerable to political challenges.

5   Outline of the Book

This book is part of my continuing attempt to answer some of the questions that were sketched above: what is capitalism and what is neoliberalism, how do they reproduce themselves both in theory and in daily practice, how to understand the rooting of grand historical patterns into the texture of our lives, how to transcend them, and so on. At a further remove, what can Marxist political economy offer that is, at the same time, distinctive, analytically powerful, and politically useful? There are strong tensions between these demands. Many insights offered by Marxist political economists are not unique, and the more concrete and politically relevant the analysis, the murkier become the distinctions between schools of thought. For example, many Marxian analyses of neoliberalism and financialisation can be undistinguishable from those advanced by Post-Keynesian writers, while Marxian deconstructions of 'development' can merge almost seamlessly into, on the one hand, the insights of Latin American structuralism and Evolutionary political economy and, on the other hand, into constructivist, post-modern or Foucauldian approaches. At the same time, the political insights of many Marxists will have much in common with a wide spectrum of progressive views; in contrast, sectarian analysts – Marxists or otherwise – will always find it hard to agree with anyone else.

We should be grateful for those analytical convergences. Academic work is, in large measure, the art of the logical and the historical, on which heterodox approaches will tend to find much in common; in contrast, politics it the art of the possible, in which effective steps are often very small, especially in phases of long historical retreat, and achievements are conditional upon broad alliances.

To my youthful disappointment, Karl Marx does not offer ready-made answers to the urgent problems of today. However, his writings provide insightful analyses of the inner workings of capitalism and the articulation between different aspects of this economic system, and they show the enormous potential of capitalism for constructive as well as spectacularly destructive outcomes. From this vantage point, Marx's writings can throw light upon the problems of our age, the boundaries of the possible solutions, and the strategies to transcend the limitations of the present. This is all that can be expected from social theory.

This book includes fifteen essays grouped into two parts; the first on value theory, and the second on neoliberalism. Part 1 includes eight essays. The first provides a very simple overview of the main categories of Marxian political economy. The second examines value theory in greater depth and detail. The third focuses on Marx's theory of money, through a review of his critique of 'labour-money'. The fourth focuses on a poorly studied but centrally important aspect of Marx's theory of value, concerning the technical, organic and value compositions of capital. The fifth reviews the vexed issue of the so-called 'transformation problem'. The sixth critically examines the structure and potential contribution of the 'new interpretation' of value theory. The seventh returns to the theory of money at a greater level of complexity, reviewing the Marxian and Post-Keynesian 'horizontalist' theories of credit money. The eighth surveys the most important Marxist theories of inflation.

Part 2 includes the following seven essays. The ninth reviews key features of contemporary (neoliberal) capitalism, and outlines the Marxist critique. The tenth and eleventh offer very different examinations of neoliberalism, as the contemporary form or mode of existence of capitalism. The twelfth critically reviews the relationship between neoliberalism and political democracy. The thirteenth examines the institutions, policies and ideologies of monetary policy under neoliberalism, through the notion of a 'new monetary policy consensus'. The fourteenth turns to patterns of development under neoliberalism, focusing on the relationship between the Washington and Post-Washington Consensus. Finally, the fifteenth reviews the causes and implications of the current 'Great Financial Crisis', in terms of its roots in, and implications for, neoliberalism.

PART 1

Essays on the Theory of Value

∴

Marxist Economics

This essay[1] explains the essential elements of Marxist economics or, preferably, Marxist political economy (MPE).[2] They include Marx's explanation of how and why wage workers are exploited, the systematic form taken by technical change through the growing use of machinery, the determinants of wages, prices and distribution, the role of the financial system and the recurrence of economic crises. This analysis provides the foundation for Marx's systemic critique of capitalism and his conclusion that the contradictions and limitations of this exploitative mode of production could be overcome only through the transition to a new mode, communism, through revolution if necessary. (In what follows, the terms communism and socialism are used as synonymous. For Marx, strictly speaking, socialism is the first or transition stage to communism, the latter taking an indeterminate time to be constructed).

If such approaches, concepts and conclusions appear alien, it is because they have been marginalised in most academic institutions and in the media, to the extent that most economics departments completely bypass MPE and its potential contribution to a critical understanding of contemporary society. In the current age of neoliberalism, mainstream (orthodox or neoclassical) economics has tightened its grip on the discipline, dismissing heterodoxy in general and MPE in particular as failing the tests of logical, mathematical and/ or statistical rigour. Yet, the shortcomings of the mainstream and the econom- ic, environmental and geopolitical catastrophes spawned by capitalism have nurtured the search for alternatives among students of economics and, even more so, in other social sciences that address economic analysis more toler- antly than economics itself. In a world precariously balanced and afflicted by recurrent as well as persistent crises, the case for communism is open to be made, and it can rest upon a Marxist analysis both for its critique of capitalism, and for the light it sheds on the potential for alternatives. Such a view stands in sharp contrast to the mainstream for which commitment to, the market is entirely to the fore without questioning whether the market system, and the class relations it represents, remains appropriate.

---

1   Originally published as 'Marxist Economics', in L. Fischer, J. Hasell, J.C. Proctor, D. Uwakwe, Z.W. Perkins and C. Watson (eds.) *Rethinking Economics: An Introduction to Pluralist Econom- ics*. London: Routledge, 2018, pp. 19–32 (with B. Fine).

2   For a systematic overview of MPE for the beginner, see Fine and Saad-Filho (2016). For a more advanced survey, see Fine and Saad-Filho (2013).

This is also a timely moment for the historical renewal of interest in MPE as it has always been validated as well as inspired by downturns in the capitalist economy. Nonetheless, it should also be acknowledged that Marx admired the dynamism of capitalism in developing both levels of production and productivity, what he called the productive forces, not least as he saw such developments as providing the potential for socialist alternatives both within capitalism itself (think of the welfare state and nationalised industries) and through radical break with it. He was also acutely aware that capitalism's extraordinary capacity to develop the productive forces is both constrained and misdirected by their commitment to private profit as opposed to collective forms of ownership, control, distribution and consumption. The consequences are evident in the dysfunctions and inequities of contemporary life.

1   The Method and Approach of Marxist Political Economy

At the time of writing, with the Global Financial Crisis (GFC) ongoing since 2007, many students have realised the limitations of what they are being taught as economics, and are actively campaigning for pluralism in their curriculum and for the teaching of alternative approaches, MPE amongst them. On the other hand, what they are being and have been taught as neoclassical economics has not only gone to the opposite extreme in terms of its own extraordinary narrowness but has exhibited limited willingness let alone capacity to allow for alternatives. This is despite the loss of intellectual legitimacy that has accompanied the GFC: not only did the mainstream not see it coming but it cannot explain let alone remedy the crisis after the event.

Student grievances with neoclassical economics range over a number of its features. First, and foremost, neoclassical economics depends upon mathematical models and a corresponding deductive method at the almost exclusive expense of other forms of reasoning. By the same token, this method is both ahistorical and asocial, most obviously in depending upon production and utility functions, that bear little or no relationship to the society to which they are applied. Slaves and slave owners, serfs and lords, men and women (across all societies and times) as well as capitalists and workers, are indiscriminately presumed to be motivated in exactly the same way, to maximise their self-interest, whether expressed as profit, 'utility' or whatever. By contrast, whilst economic motives play an enormous role in MPE, how they are formed and pursued in different social and historical circumstances (slavery is not capitalism, the home is not the marketplace) is of paramount importance. Indeed, for MPE, it is imperative that the concepts used and developed correspond to their object of study, as will be shown below for the centrepiece of MPE, the labour theory of value (LTV).

The arbitrary and perverse assumptions that follow from its dependence upon *homo oeconomicus*, rationality, given preferences and single motivation of self-interest are other aspects of dissatisfaction with the mainstream. This is not just because these starting points defy our experience but they also preclude many vital questions such as why do we have the preferences we have, and why do we behave in the ways that we do. Paradoxically, the mainstream's much vaunted celebration of the freedom of choice of the individual in market society is nothing of the sort. Within that theory, what the individual chooses is entirely pre-determined by given preferences (or utility function) without space for either inventiveness or identity on the part of the individual subject, thereby allowing supply and demand to be mathematically and rigidly derived.

In contrast, MPE, like much other social science other than mainstream economics, asks how such individual subjectivity is conditioned by social structures. MPE takes social classes rather than individuals as its starting point for understanding the nature of the economy both historically and socially. As already suggested by reference to slavery and capitalism, and so on, there are clear differences between forms of economic organisation. In particular, class society is about who works, how, and for whom, with what consequences and, not least, who gets to exploit whom in the sense of appropriating surplus production without having worked for it except through ownership or exaggerated rewards for exercising control and management. Just as under a monarchy, not everyone can be the king or queen, so not everyone can choose to be a capitalist under capitalism otherwise there would be no workers. For capitalism, then, MPE starts with the broad and fundamental distinction between those who are wage workers and those who employ them. It has long been recognised, not uniquely by MPE, that capitalism is based on exploitation in the sense that workers do not receive in wages all that they produce. Even setting aside the resources needed for the renewal of production and gross investment, 'rewards' also accrue to property owners in the form of profit, interest and rent as well as bloated 'salaries' for the functionaries of capitalist production and exchange and social control. As will be seen below, the uniqueness of MPE lies in how it conceptualises and explains such exploitation and draws out its consequences for understanding the nature, dynamics, contradictions and limitations of capitalism.

The contrast with neoclassical economics could not be greater. While the latter perceives the economy as a collection of individuals more or less efficiently organised through the market, MPE is systemic (holistic), identifying economy-wide structures, processes, agents and relations and classes as opposed to individuals simply related through market supply and demand. Then, on this basis, forces for change are identified that drive the economy and create tensions in doing so that can at most be temporarily resolved; that is, the capitalist economy is driven to grow but can only do so by creating the possibility of crises.

In this respect, there are two further contrasts between MPE and the mainstream. First is that it is inappropriate to understand the capitalist (or any other) economy in terms of 'equilibrium', since it is never achieved in practice, and its analytical use obscures the sources of conflicts and dynamics within the economy. Second is that the forces for change have to be identified and analysis taken further in understanding their implications and how they interact with one another. Within MPE, this is a source of continuing controversy ranging over whether, for example, the leading drivers of the economy are wages or profits, how parasitic a role is played by finance, and what is happening to the determinants of profitability.

2   The Labour Theory of Value

At the heart of debates within MPE and between MPE and other schools of thought in economics is the nature and validity of Marx's LTV. For many, the LTV is to be understood as a theory of price, for example, do commodities exchange at prices that can be derived algebraically from the labour time required to produce them? Note, first, that such labour time does not just involve what is called the 'living' labour or the time of those working on the current product, but also the ('dead', 'embodied' or 'congealed') labour that has gone previously into producing the raw materials and equipment required in production.

Many political economists have been attracted by the LTV, not least Adam Smith and David Ricardo, but each has found it unsatisfactory. One reason given is that it takes no account of the different capital intensities of production, that is, commodities produced with a higher (lower) quantity of capital (e.g., capital-intensive nuclear energy in contrast with the more labour-intensive construction industry) or which take longer (shorter) to produce (aeroplanes in contrast with restaurant meals). In either case, commodities should have a price including a premium (discount) corresponding to the amount of capital advanced and the time for which it is advanced, and on which a larger (smaller) profit will be expected in order to equalise the rate of profit of the advanced capitals. Given these logical imperatives, both Smith and Ricardo realised that prices will systematically diverge from the labour time taken to produce them. At a further remove, (changes in) demand will affect prices, however temporarily, as will rents and monopolies.

For reasons such as these, the LTV has been subject to longstanding rejection, even from those sympathetic to other aspects of MPE, especially its emphasis on class and exploitation. Significantly, Marx himself was well aware of these problems and did take them into account. How and whether satisfactorily remains a key element of debate if not covered here in detail.

There is, though, good reason for such debate because what fundamentally divides interpretations of Marx are two different ways of understanding the LTV, and these are irreconcilable. One proceeds as laid out above. How well can (labour) value explain price quantitatively – not very well so either modify or reject it. The other, and reflecting Marx's own approach, begins from a very different sort of question. Under what circumstances does value as measured by labour time exist within society rather than simply in minds of would-be economists as a good or bad explanation of the level of prices? Marx's answer is deceptively simple: only in a (basically capitalist) society where commodity production is pervasive do different types of labour become measured against one another by society itself through the exchange mechanism. Whatever labour has been contributed to the production of commodities either in the past or in the present is thrown into the great melting pot of exchange. And all the different types of labour are rendered as equivalent to, or, more exactly measurable against, one another in terms of the prices they command.

Of course, this does not mean that all labours count the same. The more skilled will count as more labour than the less skilled, and labours of the same skill and even similar tasks may count differently as price once account is taken of any number of considerations such as the capital-intensity of production (see above), presence of monopoly, payment of rent, etc. But the prior issue for Marx is to recognise that capitalist commodity production is a system that connects production by wage labour with the buying and selling of commodities for profit, and he sets himself, and us, the task of tracing the journeys taken by the products of that labour in production to their distant destinations in exchange.

As stated earlier, this is far from being a theory of equilibrium prices – the basis on which Marx's value theory tends to be rejected. More specifically, Marx's first concern is with how a system based on free market exchange can generate profits while, simultaneously, concealing the capture of surplus labour from the wage workers. In contrast, under slavery or feudalism the exploitation of the direct producers is obvious. Marx's second concern is with how profits can increase, especially through the development of new methods and processes of production under capitalism (from simple manufacture to the factory system, for example, something that tends to be overlooked by casual use of the ubiquitous production function). Furthermore, what it is like to be a worker under capitalism both individually and collectively, in the workplace as well as beyond it in society more generally (for example, what are the implications for the family, civil society and the state, that the economy is capitalistic). Marx's third concern is with the economic and social consequences of how capitalist production evolves (increasingly under corporate or, today, financial control, for example), and how such developments prepare the ground for moving beyond capitalism.

3   Commodities, Labour and Value

To meet these concerns, Marx begins his analysis on the basis that commodities exchange at their values (their labour time of production). This allows him to uncover exploitation under capitalism without entering into complex considerations of price formation. His explanation rests upon specifying the class relations of capitalism, notably between capital and labour. Whilst, as a class, capitalists own the means of production, the class of labour can only gain access to work and a reasonable livelihood by selling their ability to work as wage-labourers. For Marx, the distinction between the ability to work and the work itself is decisive in understanding capitalism, and it is the capacity to work, which he called labour-power, that is bought and sold, not labour itself (which is activity of work rather than something that can be bought and sold like cheese). With the wage being paid for labour-power, how much labour is actually performed and with what quality is a matter of conflict between capital and labour (although there are other conflicts too such as over levels of wages and working conditions). By analogy, you can hire a car (like you hire a worker) but that is quite different from how far, fast and safely you drive it (or him/her).

Consider, then, Marx's reconstruction of the LTV, starting with commodities. These are goods and services produced for sale, rather than consumption by their own producers. Commodities have two common features. First, they are use values: they have some useful characteristic. The nature of its use, whether it derives from physiological need, social convention, fancy or vice is irrelevant in the first instance as far as its value is concerned. Second, commodities have exchange value (they can command a price on a market): they can, in principle, be exchanged for other commodities in specific ratios. Exchange value or price shows that, despite their distinct use values, commodities are equivalent (at least in one respect) to one another in terms of commanding a monetary equivalent.

The double nature of commodities, as use values with exchange value, has implications for labour. On the one hand, commodity-producing labour is what is termed concrete labour, that is labour producing specific use values such as clothes, food or books (performed, respectively, by tailors, farmers and pub-lishers). On the other hand, when goods are produced for exchange they have a relationship of equivalence to one another. In this case, labour is also 'abstract' or general in some sense (the amount of labour is what counts not what type it is). Just like commodities themselves, commodity-producing labour is both general and specific. Concrete labours exist in all societies because people al-ways need to produce a variety of use values for their own survival. In contrast, abstract labour as just described is historically specific; it exists only where commodities are being produced *and* exchanged.

Abstract labour has two distinct aspects – qualitative and quantitative – that should be analysed separately. First, abstract labour derives from the re-lationship of equivalence between commodities. Even though it is historically contingent, abstract labour has real existence; it is not merely a construct of the economist's mind, as is shown by the possibility in principle of actually exchanging the product of one's labour for the product of anyone else's labour (through money). The ability of money to purchase any commodity shows that money represents the presence of this abstract labour.

Second, the reality of exchange values shows that there is a quantitative relationship between the abstract labours necessary to produce each type of different commodity. However, this relationship is not directly visible in the sense that, when we purchase something, the different types of labour that have gone into making it, and how they were performed, and how much they count, are not apparent in the price. However hard we look at a commodity, we cannot see how it has been produced, physically to a large extent, and how much and many concrete labours have gone into it, let alone the social rela-tions between capital and labour in the production process. This is so for mar-ket participants themselves as well as for those scholars of the economy purely concerned with supply and demand.

For example, in his *Inquiry into the Nature and Causes of the Wealth of Nations*, first published in 1776, Adam Smith claimed that in 'early and rude' societies goods exchanged directly in proportion to the labour time neces-sary to produce them. For example, if it usually costs twice the labour to kill a beaver as to kill a deer, one beaver should 'naturally' exchange for two deer. However, Smith believes that this simple pricing rule breaks down when in-struments and machines are used in production. The reason is that, in addition to the workers, the owners of 'stock' (capital) also have a claim to the value of the product in the form of profit (and landowners to a rent). Since these claims must be added to the price, the LTV becomes invalid.

Marx disagrees with Smith, for two reasons. First, 'simple' or 'direct' ex-change (in proportion to labour time of production) is not typical of any hu-man society; this is simply a construct of Smith's mind – in his rude society, you would just go and catch whatever you wanted rather than specialise for exchange which requires a commodity producing society. Second, and more importantly for our purposes, although commodity exchanges are based on the quantitative relations of equivalence between different types of labour, this relationship is indirect. In other words, whereas Smith abandons his own 'labour theory of value' at the first hurdle (the obscuring presence of profits and rents to the dependence of value on labour time), Marx develops his own value analysis rigorously and systematically into a cogent explanation of the values that underpin commodity prices under capitalism.

Indeed, Marx called commodity fetishism the limitation of the understanding of commodities to the surface (self-evident) relations between price and use (or utility) as opposed to labour and other invisible relations by which commodities come to the market. For Marx, the significance of his theory of commodity fetishism lay in how it went beyond treating exchange relations as relations between things (the prices at which goods exchange with one another) to unravel the social relations between those who produce those things. In short, piercing through commodity fetishism allows for the exploitative relations attached to capitalism to be revealed.

4   Capital and Capitalism

Commodities have been produced for thousands of years. However, in non-capitalist societies commodity production is generally marginal, and most goods and services are produced for direct consumption rather than for market exchange. It is different in capitalist societies. *A first distinguishing feature of capitalism is the generalised production of commodities*. Under capitalism, the market is foremost, most workers are employed in the production of commodities, and firms and households regularly purchase commodities as production inputs and final goods and services, respectively.

A second distinguishing feature of capitalism is the production of commodities for profit. In capitalist society, commodity owners typically do not merely seek to make a living – they want to (and must) make profit (to survive). Therefore, the production decisions and the level and structure of employment, and the living standards of the society, are grounded in the profitability of enterprise.

A third distinguishing feature of capitalism is wage labour. Like commodity production and money, wage labour first appeared thousands of years ago. However, before capitalism, wage labour was always limited, and other forms of labour were predominant. For example, co-operation within small social groups, slavery in the great empires of antiquity, serfdom under feudalism, and independent production for subsistence or exchange, have prevailed across all types of society. Wage labour has become the typical mode of labour only recently; three or four hundred years ago in England, and often much later elsewhere.

Neoclassical economic theory defines capital as an ensemble of things, including means of production, money and financial assets. More recently, knowledge and community relations have been designated as human or social capital. For Marx, this is nonsensical. Those objects, assets and human attributes, have always existed, whereas capitalism is historically new. It is misleading to extend the concept of capital where it does not belong, as if it were valid universally or throughout history. A horse, hammer or one million dollars may or may not be capital; that depends on the context in which they are used. If they are engaged in production for profit through the direct or indirect employment of wage labour, they are capital; otherwise, they are simply animals, tools or banknotes if in their own, different contexts.

For MPE, capital involves class relation but these relations are often reduced to their (immediately apparent) physical attributes or, as Marx puts it, as relations between things rather than people. Moreover, capital is not merely a general relationship between the producers and sellers of commodities, or a market relationship of supply and demand. Instead, it involves *class relations of exploitation*. This social relationship includes two classes, defined by their ownership, control and use of the means of production (MP), or inputs, whether human or physical. On the one hand, are the capitalists, who own the MP, employ workers and own what they produce; on the other hand are the wage workers, who are employed by the capitalist, and engage directly in production without any ownership rights over what they produce.

Most people do not freely choose to become wage workers. Historically, wage labour expands, and capitalist development takes off, only as the peasants, artisans and the self-employed lose control of the means of production, or as non-capitalist forms of production become unable to provide for subsistence. The much-repeated claim that the wage contract is the outcome of a free bargain between equals is, therefore, both partial and misleading. Even though the workers are free to apply for one job rather than another, they are almost always in a weak bargaining position when facing their (prospective) employers. The wage workers need money to attend to the pressing needs of their household. This is both the stick and the carrot with which capitalist society forces the workers to sign up 'freely' to the labour contract, 'spontaneously' turn up for work, and 'voluntarily' satisfy the expectations of their line managers.

5   From Value to Surplus Value

The capitalists combine the inputs to production, generally purchased from other capitalists, with the labour of wage workers hired on the market to produce commodities for sale at a profit. The circuit of industrial capital captures the essential aspects of factory production, farm labour, office work and other forms of capitalist production. It can be represented as follows:

$$M - C <^{MP}_{LP} ...P...C' - M'$$

The circuit starts when the capitalist advances money (M) to purchase two types of commodities (C), inputs (MP) and labour-power (LP). During production (... P ...) the workers transform the inputs into new commodities (C'), that are sold for more money (M').

Marx calls surplus value the difference between M' and M. Surplus value is the source of industrial and commercial profit and other forms of surplus revenue such as interest and rent. We now identify the source of surplus value, which Marx considered one of his most significant achievements.

Surplus value cannot arise purely out of exchange. Although some can profit from the sale of commodities above their value (unequal exchange), for example unscrupulous traders and speculators, this is not possible for every seller for two reasons. First, the sellers are also buyers. If every seller surcharged customers by 10 per cent, say, such gains would be lost to the suppliers, and no extra profit would arise from this exercise. Therefore, although some can become rich by robbing or outwitting others, this is not possible for society as a whole, and unequal exchanges cannot provide a general explanation for profit: 'cheating' only transfers value, it does not create new value. Second, competition tends to increase supply in any sector offering exceptional profits, eventually eliminating the advantages of individual luck or cunning. Therefore, surplus value (or profit in general) must be explained for society as a whole, or systemically, rather than relying on individual merit or expertise.

Now, inspection of the circuit of capital shows that surplus value is the difference between the value of the output, C', and the value of the inputs, MP and LP. Since this difference cannot be due to unequal exchange, the value increment must derive from somewhere in the process of production. More specifically, for Marx, it arises from the use in production of a commodity which must have the property not only of being able to create new value but also more new value than it did itself cost. Which input is this?

Starting from the means of production (physical inputs), Marx is very clear that, on their own, the transformation of the inputs into the output does not create new value. The presumption that the transformation of things into other things could produce value regardless of context or human intervention confuses the two aspects of the commodity, use value and exchange value. It implies that an apple tree, when it produces apples from soil, sunlight and water, creates not only the use value but also the value of the apples, and that ageing, for example, spontaneously adds value (rather than merely use value) to wine without any further labour to do so. The naturalisation of value relations begs the question of why commodities have value, whereas many products of nature, goods and services have no economic value: sunlight, air, access to public beaches and parks, favours exchanged between friends and so on.

Thus, value is not a product of nature (although dependent upon it) nor a substance physically embodied in the commodities: value is a social relation between commodity producers that appears as exchange value, a relationship between things. Goods and services possess value only under certain social and historical circumstances. The value relation develops fully only under capitalism, in tandem with the production of commodities, the use of money, the diffusion of wage labour, and the generalisation of market-related property rights.

With value understood as a social relation typical of commodity societies, its source – and the origin of surplus value – must be the performance of commodity-producing labour (the productive consumption of the commodity labour-power) rather than the using or making of things in general. As the inputs are physically blended into the output, their value is transferred and it forms part of the value of the output. In addition to the transfer of the value of the inputs, labour simultaneously adds new value to the product. In other words, whereas the physical inputs contribute value because of the labour time necessary elsewhere and previously deployed to produce them as commodities, freshly performed labour contributes new value to the output.

The value of the output is equal to the value of the inputs plus the value added by the workers during production. Since the value of the means of production is merely transferred, production is profitable only if the value added exceeds the wage costs. That is, surplus value is the difference between the value added by the workers and the value of labour-power. Put another way, wage workers are exploited because they work for longer than the time it takes to produce the goods that they can purchase with their wages. For the rest of their working time, the workers are exploited – they produce (surplus) value for the capitalists.

Just as the workers have little choice on the matter of being exploited, the capitalists cannot avoid exploiting the workers. Exploitation through the extraction of surplus value is a systemic feature of capitalism: this system of production operates like a pump for the extraction of surplus value.

The capitalists must exploit their workers if they are to remain in business; the workers must concur in order to satisfy their immediate needs; and exploitation is the fuel that moves capitalist production and exchange.

It is important to note that, although the wage workers are exploited, they need not be poor in absolute terms (relative poverty, due to the unequal distribution of income and wealth, is a completely different matter). The development of technology increases the productivity of labour, and it potentially allows even the poorest members of society to enjoy relatively comfortable lifestyles, however high the rate of exploitation might be.

6   Profit and (Increasing) Exploitation

Firm profits can increase in many different ways. For example, the capitalists can compel their workers to work longer hours or work harder (greater intensity of labour), employ better skilled workers, or change the technology of production.

All else constant, longer working days produce more profit because more output is possible at little extra cost (the land, buildings, machines and management structures being the same). This is why capitalists always claim that the reduction of the working week hurts profits and, therefore, lowers output and employment. However, in reality, other things are not constant, and historical experience shows that such reductions can be neutral or even lead to higher productivity because of their effects on worker efficiency and morale. Outcomes vary depending on the circumstances, and they may be strongly negative for some capitalists and advantageous for others.

Greater labour intensity condenses more labour into the same working time. Increasing worker effort, speed and concentration raises the level of output and reduces unit costs; therefore, profitability rises. The employment of better trained and educated workers leads to similar outcomes. They can produce more commodities, and create more value, per hour of labour.

Marx calls the additional surplus value extracted through longer hours, more intense labour or extending work to women and children absolute surplus value. This type of surplus value involves the expenditure of more labour, whether in the same working day or in a longer day, with given wages and methods of production. Absolute surplus value was especially important in early capitalism, when the working day was often stretched as long as fourteen or sixteen hours. More recently, absolute surplus value has been extracted through the lengthening of the working week and the penetration of work into leisure time (work often extends into the weekend and holidays, and the availability of mobile phones and computers allows the employees to be always on call). Moreover, the workers are frequently compelled to increase productivity through more intense labour (e.g., faster production lines or reduced breaks) or coerced into acquiring new skills in their 'free' time (e.g., attending courses). Despite its importance, absolute surplus value is limited both physically and socially. It is impossible to increase the working day or the intensity of labour indefinitely, and the workers gradually come to resist these forms of exploitation, eventually winning at least some battles (although such gains are far from universal and remain under threat when achieved).

Rather than increasing the surplus merely by extending the work done, capitalists can raise profitability by increasing productivity, primarily through the introduction of new technology and new machines, thus reducing the labour that goes into contributing to the wage. How can this be done? First, the production process is divided up into tasks to which particular labourers are allocated. Second, tools are developed for these tasks. Third, mechanical power is used. Finally, these developments are brought together in machinery, itself housed within a factory system.

Marx terms this the production of relative surplus value. On this basis, he develops a sophisticated understanding of how production develops under capitalism (not least by contrast with the eponymous production function to be found in neoclassical economics). Like Adam Smith before him, Marx also highlights how such developments tend to strip workers of their traditional skills and reduce them to machine minders (although new skills are created in caring for and developing machinery), reinforcing how much work is done with what productivity to paramount importance. Marx, however, went far beyond Smith in exploring the consequences of such capitalist development of production. In particular, he recognised how competition between capitalist producers was fought largely on the basis of size of capital controlled, in order to lead in productivity through the largest and most powerful factories. This gave rise to Marx's famous phrase describing capitalist imperatives: 'Accumulate, accumulate, that is Moses and the prophets!'

For Marx, then, the major, systematic source of productivity increase involves working up more inputs into final products by a given amount of labour in a given time (although there can be other sources of technical change, not least the invention of new products, materials and processes). In sum, relative surplus value is more flexible than absolute surplus value, and it has become the most important form of exploitation under modern capitalism, because productivity growth can outstrip wage increases for long periods.

7   Marxist Political Economy, Laws of Development and Contemporary Capitalism

Marx is universally praised for his analysis of how production develops under capitalism. But he also derives economic *and* social consequences from his analysis of production and the accumulation of capital. For the economy, he shows how capitalism: develops unevenly as a world economy, with wealth and poverty as opposite sides of the same coin both within and between nations; increases and concentrates corporate power; depends upon a sophisticated financial system that can sustain growth but prompt deep crises; and renders unemployment both inevitable and volatile. And, for the society in which the capitalist economy is embedded, Marx is acutely conscious of how the provision of health, education and welfare, let alone access to, and exercise of, political and ideological power, are subordinated to the imperatives of profitability. Progress, or not, in these is contingent on the ways and extent to which working people can press for and sustain reforms, only for these to be vulnerable to the power of capitalists and their representatives, especially in the context of crisis, recession and 'austerity'.

These insights remain of relevance for our understanding of contemporary capitalism, suitably developed to include economic and social developments, not least those concerning the rise of neoliberalism, its attachment to financialisation and the uneven incidence of, and responses to, the GFC. Dealing with these issues is beyond the scope of this essay although, as with MPE more generally, it is important to recognise how closely debated are such issues. In these respects, the contrast with mainstream economics is also sharp. Whilst the latter has sought to spread its scope of analysis by applying its methods beyond the market (as in institutional economics, development economics, economic sociology or, indeed, the 'economics of everything'), it does so on the basis of its reduced and flawed analytical principles, if possibly supplemented by an added wrinkle or two, with behavioural economics to the fore, to complement, if inconsistently, utility maximisation. This is more a plundering of the social sciences than interdisciplinarity, for which MPE seeks to explain the social in light of the economic, not to reduce it to the falsely perceived economic.

8   Conclusion

In principle, MPE offers the strongest intellectual threat to the mainstream as well as supporting the most acute political challenge to capitalism. So it is unsurprising that MPE is shunned relentlessly in mainstream teaching and research. By contrast, neoclassical economics is extreme in all respects across reliance upon methodological individualism, mathematical methods, empirical methods, the positive-normative dualism, equilibrium, and so on, whereas MPE challenges on all of these fronts, seeing other economic theories as partial reflections of reality (think of utility and production functions as exemplary illustrations of commodity fetishism!).

Despite these uncompromising critiques, MPE recognises that exploitation through the extraction of surplus value renders capitalism uniquely able to develop technology and the forces of production. This is the main reason why Marx admires the progressive features of capitalism. However, he *also* points out that capitalism is the most destructive mode of production in history. The profit motive is blind, and it can be overwhelming. It has led to astonishing discoveries and unsurpassed improvements in living standards, especially (but not exclusively) in the 'core' Western countries. In spite of this, capitalism has also led to widespread destruction and degradation of the environment and of human lives. Profit-seeking has led to slavery, genocide, brutal exploitation of the workers and the uncontrolled destruction of the environment, with long-term global implications. Capitalism also generates and condones the mass unemployment of workers, machinery and land in spite of unsatisfied wants, and tolerates poverty even though the means to abolish it are readily available. Capitalism can extend human life, but it can empty it of rewarding meaning (as with the diseases of affluence). It supports unparalleled achievements in human education and culture while, simultaneously, fostering, greed, mendacity, sexual and racial discrimination and other forms of human oppression.

These contradictory effects of capitalism are inseparable. Private ownership of the means of production and market competition *necessarily* give rise to the wage relation, exploitation through the extraction of surplus value, and they facilitate crises, war, and other negative features of capitalism. This places a strict limit on the possibility of social, political and economic reforms, and on the capacity of the market to assume a 'human face'. Limitations such as these led Marx to conclude that capitalism can be overthrown, and communism created, opening the possibility of realisation of the potential of the vast majority through the elimination of the irrationalities and human costs of capitalism.

Despite all this, MPE is not currently in a strong position to influence political developments, and this situation is unlikely to change through the 'implosion' of neoclassical economics because of its internal inconsistencies or external criticism. The continuity and renewal of MPE depends, instead, on developments outside academia, especially the fortunes of the workers in class struggle, which could potentially bring to light once again the connections between theory and practice that are at the core of Marxism. Nonetheless, revival of MPE is vital to sustain alternatives to the mainstream as part and parcel of a broader commitment to rethinking economics and those seeking the framing of alternatives.

In this light, what policy alternatives might MPE offer, especially given what are generally presumed to be the failed twentieth century attempts at constructing socialism? Marx himself was not unduly concerned to construct what he critically referred to as socialist utopias, preferring to envisage social-ism as emerging out of working class organisation and struggles against capi-talism. This certainly seemed to be on the agenda during the post-war boom when trade unions and their political organisations exercised considerable power and future prospects seem to rest on whether social reformism (and de-colonisation) might continue to allow for growth and prosperity, with socialist revolution as a potential alternative.

The end of the post-war period and the rise of neoliberalism have taken the contest between social reformism and social revolution off the agenda. In addition, the leading source of power in economic and, increasingly, social or-ganisation has been occupied by finance which, if anything, has even strength-ened its hold in the wake of the GFC, despite its guilt by association with it and powerlessness to resolve its consequences. For many, then, looking back to the so-called Keynesian 'golden age', future prospects rest on putting finance back in its place, conveniently overlooking that Keynesianism experienced its own crisis.

MPE continues to debate intensively amongst itself the extent to which finance is a cause as opposed to a symptom of the GFC and its aftermath. Where there might be agreement is that overcoming the power of finance is a necessary but far from sufficient condition for strengthening the hand of working people in developing both alternative forms of organisation and policies themselves, ones that bring to the majority the power, control and well-being from which they are currently denied in deference to an increasingly narrow and more powerful elite.

CHAPTER 2

The Relevance of Marx's Theory of Value

The title of this essay is deliberately provocative, on three grounds. First, it implies that the 'relevance' of social theories ought to be assessed historically, and it may shift as the subject of analysis changes over time. Second, it suggests the possibility that Marx's theory of value could have been relevant in the past – perhaps when it was first developed, or under what became known as 'competitive' (pre-World War I) capitalism – but it may no longer be tenable in the age of neoliberalism. Third, if this is the case, what are critics of capitalism supposed to do? – is there another theory offering a similarly powerful denunciation of the mode of production as Marx's, with suggestions of alternatives, or has capitalism addressed its contradictions and it can, finally, be embraced as the gateway to the best of all possible worlds?

It is impossible to answer these issues comprehensively in what follows. This essay addresses the questions outlined above only partially and unevenly, in three sections. The first reviews the strengths and limitations of some of the best-known interpretations of Marx's theory of value: the 'traditional Marxism' associated with Dobb, Meek and Sweezy; Sraffian interpretations of Marx; value-form theory (especially the Rubin tradition), and the 'new interpretation' of value theory. The second offers an interpretation of value theory based on the primacy of class relations. This interpretation is not entirely original, as it draws on an extensive literature developed over several decades. However, this section aims to present the principles of this interpretation of Marx's theory of value briefly and consistently, in order to highlight its most important claims and implications. The conclusion indicates how this interpretation can offer useful insights for the analysis of several important problems of our age. It should be pointed out that this essay does *not* survey the entire field of value theory, or deal with all important or polemical aspects of this theory, or offer an orderly exposition of the theory for beginners.[1]

---

1 Readers unfamiliar with Marx's theory of value may wish start from Fine and Saad-Filho (2016), Foley (1986), Harvey (1999) or Weeks (1981). This essay draws upon Saad-Filho (2002).

1   Interpretations of Marx's Theory of Value

The concept of value has been interpreted in widely different ways.[2] Two interpretations of Marx's theory of value have become especially prominent, the 'embodied labour' views, including 'traditional Marxism' and Sraffian approaches, and value form theories, including those associated with Rubin and the 'new interpretation'. Although these interpretations of value theory have contributed significantly to our understanding of capitalism, they are not entirely satisfactory for different reasons, discussed below.[3]

1.1   *Traditional Marxism*
For the 'traditional' interpretation,[4] Marx's value theory is not essentially different from Ricardo's. It may be summarized as follows:
(a)   The main subject of the theory of value is the analysis of capitalist exploitation. The categories developed in the first three chapters of *Capital 1* (commodity, value and money) are only indirectly related to this issue, because they belong to a broader set of modes of production, where capitalist exploitation does not necessarily exist.
(b)   The concept of value is necessary for the determination of the rate of exploitation. This reading focuses upon the magnitude of value, defined as the quantity of abstract labour embodied in each commodity. The substance and form of value and the links between value and money are largely neglected.
(c)   The analysis of profit requires the determination of commodity prices, including the wage rate. This is done through a set of assumptions that usually includes general equilibrium (simple reproduction). Consequently, prices are only relative to a *numéraire*. It follows that a theory of money is unnecessary, and money is effectively a veil.
(d)   The determination of relative prices has two stages; first, it is assumed that all capitals have equal value compositions, in which case the exchange ratios are determined by embodied labour alone. Second, the value compositions are allowed to vary; in this case, relative prices differ from the embodied labour ratios, but it is presumed that the latter determine the former algebraically.

---

2   '[V]irtually every controversy within Marxist economics is at bottom a controversy concerning the nature and status of value theory' (Mohun 1991, p. 42).
3   For a detailed review of these interpretations of Marx, see Saad-Filho (2002, ch.2); see also the essays in Part 1 of this Volume.
4   This section is based on Dobb (1940, 1967), Meek (1973) and Sweezy (1968).

(e)   The conceptual apparatus is elementary. Commodities are use values put out for sale; value is often conflated with exchange value, and the articulation between value and price is left unclear (even though they are presumed to be quantitatively comparable).

(f)   There is little concern with the distinction between levels of analysis and the interaction between tendencies, counter-tendencies and contingency. Theory arguably captures the basic tendencies of capitalism, and they should be translated unproblematically into empirical outcomes.

The traditional approach has important virtues, especially the focus on the mode of exploitation. This emphasis concurs with Marx's own concerns, and it highlights some of his most distinctive contributions; it is also conducive to the critique of the structures of circulation and distribution, such as private property and the market. However, traditional Marxism suffers from two significant shortcomings. First, it disconnects the analysis of the mode of production from the circulation and distribution of the output, which grossly exaggerates their independence. Second, traditional Marxism wrongly claims that Marx's analysis of commodities, value and money addresses a broad set of commodity modes of production, especially simple commodity production, and that his analysis of capitalism proper starts only in Chapter 4 of *Capital 1*. In this case, two sets of relative prices exist. One is based on embodied labour, and it rules pre-capitalist exchange, while the other is based on equal profitability, and it regulates capitalist exchanges.[5] Presumably, the transition between these stages is a historical process, in which case the transformation between the two types of relative prices (values and prices of production) can be analysed historically as well as algebraically.[6]

---

5   'Under certain conditions which prevailed between independent small producers in pre-capitalist societies (what Marx calls "simple commodity production") exchange of equal values was the rule. If under capitalist conditions there are other more complicated relations determining the quantitative exchange relations, this does not make an economic theory based on the determination of value by socially necessary labour inconsistent, provided there is a clear and consistent method of deriving prices from values' (Winternitz 1948, p. 277).

6   'The "derivation of prices from values" ... must be regarded as a historical as well as a logical process. In "deriving prices from values" we are really reproducing in our minds, in logical and simplified form, a process which has actually happened in history. Marx began with the assumption that goods sold "at their values" under capitalism (so that profit rates in the various branches of production were often very different), not only because this appeared to be the proper starting-point from the logical point of view but also because he believed that it had "originally" been so. He proceeded on this basis to transform values into prices, not only because this course appeared to be logically necessary but also because he believed that history itself had effected such a transformation' (Meek 1956, pp. 104–105). This view draws upon Engels (1981).

This approach is misguided both logically and historically. Generalised exchange at value has never existed because, in general, products become commodities only under capitalism. Moreover, although Marx often draws on historical studies in order to explain difficult points or trace the evolution of important categories, the only mode of production that he analyses systematically in *Capital* is *capitalism*. Hence, although commodities, value and money may have existed for millennia, *Capital* focuses upon their capitalist determinations only, and no systematic inferences may be drawn about their meaning and significance in other modes of production. Finally, the traditional approach fails to explain the relationships between money and commodities and between abstract labour and value, and it explains only imperfectly and superficially the mode of labour and the relations of exploitation under capitalism.[7]

1.2   *Sraffian Analyses*

Dissatisfaction with the shortcomings of traditional Marxism led to the development of two alternative approaches, the Sraffian (or neo-Ricardian) and value form theory (see below). The Sraffian approach is developed and explained by, among others, Pasinetti and Steedman, drawing upon works by Bortkiewicz, Dmitriev, Seton, Sraffa and Tugan-Baranowsky. Sraffians attempt to develop the traditional model, focusing upon the articulation between the value and the price systems.[8] The main features of this approach are the following:

(a)   Only the magnitude of value is discussed in detail; its substance and form are almost completely disregarded. The analysis usually involves two sets of equations; one represents the value system, and the other the price system.

---

7   '[T]o regard Marx's theory of value as a proof of exploitation tends to dehistoricise value, to make it synonymous with labour-time, and to make redundant Marx's distinction between surplus labour and surplus value. To know whether or not there is exploitation, we must examine the ownership and control of the means of production, and the process whereby the length of the working day is fixed ... Marx's concern was with the particular *form* that exploitation took in capitalism ... for in capitalism surplus labour could not be appropriated simply in the form of the immediate product of labour. It was necessary for that product to be sold and translated into *money* (Elson 1979, p. 116).

8   Early Sraffian developments were welcomed by traditional Marxists: 'I would ... wish to urge that this enquiry should be conducted within a rather different conceptual framework – that provided by Sraffa in his *Production of Commodities by Means of Commodities* ... I shall try to ... show how certain basic elements of this system could conceivably be adapted and used by modern Marxists' (Meek 1973, p. xxxii); see also Dobb's (1943) expression of support for Bortkiewicz's interpretation of the transformation of values into prices of production.

(b)   The value system is described by $\lambda = \lambda A + l = l(I - A)^{-1}$, where λ is the ($1{\times}n$) vector of commodity values, A is the ($n{\times}n$) technical matrix and l is the ($1{\times}n$) vector of direct labour.

(c)   The price system is described by $p = (pA + wl)(1 + r)$, where p is the ($1{\times}n$) price vector, w is the wage rate, and r is the profit rate.

(d)   As the analysis is primarily concerned with the relationship between the value and price systems, money has no autonomous role and, when considered at all, it is merely a *numéraire*.

(e)   These definitions of value and price are the basis for a wide-ranging critique of alleged inconsistencies in Marx, leading to the conclusion that the traditional Marxist project of determining value from embodied labour is flawed. Very briefly, first, the price system has two degrees of freedom, because it has n equations, one for each commodity, but $n+2$ unknowns, the n prices and the wage and profit rates. Therefore, while the value system can usually be solved (as long as the matrix A is well-behaved), the price system can be solved only if additional restrictions are introduced, for example, the identity of the value of labour power with the value of a bundle of goods (the wage is the price of this bundle), and a normalization condition such as one of Marx's aggregate equalities (*either* total prices equal total values, *or* total profits equal total surplus value). However, the other aggregate equality is not generally possible, which is allegedly destructive for Marx's analysis. Second, the Sraffian representation of Marx cannot distinguish between the role of labour and other inputs, in which case it cannot be argued that labour creates value and is exploited, rather than any other input, e.g., corn, iron or energy. Third, even if labour does create value and is exploited, the only meaningful relationship between labour and prices is through the proposition that a positive rate of exploitation is necessary and sufficient for positive profits, which has little empirical significance.

Sraffian analyses have contributed significantly, even if indirectly, to Marxian studies of the relationship between the mode of production and the structures of distribution. However, the Sraffian approach is insufficient in several respects, and its critiques of Marx have been rebutted convincingly by a vast literature.[9] In what follows two aspects of the Sraffian critique of Marx are briefly assessed, the shortcomings of the value equation and the Sraffian inability to represent capitalist relations of production satisfactorily.

---

9   See, for example, Fine (1980), Fine and Harris (1979, ch.2), Gleicher (1985–86), Rowthorn (1980, ch.1) and Shaikh (1977, 1981, 1982, 1984).

The value equation, $\lambda = \lambda A + l$, states that commodity values are equal to the input values (λA) plus the living labour necessary to process them (l). Although this equation represents correctly Marx's *definition* of value, it is unsuitable for the *calculation* of commodity values. To see why, suppose that the matrix A represents the average production technologies, however they may be determined. Suppose, also, that the vector l represents the average number of *concrete* labour-hours necessary to transform the inputs into the output. Even under these generous assumptions, the vector l cannot be directly used to calculate the value produced because it measures concrete rather than abstract labour. Since these labours are qualitatively distinct, any operation across them is meaningless.[10] By the same token, labour employed in distinct activities, whether or not vertically integrated, may produce distinct quantities of value per hour because of training and other differences. Suppose, instead, that l is a vector of *abstract* labour. Although this would avoid the problems outlined above it would still not allow the value vector to be *calculated*. For this assumption implies that, in order to calculate the abstract labour necessary to produce each commodity (λ), one needs to know how many hours of abstract labour are necessary to produce each commodity (l). Because it involves a tautology, the assumption that l is abstract labour does not allow the quantitative determination of value.[11]

The Sraffian system is such that production resembles a purely technical process, not necessarily capitalist, in which case capital is merely a collection of use values rather than a social relation of production, and the substance of value, abstract labour, is undistinguishable from average units of concrete labour time. Finally, the social aspect of production is either assumed away or projected upon the sphere of distribution, through the rate of exploitation.

The Sraffian model is not even based on consistent assumptions. It presumes that the technical relations of production are given independently of the value and price systems, and implies that, for Marx, calculation of the price vector would necessitate value magnitudes, but not the converse. Since

---

10   'The point is not that no abstraction is involved in the concept of embodied labour; rather it is not a *social* abstraction corresponding to particular historical process, but it is *arbitrary*, a mental convenience: an assumption that labour is homogeneous *when it is plainly not*' (Himmelweit and Mohun 1978, p. 81).

11   'The search for a privileged technological input in the labor process, which determines the value of the product, comes from a misunderstanding of what value is. Abstract labour is not a privileged input into production because abstract labour is *not an input into production at all* ... It is attached to the product (as a price tag) only because of the particular social relations in a commodity producing society' (Glick and Ehrbar 1986–87, p. 472).

this is not the case, value analysis is allegedly redundant. This is incorrect because, first, it misrepresents Marx's argument (see Saad-Filho 2002, chs. 2, 5, 7). Second, in the real world the structure of production is socially, rather than technically, determined. Under capitalism, competition determines the allocation of labour and means of production, the quantities produced and the technologies, in which case value relations are *causally determinant* vis-à-vis technologies and prices (see Shaikh 1982, pp. 71–72). Consequently, 'the labour theory of value is not redundant, but rather provides the explanation of price lacking in Sraffa's own account' (Gleicher 1985–86, p. 465). In sum, Sraffian analyses cannot define capitalism other than through the equalisation of rates of return, which makes it impossible to explain consistently the capitalist social relations, exploitation, the distribution of income, the sources of economic data, the process of competition and, most damagingly, the price form.

1.3   *Value Form Theories*

Value form theories (VFT) were developed in the seventies, partly as a reaction against the insufficiencies of traditional Marxism and the excesses of Sraffianism.[12] The development of VFT was supported by the rediscovery of the works of the Soviet economist Isaak Illich Rubin (1896–1937) in the West in the early seventies. In what follows, VFT is analysed critically through Rubin's work. Subsequently, a contemporary approach drawing upon VFT is examined, the 'new interpretation' of Marx's value theory.

The Rubin tradition departs from the social division of labour. It claims that the essential feature of the capitalist division of labour is the commodity relation, or the production of commodities by 'separate', or independent, producers. The commodity features of capitalism are so important that Rubin frequently refers to the subject of his analysis as the 'commodity-capitalist' economy. The counterpart to the independence of the producers is the need to produce a socially useful commodity or, in other words, one that is sold (the imperative to sell has been called the 'monetary constraint'). Because of separation and the monetary constraint, this tradition argues that commodities are produced by private and concrete labours that, at best, are potentially or only ideally abstract and social. Private and concrete labour is converted into social and abstract labour if and when its product is exchanged for money.[13]

---

12   Different versions of value form analysis are proposed by, among others, Backhaus (1974) de Brunhoff (1973, 1976), Eldred (1984), Eldred and Hanlon (1981), Reuten and Williams (1989) and de Vroey (1981, 1982, 1985).

13   'In a commodity economy, the labour of a separate individual, of a separate, private commodity producer, is not directly regulated by society. As such, in its concrete form, labour does not yet directly enter the social economy. Labour becomes social in a commodity

The Rubin tradition has contributed in at least two ways to the development of Marxian value analysis. First, the claim that abstract labour is social labour indirectly formed through sale is applicable to commodity economies only, and it provides the springboard for a forceful critique of ahistorical embodied labour views. This critique has helped to shift the focus of Marxian studies away from the calculation of values and prices and towards the analysis of the social relations of production and their forms of appearance. Second, this tradition has emphasized the importance of money for value analysis, because value appears only in and through price. Since money plays an essential role in commodity economies, non-monetary or general equilibrium interpretations of Marx's theory are fundamentally wrong, the search for an unmediated expression of abstract labour is futile, and attempts to calculate embodied labour coefficients are rarely meaningful. Emphasis on the importance money has facilitated the resurgence of interest in Marxian monetary analysis, and the critique of embodied labour views has opened avenues for the development of more cogent interpretations of Marx.

However, the claim that 'separation' and the monetary constraint are the essential features of 'commodity-capitalist' production has led the Rubin tradition to subsume capitalist relations of production under simple value relations. Consequently, in spite of its significant contribution to the analysis of value, this tradition has added little to our understanding of *capital* and *capitalism*. Focus on the value relation implies that commodity economies are essentially a congregation of producers that, in principle, do not belong in the

---

economy only when it acquires the form of socially equalized labour, namely, the labour of every commodity producer becomes social only because his product is equalized with the products of all other producers ... [A]bstract labour ... [is] labour which was made equal through the all round equation of all the products of labour, but the equation of all the products of labour is not possible except through the assimilation of each one of them with a universal equivalent ... [The] equalization of labour may take place, but only mentally and in anticipation, in the process of direct production, *before* the act of exchange. But in reality, it takes place through the act of exchange, through the equalization (even though it is mentally anticipated) of the product of the given labour with a definite sum of money' (Rubin 1975, pp. 96–97, 142; 1978, pp. 118–119). For de Vroey (1981, p. 176), 'Labour is first performed as private labour, initiated by an independent decision. It is transformed into social labour through, and only through, the sale of its product. When social labour is formed in this context, it is called abstract labour, the adjective referring to the operation of homogenization or abstraction achieved by exchange on the market'. Therefore, 'rather than being linked to a mere embodiment of labour – a technical process – value refers to the validation of private labour through the exchange of commodities against money ... private labour becomes validated (ie reckoned as a fraction of social labour, serving effectively this reproduction) only in so far as its product is sold. Otherwise, private labour is a waste' (de Vroey 1982, p. 40).

social division of labour. Because of separation and specialisation, the producers must sell their own goods or services in order to claim a share of the social product for their own consumption. In other words, in this type of society production is essentially for consumption, and private and concrete labour is analytically prior to social and abstract labour, which exist only ideally before sale. The equalisation, abstraction and socialisation of labour are contingent upon sale, and commodity values are determined by the value of the money for which they are exchanged. The inability to sell shows that the decision to produce was wrong, the good is useless, and the labour did not create value.[14]

This approach is misguided. In capitalist economies, the *essential* separation is between the wage workers and the means of production, monopolised by the class of capitalists. Production takes place when capitalists hire workers in order to supply goods for profit. Since the performance of labour is conditioned by this social form, the output is necessarily a commodity; it *has* a use value, and it *is* a value (if the commodity is not sold its use value is not realised, and its value is destroyed). In sum, whereas the labour of independent commodity producers is relatively free of social determinations and its social character is contingent upon *exchange*, under capitalism the *mode of labour* is socially determined (see below).

These limitations of the Rubin tradition are largely due to the conflation between capitalist production (the systematic production of commodities for profit) and simple commodity production (the socially unregulated production of commodities by independent producers). This is flawed both historically and theoretically:

> [In] the case of individual producers who own their own means of production and ... where none of the inputs used in production is bought, but all are produced within a self-contained labor process ... only the final product of the labor process is a commodity. Each article of the means of production is produced in social isolation by each producer, never facing

---

14   Rubin (1975, p. 147) realised that this argument is untenable: 'Some critics say that our conception may lead to the conclusion that abstract labour originates only in the act of exchange, from which it follows that value also originates only in exchange'. He attempts to evade this difficulty through the distinction between exchange as the social form of the process of production, and exchange as one phase of reproduction, alternating with production, claimin that his argument that value is determined in exchange refers to the first meaning of the term, rather than the second. However, this distinction is invalid, and Rubin himself states that the relationship between the producers is established through the *act*, rather than the social structure, of exchange (see Rubin 1975, pp. 7–9, 61, 64, 70, 80–88, 143; 1978, p. 114).

the discipline of competition. There is no social mechanism for bringing about a normal expenditure of labor time in the products that are the means of production. In such a situation, competition's only function is to impose the rule of a uniform selling price in the market place ... The only objective necessity is that his or her total labor expenditure ... be sufficient to allow for the reproduction of the family. Should some producers be able to deliver their commodities with less expenditure of effort than others, the more 'efficient' producers will enjoy a higher standard of living. *This higher standard of living of some in no way pressures the less efficient to raise their efficiency.*

> WEEKS 1981, pp. 31–32, emphasis added

The Rubin tradition's sharp focus upon the value relation has contributed to important advances in Marxian value analysis. However, its relative neglect of the wage relation and the mode of labour have limited its ability to distinguish capitalism from other (commodity) modes of production. The Rubin tradition wrongly presumes that commodity exchange is the determinant aspect of capitalism, conflates money with the substance of value, and eschews the mediations that structure Marx's value analysis. Lack of analytical depth explains its failure to illuminate important real relations identified by Marx, for example, the capitalist monopoly of the means of production, the subordination of the workers in production, the social regulation of production through competition, mechanisation and deskilling, and the mediations between value and price. Because of these limitations, the Rubin tradition is poorly equipped to explain the main features of capitalism and to analyse their social, economic and political consequences empirically.

1.4   The 'New Interpretation'

In the early 1980s Gérard Duménil and Duncan Foley independently outlined a 'new interpretation' (NI) of Marx's value theory,[15] drawing upon Aglietta (1979) and Rubin (1975, 1978). The NI has helped to shift the value debate away from the relatively sterile polemics against the Sraffian critics of Marx and the highly abstract analyses of the Rubin tradition, and into more substantive issues. The distinctive contribution of the NI is based on its emphasis on the net, rather than gross product, and its unconventional definitions of value of money and value of labour power.

---

15   Duménil (1980) and Foley (1982). This section draws upon Fine, Lapavitsas and Saad-Filho (2004) (see Chapter 6) and Saad-Filho (2002, ch.2). See also Moseley (2000a).

The NI stems from a value form interpretation of Marx, whence labour becomes abstract, and is socialised, through sales.[16] Two implications follow; first, money is the immediate and exclusive expression of abstract labour and, second, the value created by (productive) labour is measured by the quantity of money for which the output is sold. This interpretation bypasses the conceptual difficulties involved in the relationship between values and prices, since it remains at the aggregate or macroeconomic level. At this level, money is essentially command over newly performed abstract labour. There is no necessary relationship between individual prices and values, and this theory cannot discriminate between alternative price systems. This allegedly increases its generality in the light of potentially pervasive imperfect market structures (for an algebraic analysis of the NI, see Chapter 6).

Let us consider the contribution of the NI more closely, starting with the operation in the net product. There are two ways to conceptualise the economy's net product. In use value terms, it comprises the means of consumption and net investment, or that part of the gross output over and above that necessary to maintain the productive system, or to repeat the same pattern and level of production. In value terms, it is identical with the newly performed labour. This raises the problem of the value of the gross product, since labour creates the entire gross product but only part of its value. The NI implies that the conventional definition of Marx's equalities in terms of the gross product is inconsistent because the value of the means of production is counted twice in the value of the gross product. It counts, first, as the value of the newly produced means of production and, again, as the new value of the means of production used up. However, the latter does not correspond to labour actually performed either in the current period or previously; this is merely a reflection of labour carried out and value created elsewhere. These insights are persuasive. However, the NI's exclusive focus on the net product may be misleading, for two reasons. First, empirically, the net product is defined over a

time period other than the turnover period of capital. Net national product, for example, is defined for a year or a quarter. In consequence, the two components of net capital value (variable capital and surplus value) are aggregated over several turnovers, and conceptually one loses sight of

---

16   For Foley (1982, p. 37), the labour theory of value is 'the claim that the money value of the whole mass of net production of commodities expresses the expenditure of the total social labor in a commodity-producing economy ... The concept of value as a property of the whole mass of the net commodity product in this approach is analytically prior to the concept of price, the amount of money a particular commodity brings on the market'.

the fundamental aspect of circulation, which is the recapture of capital advanced through sale of commodities and the replacement of the material components of production.

WEEKS 1983, p. 220

Second, and more importantly, focus on the net product eliminates the production of the means of production (other than that required for expanded reproduction). As a result, a significant proportion of current production is rendered invisible as if it were redundant, and the largest proportion of commodity exchanges, those between the producers, vanishes as if it were inconsequential. The use of money as capital and as means of payment, and the role of the credit system, are inevitably minimised unwarrantedly.

Because of the alleged double counting of the input values in the value of the gross output, the NI defines the value of money on the net, rather than gross, product. This definition of value of money is seductive for three reasons; first, it avoids the simplifying assumptions that encumber the traditional and Sraffian approaches. Second, it appeals to the contemporary experience with inconvertible paper currencies and the perceived importance of the macroeconomic determinants of the value of money, especially through fiscal and monetary policy. Third, it facilitates the analysis of imperfect market structures and monopoly power, which can hardly be achieved by the traditional approach.

In spite of these significant advantages, this concept of value of money is limited in two important ways. On the one hand, it is merely the *ex post* reflection of the relationship between (abstract, productive) labour performed and the money-value added in the period. It is known only *after* labour is performed, commodities are produced and priced, and the technologies are determined. In this respect, it is unrelated to the Marxian concept of value of the money-commodity, that is determined *before* circulation. On the other hand, this concept of value of money cannot capture the distinct levels of complexity of the value relation, including the social relations of production and distribution, the labour performed, the relations between supply and demand, monopoly power, the quantity and velocity of money, and the credit system. Each of these factors can affect the price system in different ways, but the NI is unable to distinguish systematically between them, or to ground them analytically and explain their implications.

In short, the value of money short-circuits the real structures and relations between social labour and its representation in money, in order to address the extant macroeconomic relationships. Unfortunately for the NI, these mediations inherently contain the possibility of disequilibrium and crisis. To collapse the mediated expression of value as price into the simple division of the total hours worked over the price of the total net product is to set aside the complexity of the real processes involved and to obscure the inherent potential for disequilibrium in the economy, which weakens the theory's ability to address the very relations which it wishes to confront.[17]

The NI concept of value of labour power suffers from similar shortcomings. For the NI, the value of labour power is the workers' share of the national income, which is determined by class struggle. However, this definition of the value of labour power does not extend beyond one of the effects of exploitation, the inability of the workers to purchase the entire net product.[18] This notion of value of labour power can be misleading, first, if it dilutes the ability of theory to explain the primary form of class conflict in capitalism, that takes place in production rather than distribution. Second, it may create the illusion that the net product is somehow 'shared' between workers and capitalists at the end of each production period, or that exploitation is due to the unfair distribution of income. Third, it may support the Classical dichotomy between ordinary commodity values, determined by labour embodied, and the value of labour power, given by supply and demand.

In sum, there are two distinct aspects to the contribution of the NI for the development of value analysis. On the one hand, it bypasses the transformation problem (especially the spurious debate about the 'correct' normalisation condition), and it rightly rejects the equilibrium framework in which value theory and, especially, the transformation problem, were discussed in the past. These important contributions are part of a broader reconsideration of Marx's value theory, providing the foundation for a new, critical macroeconomics. These achievements are important, and the objective is worthwhile. On the other hand, the NI is open to criticism on several grounds. This approach has been developed in order to address the appearances directly, through empirical studies, but this important objective exacts a heavy toll. The NI has little analytical 'depth', emphasizes exchange and distribution at the expense of production, and it eliminates the mediations and the complex relationship

---

17   In his ground-breaking paper on the NI, Foley (1982, p. 41) invites the reader to 'Suppose ... we have a commodity-producing system in which, for one reason or another, the money prices of commodities are not proportional to labor values. One reason might be that prices deviate from labor values so that profit rates can be equalized when invested capital per worker varies over different sectors. Other reasons might be monopoly, government regulations, the exploitation of information differentials in markets by middlemen, and so on'. Collapsing categories at distinct levels of complexity in order to employ macroeconomic identities may be useful for policy analysis, but it can be unhelpful analytically because it obscures the structures of determination of the mode of production.

18   Marx was heavily critical of theories of exploitation that focused primarily upon the distribution of income, see Marx (1974, pp. 344–345) and Saad-Filho (1993, see also Chapter 3).

between value and price and surplus value and profit, treating them as if they were identical. As a result, the NI becomes unable to incorporate some of Marx's most important insights into the analysis, including technical change, accumulation, the credit system and crises, other than as exogenous accretions. These limitations are due to the internal structure of the NI, and they explain why it has been accused of tautology (because of the way in which it validates Marx's equalities) and empiricism (because it does not highlight the structures whose development underpins value analysis). Therefore, it is difficult to develop the NI further without making use of arbitrariness in the choice of phenomena to be explained, the judgement of their importance and their relationship with the other features of reality.

2   Value Theory and Class Analysis

The previous section has shown that the capitalist economy can be approached in two ways. From the viewpoint of circulation (exchange), it appears as an unco-ordinated collection of competing activities, distinguished from one another by the commodities produced in each firm and their possibly distinct technologies. This approach tends to emphasize the processes that bring coherence to decentralised economies and ensure that needs are satisfied, subject to constraints, in which case the relative prices and the distribution of labour and income become prominent. The inquiry may be extended subsequently into why the 'invisible hand' can fail, in which case there are disproportions and crisis. These issues are worthy of detailed study and bring to light important aspects of capitalism. However, they do not directly or easily lead to the analysis of the mode of *production*. This is a severe limitation, because the essential differences between capitalism and other modes of production stem primarily from the relationship between the workers and the owners of means of production and the mode of labour associated with it.

In contrast, analyses that emphasise production at the expense of exchange tend to impose equilibrium conditions arbitrarily, in order to focus upon the technologies of production. In this case, it can become difficult to grasp the significance of money, the relationship between concrete and abstract labour, the meaning of competition, the process of technical change, capital migration and class conflicts. More generally, this approach obscures the historical limits of value analysis.

These shortcomings imply that value analysis ought to consider both production and exchange, and the mediations between these spheres and the different levels of analysis. While it can be appropriate, or even indispensable, to short-circuit certain mediations in order to focus upon specific aspects of capitalism, this can be risky because it could become difficult to know where and how to introduce important structures or tendencies into the analysis. In this case, it may be necessary to resort to arbitrariness, or to plug into value analysis unrelated studies uncritically, which smacks of eclecticism and is rarely fruitful.

In what follows, this view is developed into a *class interpretation* of Marx's theory of value, which attempts to address the shortcomings identified above. This interpretation is based on three principles.

2.1   *Principles*

(a) *The subject of analysis:* Marx's theory of value is a *theory of the class relations of exploitation in capitalist society*. It explains systematically the process of production of the material conditions of social reproduction in capitalism or, alternatively, the reproduction of the capitalist relations of exploitation through the process of material production.[19] This includes such issues as the social form of the property relations, labour, labour control and exploitation, the social form of the products of labour, and the objective of social production. They are studied in relation to the form of interaction between different classes, the material (objective) form of the process of economic and social reproduction, and the revolutionary action necessary to overthrow this mode of production. Therefore, value theory is not limited to the description of events, the study of individual behaviour, preferences or objectives, or the analysis of disparate aspects of contemporary society – it is a holistic and dialectical theory.[20]

The exclusive focus of Marx's value theory on capitalism has been disputed. For example, the focus of traditional Marxism, Sraffianism and the abstract labour version is broader, encompassing commodity societies or economies subject to rules of equalisation of rates of return regardless of the employment

---

19   'Interpreted on very narrow terms, social reproduction includes the processes necessary for the reproduction of the workforce, both biologically and as compliant wage-labourers. More generally, social reproduction is concerned with how society as a whole is reproduced and transformed over time' (Fine 2001b, p. 32).

20   '[V]alue theory is not primarily a theory of exchange or allocation, but a theory that reveals the class relations underlying a commodity-producing society ... The theory of value that Marx developed provides at the same time (1) the revelation that capitalism is merely one form of exploitative (class) society; (2) the explanation of the historical transition from precapitalist to capitalist society; (3) a theory of the concrete operation of a capitalist economy; and (4) an explanation of why others would explain the workings of a capitalist economy in an alternative theoretical framework' (Weeks 1981, pp. 8, 11).

of wage labour (see above). These approaches do not correspond to Marx's own. *Capital 1* opens with the following statement (p. 125):

> The wealth of societies in which the capitalist mode of production prevails appears as an "immense collection of commodities"; the individual commodity appears as its elementary form. Our investigation therefore begins with the analysis of the commodity.

The expression 'in which the capitalist mode of production prevails' is essential, because it situates the subject of Marx's analysis and the historical limits of its validity. Although commodities have been produced for thousands of years, and commodity production and exchange are historical premises of capitalism, commodities produced under capitalism are essentially distinct from those produced in other modes of production. This difference arises because, under capitalism, the social output typically takes the commodity form and, more importantly, labour power also takes this form:

> Two characteristic traits mark the capitalist mode of production right from the start ... *Firstly.* It produces its products as commodities. The fact that it produces commodities does not in itself distinguish it from other modes of production; but that the dominant and determining character of its product is that it is a commodity certainly does so. This means, first of all, that the worker himself appears only as a seller of commodities, and hence as a free wage-labourer – i.e., labour generally appears as wage-labour ... [T]he relationship of capital and wage-labour determines the whole character of the mode of production ... The *second* thing that particularly marks the capitalist mode of production is the production of surplus-value as the direct objective and decisive motive of production. Capital essentially produces capital, and does this only as long as it produces surplus-value.
>
> *Capital 3*, pp. 1019–1020.

(*b*) *Methodology:* The class interpretation of value theory is firmly grounded on a *materialist dialectic* understanding of Marx's method, eschewing methodological individualism and formal logic.[21] Marx's theory of value is structured by the articulation of concepts at different levels of analysis, departing from relatively high levels of abstraction and moving, dialectically, to increasingly concrete levels. At the relatively abstract level of analysis where the key

---

21   This methodological approach is explained in Saad-Filho (2002, ch.1).

theoretical categories (commodity, value, capital, labour power, surplus value, and so on) are initially posited, individuals are only the representatives of economic categories. The study of the structural motives underpinning the behaviour of different classes – large groups of people playing key roles in the process of economic and social reproduction – permits the systematic development of Marx's materialist dialectic analysis of capitalism, the orderly introduction and development of the essential analytical categories that are recognised as forms of existence of social relations in capitalism. Finally, it permits the integrated study of problems that are often treated separately or inconsistently in other interpretations, especially abstract labour, money, prices, exploitation, the labour process and the critique of technology. These categories are explained primarily from the aggregate, or at the level of class, rather than starting at the individual level or from purely arbitrary deductions.

(c) *The role of value:* The concept of value expresses the systematic features of exploitation in capitalism. Value analysis helps to overcome the fragmented perception of exploitation through individual experiences, and the misleading appearances fostered by market exchanges.[22] It also relates the basic principles of Marx's theory to the dynamic outcomes of accumulation, including technical progress, crises, fluctuations in the levels of unemployment, credit and inflation and, more broadly, with the possibility of eliminating these relations of exploitation. This interpretation can also help to understand the historical transition from non-capitalist societies to capitalism, and offer a critique of social theories that assess these processes differently. Finally, this interpretation implies that the relevance of Marx's value theory depends upon the prevalence of capitalist relations of production and exploitation in any particular society. Since these relations have become increasingly widespread and dominant in the last two centuries, Marx's theory of value has become *more* relevant for understanding modern society.[23]

---

22   '[T]he theory of value enables us to analyse capitalist exploitation in a way that overcomes the fragmentation of the experience of that exploitation ... it enables us to grasp capitalist exploitation as a contradictory, crisis-ridden process, subject to continual change ... [and] it builds into our understanding of how the process of exploitation works, the possibility of action to end it' (Elson 1979, p. 171).

23   The scientific relevance of this (or any other) theory is determine by its ability to illuminate the phenomena belonging to its areas of concern. This is entirely unrelated to the 'popularity' of the theory, or the recognition of its potential usefulness by large numbers of people. This essay is concerned with the former, rather than the latter, which belongs to the realm of ideology.

2.2   *Implications*

1. Marx's critique of the capitalist mode of production starts from human labour in general. For Marx, labour is the process of transformation of given natural and social conditions in order to achieve predetermined outcomes – the goods and services necessary for social reproduction (use values). In every society, the social labour power (the capacity to work of all individuals, including their knowledge, ability and experience) is a community resource employed according to cultural, natural and technological constraints. Labour is always divided according to such principles as gender, age, lineage or class, and the product of social labour must be similarly divided. In addition to this, in most societies, groups or classes of non-producers live off transfers due to the exploitation of the producers.[24]

2. Modes of production and class relations of exploitation are determined by the form of extraction of surplus labour from the direct producers, and the mode of appropriation of the surplus in each of them.[25] These relations include the structures and processes that compel the producers to produce more than they consume or control, and the mechanisms of appropriation of the surplus by the exploiters. Even when narrowly defined in purely economic terms exploitation is a totality, including several aspects of social life, among them the property relations, the distribution of labour, control over the production process, and the distribution of the output. The existence of necessities and the surplus, and the division of social labour time between necessary and surplus labour, are consequences of exploitation in all modes of production. However, the existence of the value of labour power and surplus value, and their manifestation as wages and profits, are typical of capitalism, because only in this mode of production exploitation is mediated by the value form.

3. Capitalism is a mode of production, social reproduction and exploitation with three essential features: the diffusion of commodity production; the separation between the workers and the means of production (monopolised by the capitalist class), the commodification of labour power and the generalisation of the wage relation; and the subordination of production by the profit motive. These features, and their relations of mutual implication, mean that capitalism

---

24   There is exploitation if some people are compelled to act in ways that are systematically advantageous to others: 'To exploit a person is to use them toward the exploiter's ends. Exploiter status differs qualitatively, not quantitatively, from being the one exploited' (Naples 1989, p. 149).

25   'What distinguishes the various economic formations of society – the distinction between for example a society based on slave-labour and a society based on wage-labour – is the form in which surplus labour is in each case extorted from the immediate producer, the worker' (*Capital 1*, p. 325).

is a totality: it exists only at the level of society. It is meaningless to speak of capitalism at the 'individual' level (e.g. in a small number of farms or factories submerged in a sea of non-capitalist social relations) or of 'wage relations' between isolated employers and temporary workers producing small quantities for largely closed communities, in which most needs are not satisfied by commodity exchanges.

4. *Capital is a relationship of exploitation between two social classes*, through which the capitalists compel the wage workers, as a class, to produce more than the working class consumes or controls. The capitalist class absorbs the surplus value produced by the class of wage workers and, through it, commands part of the social product (the surplus).[26] This class relation is established when the means of production (the buildings, machinery, tools, vehicles, land, and so on) are monopolised by a class (the capitalists) that employs wage workers in the production of commodities for profit.[27] In contrast with pre-capitalist modes of production, wage workers under capitalism are forced – by structural-economic coercion, rather than personal-political relations – to sell their labour power regularly and continually because they do not own means of production, cannot produce independently, and need money to purchase part of the use values that, as a class, they have produced previously.[28] Therefore, capitalist exploitation is not determined primarily at the level of the individual farm, firm, or office and it would be meaningless to seek to analyse it at the individual level. It is determined at the social level, and mediated by the market-led distribution of labour and its products.[29] The capitalists' ownership of the means of production and their command over the production process allows them to control the level and composition of the output (including the relations between consumption and investment) and the allocation of labour

---

26 'Marx's starting point in the treatment of capital is conceiving capital as a social totality, capital representing a *class* opposed not so much to the individual laborers as to the wage laborers as a *class*' (Chattopadhyay 1994, p. 18).

27 The transformation of labour power into a commodity is the historical result of the primitive capital accumulation (see *Capital 1*, chs.26–32 and Perelman 1999). This process includes the elimination of the capacity of the workers to satisfy their own needs except through commodity exchanges, and the establishment of a pliant and reliable wage labour force.

28 'Exploitation is a matter of structural coercion. Circumstances are so arranged that a large mass of people must agree to do as they are told by others in order to support themselves and their families' (Nell 1992, p. 66).

29 'To Marx ... the essence of capitalist property is the control of the productive process and therefore the control over laborers. Forced labor rather than low wages, alienation of labor rather than alienation of the product of labor are, according to Marx, the essence of capitalist exploitation' (Medio 1977, p. 384).

in the economy. It also determines the mode of exploitation of the wage workers, through the extraction of surplus value.

   5. The value relation can be analysed at different levels. At a relatively abstract level of analysis, or in non-capitalist societies where commodity production and exchange are marginal, value is significant only as exchange value, a mental generalisation that expresses the rate of exchange of one commodity for another.[30] At this level, or at this stage in history, abstract labour is also a mental generalisation because, first, production aims primarily at the creation of specific use values, rather than the valorisation of capital. Second, labour markets are thin, highly fragmented and, often, absent. Third, the division of labour across society and within the workplace remains relatively undeveloped. Fourth, the exchange values are highly dependent upon non-market relations, rather than being determined primarily by the forces of production and competition, as in developed capitalism. Consequently, the labour process has few social determinations, the products of labour take the form of commodities only if they find their way into exchange, and the abstraction of labour is contingent on their sale.

   6. In capitalism, the social product has the form of value, and the value relation is expressed through the exchange value of the products of social labour.[31] In order to explain the capitalist mode of exploitation, Marx starts from its most abstract feature, the value relation. Value is the general form of human intercourse in capitalism, and its creation in production is a social process determined by the mode of division of labour and the social form of labour.[32]

---

30   In this case, '[t]he category of exchange-value leads an "antediluvian existence". One can find exchange-values in ancient Rome, in the Middle Ages and in capitalism; but different contents are hidden behind each of these forms of exchange-value. Marx stresses that "exchange-value" detached from the concrete relations under which it has arisen is an unreal abstraction, as exchange-value "can never exist except as an abstract, one-sided relation to an already given concrete and living whole"' (Grossman 1977, p. 46).

31   'For Marx the value of a commodity expresses the particular historical form that the social character of labour has under capitalism ... This suggests first, that the generalisation of the commodity form of human labour is quite specific to capitalism and that value as a concept of analysis is similarly so specific. Secondly, it suggests that value is not just a concept with a mental existence; it has a real existence, value relations being the particular form taken by capitalist social relations' (Mohun 1991, p. 564).

32   For Marx, the value relation and its grounding upon the social division of labour do not need to be demonstrated; they are *facts*: 'even if there were no chapter on "value" at all in my book, the analysis I give of the real relations would contain the proof and demonstration of the real value relation. The chatter about the need to prove the concept of value arises only from complete ignorance both of the subject under discussion and of the method of science. Every child knows that any nation that stopped working, not for a year, but let us say, just for a few weeks, would perish. And every child knows, too, that the

In capitalism, commodities are produced by a co-ordinated set of concrete labours usually performed at the farm, factory or office. These labours are performed with varying degrees of efficiency, diverse skills and distinct technologies, and at different points in time. In spite of these differences, all commodities of the same kind (with the same use value) have the same value, which appears through their price. The labour time that determines value is socially, rather than individually, determined, and commodity values express the abstract labour time necessary to produce each kind of commodity, rather than the concrete labour time required by any individual worker or firm to produce a sample of the object. Output values cannot be identified at the firm or sectoral levels for two reasons. First, value creation is a social process determined by the predominance of specific relations of production, in which case individual production has meaning and significance only as part of the whole. Second, values and prices are determined by the *abstract* labour time necessary to reproduce each type of commodity, including its inputs. In sum, the value form of the product is due to the social division of labour, values are quantitatively determined by the collective effort and the productive potential of society, and prices are determined for the mass of commodities rather than good by good or at the level of the firm or sector.

7. *Values are determined quantitatively by the normalisation, synchronisation and homogenisation of labour.*[33] *Normalisation* is the subsumption of the labours performed in each firm and sector under the social process of production of each type of commodity, by which individual labours are averaged out within each capitalist firm and sector, including not only those labours performed in the last stage of production but also the labours that produced the inputs used up. Because of normalisation, commodities with identical use values have the same value whatever their individual conditions of production. The simultaneous sale, at the same price, of commodities produced in different moments shows that individual concrete labours are *synchronised* across those that have produced the same kind of commodity at other times, or with distinct technologies. Because labours are normalised and synchronised, all commodities of a kind have the same value, regardless of how, when and by whom they are produced. Normalisation explains why the labour time

---

amounts of products corresponding to the differing amounts of needs demand differing and quantitatively determined amounts of society's aggregate labour ... And the form in which this proportional distribution of labour asserts itself in a state of society in which the interconnection of social labour expresses itself as the private exchange of the individual products of labour, is precisely the exchange value of these products' (Marx 1988a, p. 68).

33   See Lee (1990) and Saad-Filho (2002, ch.5).

necessary to produce a type of commodity is socially determined, and includes that necessary to produce the inputs. Synchronisation implies that this labour time is indistinguishable from and, therefore, is equivalent to living labour.[34] The equivalence between labours producing the same commodities at different points in time or with distinct technologies is due to the fact that value is a social relation established by, and reproduced through, capitalist production, rather than a substance ahistorically embodied in the commodities by concrete labour.

The social reality of value implies that *only living labour creates value* or, alternatively, that Marx's value theory is based on *social reproduction costs*.[35] More specifically, values are determined by the current ability of society to reproduce each kind of commodity, or the *socially necessary labour time for the reproduction* of each commodity (SNLTR).[36] Qualitatively, values are not set in

---

34   'All the labour contained in the yarn is past labour; and it is a matter of no importance that the labour expended to produce its constituent elements lies further back in the past than the labour expended on the final process, the spinning. The former stands, as it were, in the pluperfect, the latter in the perfect tense, but this does not matter. If a definite quantity of labour, say thirty days, is needed to build a house, the total amount of labour incorporated in the house is not altered by the fact that the work of the last day was done twenty-nine days later than that of the first. Therefore the labour contained in the raw material and instruments of labour can be treated just as if it were labour expended in an earlier stage of the spinning process, before the labour finally added in the form of actual spinning' (*Capital 1*, pp. 294–295).

35   Somewhat counter-intuitively, the original value of the inputs used up, and the money-capital spent buying them, are *irrelevant* for the determination of the output value: 'the values of the material and means of labour only re-appear in the product of the labour process to the extent that they were preposited to the latter as values, i.e. they were values before they entered into the process. Their value is equal to the ... labour time necessary to produce them under given general social conditions of production. If later on more or less labour time were to be required to manufacture these particular use values ... their value would have risen in the first case and fallen in the second ... Hence although they entered the labour process with a definite value, they may come out of it with a value that is larger or smaller ... These changes in their value, however, always arise from changes in the productivity of the labour of which they are the products, and have nothing to do with the labour process into which they enter as finished products with a given value' (Marx 1988b, pp. 79–80).

36   'The value of any commodity ... is determined not by the necessary labour time that it itself contains, but by the *socially* necessary labour-time required for its reproduction. This reproduction may differ from the conditions of its original production by taking place under easier or more difficult circumstances. If the changed circumstances mean that twice as much time, or alternatively only half as much, is required for the same physical capital to be reproduced, then given an unchanged value of money, this capital, if it was previously worth £100, would now be worth £200, or alternatively £50' (*Capital 3*, p. 238). For similar statements, see *Capital 1*, pp. 129–130, 317–318, 676–677, *Capital 2*, pp. 185–188,

stone when the commodities are produced; rather, they express the conditions of social reproduction, including the ability of society to *re-start* production in the next period. Quantitatively, they are socially determined continuously, and they can shift because of technical change anywhere in the economy. Normalised and synchronised labours in distinct sectors of the economy generally create different quantities of value in a given time, for example, in window cleaning and computer programming. The *homogenisation* of labour translates the different value-productivities of normalised and synchronised labour into distinct quantities of abstract labour (SNLTR). Labours are homogenised for all commodities simultaneously as they receive a price, or when money fulfils the function of measure of value. At this level of analysis, the law of value ensures that commodity prices correspond to their SNLTR. Although homogenisation is conceptually clear, the assessment of the value produced is uncertain because prices are affected by a wide range of variables at distinct levels of complexity. For example, price reductions may be due to technical progress, the possibility of capital migration, excess supply, industrial, financial, tax, trade or exchange rate policies, and other variables.

Value determination through SNLTR, its expression as price through normalisation, and the possibility of differences between the value production and realisation because of the misallocation of social labour or economic crises, belong to distinct levels of analysis. The latter is more complex, because it includes not only the production conditions, but also the circumstances of exchange, the distribution of labour and the possibility of crisis. Finally, firms whose profit rates are lower than the average are always penalised. Within each branch, inefficient firms produce less value than their competitors, and may go bankrupt or become the target of takeover bids. These pressures can become stronger if the sector produces in excess of demand, which depresses the profit rate of all firms. Differences between individual and sectoral profit rates vis-à-vis the average are the capitalist mechanism of reallocation of labour across the economy and, simultaneously, the main lever of technical change.

8. Abstract labour, value and price can be viewed at distinct levels. At a highly abstract level, value is a social relation that derives from the mode of production; therefore, labour performed within the relations of production typical of capitalism produces value regardless of the circumstances in exchange or distribution. The quantity of value produced is determined by SNLTR, and it

---

222–223, 366–368, *Capital* 3, p. 522, *Theories of Surplus Value 1*, pp. 232–233, *Theories of Surplus Value 2*, p. 416, *Theories of Surplus Value 3*, p. 280, *Grundrisse*, pp. 135, 402, 657, and Marx's letter to Engels dated 14 September 1851 (cited in Rosdolsky 1977, p. 318n3). For an exhaustive survey of Marx's texts, see Moseley (2000b).

appears initially as 'value', 'direct' or 'simple' price. The relationship between value and price can be analysed more concretely, but there is often a trade-off between conceptual detail and quantitative determinacy. For example, the transfer of the value of the means of production introduces a quantitative indeterminacy in the output value and, correspondingly, arbitrariness in the price level, because the rate of technical depreciation of the fixed capital is unknowable. By the same token, price can be seen as the mode of existence of value, as the condition of supply, or as the money that can be commanded on sale, which are, *prima facie*, unrelated to the mode of labour. In addition to these difficulties, discrepancies between supply and demand and economic crises blur the relationship between values and prices even further. In sum, shifts in the level of analysis modify the relationship between value and price and, therefore, the homogenisation of labour. In contrast, normalisation and synchronisation remain unaffected, because they are determined exclusively in production. These limitations show that attempts to calculate values independently of prices through estimates of the vector of abstract labour are limited both conceptually and empirically, because they presume that value can appear in two different ways, both directly (as if it could be measured by concrete labour time) and through price. Simply put, the value analysis developed here does not allow the quantitative determination of long-run prices better than alternative approaches. Its main advantage is theoretical; it *explains* the social relations underlying economic activity more clearly than alternative views.

9. *In capitalist societies wage labour is the form of social labour*, and the products, other assets and social relations generally have the commodity form. Consequently, wage labour employed by capital in the production of commodities for profit produces value regardless of the form or destination of the product, or whether or not it is sold. Under capitalism, labour has a double determination; it is both concrete and abstract. As concrete labour, work is a transformative activity; as abstract labour, work is subsumed by, or exists in and through, a specific social form, wage labour employed for profit. The generalisation of the value form, wage labour and production for profit – i.e., the performance of concrete labour generally depends upon the extraction of surplus value rather than, for example, need for the output – establish in practice (rather than simply conceptually) the primacy of abstract over concrete labour.[37] The abstraction of labour and the commodification of

---

[37] This is not always accepted by different interpretations of Marx; for example, it was shown above that traditional approaches claim that absolute and concrete labour are merely distinct aspects of labour, existing in parallel.

the social product can be analysed at two levels. First, in production, the wage workers are typically hired on the labour market and compelled to work in order to produce goods and services primarily for profit (surplus value) rather than need (use value), using commercially available inputs. Consequently, the products are commodities since their inception, and abstract labour predominates over concrete labour in production. Second, the exchangeability of the products demonstrates, in the sphere of exchange, the substantive identity (i.e., abstraction) of all types of labour, regardless of the concrete form of the output.[38]

10. Surplus value is the difference between the value produced by the working class and the value of labour power. From the point of view of the extraction of surplus value, capital is a class relation of exploitation defined by the capitalists' ability to compel the working class to produce more value than it consumes or controls (which Marx calls 'necessities', produced by necessary labour, and whose value is the value of labour power), and the capitalist command of the surplus in value form.[39] Alternatively, the workers are exploited because they produce more value than they control or receive as wages.[40] Surplus value is

---

38 Marx contrasts the determinations of labour in simple commodity exchange and in capitalism as follows: 'what is it that forms the bond between the independent labours of the cattle-breeder, the tanner and the shoemaker? It is the fact that their respective products are commodities. What, on the other hand, characterizes the division of labour in manufacture? The fact that the specialized worker produces no commodities. It is only the common product of all the specialized workers that becomes a commodity ... The division of labour within manufacture presupposes a concentration of the means of production in the hands of one capitalist; the division of labour within society presupposes a dispersion of those means among many independent producers of commodities ... Division of labour within the workshop implies the undisputed authority of the capitalist over men, who are merely the members of a total mechanism which belongs to him. The division of labour within society brings into contact independent producers of commodities, who acknowledge no authority other than that of competition' (*Capital 1*, pp. 475–477).

39 The primacy of surplus value over the extraction of material surplus in capitalist exploitation is grounded on the motivation of the labour process (profit rather than goods) and the form of the appropriation of the surplus (monetary profit). Obviously, capitalists only acquire command over commodities (and over future production cycles) through their money-capital, rather than directly through their use of leftovers from the previous production cycle.

40 'The wage-form thus extinguishes every trace of the division of the working day into necessary labour and surplus labour, into paid labour and unpaid labour. All labour appears as paid labour. Under the *corvée* system it is different. There the labour of the serf for himself, and his compulsory labour for the lord of the land, are demarcated very clearly both in space and time. In slave labour, even the part of the working day in which the slave is only replacing the value of his own means of subsistence, in which he therefore actually works for himself alone, appears as labour for his master. All his labour appears as unpaid labour. In wage-labour, on the contrary, even surplus labour, or unpaid labour, appears as

the part of the social value product appropriated by the capitalist class. It appears as profit, the residual left after the payment of the production costs.

11. The ratio between the surplus value and the value of labour power (or between surplus and necessary labour time) is the rate of exploitation (rate of surplus value). From the point of view of distribution, capitalist exploitation can be conceptualised and measured at three levels, the physical, macromonetary and value levels. For the physical or surplus approach, associated with traditional Marxism and Sraffian views, there is exploitation when the producers (individually and, by aggregation, as a class) are compelled to produce more than they themselves consume or control, the residual being appropriated by their masters, lords or employers by custom or law, or under the threat or use of force, or because refusal to comply might disorganise the social reproduction. This approach is not wrong but it is transhistorical and excessively general. It is valuable because it highlights the similarities between different modes of exploitation. However, this generality is also a source of weakness, because the analysis is unable to distinguish clearly between different modes of exploitation.[41] At the macro-monetary level of analysis, associated with value-form theories, capitalist exploitation is revealed by the existence of profits (including interest, rent and other forms of profit), and the rate of exploitation is measured by the profit-wage ratio.[42] This approach is useful because it lends itself to empirical studies. However, it suffers from two shortcomings: it focuses on the symptoms (the inability of the workers to command the entire net product) rather than the cause of exploitation, and it can be misleading because the profit-wage ratio is an imprecise measure of exploitation.[43] Finally, value analysis can identify the essence of capitalist

---

paid. In the one case, the property-relation conceals the slave's labour for himself; in the other case the money-relation conceals the uncompensated labour of the wage-earner' (*Capital 1*, p. 680).

41   'The specific economic form in which unpaid surplus labour is pumped out of the direct producers determines the relationship of domination and servitude, as this grows directly out of production itself and reacts back on it in turn as a determinant ... It is in each case the direct relationship of the owners of the conditions of production to the immediate producers ... in which we find the innermost secret, the hidden basis of the entire social edifice' (*Capital 3*, p. 927).

42   There are significant difficulties for the empirical estimation of the rate of exploitation because of the influence of the accounting conventions, taxes, savings, unproductive labour, and so on.

43   First, empirically, profits and wages are originally assessed at the firm level, then aggregated for the entire economy. This does not correspond to the actual process of exploitation, that is determined by the class structure of society, the mode of production that corresponds to it, and the appropriation of part of the social product by the capitalist class. In other words, exploitation takes place at the level of capital in general and

exploitation, distinguish it from other modes of exploitation, and facilitate empirical studies. In common with the surplus approach, value analysis implies that the workers are exploited because they work for longer than what is necessary to produce the commodities that they consume or control. However, it claims that the rate of exploitation cannot be measured directly because it is determined by abstract rather than concrete labour.

12. *The value of labour power is a quantity of value*, the labour time spent by the working class producing necessities (the goods and services appropriated or controlled by the workers). This value is determined at the aggregate (class) level through the exchange between capital and labour as a whole and, subsequently, the performance of labour and exploitation in production.[44] This form of conceptualising the value of labour power is distinct from the traditional and Sraffian views, where it is a quantity of goods, and from the abstract labour version or the 'new interpretation' definition of value of labour power as a quantity of money. The class concept of value of labour power implies that the working class is exploited because part of what it produces is appropriated, through money, by the capitalists, and it acknowledges that capitalist exploitation includes an irreducibly monetary and macroeconomic aspect (rather than being encapsulated by the transhistorical inability of the workers to command the entire net product). However, this does not imply that a fixed bundle must be consumed in order to obtain specific outcomes and, consequently, it avoids the conflation between the workers and draught cattle, machines or electricity. The level of wages and the workers' norm of consumption are part of the conditions of reproduction of the working class. They should be understood starting from the aggregate, rather than as the ex post average across firms or labour market segments.[45] The levels of consumption and wages, and the incidence

---

it is mediated by generalised commodity relations, in which case wage workers are exploited *qua* workers, regardless of the profitability of the firms where they are currently employed. Second, transfers create systematic discrepancies between commodity prices and values. As a result, the profit-wage ratio may be different from the ratio between the abstract labour required to produce the necessities and the surplus, which Marx called necessary and surplus labour time. Third, wages, prices and profits are determined at market prices, and they can fluctuate widely regardless of changes in the conditions of production, especially after the development of the credit system.

44 'The value of wages has to be reckoned not according to the quantity of the means of subsistence received by the worker, but according to the quantity of labour which these means of subsistence cost (in fact the proportion of the working-day which he appropriates for himself), that is according to the *relative share* of the total product, or rather of the total value of this product, which the worker receives' (*Theories of Surplus Value 2*, p. 419).

45 The value of labour power provides the clearest example of *reproduction* SNLT: the value of labour power is determined by the workers' reproduction needs, rather than the

of needs, are the outcome of dynamic socio-economic processes including the structure of the labour market, struggles within them, and the social processes of production and satisfaction of wants. What those wants and patterns of consumption are, and how they are determined, can be very different from one commodity to another and from one section of the working class to another. Distinct commodities are not only differentially consumed across the working class but their patterns and levels of consumption derive from very different structures and processes of causation, including the structure of employment, the role of the state, the structure and content of housework, (changes in) skill levels, the role of trade unions and the political leverage of each section of the working class.

13. As a totality engaged in self-expansion through the employment of wage labour, capital is primarily capital in general – this is the general form of capital. Capital in general is represented by the circuit of industrial capital, M-C-M', where M is the money advanced to buy commodities (means of production and labour power), C, for processing and, later, sale for more money M'. The difference M' – M is the surplus value, which is the foundation of industrial and commercial profit and other forms of profit, including interest and rent. The circuit of industrial capital represents the essence of capital, valorisation through the production of commodities by wage labour.[46] In this circuit, capital shifts between different forms, money, productive and commodity capital, as it moves between the spheres of exchange, production and, upon its completion, exchange. Although this movement is critical for the process of valorisation, profit is due to the surplus labour performed in production only.[47] But profit is not the only thing that capital produces; the social outcome of its

---

concrete labour time embodied in the workers or in the goods that they consume, or have consumed in the past.

46   'Industrial capital is the only mode of existence of capital in which not only the appropriation of surplus-value or surplus product, but also its creation, is a function of capital. It thus requires production to be capitalist in character; its existence includes that of the class antagonism between capitalists and wage-labourers ... The other varieties of capital which appeared previously, within past or declining conditions of social production, are not only subordinated to it and correspondingly altered in the mechanism of their functioning, but they now move only on its basis, thus live and die, stand and fall together with this basis. Money capital and commodity capital, in so far as they appear and function as bearers of their own peculiar branches of business alongside industrial capital, are now only modes of existence of the various functional forms that industrial capital constantly assumes and discards within the circulation sphere' (*Capital* 2, pp. 135–136).

47   Interest-bearing capital (IBC), whose general form is M-M' (money that becomes more money), does not *produce* profit, any more than money left inside a mattress begets more money simply by lying there. The expansion of IBC is due to transfers from productive capital, see Fine and Saad-Filho (2016, ch.12).

circuit is the expanded reproduction of capital, the renewal of the separation between capitalists and wage workers. In this sense, 'Accumulation of capital is ... multiplication of the proletariat'.[48]

14. Capitalist production is necessarily mass production. Pre-capitalist production is characterised by small scales and market fragmentation. In contrast, in developed capitalism firms produce an extraordinarily varied assortment of goods and services, in large quantities. Mass production necessitates the employment of millions of workers. Even when individual firms are small, or downsize, or spin-off independent companies, or if the products are made to order, capitalist production – including finance, accounting, design, planning, logistics, hiring, training and managing the workforce, manufacturing, marketing, distribution, and so on – remains tightly integrated vertically into systems of provision employing large numbers of workers in large-scale and continuous operations managed professionally, often by large organisations. Each stage of this process is closely intertwined with the others, and with production carried out elsewhere. In these systems of provision, the labour of individual workers exists, and can be analysed, only as part of the whole. This labour is performed according to the rhythm dictated by technology, management, machinery and competition, limited by collective resistance on the shopfloor. Mass production and collective (co-operative) work harnessed by capital raise the productivity of labour, and this power is appropriated by the capitalists. At the same time, the organisation, integration and mechanisation of mass production for profit tends to average out the labour of the wage workers, creating the 'collective worker'. The averaging out of labour in production rather than on the market, as is the case under simple commodity production, is due to the organised, integrated and mechanised character of capitalist production.[49]

---

48   *Capital 1*, p. 764. In other words, 'The capitalist process of production, therefore, seen as a total, connected process, i.e. a process of reproduction, produces not only commodities, not only surplus-value, but it also produces and reproduces the capital-relation itself; on the one hand the capitalist, on the other the wage-labourer' (*Capital 1*, p. 724).

49   '[E]ach worker, or group of workers, prepares the raw material for another worker or group of workers. The result of the labour of the one is the starting-point for the labour of the other. One worker therefore directly sets the other to work ... [T]he direct mutual interdependence of the different pieces of work, and therefore of the workers, compels each one of them to spend on his work no more than the necessary time. This creates a continuity, a uniformity, a regularity, order, and even an intensity of labour, quite different from that found in an independent handicraft or even in simple co-operation. The rule that the labour-time expended on a commodity should not exceed the amount socially necessary to produce it is one that appears, in the production of commodities in general, to be enforced from outside by the action of competition: to put it superficially, each single producer is obliged to sell his commodity at its market price. In manufacture, on

This process subsumes the labours performed in each firm and sector under the social (class-based) process of production of each type of commodity. The tendencies towards averaging out labour in production and creating the collective (class) worker does not imply unambiguous outcomes, because they are counteracted by workers' resistance, changes in work practices, technical innovations within firms, demand shifts, and other factors.[50]

15. *Capital controls the workers in three principal ways.* First, capital owns the means of production, whereas the workers must seek paid employment in order to survive. Second, having purchased labour power, capital claims the right to control the labour process in its entirety, and machinery helps management to dictate the structure and pace of the labour process. Third, ownership of the means of production and control of the labour process allow capital to influence the state, economic policy, the legislature, interpretation and enforcement of law, and other social institutions. In other words, exploitation is a class relationship with two aspects, the capitalist command over part of the output, and their exclusive control over its composition, including the investment goods and the sources of growth. Both aspects of exploitation derive from the capitalist monopoly of the means of production, the transformation of commodities into the general form of the product, and the capitalist control of the labour process.

16. *Capitalist domination is invariably contested, and capitalist production invariably involves conflicts in production and in distribution.* These conflicts are unavoidable, because they spring from the relations of production that define this social system. For example, the workers constantly strive for alternatives to paid employment and subordination in the workplace, seek higher wages and better working conditions, and may engage in collective activity in order to defend their interests in the production line and elsewhere. The distributive conflicts resemble those in other class societies, for they involve disputes about how the cake (the national product) is shared among competing claims,

---

the contrary, the provision of a given quantity of the product in a given period of labour is a technical law of the process of production itself' (*Capital 1*, pp. 464–465).

50   'Capitalist production only really begins ... when each individual capital simultaneously employs a comparatively large number of workers, and when, as a result, the labour-process is carried on an extensive scale, and yields relatively large quantities of products ... This is true both historically and conceptually ... *The labour objectified in value is labour of an average social quality, it is an expression of average labour-power* ... The law of valorization therefore comes fully into its own for the individual producer only when he produces as a capitalist and employs a number of workers simultaneously, i.e. when from the outset he sets in motion labour of a socially average character' (*Capital 1*, pp. 439–441, emphasis added).

while maintaining systemic stability. In contrast, conflicts in production derive from the class relations that distinguish capitalism from other modes of production. They are due to disputes about how much wage labour is performed and under what conditions, and their outcome plays a limiting role upon the distributive conflicts.

17. Capital always exist in and through competition, or as many capitals. Two types of competition are especially important in *Capital*. Intra-sectoral competition (between capitals producing the same use values) compels firms to minimise costs in order to maximise its profit rate. The most important tools available to capitalist firms are, on the one hand, the extension of the working day, increasing labour intensity, and increasing the training and discipline of the workforce, leading to the extraction of absolute surplus value. On the other hand, firms can introduce new technologies, raising the value-productivity of their employees.[51] These innovations will be copied or emulated elsewhere, eroding the advantage of the innovating firm while preserving the incentives for further technical progress across the economy. This process tends to reduce the value of all goods, including those consumed by the workers and, all else constant, it permits the extraction of relative surplus value. This type of competition tends to disperse the individual profit rates, because more profitable capitals can invest larger sums for longer periods, select among a broader range of production techniques and hire the best workers, which reinforces their initial advantage. Important counter-tendencies are the diffusion of technical innovations among competing firms, the potential ability of smaller capitals to undermine the existing technologies through invention and experimentation, and foreign competition. In contrast, inter-sectoral competition (between capitals producing distinct use values) creates a tendency towards the convergence of profit rates, because capital migration redistributes the productive potential of society and increases supply in the more profitable branches, thus reducing excess profits. The financial system plays an important role in both processes. In sum, competition within sectors explains the sources of profit rate *differences* between capitals producing similar goods with distinct technologies, the necessity of technical change, and the possibility of crisis of disproportion and overproduction. Competition between capitals in different sectors explains the possibility of capital migration to other sectors due to profit rate differentials, the tendency towards the

---

51   New technologies allow firms to introduce new goods or to improve existing goods. The latter is ignored here because it merely replicates the same type of competition across new markets.

equalisation of the profit rates of competing capitals, and other equilibrating structures and processes associated with competition and market relations.

18. Intra-sectoral competition leads to mechanisation, or the introduction of new technologies and new machines. Mechanisation increases the degree of integration between labour processes within and across firms, and the potential scale of production. Mechanisation can fulfil three capitalist objectives: higher profitability, socialisation of labour, and social control. At the level of individual capitals, mechanisation reduces unit costs, increases the value-productivity of labour, and raises the profit rate of the innovating capitals. At the level of capital in general, mechanisation facilitates the extraction of relative surplus value. Mechanisation also allows increasingly sophisticated goods to be produced with higher investment, which tends to reduce the scope for competition by independent producers, and their ability to survive except as wage workers or dependent contractors. Within firms, mechanisation socialises production because it imposes production norms that reduce the scope for worker control over the expenditure of their labour power. However, and contradictorily, mechanisation can also give workers more control over their job conditions and reduce the drudgery associated with difficult and repetitive tasks. Finally, the socialisation of production is closely associated with capitalist control of the production process. Underneath their seemingly neutral, scientific and productivist guise, machines are despotic dictators of the rhythm and content of the labour process.[52] Machines dilute the workers' individuality through collective labour, and they have been often deployed deliberately in order to wrestle both the knowledge and the control of production away from the workers. Machinery is often introduced even at the expense of profitability.[53] On the shopfloor, capital appears in its simplest form, as a conflict-ridden

---

52   '[T]echnology is not merely control over Nature, it also provides control over Man. The division of labor and the factory system provided ways of *controlling* the pace and quality of work, as do modern assembly-line methods. Technology provides for social control and discipline in the workplace. So the development of technology is not socially neutral; it will reflect class interests and sociopolitical pressures' (Nell 1992, p. 54).

53   '[M]machinery does not just act as a superior competitor to the worker, always on the point of making him superfluous. It is a power inimical to him, and capital proclaims this fact loudly and deliberately, as well as making use of it. It is the most powerful weapon for suppressing strikes, those periodic revolts of the working class against the autocracy of capital ... It would be possible to write a whole history of the inventions made since 1830 for the sole purpose of providing capital with weapons against working-class revolt' (*Capital 1*, pp. 562–563). For modern accounts of the role of technology in social conflicts, see Levidow and Young (1981, 1985) and Slater (1980). In general, '[a]s the case studies proliferate, the evidence accumulates against a technological-determinist reading of organizational history and in favor of a conflict approach that views organizational structures as embodiying strategies for controlling workers' behavior' (Attewell 1984, p. 119).

social relation of production and exploitation, in which machinery, law, and the threat of unemployment and social exclusion play an essential role in its reproduction. In spite of the widespread perception that capitalism and productivity growth are inseparable (because of competition within sectors), this relationship is not straightforward for two reasons. First, firms do not select the technologies that are most productive of use values, but those that are most profitable, and these criteria may lead to distinct outcomes. Second, the imperative of social control, in the production line as well as in society, introduces biases in the choice of technology, systematically favouring control and profitability rather than the imperatives of health, safety and social welfare.

19. *The existence of different types of competition does not lead to static outcomes*, for example, the equalisation of profits rates across the economy or the relentless concentration of capital, as may be expected in mainstream microeconomics. Rather, both types of competition interact continually within and between sectors, and they are among the most important factors responsible for the dynamics of capitalism. Attempts to 'add up' the impact of competition within and between sectors are analytically illegitimate, because of their distinct levels of abstraction: competition within sectors is relatively more abstract, and more important, than competition between sectors, for two reasons. First, profit must be produced before it can be distributed and equalised, in which case analysis of technologies, strategies and work practices should precede the study of outcomes, both at the level of the firm and the sector. Second, although migration can raise the profit rate of individual capitals, for Marx changes in the profitability of capital as a whole are contingent upon technical progress. Capital accumulation and competition are normally conflicting processes, tending to generate instability, crisis, overwork, unemployment and poverty. For these reasons, capitalism is not only a highly efficient system of production: it is also the most structurally unstable and systematically destructive mode of production in history, because of the conflicting forces of extraction, realisation, and accumulation of surplus value under competitive conditions. Capitalist instability in the social, economic and ecological domains is systemic and structural, and the ensuing destructiveness affects both peoples and nature. They cannot be entirely avoided whatever the combination of economic policies.

20. *Competition destroys the capitalist basis of production.*[54] Intrasectoral competition creates a tendency towards rising labour productivity

---

54 '[C]apital ... increases the surplus labour time of the mass by all the means of art and science ... It is thus, despite itself, instrumental in creating the means of social disposable time, in order to reduce labour time for the whole society to a diminishing minimum, and thus to free everyone's time for their own development. But its tendency always, on

and increasing technical and organic compositions of capital. They objectively permit living standards to increase and labour time to decline simultaneously.[55] However, there is are severe contradictions between the workers' desire to reduce working time to a minimum, while demanding the highest possible wages, and the capitalists' demand for the longest possible working days with (in their own firms) the highest possible levels of productivity, and the highest possible rates of productivity growth. Systemically, excessively low rates of exploitation lead to high unemployment and low productivity growth, while excessively high rates of exploitation render the economy prone to overproduction crises. These contradictions between the classes of workers and capitalists, and within the capitalist class, make it difficult to implement (through the state) the collective capitalist interest in regulating the length of the working day in order to preserve economic stability. In the absence of this regulating mechanism, other policies must be used even if they achieve this objective only indirectly. Limitations such as these make it unlikely that maximum rates of exploitation and rapid economic growth can be compatible for long periods. Over the long term, rising labour productivity reduces the significance of living labour for the production of use values and, consequently, its importance for the determination of value. In spite of its potential welfare implications, under capitalism technology is unlikely to eliminate drudgery and long hours of work. Their perpetuation is due to social, rather than technical, barriers. More specifically, technical progress facilitates the satisfaction of needs through non-market processes, the reduction of labour time, and the automation of repetitive, dangerous and unhealthy jobs. However, they are

the one side, *to create disposable time, on the other, to convert it into surplus labour.* If it succeeds too well at the first, then it suffers from surplus production, and then necessary labour is interrupted, because *no surplus labour can be realised by capital.* The more this contradiction develops, the more does it become evident that the growth of the forces of production can no longer be bound up with the appropriation of alien labour but that the mass of workers must themselves appropriate their own surplus labour ... *Labour time as the measure of value* posits wealth itself as founded on poverty, and disposable time as existing *in and because of the antithesis to surplus labour time*; or, the positing of an individual's entire time as labour time, and his degradation therefore to mere worker, subsumption under labour. *The most developed machinery thus forces the worker to work longer than the savage does, or than he himself did with the simplest, crudest tools*' (*Grundrisse*, pp. 708–709).

55   This has been the case historically in the rich countries. However, reductions in the working week generally fail to keep pace with technical progress, because the capitalists tend to resist against measures that reduce the rate of exploitation. Experience shows that the success of attempts to curtail labour time depends upon the strength and political leverage of the working class, whilst the state of technology is an important, but secondary influence.

anathema for capitalism, because they conflict with the valorisation of capital and the reproduction of the relations of exploitation. At some stage, Marx believes that the majority will no longer accept these limits to the achievement of their individual and collective potential, and they will revolt against capitalism and build another social and economic system, communism.

3   Conclusion

The interpretation of Marx's theory of value outlined above can be summarised as follows. Marx's theory departs from the principle that human societies reproduce themselves, and change, through labour. Labour and its products are socially divided and, under capitalism, these processes and their outcomes are determined by the monopoly of the means of production by the class of capitalists, the commodification of labour power and the commodity form of the products of labour. In these circumstances, the products of labour generally take the value form, and economic exploitation is based on the extraction of surplus value. Hence, the capital relation includes the monopoly of the means of production, wage labour, and the continuous reproduction of the two large and mutually conditioning social classes, the capitalists and the workers. When analysed from this angle, the theory of value is a theory of class, class relations, and exploitation. The concept of value is essential because it expresses the relations of exploitation under capitalism, and allows them to be explained in spite of the deceptive appearances created by the predominance of voluntary market exchanges.

This approach to Marx's theory implies that value theory is *not* essentially a theory of the 'separation' of commodity producers, commodity exchange ratios, labour embodied in products, or of the allocation of labour in the economy, as is the case in alternative interpretations discussed previously. Quite the opposite, the class interpretation of Marx's theory of value highlights the *social form of the property relations* (the means of production are owned by the class of capitalists), the *social form of labour* (wage labour), the *mode of labour control* (capitalists hire and manage the expenditure of labour power), the *social form of the products of labour*, and of goods and services more generally (commodities) and the *objective of social production* (profit rather than, say, need, exchange, consumption or investment).

It is impossible to draw together, in the limits of this essay, all the implications of the class interpretation approach outlined above. Moreover, Marx's writings on value, and the interpretation outlined above, are pitched at a level of abstraction that is too high to offer ready-made answers to the urgent problems of today. In spite of this, a class interpretation of Marx's value theory can provide a uniquely insightful explanation of the inner workings of capitalism and the articulation between distinct aspects of this economic system, showing the enormous potential of capitalism to achieve constructive as well as destructive and degrading outcomes. In particular, Marxian analysis can explain important features of capitalism which other schools of thought, including the neoclassical, Keynesian and institutionalist, have difficulty analysing. For example, the necessity and origin of money, technical progress and the rising productivity of labour, conflicts over the intensity of labour and the length of the working-day, the growth of the wage-earning class, the inevitability of uneven development, cycles and crises, and the impoverishment of the workers – not because of declining living standards but, rather, because of the growing distance between their 'needs' and what they can afford to buy, often leading to debt and overwork.

Another distinguishing contribution of Marx's theory of value is its capacity to point out the root cause of several contemporary problems and the limits to their potential solution under capitalism. Some of these problems can be remedied within the current system, for example, relative economic stagnation, high unemployment, the erosion of political democracy, lack of corporate responsibility, and absolute poverty. In contrast, other problems cannot be resolved, because they are *features* of capitalism; among them, the existence of unemployment and exploitation of the workforce, economic inequality, the encroachment of work upon free time, systematic environmental degradation, lack of economic democracy, and production for profit rather than need. Problems such as these can be, at best, concealed by propaganda and mitigated by economic prosperity.

Mass action is necessary in order to address important problems of our age, among them environmental degradation, long-term unemployment, poverty amidst plenty in developed and developing countries, the dissemination of curable or controllable diseases, illiteracy, cultural, ethnic and economic oppression, and other problems. In addressing these problems and their potential solutions, Karl Marx offers an analysis that is unencumbered by current prejudices and that can inspire creative solutions. Marxists can, therefore, contribute to the advance of these movements and, in doing so, familiarise large numbers of people with Marxian views. This has become especially urgent. The reproduction of Marxist theory is in danger, as the 'generation of 1968' approaches retirement age and draws to a close its militancy in the universities, trade unions and workplaces. There is a great risk that Marxism will face a historical decline similar to that experienced between the late twenties and the mid-sixties, with irretrievable losses in terms of theory and political experience.

CHAPTER 3

Labour, Money and 'Labour-Money': A Review of Marx's Critique of John Gray's Monetary Analysis

A hundred guinea premium is offered to the man who may be able most effectually to refute my arguments.

JOHN GRAY 1848, pp. 256–257

∙ ∙ ∙

All the illusions of the monetary system arise from the failure to perceive that money, though a physical object with distinct properties, represents a social relation of production.

KARL MARX 1987, p. 276

∙ ∙
∙

Throughout his mature work, Marx often criticises the 'Ricardian socialist' economists whom he regarded as utopians. This essay[1] concentrates on Marx's attack against one of their main proposals: a monetary reform aiming at the institution of a 'labour-money'. Although several authors advanced some version of this idea, this essay focuses on John Gray's formulation, as his is probably the best-argued case for such a reform. However, the main goals of this essay are neither to review Gray's plans nor to present Marx's critique. Marx's polemic against Gray's 'labour-money' scheme is used as a means of scrutinising his own theory of money and of shedding light on its remarkably rich perspectives. In particular, this essay focuses on the relationship between labour and value, and the study of the functions of money.

Limited to these aims, this essay does not offer a comprehensive account of the various formulations of the idea of labour-money, nor does it

---

1 Originally published as 'Money, Labour and "Labour-Money": A Review of Marx's Critique of John Gray's Monetary Analysis', *History of Political Economy* 25 (1), 1993, pp. 65–84. Reproduced with minor changes.

examine Gray's influence on the evolution of Marx's own thought. After this introduction, the first section offers a summary of Gray's proposals, occasionally supported by recourse to similar approaches by John Bray, P.-J. Proudhon and A. Darimon. The second section discusses the relationship between labour and value in Marx, using the concepts of normalisation, synchronisation and homogenisation of labour, that are applied to Marx's critiques of labour-money. The third concentrates on the relationship between value, money and prices in Marx and in Gray, and examines how value is measured and how prices are set in each view. The fourth analyses the other functions of money in Marx, in contrast with Gray. The fifth section concludes, showing why, for Marx, 'labour-money' could not be money.

1   Labour, Money, Exploitation

In the early and mid-nineteenth century, capitalist development was seen by many as generating widespread misery among the working class, manifest disproportionalities in production and frequent economic crises. In addition, unequal exchanges apparently took place between 'capital' and 'labour' (the workers not receiving back the 'full fruit of their labour') and between capitalists themselves (some of whom did not command a 'just price' for their commodities or were exploited when taking credit). Based on this framework, authors such as Gray, Bray, Proudhon and Darimon elaborated plans to change the economic system.

They saw the monetary sphere as the main root of economic troubles, since it was 'wrongly' organized around the 'privilege' of precious metals such as gold and silver that, because of their monopoly of exchange equivalencies, were the sole form of money:

> A defective system of exchange is not one amongst many other evils of nearly equal importance: it is the evil – the disease – the stumbling block of the whole society.
>
> GRAY 1831, p. 90

According to Gray (1831, pp. 58–59), society creates money as a scale to measure the relative values of commodities and to enable them to be exchanged in correct proportions; as such, the quantity of money in circulation should equal the sum of all prices, and money should be promptly available wherever its services were needed. However, since for Gray it was easier to increase the production of commodities as a whole than to increase the production of gold, the requirement that the aggregate value of gold in circulation should equal the value of commodities for sale implied that commodities' prices would tend to *fall* as their quantity increased faster than the quantity of gold, bringing distress instead of rewards for the producers:

> money ... must increase just exactly and precisely as fast as all other marketable commodities put together; for if it do not do this, every commodity multipliable by the exercise of human industry faster than money itself ... will fall in money-price; and from that instant, the greatest and most important principle in Political Economy ... – Production the cause of Demand is expelled from our commercial system.
>
> GRAY 1848, p. 69

As such, Gray considered the underproduction of money as the main evil of capitalism, while the overproduction of commodities was seen as impossible. However, he believed that all difficulties could be overcome:

> it would be by no means difficult to place the commercial affairs of society upon such a footing, that production would become the uniform and never failing cause of demand; or, in other words, that to sell for money may be rendered, at all times, precisely as easy as it now is to buy with money.
>
> GRAY 1831, p. 16, original in italics

Gray assumed that labour alone bestows value and that labour itself should be the measure of values. The problems caused by the use of gold (a valuable commodity) as a measure of values and by unequal exchanges could be solved through the creation of a valueless (paper) money, with average labour time as its unit. The privileges enjoyed by gold would be abolished; all commodities would be directly exchangeable for money and thus also for one another. As a result, society would no longer have its progress hampered by a defective monetary system, 'justice' would prevail, and no exploitation would take place.

The possession of a given amount of labour-money would certify a labourer's true contribution to social production, and would enable him or her to draw commodities of an equivalent value from the whole of that produce. At the same time, prices, determined by the costs of material inputs, wages and profits, would at last find stability (of course, if the conditions of production changed they would be modified accordingly).

At the centre of Gray's system was the 'National or Standard Bank' that would print labour-money. The producers would first 'sell' all their capital stock and properties to that Bank, receiving for them a 'just' amount of labour-money; they would then be paid with the usual rate of profits to manage their old businesses. When they had produced commodities, they would 'sell' them to a network of 'National Warehouses', again receiving labour-money in return. As the value of all commodities for sale plus the value of the social stock of wealth would be exactly matched by the amount of money in circulation, money could always buy all goods at once:

> Under the Social System, the money in circulation and the goods in the national stores would always be exactly equivalent, increasing and decreasing together. The money would be the demand, the property would be the supply, and the one would ever be equal to the other.
>
> GRAY 1831, pp. 251–252

As demand would never fail, crises would be abolished forever:

> by the adoption of the plan of exchange that is here described, goods of every kind would be made to pay for each other. Selling would be merely the act of lodging property in a particular place; buying would be merely the act of taking of it back again; and money would be merely the receipt which every man would require to keep in the interim between the period of selling and that of buying.
>
> GRAY 1831, p. 86

If, for whatever reason, the Warehouses could not sell a commodity, its producer would have to return the money previously received; if it could only be sold at a reduced price, he or she would have to return the difference and, if sold at a higher price, the producer would get the extra profit (see Gray 1848, p. 117). Thus, in the end, producers would receive the sale price of commodities, and the Warehouse would be a neutral intermediary.

The same group of authors also criticised credit and interest, although there is again no uniformity in their opinions. Gray himself did not have a firm point of view on these matters and changed his (superficial) judgement between 1831 and 1848. At first he considered interest as a source of injustice, since its 'addition' to commodities' values would both prevent workers from 'buying back' the product of their labour and prevent borrowers from having a fair reward for their efforts. Later on, however, he saw it as a fair 'remuneration for capital', to be preserved at least while his ideas were not fully implemented (see Kimball 1948, pp. 33 et. seqs.).

The discussion above could be summarized by saying that, in order to establish 'equivalent exchanges', Gray, Proudhon and others argued that society needs to have both a form of money allowing for a full reward of the labour performed, *and* the elimination of interest. These reforms would render harmonious and fair an otherwise anarchic and unjust economic system.

2   Marx on Labour and Money

A discussion of Marx's critique of the labour-money scheme requires a brief exposition of his theory of money; thus, the analysis of commodities must be the starting point. For Marx, a commodity has to be first of all a use value, thus requiring the application of concrete and useful labour for its production. But commodities are not only that: the abstraction of their use value shows us that they share a common essence amidst their apparent diversity – abstract human labour (see Marx 1983, pp. 45–46).

Every commodity-producing labour process is, therefore, an expenditure of human labour-power with a double character: as concrete labour it creates the useful properties of commodities, or their use value; as abstract labour it creates their value. Although producers are formally independent from each other, their underlying articulation prevails as they are compelled to sell their own commodities in order to buy any commodity. Private activities are thus subordinated to the social division of labour, and to provision to satisfy social needs.

The character of social utility that commodities must possess in order to be sold implies a double condition: they must have use value for other producers, and the labour that has produced them must be equalised with other kinds of labour, making the product of one's labour exchangeable for the products of others' labour:

> the labour of the individual producer acquires socially a two-fold character. On the one hand, it must, as a definite useful kind of labour, satisfy a definite social want, and thus hold its place as part and parcel of the collective labour of all, as a branch of a social division of labour ... On the other hand, it can satisfy the manifold wants of the individual producer himself, only in so far as ... [it] ranks on an equality with that of all others. The equalization of the most different kinds of labour can be the result only of an abstraction from their inequalities, or of reducing them to their common denominator, viz., expenditure of human labour-power or human labour in the abstract.
>
> MARX 1983, p. 78

When a commodity reaches the market the private labour that produced it loses its individuality in a process including three stages: (a) it is normalised with all individual labours producing the same kind of commodity, converting each good into a mere sample of its kind; (b) it is synchronised with other labours that have produced the same kind of commodity in the past but which are concurrently for sale; and (c) it is homogenised with all other kinds of labour as the commodity is equalised with ideal money. Let us investigate these processes more closely:

(a) *Normalisation:* The labours of the distinct individuals producing the same kind of commodity, say silk, are normalised as every individual piece of silk reaches the market, where they are identified as samples of a single general piece of silk put up for sale. As such, all these labours become links of a unique silk-producing process carried out throughout society. Although each piece of silk will come from distinct labour processes, they will all have the same value. The value of a specific piece of silk will not, then, be given by its individual production time; instead, it will be determined by the normal time that it takes society as a whole to produce it, or by the socially necessary labour time. The two hours (say) that it takes society to produce each yard of silk are, then, a composition of the one hour it takes A to produce one yard with the three hours it takes B, and so on, without presumption that an arithmetic average would result: it is, instead, a matter of establishing the *dominant* process of production in society. Hence, when silk-producing labours are normalised their diverse individual efficiencies are ironed out and the individual labour times are put into correspondence with a socially determined one (which may be taken to be the numerical average only by way of illustration; see Marx 1983, pp. 46–47).

(b) *Synchronisation:* On the market, commodities produced in diverse moments in time are also assimilated, and silk produced in the past will equal silk produced now as they are parts of the same silk for sale. Without this synchronisation of inherently diachronous concrete labour processes, production and exchanges could not be continuous in time, and the necessary and inevitable non-simultaneity of human actions would bring about a paralysis of the economy.

It can be concluded that, for Marx, the value of a commodity is determined neither by the particular labour-time concretely necessary to produce it, nor on the labour time socially necessary when it was made. Instead, the value of a commodity depends on the social labour time presently necessary for its production, or the *labour time socially necessary for its reproduction*. Values in Marxist analysis are not given to commodities once and for all when they are produced, but are socially attributed to them at every moment.

This does not contradict the fact that commodities themselves have value; it does, however, illuminate the social nature of this concept: as commodity production is a social division of labour, individual commodities only exist as samples of their kind, and each kind of commodity only exists as one among several others. It is the general, historical process of production of each commodity, alongside all other production processes, that determines their values – not the amount of physical labour one applies to produce a given good.

(*c*) *Homogenisation:* When different kinds of commodities are related to money, the heterogeneous qualities of the concrete labours applied in their production are abstracted, and they are treated as materialisations of equal human labour. Those labours are then homogenised; only their essence of abstract labour becomes relevant, and only their quantitative relationship matter. The value that commodities have may now be observed, through their prices.

The processes of normalisation, synchronisation and homogenisation are carried out simultaneously, and each of them depends on the other two: the normalisation of labours requires their synchronisation; the latter occurs among normalised labours; and only normalised and synchronised labours can be homogenised. These demands are not contradictory, since all those processes are unceasingly performed in a continuous flow of production that culminates in individual exchanges for money. As all private labours have this common need, they are normalised, synchronised and homogenised as they are performed and even as they are conceived.

Let us now see how Marx criticises Gray's value analysis, starting with the 'sale' of commodities to his Warehouses. A preliminary point is that if a Warehouse would buy commodities and later on return to the same producer to give him or her the 'true' price paid by the final consumers, then the Bank, the Warehouses and the labour-money are all unnecessary – they change nothing in the capitalist reality of uncertain sales, floating prices, and possible bankruptcies. If we ignore this clumsy scheme, three cases are worth discussing:

(a) If the 'just price' that the Warehouses would pay for a commodity were solely determined by the time that each producer had worked, the economy would fall into disarray: a chair produced in six hours would be 'worth' twice as much as a similar one that took a more efficient producer only three hours to make. The first chair could be exchanged for ten pounds of potatoes, say, while the second one would only equal five pounds. Total productivity would then quickly fall, because everyone would try to make his or her commodities more 'valuable' by working less efficiently. This absurd outcome stems from the inconsistent assumptions that (i) commodity-producing labours do not need to be normalised, and that (ii) their homogenisation could be reduced to a direct identity between individual labour-time and money.

(b) Although in Gray's scheme metals would be unfit to act as a measure of value, coins could be used as 'auxiliary instruments of exchange' (1831, pp. 75–76), bought and sold for money. In the case of copper and silver, if their production times varied their weights would change to preserve their money prices, while gold coins, given their importance and traditional use, would vary not in weight but in value (see Gray 1848, pp. 180–184). Let us analyse the second case, supposing that the Bank charged for gold coins the social labour time required for their reproduction and that all labour productivities were kept constant, except in gold-mining. If the latter constantly increased, the synchronisation of gold-producing processes would subject all coins to a constant depreciation and to the idealisation of their name, or to a specific form of inconvertibility – between an old 'six-hour' coin and a new commodity 'worth' six-hours.

This would happen because, as gold productivity rose, the labour-time necessary to produce a given coin would decrease, and so would its 'value'. Had labour productivity in gold-mining doubled, a coin of a given size would be devalued, exchanging for only half as many commodities as it once did, and an old 'six-hour' coin, say, would now equal commodities that took only three hours to make:

> Gold money with the plebeian title x hours of labour would be exposed to greater fluctuations than any other sort of money and particularly more than the present gold money, because gold cannot rise or fall in relation to gold (it is equal to itself), while the labour time accumulated in a given quantity of gold, in contrast, must constantly rise or fall in relation to present, living labour time. In order to maintain its convertibility, the productivity of labour time would have to be kept stationary.
>
> MARX 1981, p. 135

(c) Let us now consider paper labour-money, what Marx called 'labour-chits', as proposed by 'Weitling ... with Englishmen ahead of him and French after, Proudhon Co. among them' (1981, p. 135). In this case, other difficulties would arise. As labour productivity increased generally, a chair that yesterday could be exchanged for a six-hour chit, say, would today command only a three-hour one, money being constantly appreciated in relation to commodities – to the benefit of the cursed creditors. Moreover,

> The time-chit, representing average labour time, would never correspond to or be convertible into actual labour time; i.e. the amount of labour time objectified in a commodity would never command a quantity of labour time equal to itself, and vice versa, but would command,

rather, either more or less, just as at present every oscillation of market values expresses itself in a rise or fall of the gold or silver prices of commodities.

> MARX 1981, p. 139

3   Money, Value, and Price

For Marx money is a special commodity, equivalent to all the others and with the formal use value of representing values. Money is, therefore, a social relation that derives from the form of social articulation and reflects the reciprocal dependence of commodity-producers. As the money-commodity is, for Marx, a social value *a priori*, the concrete labour of the individuals producing (say, gold miners) is directly social labour, or the medium for the material expression of abstract labour (see Marx 1983, p. 64).

Commodities' values are disclosed in a relation between each of them and money; as such, money is their measure of value:

> The first chief function of money is to supply commodities with the material for the expression of their values, or to represent their values as magnitudes of the same denomination, qualitatively equal, and quantitatively comparable. It thus serves as a universal measure of value ... It is not money that renders commodities commensurable. Just the contrary. It is because all commodities, as values, are realised human labour, and therefore commensurable, that their values can be measured by one and the same special commodity, and the latter be converted into the common measure of their values i.e., into money. Money as a measure of value, is the phenomenal form that must of necessity be assumed by that measure of value which is immanent in commodities, labour-time.
>
> MARX 1983, p. 97

Marx stresses that as a measure of value money is merely ideal money:

> Every trader knows, that he is far from having turned his goods into money, when he has expressed their value in a price or in imaginary money, and that it does not require the least bit of real gold, to estimate in that metal millions of pounds' worth of goods. When, therefore, money serves as a measure of value, it is employed only as imaginary or ideal money.
>
> MARX 1983, pp. 98–99

The comparison of a commodity with money relates the values of them both. As the value of money is already social, the value of the commodity is then expressed in a price, as soon as the measure of value is divided into the conventional units of a standard of prices. Thus, as de Brunhoff and Ewenczyk (1979, pp. 49–50) rightly put it,

> As measure of value and standard of prices, money gives a price form to commodities; it expresses the value of commodities in quantities of the money commodity (gold), and relates at the same time these magnitudes to a fixed unitary quantity of weight of gold, that is the standard of prices. The monetary name – the price form – expresses at the same time these two functions.

It is this step that allows the heterogeneous labours that create each commodity to be reduced to homogeneous labour:

> the price relations between commodities is the form in which an equivalence is established between different concrete labours, the means by which these are reduced to homogeneous labour that counts as value, what Marx called abstract labour.
>
> FINE 1980, p. 124

In contrast, for Gray, no commodity could be a good measure of value, since it would itself have a value; as such, changes in the value of the money-commodity would modify the prices of all commodities irrespective of the stability of their own production times, disturbing the exchange process. Moreover, since for Gray increases in the production of metals tended to be more difficult than increases in the production of other commodities, those price changes would generally be downwards, reducing profits and, ultimately, triggering deflation and crises.

However, this is neither a reasonable theory of value nor a good theory of crisis. Gray's valueless measure of value is simply not a measure since, as we have seen, the Bank-Warehouses complex would be the true 'measurers of value' in his scheme. Furthermore, even if prices tended to fall over time this would not by itself lead to the interruption of sales. Gray's conceptions show his flawed understanding of the synchronisation and normalisation of labours inherent in commodity production, which imply that increases in the value of money reduce the price of the outputs at the same time as they lower the price of the inputs.

Another side of Marx's critique of the labour-money scheme regards its identification of prices with values. For Marx, at the same time that prices express commodities' values they allow for the possibility of differences between values and prices, for him an intrinsic characteristic of the price form (see Marx 1983, p. 104). For him, the distinction between prices and values derives from the private nature of commodity-producing labours, and it has a role in the social regulation of the amounts of concrete labour applied in the production of each use value. For example, although the relationship between supply and demand does not affect commodity values, it may cause changes in prices, signalling to the producers the wants of society, and guiding their expenditures of labour.

According to Marx, the identification of prices with values reveals the unfamiliarity of Gray and others with the nature of commodity production. As Gray considered labour-time to be the measure of values and proposed a labour-money, *time* would become the unit of both values and prices. In addition, the automatic purchase of any commodity by the Warehouses would make private labour immediately social, rendering prices equal to values. Values would then either directly express commodities' individual labour times (depriving society of the relations between supply and demand as a signalling mechanism and leading to the collapse of production examined above), or they would result from determinations made by the Bank and the Warehouses (which would make them the signallers, instead of the market).

These ideas would, for Marx, imply the end of commodity production and thus of capitalism itself. Commodities are products of private labour, and money is an immediately social value. The 'identity' between commodities and money – to which Gray aspires – makes private labour social from the outset, or makes it produce *money*, and no longer commodities. As such, it becomes meaningless to discuss the conditions for the conversion of commodities into money:

> The first basic illusion of the time-chitters consists in this, that by annulling the nominal difference between real value and market value, between exchange value and price – that is, by expressing value in units of labour time itself instead of in a given objectification of labour time, say gold and silver – ... they also remove the real difference and contradiction between price and value. Given this illusory assumption it is self-evident that the mere introduction of the time-chit does away with all crises, all faults of bourgeois production. The money price of commodities their real value; demand supply; production consumption; money

is simultaneously abolished and preserved; the labour time of which the commodity is the product, which is materialized in the commodity, would need only to be measured in order to create a corresponding mirror-image in the form of a value-symbol, money, time-chits. In this way every commodity would be directly transformed into money; and gold and silver, for their part, would be demoted to the rank of all other commodities.

MARX 1981, p. 138; see also 1987, pp. 321–322

In Gray's economy, the 'Bank' would necessarily control every aspect of production and enjoy absolute power. As the general buyer and seller of commodities, it would evaluate the social labour time necessary to produce each commodity and, consequently, oversee all production processes. It would also have to become the general planner – both because the average productivity in all sectors of the economy would have to be kept constant (or grow at identical rates) to avoid disproportions, and because supply would have to balance demand, both in the aggregate and in each market, to make the labour-money really convertible into commodities. In the end, the Bank would order, control, receive and pay for all products, and all individuals would be subordinated to it. But then we are no longer in commodity production and thus no longer in a capitalist society – an inevitable result of Gray's proposals to 'reform' the economic system.

4   The Other Functions of Money

This section follows Marx's analysis of the other functions of money, in order to understand more thoroughly his critique of the labour-money scheme.

As money personifies abstract labour, its concrete equivalence with commodities, achieved on sale, makes them 'acquire the properties of a socially recognised universal equivalent' (Marx 1983, p. 108). When commodities are exchanged for money and money occupies their place, it acts as a means of circulation.

Since, for Marx, exchanges occur between commodities with equal value, the role of money as a means of circulation requires the previous normalisation, synchronisation and homogenisation of the labour processes involved. However, the use of gold coins as a means of circulation causes their wear and tear, and commodities are soon exchanged for coins worth less than their face value. The continuity of exchanges in these circumstances shows that, although it is essential that, in an abstract exchange, the value of the amount of money involved equals the value of the commodity, in circulation as a whole matters are different: what has to be preserved is no longer the value each participant at all times holds, but the value-equivalence of the commodities being exchanged, with money operating merely as a representative or symbol of their value. Symbols of money may, then, perform exactly the same service as pure gold:

> The fact that the currency of coins itself effects a separation between their nominal and their real weight, creating a distinction between them as mere pieces of metal on the one hand, and as coins with a definite function on the other – this fact implies the latent possibility of replacing metallic coins by tokens of some other material ... Therefore things that are relatively without value, such as paper notes, can serve as coins in its place.
> MARX 1983, pp. 126–127

Many divergences between Marx and Gray stem from their different views of money. For Marx, money is the unity of a measure of value and a means of circulation:

> The commodity that functions as a measure of value, and, either in its own person or by a representative, as the medium of circulation, is money.
> MARX 1983, p. 130

In contrast, Gray sees money as a unique, static object that, as measure of value standard of prices (he cannot distinguish between them), would concretely, in a sale, certify the labour-time necessary to the production of each commodity. Money should not be any valuable object, so that it could be reproduced easily and, thus, capable of preserving the values of commodities. In its role as means of circulation, Gray wanted labour-money to be present in the same quantity as all goods and wealth put together, enabling it to purchase all commodities at the same time. In sum, Gray's misunderstanding of the synchronisation of labour leads him to confuse the fact that the sum of prices of all commodities must equal the sum of money paid for them, with the idea that that sum of prices must equal the total of money in circulation, or that the velocity of circulation of money should be unity.

For Marx (1981, p. 213), Gray makes no more than a 'clumsy confusion between the contradictory functions of money'. To be a measure of values money must itself have value, since the determination of the amount of social labour in a private product is made, first, through the ideal comparison of the commodity with money. The result of this comparison is a price, given in the units of the standard of prices, that floats around the commodity's value. This is necessarily followed by a concrete equivalence between commodities and money, in a market sale. Such sales may, however, be made against mere token representatives of money, such as paper notes.

Marx claims that the exchangeability of commodities is not due to the intervention of money (as is the case in Gray) but is a feature of commodity production. The units that compose the means of circulation participate in several exchanges during their lifetime, simply by circulating more than once. They may thus realise, in the aggregate, values several times greater than their own, while in each exchange they are present in amounts whose value equals that of the commodity they are exchanged for. All in all, Marx's money contrasts sharply with Gray's: it is the dialectical unity of a measure of value, that works as an ideal body, with a means of circulation that may be substituted by symbols.

Let us now see how the functions of reserve value, means of payment, and world money derive in Marx from the unity of the measure of values and the means of circulation. The value of money, like the value of any other commodity, is given at each moment by the social conditions of its reproduction; it is not 'preserved' through time inside the physical body of a coin, and changes in this value surface in the form of generalised variations in commodities' prices. At the same time, money is always exchangeable for any commodity, due to the unvarying nature of values and of value-producing labour processes.

Only on this double basis may interruptions in the circulation of money lead to its use as a reserve value and to the formation of hoards. Hoarding plays in Marx a very important role, both because the volume of circulating money must respond to the needs of circulation itself, and because money represents universal wealth, that may be retained to secure a general power of purchase. This power is not, however, absolute, since the value of the hoard depends on its size and the current value of money.

If commodities are sold today to be paid for only later (or if they are rented), their buyer becomes a debtor. To close that transaction, he or she must either sell commodities and then transfer a given amount of means of circulation to the creditor, or gradually hoard money as reserve value and, later on, use it as a means of circulation to settle the debt. As such, money is used as a means of payment.

All functions of money are performed in the international sphere by world money, that is value in pure form and an incarnation of abstract labour recognised as such in every nation. Of course, all domestic currencies must be convertible into world money to allow national commodities to be exchanged for foreign ones, or to insert nationally performed labours into worldwide commodity production.

Gray offers no careful discussion of money as reserve value, means of payment, or world money. It was shown above that, in the best-case scenario, his labour-money would lead to an appreciating currency and to disturbances in creditor-debtor relations, at the same time as hoards would systematically gain value. Money hoards would not be, however, 'normal' since, for Gray, production was directly aimed at consumption:

> A man ... having acquired property in the standard stock of the country, as proved by his possession of standard bank-notes, is sure to require something in exchange for them – the notes themselves being of no value whatever.
>
> GRAY 1848, pp. 118–119

In the international sphere, gold would continue to perform the role of world money:

> gold, silver, and copper goods, (coins,) of two distinct kinds, or classes, should be manufactured ... The first class would be required to pay balances to foreign countries; to buy goods from foreign countries ... to enable persons, disposed to store up metallic property, to do so [etc.].
>
> GRAY 1831, pp. 77–78

Since Gray's valueless labour-money would merely reflect the intrinsic values of commodities, it could – at most – be a means of circulation (which is ironic, since in his economy commodities would not really circulate). The functions of measure of value, means of payment, reserve value and world money, that are intrinsically linked to gold's cursed 'exclusivity', would either not be performed by money but, instead, by the Bank-Warehouses complex, or would still be carried out by gold.

5   Labour-Money in Retrospect

The proposers of labour-money schemes recognised labour as the source of value and wished to eliminate economic crises and 'unjust' exchanges. To do so, they imagined a 'Bank' that, in Marx's analysis, would take as its starting point the fact that, in simple commodity production, if supply equals demand prices equal values. The Bank would then try to do the converse – identify prices with values in order to make supply match demand. As the Bank guarantees an 'equivalent exchange' for anything produced, private labour would become social *a priori* and, thereby, every commodity would also be money. Since prices would be identical with values, money would lose its role, products would no longer be commodities – and the very basis of capitalism would be abolished through the attempt to make Say's law a reality.

It was shown above that labour-money could not fulfil all the functions of money and that it would, in fact, be a non-money, in Marx's sense. This is a consequence of the fact that labour-money is incapable of socialising commodity-producing labours, a task that is carried out by the Bank and the Warehouses, which occupy in Gray's scheme the role of money in Marx's. This does not happen by chance. When the authors proposing a labour-money declare 'labour' to be the essence of value, but do not admit a commodity to be the general equivalent, they make it clear that their 'labour' is not what Marx calls 'abstract labour'. This notion of labour comes hand-in-hand with the belief that commodity production and capitalism are eternal, ahistorical relations of production. As such, the labour they see in every commodity is merely labour devoid of the concrete forms it acquires in use values; it is the expenditure of human energy required by any enterprise, all over history – in this respect, it is equivalent to *physiological labour*. It follows that all goods could become immediately exchangeable, since production always demands the expenditure of this kind of labour.

Physiological labour is distinct from Marx's abstract labour, with the former being incompatible with the historicity of Marx's concept and the transitory nature of commodity production itself. As a result of his inconsistent views, Gray cannot arrive at the Marxian concept of value, but only at the contradictions examined above, that lead his monetary system to the paradox of ultimately rejecting the very kind of social division of labour that he sees as eternal.

According to Marx, Gray's mistaken appreciation of commodity production and money lead him to the utopian view that alterations in money would suffice to modify the form of socialisation of private labour and change the capitalist economy as a whole. Similarly, for Marx, it is not through 'equivalent exchanges' that capitalism, exploitation and crises can be eliminated – and he examines surplus value on the assumption of equivalent exchanges between capitalists and workers.

Marx's critique of the case for 'free credit' was equally emphatic, but it will not be detailed here. He considers that the elimination of interest would neither prevent exploitation nor allow workers to buy back the products of their labour, but would only do away with one of the forms taken by surplus value. Marx would use this as an example of what was, for him, the utter ignorance of the nature of capitalist credit shared by those who made such proposals.

Gray misapprehends the relations between money and commodities, which leads him either to assume away the contradictions of commodity production and transfer their solution to a 'Bank'. When analysing money, he says that gold is a commodity like any other, being a mere symbol of value. In this case any commodity, or all of them, could also be money, since gold's privileges have no objective basis. At the same time, Gray shares the opposite (and also mistaken) view that money is totally different from commodities, the former being added to the world by convention, after the full development of commodity production.

6   Conclusion

This essay reviews the case for the institution of a form of money based on labour-time, as it was advanced by John Gray; it also comments on similar ideas held by, among others, Bray, Proudhon and Darimon. These conceptions were criticised following Marx's line of argument, showing that their theoretical weaknesses are symptoms of an ahistorical approach to economics and an undeveloped analysis of commodity production. It was concluded that labour-money cannot be money and that, if it were to exist, money could no longer be what it now is.

The main goal of this essay, however, concerns the study of Marx's own theory of money. Analysis of his critiques of the labour-money scheme underpinned the examination of how Marx's views the attribution of values and prices to commodities. For him, this is neither direct nor straightforward, but is composed of three processes that relate individual commodity-producing labours to the world of commodities – the normalisation, synchronisation and homogenisation of labour. This essay also stresses the close relation between value and money theories in Marx, and the functions of money were analysed from this perspective. The use of Marx's critiques of the 'labour-money' scheme with these purposes is not fortuitous: by showing how Marx unveiled the contradictions in that proposal, key aspects of his own theory of money could be brought to light.

CHAPTER 4

Capital Accumulation and the Composition of Capital

This essay examines Marx's concept of the composition of capital.[1] Although this concept is essential for understanding the relationship between values and prices, technical change, accumulation, and other critically important structures and processes under capitalism – for example, the occ is the pivot of the transformation problem and the tendency of the rate of profit to fall, and it plays a critical role in Marx's theory of rent – the composition of capital has tended to be explained cursorily and understood only superficially and – often – incorrectly in the literature.

This essay shows that a clear understanding of the composition of capital can contribute to the development of Marx's theory of value, exploitation and capital accumulation. The argument is developed in five sections. The first summarises Marx's theory of capital, exploitation and accumulation, which underpins the concepts of composition of capital. The second briefly reviews some of the best-known interpretations of the composition of capital, in order to illustrate the diversity of the literature on this topic. The third follows Marx's analysis of the composition of capital in the absence of technical change. Each concept used by Marx is defined and its introduction justified. The fourth discusses how the technical (TCC), organic (OCC) and value composition of capital (VCC) are affected by technical progress. It will be shown that one of Marx's aims in distinguishing the OCC from the VCC is for a focused analysis of a particular case, where the accumulation of capital occurs with technological change. The fifth summarises the main findings. The contrast between the static and dynamic cases is essential, not only to the orderly introduction of the concepts, but also to the appreciation of their contradictions, limits and shifts. Moreover, this arrangement is useful in its direct connection with the levels of analysis of the composition of capital.

---

1 Based on *The Value of Marx*, London: Routledge, 2002, ch.6, 'Capital Accumulation and the Composition of Capital', *Research in Political Economy* 19, 2001, pp. 69–85, and on 'A Note on Marx's Analysis of the Composition of Capital', *Capital & Class* 50, 1993, pp. 127–146.

1 Capital and Exploitation

For Marx, capital is a social relation between two classes, capitalists and workers. This relation is established when the means of production are monopolised by the capitalists, that employ wage workers in production for profit. Once this class relation of production is posited, capital exists in and through things, namely, the means of production, commodities, money and financial assets employed in the process of valorisation:

> Capital is not a *thing*, any more than money is a *thing*. In capital, as in money, certain *specific social relations of production between people* appear as *relations of things to people*, or else certain social relations appear as the *natural properties of things in society* ... Capital and wage-labour ... only express two aspects of the self-same relationship. Money cannot become capital unless it is exchanged for labour-power ... Conversely, work can only be wage-labour when its *own* material conditions confront it as autonomous powers, alien property, value existing for itself and maintaining itself, in short as capital ... Wage-labour is then a necessary condition for the formation of capital and remains the essential prerequisite of capitalist production.[2]
>
> *Capital 1*, pp. 1005–1006

There is a relationship of mutual implication between capitalism (the mode of social production), wage labour (the form of social labour), and the commodity (the typical form of the output):

> [The] relation between generalised commodity production [GCP] ... wage labor and capitalist production is one of reciprocal implication. First ... when labor becomes wage labor ... commodity production is generalised. On the one hand wage labor implies GCP ... On the other hand, GCP implies wage labor ... Marx shows ... that capitalist production is commodity production as the general form of production while, at the same time, emphasizing that it is only on the basis of the capitalist mode of production that all or even the majority of products of labor assume commodity form ... Finally, the relation of wage labor and capital is also

---

2 Chattopadhyay (1994, p. 18) rightly argues that 'Marx's starting point in the treatment of capital is conceiving capital as a social totality, capital representing a *class* opposed not so much to the individual laborers as to the wage laborers as a *class*'.

one of reciprocal implication for Marx. Capital is a production relation between the immediate producers and their conditions of production which, separated from them and passing under the control of non (immediate) producers, dominate them as capital ... [T]he rest of the features of capitalism could be seen as the necessary resultants following from any one of these essentially equivalent central categories.

CHATTOPADHYAY 1994, pp. 17–18

As a totality engaged in self-expansion through the employment of wage labour, capital is primarily *capital in general*. This is the general form of capital.[3] Capital in general can be represented by the circuit of industrial capital, M-C-M', where M and M' are sums of money-capital and C represents the inputs, including labour power and means of production; the difference between M' and M is the surplus value.

The circuit of industrial capital represents the essence of capital, valorisation through the production of commodities by wage labour. However, capital produces not only surplus value; at the social level, the outcome of the circuit is the *expanded reproduction* of capital or, following from the concept of capital, the renewal of the separation between capitalists and wage workers. For this reason, Marx claimed that 'Accumulation of capital is ... multiplication of the proletariat' (*Capital 1*, p. 764). In other words,

> The capitalist process of production ... seen as a total, connected process, i.e. a process of reproduction, produces not only commodities, not only surplus-value, but it also produces and reproduces the capital-relation itself; on the one hand the capitalist, on the other the wage-labourer.
>
> *Capital 1*, p. 724

The capital relation implies that the means of production have been monopolised by a relatively small number of people. In contrast, the majority is forced to sell their labour power in order to purchase commodities that, as a class, they have produced previously (see *Theories of Surplus Value 3*, pp. 490–491). Therefore, capital is a *class relation of exploitation*, allowing the class of capitalists to live off the surplus value extracted from the working class:

> Capitalism, and hence capital, requires a lot more by way of the social than private property and the market ... What it does depend upon is wage labour, able and willing to produce a surplus for capital. By implication,

3 See *Grundrisse*, pp. 310, 449, 852.

> the social attached to capital takes the form of class relations ... Capital
> and labour confront one another as classes with the capitalist class mo-
> nopolising the means of production or access to livelihood through work.
> Consequently, workers can only survive by selling their capacity to work
> for a wage that represents less in terms of labour time than is performed
> for the capitalist. The surplus labour performed over and above that nec-
> essary to provide the wage gives rise to what Marx termed exploitation,
> and provides for the profits of the capitalists.
>
> FINE 2001a, p. 29

For Marx, the defining feature of capitalism is the exploitation of the class of
wage workers by the capitalist class, through the extraction of surplus value.[4]
The ratio between the surplus value (surplus labour time) and the value of labour power (necessary labour time) is the rate of exploitation or rate of surplus
value. All else constant, the rate of exploitation can increase for at least three
reasons: if more hours are worked, if the intensity of labour increases, or if
the necessary labour time declines because of productivity growth in the sectors producing necessities (given the real wage). Marx calls the first two cases
the production of *absolute surplus value*, while the third produces *relative surplus value* (see *Capital 1*, pp. 430–437, 645–646, and *Theories of Surplus Value 1*,
p. 216). Absolute surplus value is generally limited, because it is impossible to
increase the working day or the intensity of labour indefinitely, and the workers gradually learn to resist against these forms of exploitation. In contrast,
relative surplus value is more flexible and harder to resist, because productivity growth can outstrip wage increases for long periods (see Fine and Saad-
Filho, 2016, ch.6).

Intra-sectoral competition between firms producing the same use values
compels each firm to minimise costs in order to maximise its profit rate. This
type of competition may be associated with different firm strategies. For example, a longer working day increases the output and may reduce unit costs,
because the transfers from fixed capital are spread across larger batches, and
there is a reduced risk of technical obsolescence (that Marx called moral depreciation) because the machines depreciate physically more quickly. In contrast,
greater labour intensity increases the output, because more simple labour is
performed in the same period, but this does not affect directly the unit value

---

4   'To Marx ... the essence of capitalist property is the control of the productive process and
    therefore the control over laborers. Forced labor rather than low wages, alienation of labor
    rather than alienation of the product of labor are, according to Marx, the essence of capitalist
    exploitation' (Medio 1977, p. 384).

of the product. Finally, technical progress reduces the simple labour necessary
to produce a unit of the product and, consequently, tends to lower its value:

> Production for value and surplus-value involves a constantly operating
> tendency ... to reduce the labour-time needed to produce a commodity,
> i.e. to reduce the commodity's value, below the existing social average
> at any given time. The pressure to reduce the cost price to its minimum
> becomes the strongest lever for raising the social productivity of labour,
> though this appears here simply as a constant increase in the productiv-
> ity of capital.
>
> *Capital 3*, p. 1021

These technical innovations will be copied or emulated by the rival firms. This
process continually erodes the advantage of the innovating firms, while preserving the incentives for further technical progress across the economy. At the
level of capital in general, competition and technical change constantly reduce
the value of all goods, including those consumed by the workers. All else constant, they permit the extraction of relative surplus value:

> Capital therefore has an immanent drive, and a constant tendency,
> towards increasing the productivity of labour, in order to cheapen
> commodities and, by cheapening commodities, to cheapen the worker
> himself.
>
> *Capital 1*, pp. 436–437

The most important aspect of intra-sectoral competition is mechanisation,
or the introduction of new technologies and new machines by the innovating firms. Mechanisation has three principal aspects, two of which were discussed above; it increases the value-productivity of labour and the profit rate
of the innovating capitals, facilitates the extraction of relative surplus value
and, finally, it is a tool of capitalist control. The Marxian critique of technology has demonstrated that, underneath their seemingly neutral, scientific
and productivist (of use value) guise, machines are despotic dictators of the
rhythm and content of the labour process (see Saad-Filho 2002, ch.5). Therefore, despite the perception that competition invariably increases physical
productivity, reduces commodity values and potentially leads to higher real
wages, the relationship between competition and machinery is complicated
by two factors. First, firms do not select the technologies that are most productive of use values, but those that are most profitable, and these criteria may
lead to distinct outcomes. Second, capitalist attempts to establish control in

the production line and in society may introduce further biases in the choice of technology, including the adoption of technologies that are not *prima facie* more profitable, but that facilitate control (see Levidow and Young 1981, 1985 and Slater 1980). In sum, conflicts between competing capitals, between capital and labour on the shopfloor, and between social groups can influence the choice of technology and the output mix with consequences that cannot always be anticipated.

2   Understanding the Composition of Capital

Widely different understandings of the composition of capital found in the literature may, at least partly, result from Marx's use of three forms of the concept, the TCC, OCC and VCC, which he uses to examine in detail the processes of accumulation outlined in the previous section. While the content of each term is evident at times, there are moments when Marx seems to use them contradictorily; consequently, his work may look arbitrary and puzzling. A brief review of differing views of the composition of capital may give a better idea of the difficulties involved in this study.

Paul Sweezy (1968, p. 66) argues that the composition of capital is the relation of constant (c) to variable capital (v) in the total capital used in production. For him, although '[s]everal ratios would serve to indicate this relation ... the one which seems most convenient is the ratio of constant capital to total capital'. Sweezy defines the OCC as $c/(c + v)$. This formulation has its roots in Bortkiewicz's work, and it is also adopted by Seton and Desai.[5] In his discussion of the transformation problem Sweezy also follows Bortkiewicz's treatment and, as may be gathered from the discussion below and in Chapter 4, attributes the different sectoral rates of profit to the distinct value rather than organic compositions of the invested capital, which is contrary to Marx's argument.

Michio Morishima (1973) is closer to the mark in his understanding of the TCC and the VCC, but misinterprets the OCC by defining it as the name Marx would have given to the VCC, in case the TCC underwent changes such that all relative values were left unaltered (in other words, for him OCC is the name of the VCC when the changes in the TCC are precisely reflected by changes in the VCC – as if productivity increase is identical across all sectors). Morishima believes that Marx only defined the OCC to simplify his treatment of technical changes, but it will be shown below that this is insufficient.

---

5   See Bortkiewicz (1949), Desai (1989, 1992) and Seton (1957).

Nobuo Okishio (1974) works with the value composition of capital under the name of the organic composition in his treatment of the transformation, and he is by no means the only one to do so. Much of the current literature argues that the OCC can be defined unproblematically as c/v, as if the VCC did not exist, and they transform values into prices on this basis.[6] However, for Marx, matters were more complicated than that. In his analysis of the law of the tendency of the rate of profit to fall, Roemer (1979) also calls OCC what should really be termed VCC, and his discussion of the falling profit rate bears the mark of this misconception.

In his classic paper proposing an iterative solution to the transformation problem, Shaikh calls OCC the ratio (c + v)/v.[7] In contrast, Sherman defines the OCC as v/(c + v), while Smith and Wright, following Mage, call OCC the ratio c/(v + s). Foley, in his outstanding textbook, defines the 'composition of capital' as v/(c + v), and the 'OCC' as c/v.[8] Finally, Groll and Orzech (1987, 1989) in their detailed discussion of the composition of capital (one of whose merits is the careful distinction of the TCC, OCC and VCC from each other) argue that the OCC is a long-run value-concept while the VCC is measured in market prices and refers to the short-run, something with which Marx would probably disagree.

These problems are merely a sample of the difficulties one encounters in literature on the composition of capital. In order to understand Marx's use of these concepts, this essay reviews their development. In what follows it is shown that, while in the *Grundrisse* Marx does not yet employ the concepts which he would later call the composition of capital, in the *Theories of Surplus Value* he introduces the physical (technical) composition of capital and the organic composition of capital and, finally, in *Capital* he uses the technical composition of capital, the organic composition of capital and the value composition of capital in their most developed form. The progressive introduction of these terms reflects the increasing refinement of Marx's own perception of the matter, and allows him to clarify his own arguments. It will be shown below that, although the form of Marx's arguments changes, the problems with which he deals and the results he reaches are essentially unaltered through the years.

---

6   See, for example, Bortkiewicz (1952), Howard (1983), Lipietz (1982), Meek (1956, 1973, p. 313) and Winternitz (1948).

7   Shaikh (1977, p. 123); see also Shaikh (1973, p. 38).

8   See Foley (1986, p. 45), Mage (1963), Smith (1994, p. 149) and Wright (1977, p. 203).

3 Production and the Composition of Capital

The productivity of labour is determined by the mass of means of production that can be processed into final commodities in a given labour time or, alternatively, by the output per hour.[9] This notion is captured by the *technical composition of capital* (TCC, called earlier the physical composition of capital). The TCC is the physical ratio between the mass of material inputs (the products of past labour) and the living labour necessary to transform them into the output:

> A certain quantity of labour-power, represented by a certain number of workers, is required to produce a certain volume of products in a day, for example, and this involves putting a certain definite mass of means of production in motion and consuming them productively – machines, raw materials etc ... This proportion constitutes the technical composition of capital, and is the actual basis of its organic composition.
>
> *Capital 3*, p. 244. See also *Theories of Surplus Value 2*, pp. 455–456

The TCC cannot be measured directly or compared across sectors of the economy because it is the ratio between a heterogeneous bundle of use values (the material inputs) and a quantity of sectorally-specific average (normalised and synchronised) labour, rather than abstract labour (see Chapter 2). For example, it is impossible to contrast directly the TCC in the construction and electronic industries, where the use value of the inputs processed per hour of labour, and the value-productivity of labour, can be very different. However, the TCC can be assessed in value terms because in capitalism all produced inputs tend to become commodities. The value-assessment of the TCC defines the *organic composition of capital* (OCC), or the value of the means of production which absorb one hour of living labour in a given firm, industry or economy:

> The organic composition can be taken to mean the following: Different ratios in which it is necessary to expend constant capital in the different spheres of production in order to absorb the same amount of labour.[10]

---

9   See *Capital 1*, pp. 136–137, 332, 431, 773, 959 and *Capital 3*, p. 163.

10   *Theories of Surplus Value 3*, p. 387. The term 'organic' refers to the 'intrinsic' composition of capital. When analysing the general rate of profit (see Chapter 4), Marx says: 'Because the rate of profit measures surplus value against the total capital ... surplus value itself appears ... as having arisen from the total capital, and uniformly from all parts of it at that, so that the *organic* distinction between constant and variable capital is obliterated in the concept of profit' (*Capital 3*, p. 267, emphasis added).

For Marx, the OCC is the value-reflex of the TCC, or a 'technological composition' determined *in production*, and that expresses, in value terms, the technical relations in production. The OCC relates the *total* value of the constant capital (including fixed and circulating capital) to the *total* labour time required to transform the inputs (whether paid or unpaid). Marx refers to the OCC as follows:

> The ratio between the different elements of productive capital ... [can be] determined ... [b]y the organic composition of productive capital. By this we mean the technological composition. With a *given productivity* of labour, which can be taken as constant so long as no change occurs, the amount of raw material and means of labour, that is, the amount of constant capital – in terms of its *material elements* – which corresponds to a definite *quantity of living labour* (paid or unpaid), that is, to the *material elements* of *variable capital*, is determined in every sphere of production.
> *Theories of Surplus Value 3*, p. 382. See also *Theories of Surplus Value 2*, pp. 276, 279

There is, however, a severe difficulty with the OCC. As the value of a bundle of means of production is the product of the values of its components by the quantities used up, it seems impossible to tell whether differences or changes in the OCC are to differences or changes in the TCC (and, consequently, to differences or changes in the productivity of labour in *this* industry) or from differences or changes in the value of the means of production used up (that reflect the circumstances in *other* industries). However, for Marx there was no ambiguity. As the OCC is an immediate value-reflex of the TCC, it does *not* change if the TCC is kept constant, even if the value of the elements of capital changes. Having made this highly abstract claim, Marx says:

> if one assumes that the organic composition of capitals is given and likewise the differences which arise from the differences in their organic composition, then the value ratio can change although the technological composition remains the same ... If there is any change in [e.g.] the value of variable capital independent[ly] of the organic composition, it can only occur because of a fall or a rise in the price of means of subsistence that are not produced in the sphere of production under consideration but enter into it as commodities from outside ... The organic changes and those brought about by changes of value can have a similar effect on the rate of profit in certain circumstances. They differ however in the following way. If the latter are not due simply to fluctuations of market prices and are therefore not temporary, they are invariably caused by an

organic change in the spheres that provide the elements of constant or of variable capital.[11]

Marx is clearly aware that, for a given production process, changes in the value-ratio between the (fixed and circulating) constant capital and the (paid and unpaid) quantity of labour technically required can stem from either variations in the value of the inputs *or* from technological ('organic') changes in production. Based on this definition of the OCC, and aware that technical and value changes should not be conflated, Marx planned to discuss in Chapter 2 of Part 3 of *Capital*:

1. Different organic composition of capitals, partly conditioned by the difference between variable and constant capital in so far as this arises from the *stage of production* – the absolute quantitative relations between machinery and raw materials on the one hand, and the quantity of labour which sets them in motion. These differences relate to the labour-process. The differences between fixed and circulating capital arising from the circulation process have also to be considered...

2. Differences in the relative value of the parts of different capitals which do not arise from their organic composition. These arise from the difference of value particularly of the raw materials, even assuming that the raw materials absorb an equal quantity of labour in two different spheres.

3. The result of those differences is diversity of the rates of profit in different spheres of capitalist production.[12]

Marx eventually realised that an adequate treatment of these problems would require a more refined distinction between the effects of the application of different technologies and the consequences of the use of inputs of distinct values. For this reason, he introduces, in *Capital*, the concept of *value composition of capital* (VCC). The VCC is a concept of *exchange*. This is the ratio between the value of the circulating part of the constant capital (including the depreciation of fixed capital) and the variable capital required to produce a unit of the commodity.[13]

Let us follow Marx's discussion of the same problem both before and after the introduction of the VCC. This will show the place of the VCC in his analysis, and its relation to the TCC and the OCC. Marx wants to argue that if the

---

11   *Theories of Surplus Value 3*, pp. 383–386, various paragraphs; see also *Theories of Surplus Value 2*, pp. 376–377.

12   *Theories of Surplus Value 1*, pp. 415–416.

13   See D. Harvey (1999, p. 126) and Weeks (1981, pp. 197–201).

technical and organic compositions of two capitals are equal, but the value of the means of production used up is different, the value-assessment of their TCCs from the point of view of circulation may mislead the analyst into believing that their TCCs are distinct. In the *Theories of Surplus Value* he says:

> In the case of capitals of equal size ... the *organic composition* may be *the same* in *different spheres of production*, but the *value ratio* of the primary component parts of constant and variable capital may be *different* according to the different values of the amount of instruments and raw materials used. For example, copper instead of iron, iron instead of lead, wool instead of cotton, etc.[14]

The VCC allowed Marx to become more rigorous and elegant. In *Capital*, he says:

> it is possible for the proportion [the TCC] to be the same in different branches of industry only in so far as variable capital serves simply as an *index* of labour-power, and constant capital as an *index* of the volume of means of production that labour-power sets in motion. Certain operations in copper or iron, for example, may involve the same proportion between labour-power and means of production. But because copper is dearer than iron, the value relationship between variable and constant capital will be different in each case, *and so therefore will the value composition of the two capitals taken as a whole.*
>
> > *Capital 3*, p. 244, emphasis added

These examples explain the impact of differences in the value of the means of production consumed per hour of labour in distinct sectors with equal TCCs and OCCs. For example, if copper and iron implements (or wool and cotton clothes, or silver and gold jewellery) are manufactured with identical technologies and, therefore, by capitals with the same technical and organic compositions, Marx says that their value compositions are different because of the distinct value of the material inputs. In the first quote, he measures the TCCs only through the OCCs. As the OCC reflects the TCC from the point of

---

14   *Theories of Surplus Value 3*, p. 386. Alternatively, 'With capitals in *different branches of production* – with an otherwise equal physical [technical] composition – it is possible that the higher *value* of the machinery or of the material used, may bring about a difference. For instance, if the cotton, silk, linen and wool {industries} had exactly the same physical composition, the mere difference in the cost of the material used could create such a variation' (*Theories of Surplus Value 2*, p. 289).

view of production, it disregards the distinct value of the inputs used up. Marx can only point out that capitals may have equal TCCs and OCC, even though they employ means of production with distinct values. In the second example, Marx argues differently, directly claiming that if two capitals in distinct sectors have the same technical (and, therefore, organic) composition, but use means of production with different value, the equality of their TCCs and OCCs would appear distorted by their distinct VCCs.

The opposite case was also the subject of Marx's attention. If two sectors had equal VCCs, could they have different OCCs (and, therefore, distinct TCCs)? Marx's answer is in the affirmative:

> A capital of lower organic composition ... considered simply in terms of its value composition, could evidently rise to the same level as a capital of higher organic composition, simply by an increase in the value of its constant parts ... Capitals of the same organic composition can thus have a differing value composition, and capitals of the same percentage {value} composition can stand at varying levels of organic composition, displaying various different levels of development of the social productivity of labour.
>
> *Capital 3*, pp. 900–901

Therefore, if in two distinct production processes a given quantity of homogeneous labour power transforms different *masses* of means of production into the final product, the capitals will have different TCCs and OCCs. However, if the value of these inputs is such that the ratio between the constant and the variable capitals used up is equal, then their VCCs will be equal.[15]

These examples show that differences in the *value* of the constant and variable capital consumed in distinct industries are captured by the VCC but not the OCC; in contrast, differences in the *technologies of production* affect the OCC but they may not be accurately reflected by the VCC. The concept of OCC is important because it allows the study of technical differences (or changes, see below) in production, regardless of the corresponding value differences (or changes), while the VCC cannot distinguish between them.

---

15 '[W]e immediately see, if the price of the dearer raw material falls down to the level of that of the cheaper one, that these capitals are none the less similar in their technical composition. The value ratio between variable and constant capital would then be the same, although no change had taken place in the technical proportion between the living labour applied and the quantity and nature of the conditions of labour required' (*Capital 3*, p. 900).

One final example illustrates the scope and limitations of the concept of OCC, and the role of the VCC:

> let us assume that the raw material is dearer and labour (of greater *skill*) is dearer, in the same proportion. In this case {capitalist} A employs 5 workers, where {capitalist} B employs 25, and they cost him £100 – as much as the 25 workers, because their labour is dearer (their surplus labour is therefore also worth more). These 5 workers work up 100 lbs. of raw material, y, worth {£}500 and B's workers work up 1,000 lbs. of raw material, x, worth {£}500 ... The value ratio here – £100 v to {£}500 c is the same in both cases, but the *organic composition* is different.
>
> *Theories of Surplus Value*, p. 387

This example is clear enough. Although capitalists A and B spend equal amounts of money on means of production and labour power – which implies that their capitals have *equal* value compositions – their organic compositions are *different* because of the distinct production technologies.

In sum, although the OCC and the VCC are value-assessments of the TCC, they are distinct concepts because of the different evaluation of the means of production and labour power. An OCC-comparison of the technologies of production adopted in two industries is independent of differences in the values of the components of capital, because the OCC is defined in production. In contrast, distinctions (or variations, see below) in the values of constant and variable capital are detected by the VCC, a concept of exchange.[16] Only in this case is it possible to capture Marx's definition in full:

> The composition of capital is to be understood in a two-fold sense. As value, it is determined by the proportion in which it is divided into constant capital ... and variable capital ... As material, as it functions in the process of production, all capital is divided into means of production and living labour-power. This latter composition is determined by the relation between the mass of the means of production employed on the one hand, and the mass of labour necessary for their employment on the other.

---

16   For example: 'in this part of the work we ... assume in each case that the productivity of labour remains constant. In effect, *the value-composition* of a capital invested in a branch of industry, that is, a certain proportion between the variable and constant capital, *always expresses a definite degree of labour productivity*. As soon, therefore, as this proportion is altered by means *other* than a mere change in the value of the material elements of the constant capital, or a change in wages, the productivity of labour must likewise undergo a corresponding change' (*Capital 3*, pp. 50–51, emphasis added).

I call the former the value-composition, the latter the technical composition of capital. There is a close correlation between the two. To express this, I call the value-composition of capital, in so far as it is determined by its technical composition and mirrors the changes in the latter, the organic composition of capital.[17]

4   Capital Accumulation

One of the essential features of capitalism is the tendency towards the development of technology. Technical change is usually introduced in individual firms, raising their TCCs and, consequently, their OCCs and VCCs.[18] Because of their higher productivity, the innovating firms enjoy higher profit rates. Competition between firms in the same branch tends to generalise these technical advances, which reduces the commodity values and eliminates the advantage of the innovating firms. More generally, the technical and the organic compositions of capital in general tends to rise in every turnover and, all else constant, commodity values tend to fall.[19]

Since technical change potentially modifies the values of all commodities, whether directly or indirectly, the determination of the composition of capital in a dynamic environment is contingent upon the way changes in production affect commodity circulation. This is best analysed at the level of capital in

---

17   *Capital 1*, p. 762. Alternatively, 'The *organic* composition of capital is the name we give to its value composition, in so far as this is determined by its technical composition and reflects it' (*Capital 3*, p. 245).

18   Although the three compositions change simultaneously, in logical terms the TCC changes first, and this shift is reflected by the OCC and, subsequently, the VCC.

19   In the *Grundrisse* Marx was already aware of this, but he had not yet defined the concepts necessary to to develop the analysis of the composition of capital: 'if the total value of the capital remains the same, an increase in the productive force means that the constant part of capital (consisting of machinery and material) grows relative to the variable, i.e. to the part of capital which is exchanged for living labour and forms the wage fund. This means at the same time that a smaller quantity of labour sets a larger quantity of capital in motion' (p. 389, emphasis omitted). In p. 831 he adds: 'The fact that in the development of the productive powers of labour the objective conditions of labour, objectified labour, must grow relative to living labour ... appears from the standpoint of capital not in such a way that one of the moments of social activity - objective labour - becomes the ever more powerful body of the other moment, of subjective, living labour, but rather ... that the objective conditions of labour assume an ever more colossal independence, represented by its very extent, opposite living labour, and that social wealth confronts labour in more powerful portions as an alien and dominant power' (see pp. 388–398, 443, 707 and 746–747).

general, where the values that exist at the beginning of the circuit ('earlier values'), at which the inputs are purchased, are higher than those at which the output is sold ('later values').[20] This conceptual distinction is essential for the analysis of accumulation:

> since the circulation process of capital is not completed in one day but extends over a fairly long period until the capital returns to its original form ... great upheavals and changes take place in the *market* in the course of this period ... [and] in the productivity of labour and therefore also in the *real value* of commodities, [and] it is quite clear, that between the starting-point, the prerequisite capital, and the time of its return at the end of one of these periods, great catastrophes must occur and elements of crises must have gathered and develop ... The *comparison* of value in one period with the value of the same commodity in a later period is no scholastic illusion ... but rather forms the fundamental principle of the circulation process of capital.[21]

Now, which values should be used in the calculation of the OCC and the VCC, the older and higher or the newer and lower? For Marx, the answer is unambiguous. The OCC reflects the TCC at the *initial* (higher) values of the component parts of capital, *before* the new technologies affect the value of the output. In contrast, the VCC reflects the TCC at the *final* (lower and synchronised) values of the elements of constant and variable capital, determined by the modified conditions of production and newly established in exchange. Therefore, changes in the social VCC capture the rise in the social TCC as well as the ensuing fall in commodity values, including those that have been used as inputs. Consequently, the VCC tends to increase more slowly than the social TCC and OCC:

> This change in the technical composition of capital ... is reflected in its value-composition by the increase of the constant constituent of capital at the expense of its variable constituent ... However ... this change in the composition of the value of the capital, provides only an approximate indication of the change in the composition of its material constituents ... The reason is simple: with the increasing productivity of labour, the mass of the means of production consumed by labour increases, but their

---

20   See Fine (1990, 1992) and Weeks (1981, ch.8).
21   *Theories of Surplus Value 2*, p. 495. See also *Capital 2*, p. 185 and *Theories of Surplus Value 3*, p. 154.

value in comparison with their mass diminishes. Their value therefore rises absolutely, but not in proportion to the increase in their mass.

Capital 1, pp. 773–774. See also *Capital 3*, pp. 317–319, 322–323

In contrast, the social OCC is measured at the 'earlier' values, and rises in tandem with the social TCC. In advanced capitalism, when technical progress is the main lever of accumulation, we may well find that the TCC and the OCC grow even faster than social capital itself:

> the development of the productivity of labour ... and the change in the organic composition of capital which results from it, are things which do not merely keep pace with the progress of accumulation, or the growth of social wealth. *They develop at a much quicker rate*, because simple accumulation, or the absolute expansion of the total social capital, is accompanied by the centralization of its individual elements, and because the change in the technical composition of the additional capital goes hand in hand with a similar change in the technical composition of the original capital.[22]

5   Conclusion

The OCC is distinguished from the VCC only through the comparison between contrasting situations. If one compares two capitals at the same moment of time, one would contrast the value of the constant capital productively consumed per hour of labour (which defines the VCC) with the mass of means of production processed in the same time (that determines the TCC and the OCC). This case is important theoretically, and it was through the static comparison of capitals with distinct organic compositions that Marx developed, in Part 2 of *Capital 3*, his transformation of values into prices of production (see Chapter 4).

In a dynamic environment, both the OCC and VCC of a capital undergoing technical change can be calculated. It was shown above that they diverge

---

22   *Capital 1*, p. 781. Moreover, 'Since the demand for labour is determined not by the extent of the total capital but by its variable constituent alone, that demand falls progressively with the growth of the total capital, instead of rising in proportion to it, as was previously assumed. It falls relatively to the magnitude of the total capital, and at an accelerated rate, as this magnitude increases. With the growth of the total capital, its variable constituent, the labour incorporated in it, does admittedly increase, but in a constantly diminishing proportion' (*Capital 1*, pp. 781–782).

because the OCC is an *ex ante* evaluation of the (fixed and circulating) constant capital technically required per hour of (paid and unpaid) labour, while the VCC is the *ex post* ratio between the new value of the (circulating) constant and the variable capital spent in the last phase of production. Thus, the OCC is measured at the time of production, while the VCC is determined in circulation and calculated when labours are normalised, synchronised and homogenised, new values are determined and commodities are about to enter the sphere of exchange. It was in this context that Marx presented his law of the tendency of the rate of profit to fall, in Part 3 of *Capital 3*.

Marx's use of the TCC, OCC and VCC may at times look ambiguous, since both the OCC and the VCC assess the TCC in value terms. However, these concepts have very distinct meaning and significance, and the terminological changes that Marx gradually adopts almost certainly reflect his growing awareness of the importance of the composition of capital for the analysis of accumulation, the transformation of values into prices of production, the tendency of the rate of profit to fall, different types of rent and so on. However, and probably more importantly, it helps to illuminate the impact of accumulation upon the reproduction of the social capital. Continuous technical change raises the TCC, the OCC and gross input values. However, output values, future input prices, and the VCC tend to fall. How the actual process of adjustment happens – especially for large blocs of fixed capital – is crucial to the process of accumulation, because the sudden devaluation of large masses of capital can lead to financial upheaval and crises.

CHAPTER 5

The 'Transformation Problem'

The transformation of values into prices of production (TVPP) is one of several shifts in the form of value examined in *Capital*.[1] These shifts are introduced sequentially, as Marx gradually reconstructs the processes of capitalist reproduction and accumulation across increasingly complex levels of analysis. Briefly, in *Capital 1* Marx reviews the process of production of (surplus) value, including the determination of commodity values through the competition between capitals producing identical use values (intra-sectoral competition). *Capital 2* examines the conditions of social and economic reproduction through the circulation of the (surplus) value produced across the economy. Finally, *Capital 3* addresses two aspects of the distribution of (surplus) value. First is distribution across competing industrial capitals in different sectors, which concerns the possibility of capital migration and, consequently, the allocation of resources (principally capital and labour) across the economy and, correspondingly, the composition of the output. Competition between capitals in different sectors transforms the expression of value as price; the latter – previously examined at a more abstract level in *Capital 1* – take up a more complex and concrete form as *prices of production*. This transformation of the form of value is due to the distribution of surplus value according to the size of each capital, regardless of where value was originally produced. In sequence, Marx examines the relationships between industrial, commercial and financial capital and the landowning class, showing how part of the surplus value can be captured in exchange as commercial profit, interest and rent. This, too, transforms the form of value, but these processes have tended to be ignored by the literature.

When examining the TVPP, the Anglo-Saxon literature has tended to focus narrowly on the quantitative relationship between vectors of equilibrium values and prices, and the corresponding redistribution of surplus value and profit across analytically separate forms of valuation of commodities. This separation is misguided, because values and prices are integrally related to one another, to the logic of capital accumulation, and to the logical structure of Marx's *Capital*. Nevertheless, this separation has become traditional, and

---

1 Based on *The Value of Marx*, London: Routledge, 2002, ch.7, and 'Transformation Problem', in B. Fine and A. Saad-Filho (eds.) *The Elgar Companion to Marxist Economics*. Aldershot: Edward Elgar, 2012.

it is, largely, due to the fact that the conventional literature tends to perceive the TVPP as the unique point of articulation between the intangible domain of values and the visible realm of prices. Other contributory factors include the flirting engagement of mainstream economists, who saw in the TVPP an opening to attack the logical consistency of Marxism, and the wish of Sraffian economists to sideline their most significant rivals amongst the heterodoxy in the 1970s (for a review, see Elson 1979, and Fine 1986). In other words, the TVPP has often provided the canvas for contrasting rival interpretations of Marx's theory of value (MTV), and the pretext for shunning it altogether.

1   The 'Problem'

The third volume of *Capital* opens with the distinction between the concepts of surplus value (s) and profit. Surplus value is the difference between the newly produced value and the value of labour power, and profit is the difference between the value of the product and the value of the constant (c) and variable (v) capital (for a detailed explanation of these concepts, see Fine and Saad-Filho 2016, chs.1–3).

The rate of exploitation, e = s/v, measures the surplus value created per unit of variable capital. In contrast, the rate of profit (r) measures capital's rate of growth, in which case the distinct role in production of the means of production and labour power is immaterial. The rate of profit is:

$$r = \frac{s}{c+v} = \frac{e}{\left(c/v\right)+1}$$

Marx subsequently considers the impact on the profit rate of changes in the quantity, quality and value of the inputs, and the implications of changes in the turnover time and the rate of surplus value. In Chapter 8 of *Capital 3*, Marx points out that the same factors that affect the general rate of profit may also lead to differences between the profit rates of individual capitals in distinct sectors:

> the rates of profit in different spheres of production that exist simultaneously alongside one another will differ if, other things remaining equal, either the turnover times of capitals invested differ, or the value relations between the organic components of these capitals in different branches of production. *What we previously viewed as changes that the same capital underwent in succession, we now consider as simultaneous distinctions*

> *between capital investments that exist alongside one another in different spheres of production.*
>
> *Capital 3*, p. 243, emphasis added. See also *Theories of Surplus Value 2*, p. 384

This passage introduces the concept of inter-sectoral competition, and it marks the shift in the level of analysis. This shift posits the need for the TVPP.

It may therefore come as a surprise that Marx does not immediately address this issue. Rather, in the following pages he analyses (differences between) the technical, organic and value compositions of capital (TCC, OCC and VCC, see Chapter 4). It is only after this apparent detour that Marx looks into the transformation, in Chapter 9 of *Capital 3*.

In that chapter, Marx contrasts five capitals equal to 100 but with different proportions of c and v, illustrating that capitals produce distinct use values with varying combinations of living labour, raw materials and machinery. Marx points out that these capitals will produce different amounts of surplus value because of their distinct OCCs, defined as c/v. For example, and using only two sectors instead of Marx's five, one unit of capital invested in the steel industry typically employs less workers – and, therefore, directly produces less surplus value – than one unit of capital in the textile industry. Using Marx's notation, these capitals might be represented as, say, $80c + 20v$ and $20c + 80v$. Supposing the rate of surplus value is 100% ($s/v = 1$), the output values will be $80c + 20v + 20s = 120$ in the steel industry, and $20c + 80v + 80s = 180$ in the textile industry. Therefore, their profit rates, defined above, are, respectively, 20% and 80%.

Classical Political Economy recognised that this difference is incompatible with inter-sectoral competition, which creates a tendency towards the equalisation of profit rates. For Ricardo, a more sophisticated analysis was required, which he unsuccessfully endeavoured to provide (and for which Sraffa is presumed to have found a solution albeit at the expense of MTV; see Milonakis and Fine, 2009). In contrast, for Marx, while the abstraction that commodities exchange at their values permits the explanation of the production of (surplus) value, this level of analysis is insufficiently developed to account for inter-sectoral competition and, therefore, the composition of output and the distribution of labour. Their explanation requires a more complex form of value, which Marx called prices of production.

This shift, or transformation, in the form of value does not simply 'erase and replace' the previous abstraction (commodity values determined by socially necessary labour time) as if it were wrong or merely a special case (of equal OCCs). Nor is Marx confronting a purely logical (neoclassical) problem of finding a price vector that satisfies arbitrary static equilibrium conditions. Finally,

Marx was fully aware that the input values had not been transformed in his presentation in *Capital*. Rather, in Marx's presentation the abstract content of value is being reproduced in a more complex and concrete form as prices of production, preserving the prior analysis and addressing additional (more concrete) aspects of capitalism on this basis. Unfortunately, Marx's presentation of the transformation is hampered by the unfinished status of *Capital 3*. This has contributed to overlapping disagreements about what Marx really said, what he would have said if he had been able to finish this Volume, and what he should have said in order to be 'right' according to differing interpretations.

In *Capital 3*, Marx calculates the average of the profit rates of the five capitals in his example, and derives the prices of production of the output as $p_i = (c_i + v_i)(1 + r)$, where i represents the capital ($i = 1, \dots, 5$) and the average profit rate is $r = S/(C + V)$, where S, C and V are the total surplus value and constant and variable capital. Therefore, while commodity values include the surplus value produced by each capital, the prices of production distribute the surplus value produced to equalise the profit rates across different sectors. In the numerical example provided above, the values of the output are 120 and 180, the average profit rate is 50% ($r = 100/200$), and the prices of production of the output are 150 and 150.

The distribution of surplus value to equalise profit rates amongst competing capitals gives rise to *profit* as a form of surplus value: this conceptual difference mirrors the difference between the *production* of surplus value, and its *appropriation* as industrial profit (at this level of analysis, other forms of profit, as well as interest and rent, are not present yet). Marx claims that the sum of prices is equal to the sum of values (in our case, 120 + 180 = 150 + 150), *and* that the sum of surplus values is equal to the sum of profits (20 + 80 = 50 + 50). These aggregate equalities illustrate Marx's claims that prices of production are transformed values, and that profit is transformed surplus value. In other words, each capitalist shares in the surplus value produced according to their share in capital advanced, as if receiving a dividend on an equity share in the economy's social or total capital as a whole.

Marx's transformation procedure, outlined above, has been criticised primarily because of a supposed logical inconsistency: he calculates the price of production of the output (steel and textiles) based on *untransformed* values of the inputs – whereas capitalists will have bought their inputs (*including* steel and textiles) at prices of production, not values. However, these commodities cannot be purchased as inputs at one set of prices (120 and 180) and sold at *different* prices (150 and 150) as outputs, because every sale is also a purchase for one or other capitalist. Further, this implies that the 'value rate of profit', as calculated by Marx as S/(C+V), is also not the monetary rate of profit at all, since both numerator and denominator need to be recalculated at their prices of production as opposed to their values. In other words, Marx gets the rate of profit wrong and, even if he did not, he still gets prices wrong!

2 Alternative Interpretations

The charge of inconsistency was issued soon after the publication of *Capital 3*, and it was brought into prominence in the Anglo-Saxon literature by Paul Sweezy (1968, originally published in 1942). The subsequent debate has focused on the algebraic difficulties of transferring monetary quantities across sectors in an economy in static equilibrium, starting from direct (untransformed) prices, a single value of labour power and equal rates of exploitation, and arriving at an identical material equilibrium with a single wage rate and an equalised profit rate, while, at the same time, validating Marx's aggregate equalities between total price and total value, and total surplus value and total profit.

These controversies became especially prominent with the emergence of radical political economy in the late 1960s, and even attracted the attention of leading mainstream economists, especially Paul Samuelson, Michio Morishima and William Baumol (for a review, see Saad-Filho 2002, ch.7). Alternative solutions to the 'transformation problem' proliferated, depending on the structure of value theory envisaged by competing authors and their choice of starting conditions, constraints and desired outcomes including, almost invariably, which aggregate equality should be sacrificed in order to 'preserve' the other. These transformation procedures were deemed to be significant because they would either 'validate' or 'deny' selected aspects of Marx's theory of value – or, even, the entire logical core of Marx's theory.

2.1 *Neoclassical and Sraffian*

The neoclassical and Sraffian critiques of Marx are essentially identical if differently motivated and rooted. They postulate two equilibrium exchange value systems, one in values (defined as quantities of embodied labour) and the other in equilibrium prices. The value system is described by $\lambda = \lambda A + l = l(I - A)^{-1}$, where λ is the ($1 \times n$) vector of commodity values, A is the ($n \times n$) technical matrix and l is the ($1 \times n$) vector of direct labour. Given the same technical matrix, the price system is described by $p = (pA + wl)(1 + r)$, where p is the ($1 \times n$) price vector, w is the wage rate, and r is the profit rate.

These systems provide the basis for a critique of both alleged inconsistencies and incompleteness in Marx, leading to the conclusion that the attempt to determine values from embodied labour, and prices from values, is logically flawed. In brief, while the value system can usually be solved, the price system has two degrees of freedom (it has n equations, but $n+2$ unknowns: the n prices, w and r). A solution would require additional restrictions, for example, defining the value of labour power as the value of a fixed bundle, b, of workers' consumption goods (with wages given by $w = pb$), plus one of Marx's aggregate equalities – however, the other aggregate equality would normally not hold, which is allegedly destructive for Marx's analysis. Furthermore, this representation of Marx can scarcely distinguish between the role of labour and other inputs, in which case it cannot be argued that labour creates value and is exploited, rather than any other input, such as corn, iron or energy.

This critique of Marx is insufficient for four reasons. First, it presumes that the production structure is determined exogenously and purely technically while, for Marx, technologies and social forms are mutually constituting (on the one hand, capital accumulation and the development of productive forces do not rest on equilibrium foundations regardless of growth; on the other hand, production technologies are irreducibly *capitalist*; see, for example, Marglin 1974, Levidow and Young 1981 and Slater 1980). Second, it assumes that, for values to have conceptual legitimacy, they should be both necessary and sufficient for the calculation of the profit rate and the price vector. Since this is not the case in this model (in which, incidentally, the 'value' rate of profit has no significance for economic behaviour), value analysis is allegedly redundant. However, these claims are based on a misrepresentation of Marx's theory, where labour values, direct prices, prices of production and market prices are forms of value belonging to distinct levels of complexity, rather than sequences in (deductive) calculation. Third, the neoclassical and Sraffian value equation is inconsistent, for, if l represents concrete labour time, these labours are qualitatively distinct and cannot be aggregated; but if l is a vector of abstract labour values cannot be calculated in practice because abstract labour data are not directly available. Fourth, in this system the social aspect of production is either assumed away or projected upon the sphere of distribution, through the inability of the workers to purchase the entire output with their wages (see Rowthorn 1980).

2.2 *Value-Form Theories*

Value-form interpretations of Marx draw upon the social division of labour and the production of commodities by 'separate' (independent) producers. Separation brings the need to produce a socially useful commodity, that is, one that can be sold. Consequently, for this tradition, commodities are produced by private labours that are only potentially abstract and social; the conversion to value form only happens when the product is exchanged for money.

Value-form approaches have helped to shift the focus of Marxian studies away from the algebraic calculation of values and prices and towards the analysis of the social relations of production and their forms of appearance. Nevertheless, the claim that 'separation' is the essential feature of commodity production subsumes capitalist relations under simple commodity relations of production. This limitation helps to explain this tradition's stunted contribution to the theory of *capital*(*ism*) – including the TVPP, which is frequently bypassed through the direct assimilation of values with market prices.

The 'new interpretation' (NI) of Marx's value theory was developed in the early 1980s, drawing heavily upon value-form analysis (see Fine, Lapavitsas and Saad-Filho, 2004, see also Chapter 6). The NI eschews equilibrium analysis, and postulates that money is the immediate and exclusive expression of abstract labour, as well as its measure. Since this interpretation remains at the aggregate level, it bypasses the relationship between individual prices and values that was normally associated with the TVPP. Furthermore, the NI defines the value of money as the quantity of labour represented by the monetary unit or, conversely, the abstract labour time that adds £1 to the value of the output. The newly produced money-value is allocated as price across the net product. Finally, the NI defines the value of labour power as the *ex post* wage share of national income (i.e. the wage rate times the value of money), while the surplus value is the residual, which confirms that profit is merely redistributed surplus value.

The NI has contributed to closer attention to Marx's value analysis, as opposed to imposing equilibrium interpretations of price theory, and it established a channel for empirical and policy studies. Nevertheless, the NI is limited at three levels. First, its focus on the net product short-circuits the production of the means of production (other than the part incorporated into net product for expanded reproduction), rendering invisible a significant proportion of current production and the entire sphere of exchanges between capitalist producers. Second, the NI's concept of value of money short-circuits the real structures, processes and relations mediating the expression of social labour into money, which Marx was at pains to identify across the three volumes of *Capital*. This weakens the NI's ability to examine disequilibrium, conflict and crises logically, rather than arbitrarily. Third, the NI definition of value of labour power is limited to one of the effects of exploitation, namely, the inability of the workers to purchase the entire net product. This was also the same aspect of exploitation that the Ricardian socialist and Sraffian economists contemplated (see Chapter 3 and Saad-Filho 2002, ch.2). However, for Marx, capitalist exploitation is not due to the unfair distribution of income, and the net product is not 'shared' between the classes at the end of each production cycle. Rather, wages are part of the advance of capital (regardless of when they are paid), whilst profit is the consequence of how much surplus value is extracted. In sum, while addressing crucial issues for value theory, the NI resolves none of them. Instead, it confines value theory to a sequential if not static sociological theory of exploitation in which selective aspects of Marx's transformation are subject to piecemeal (and arbitrary) attention, independently of the structures and processes by which surplus value is produced and distributed competitively through the market.

2.3   *Dynamic Analysis*

Ben Fine (1983) offered a dynamic interpretation of the TVPP. This interpretation starts from (a critique of) conventional views, which tend to focus on the differences in the *value* composition of capital across different sectors (although often, incorrectly, referring to as differences in OCCs; see Chapter 4). Paradoxically, nearly all treatments of the TVPP, especially but not exclusively those who reject Marx, deploy the OCC in terminology but the VCC conceptually. However, this is not the case for Marx, who examines the transformation entirely in terms of the OCC, properly conceived and distinguished from the VCC: for him, the TVPP is concerned with the effects on prices of the differing *rates of increase* at which raw materials are transformed into outputs (rather than the effect of differences in the input values, which are captured by the VCC). This attaches Marx's TVPP to the theory of accumulation and productivity growth in *Capital 1*, the circulation of capital from *Capital 2*, and to the law of the tendency of the rate of profit to fall that immediately follows the TVPP in *Capital 3*. For standard interpretations of the TVPP, there is no reason why it should not come earlier than *Capital 3*, and none why it should have any connection to falling profitability (and, not surprisingly, equilibrium interpretations of the TVPP as transformation problem are heavily associated with denial of Marx's treatment of falling profitability).

For this dynamic view, then, Marx's problem is the following. If a given amount of living labour employed in sector i (represented by v_i) works up a greater quantity of raw materials (represented by c_i) than in another sector j, *regardless of their respective costs*, the commodities produced in sector i will command a higher price relative to value. That is, the use of a greater quantity of labour in production creates more (surplus) value than a lesser quantity, regardless of the sector, the use value being produced, and the cost of the raw materials. This completely general proposition within value theory underpins Marx's explanation of prices and profit.[2]

---

2   'When the rate of surplus-value ... is given, the *amount* of surplus-value depends on the organic composition of the capital, that is to say, on the *number of workers* which a capital of given value, for instance £100, employs' (*Theories of Surplus Value* 2, p.376, emphasis added).

Marx's focus on the OCC rather than the VCC in the transformation is significant, because it shows that Marx is mainly concerned with the impact on prices of the different *quantities* of labour transforming the means of production into the output – that is, the *production* of value and surplus value by living labour, regardless of the value of these means of production. In contrast, the VCC links profits with the sphere of *exchange*, where commodities are traded and where the newly established values measure the rate of capital accumulation. Marx's choice is analytically significant because it pins the source of surplus value and profit down to unpaid labour, substantiating the claims that machines do not create value, that surplus value and profit are not due to unequal exchange, and that industrial profit, interest and rent are shares of the surplus value produced by the productive wage workers.

3   Marx's Transformation: A Review

The literature generally ignores completely the reason why Marx includes capitals with the *same size*, £100, in his analysis of the TVPP, and the reason why he determines the price of production of the *entire* output of each capital, rather the unit price. These analytical choices have probably been attributed to convenience or ease of exposition. However, since Marx is interested in the OCC, this procedure is *necessary*. Let us start from the equal size of the advanced capitals:

> the organic composition of capital ... *must* be considered in percentage terms. We express the organic composition of a capital that consists of four-fifths constant and one-fifth variable capital by using the formula 80c + 20v.
>
> *Capital 3*, p. 254, emphasis added

Marx uses the per cent form several times, in the transformation and elsewhere. He does this because this is the *only* way to assess the OCC in the static case, when it cannot be measured directly. If we assume, as Marx does, that the value-productivity of labour is the same in every firm and that the rate of surplus value is determined for the entire economy, the per cent form (e.g., 60c+40v rather than 6c+4v or 180c+120v; and 80c+20v rather than 8c+2v or 2400c+600v) has striking consequences: variable capital becomes an *index* of the quantity of labour power purchased, labour performed, and value and surplus value produced.[3] Moreover, there is a direct relationship between

---

3   '[T]he rate of profit depends on the amount of surplus-value, and by no means on the rate of surplus-value. When the rate of surplus-value ... is given, the amount of surplus-value

the quantity of labour put in motion, the value of the output and the rate of profit. This is precisely what Marx wants to emphasize in the transformation. As these relationships are established in production, they involve the *organic* (rather than value) composition of capital:

> Capitals of the same size, or capitals of different magnitudes reduced to percentages, operating with the same working day and the same degree of exploitation, thus produce very different amounts of surplus-value and therefore profit, and this is because their variable portions differ according to the differing organic composition of capital in different spheres of production, which means that different quantities of living labour are set in motion, and hence also different quantities of surplus labour, of the substance of surplus-value and therefore of profit, are appropriated ... At any given level of exploitation of labour, the mass of labour set in motion by a capital of 100, and thus also the surplus labour it appropriates, depends on the size of its variable component ... Since capitals of equal size in different spheres of production, capitals of different size considered by percentage, are unequally divided into a constant and a variable element, set in motion unequal amounts of living labour and hence produce unequal amounts of surplus-value or profit, the rate of profit, which consists precisely of the surplus-value calculated as a percentage of the total capital, is different in each case.[4]

Use of the per cent form helps to illustrate the principle that profit is created in production, and that it depends primarily upon the *quantity* of labour power put in motion, rather than the value of the means of production. For Marx, this shows that profit is a 'dividend' drawn from the social surplus value.[5] Finally,

---

depends on the organic composition of the capital, that is to say, on the *number* of workers which a capital of given value, for instance £100, employs' (*Theories of Surplus Value 2*, p.376, emphasis added). See also *Capital 3*, pp. 137, 146, 243–246, D. Harvey (1999, p.127) and Rubin (1975, pp. 231–247).

4   *Capital 3*, pp. 248–249. Alternatively, 'As a result of the differing organic compositions of capitals applied in different branches of production, as a result therefore of the circumstance that according to the different percentage that the variable part forms in a total capital of a given size, very different amounts of labour are set in motion by capitals of equal size, so too very different amounts of surplus labour are appropriated by these capitals, or very different amounts of surplus-value are produced by them. The rates of profit prevailing in the different branches of production are accordingly originally very different' (p.257). See also *Capital 1*, pp. 421, 757, *Capital 3*, pp. 137–138, and *Theories of Surplus Value 3*, p.483.

5   See *Capital 3*, pp. 257–258, 298–99, 312–313, *Theories of Surplus Value 2*, pp. 29, 64–71, 190, *Theories of Surplus Value 3*, pp. 73, 87 and *Grundrisse*, pp. 435, 547, 760. In other words, differences

the per cent form shows clearly that total value equals total price of production, and that total surplus value equals total profit.

Next is the two aggregate equalities, which are essential for Marx. They should not be understood as two independent conditions, nor as 'testable hypotheses', as if Marx's value theory would be falsified unless they are verified empirically. For Marx, these equalities are one and the same and they necessarily hold, but they refer to distinct levels of analysis. Total price is equal to total value *because* price is a form of value or, alternatively, *because* total profit is equal to total surplus value. Conversely, individual prices differ from values *because* profits differ from surplus values, due to the redistribution of surplus value in the TVPP. These equalities always hold because they express the development of the same concept, social labour, across distinct levels of analysis.

Marx's abstraction from the transformation of the value of the inputs and the value of the money-commodity, which naturally follow from his analysis based upon the OCC, confirm that these equalities should be understood conceptually rather than arithmetically. They express the relationship between value and surplus value with their own forms of appearance, price and profit. Prices of production are a relatively complex form of value, in which price-value differences redistribute surplus value across the economy until the average capital in each branch of industry has the same profit rate.[6]

These relationships can be examined from another angle. In *Capital*, commodity values and prices can be analysed at distinct levels. At a very abstract level, value is a social relation of production or, in quantitative terms, it is the labour time socially necessary to reproduce each kind of commodity. Value can also be seen as the monetary expression of labour time as direct price, price

---

in the profit rates between capitals in the same sector arise because they *produce* distinct quantities of value per hour, while the equalisation of profit rates of capitals in distinct branches is due to value *transfers*: 'What competition within *the same* sphere of production brings about, is the determination of the *value of the commodity in a given sphere* by the average labour-time required in it, i.e., the creation of the *market-value*. What competition between the *different* spheres of production brings about is the *creation of the same general rate of profit in the different* spheres through the levelling out of the different market-values into market-prices, which are [*prices of production*] that are different from the actual market-values. Competition in this second instance by no means tends to assimilate the prices of the commodities to their values, but on the contrary, to reduce their values to [prices of production] that differ from these values, to abolish the differences between their values and [prices of production]' (*Theories of Surplus Value 2*, p.208). See also pp. 126, 206–207.

6 'Values cannot be literally transformed into prices because the two play theoretical roles at different levels of explanation; for each commodity there is thus *both* a value and a price' (Mattick Jr 1991–92, p.40). See also Rubin (1975, pp. 176, 250–257) and Weeks (1981, p.171). In this sense, procedures that focus upon these aggregate equalities miss the point of the transformation.

of production, or market price. These shifts are due to the gradual refinement of the concept of value through its reproduction at greater levels of complexity, which captures the determinations of the price form and, therefore, of the value relation. The study of these determinations comprises a large part of the body of Marx's work, and of Marxian value theory more generally.

It follows, then, that the TVPP has two stages. The *first* stage, explained above, is the distribution of the surplus value newly produced by all capitals in order to equalise the profit rates across the economy. In the *second* stage, the input values and the value money are transformed. This stage is analytically secondary, and it received little attention from Marx; however, this has been the source of most disputes about the meaning and significance of the transformation.

Distinguishing between the two stages in the TVPP helps to explain Marx's supposed 'omission' of the transformation of the input values. In reality, however, Marx *abstracts* from the input values, for two reasons. First, the input values are irrelevant for his argument that prices are the form of appearance of values, and that profit is the form of appearance of surplus value. Second, the simultaneous transformation of input and output values would make undetectable the production and distribution of surplus value, which is the conceptual core of the transformation. If the inputs and outputs were transformed simultaneously, only two opposing and seemingly unrelated relative price systems would exist, one in values and the other in prices. Price and profit could not be assessed in the former, and value and surplus value would be absent in the latter. Their intrinsic relationship would be invisible. In contrast, if we follow Marx's procedure and abstract from the value of the means of production, this dichotomy is avoided and the change in the level of abstraction can be 'seen' through the shift of surplus value across branches of industry.

Abstraction from the value of the inputs reveals the distribution of surplus value and the ensuing determination of prices of production, regardless of the systematic modification of the exchange ratios brought about by the transformation. Moreover, it nets out the impact of the transformation of the value of the money-commodity, which would complicate further the relationship between values and prices and obscure the concepts being introduced, especially if the VCC of the money-producing sector were distinct from the social average.

In sum, there are three reasons why the price vector cannot be calculated from Marx's transformation procedure: (a) Marx works with the price of production of the mass of commodities produced per £100 advanced, rather than their unit price; (b) Marx abstracts from the transformation of the input values, and (c) Marx abstracts from the transformation of the value of the money-commodity. This implies that the age-old objection that Marx's transformation is 'wrong' because he failed to transform the value of the inputs is beside the point. For, if the transformation pivots around the OCC, the value of the means of production is immaterial, and their transformation cannot affect the outcome. The same argument can be used to dismiss the critique that Marx 'forgot' to transform the value of the money-commodity (or was mathematically incompetent to handle this problem), or that he 'unwarrantedly' failed to define the problem in terms of unit values and unit prices of production. Marx's procedure is adequate for the derivation of the concept of price of production (although not immediately for its calculation), because it separates *cause* (the performance of labour in production and exploitation through the extraction of surplus value) from *effect* (the existence of a positive profit rate, and the forces leading to its equalisation across branches).[7]

Having introduced the concept of price of production Marx's analysis reaches a more complex level, and the second stage of the transformation may be considered. When the realm of the OCC is superseded and the prices of the means of production and labour power enter the picture, there are two reasons why commodity prices may diverge from their value:

(1) because the average profit is added to the cost price of a commodity, instead of the surplus-value contained in it;

(2) because the price of production of a commodity that diverges in this way from its value enters as an element into the cost price of other commodities, which means that a divergence from the value of the means of production consumed may already be contained in the cost price, quite apart from the divergence that may arise for average profit and surplus-value.[8]

---

7   'One must ... reject the assertion that Marx thought prices had to be *deduced* from values via his transformation calculation. Marx knew very well that his 'prices of production' were the same as the 'natural values' of classical economics ... Thus, he does *not* accuse the classical authors of having erred in deducing their price relationships without using Marxian values in the process. Rather, the charge repeatedly reasserted is that they dealt only with "this form of appearance" ... To Marx, prices and values are ... not the same thing. Values are not approximations to prices nor a necessary step in their calculation. Rather, one is a surface manifestation, while the latter is intended to reveal an underlying reality' (Baumol 1992, p.56).

8   *Capital 3*, pp. 308–309. In other words the cost price, previously the value of the inputs, is now their *price*: 'It was originally assumed that the cost price of a commodity equalled the *value* of the commodities consumed in its production. But ... [as] the price of production of a commodity can diverge from its value, so the cost price of a commodity, in which the price of production of others commodities is involved, can also stand above or below the portion of its total value that is formed by the value of the means of production going into it. It is necessary to bear in mind this *modified significance* of the cost price, and therefore to bear in mind too that if the cost price of a commodity is equated with the value of the means of production used up in producing it, it is always possible to go wrong' (*Capital 3*, pp. 264–265,

This change in the point of view, from the conceptual derivation of price to the study of the economy at the level of price, leads to the further determination of the concept of price of production and concludes Marx's transformation procedure. Whilst the derivation of price departs from the distribution of surplus value abstracting from the value of the means of production and labour power, the calculation of the price vector involves, as is well known, the current technologies of production, the wage rate and the (price-) rate of profit.[9]

4   The Transformation and its Method

Examination of the TVPP shows that Marx's method involves not only the progressive transformation of some concepts into others, but also gradual shifts in the meaning of each concept, whenever this is necessary to accommodate the evolution of the analysis.[10] Having done this, Marx can claim that his prices of production are:

> the same thing that Adam Smith calls 'natural price', Ricardo 'price of production' or 'cost of production', and the Physiocrats '*prix nécessaire*', though none of these people explained the difference between price of production and value ... We can also understand why those very economists who oppose the determination of commodity value by labour-time ... always speak of prices of production as centres around which market prices fluctuate. They can allow themselves this because the price of production is already a completely externalized and *prima facie* irrational form of commodity value, a form that appears in competition and is therefore present in the consciousness of the vulgar capitalist and consequently also in that of the vulgar economist.
>
>   *Capital 3*, p. 300. See also p. 268, *Capital 1*, pp. 678–679 and Marx (1998, p. 38)

At this stage,

> The value of commodities appears directly only in the influence of the changing productivity of labour on the rise and fall of prices of production; on their movement, not on their final limits. Profit now appears as

---

           emphasis added). See also pp. 1008–1010, *Theories of Surplus Value 3*, pp. 167–168, The italicised passage highlights the shift in the concept of cost price.

9   See *Capital 3*, pp. 259–265, 308–309, 990–920.

10   The concepts of price of production and general rate of profit are modified again when Marx discusses commercial capital, see Saad-Filho (2002, ch.1) and *Capital 3*, pp. 398–399.

determined only secondarily by the direct exploitation of labour, in so far as ... it permits the capitalist to realize a profit departing from the average.

Capital 3, pp. 967–968

It follows that Marx's price theory is two-fold; on the one hand, it is a production cost theory similar to the Classical. On the other hand, Marx's theory is distinctive because he explains the price form through the social division of labour in capitalism, analysed at increasing levels of complexity.

The TVPP has a four-fold impact upon the structure of *Capital*. First, it explains why market exchanges are not directly regulated by the labour time socially necessary to reproduce each commodity. Second, it shows that price is a relatively complex form of social labour. Third, it allows a more complex understanding of Marx's analysis of the forms of value (see below). Fourth, it explains the distribution of labour across the economy.

Even though it was left incomplete, Marx's procedure is important because it develops further his reconstruction of the capitalist economy, and substantiates the claim that *living labour alone*, and *not* the dead labour represented by the means of production, creates value and surplus value. In contrast, approaches that argue that the input values should be taken into account from the start, and that they should be transformed together with the output values, often conflate the roles of living and dead labour in the production of value, and can hardly distinguish between workers and machines in production. The 'non-transformation of the inputs' cannot be considered a defect. Rather, it is a *feature* of Marx's method. By abstracting from (changes in) the value of the inputs and the money-commodity, Marx locates the source of profit in the performance of labour in production, and carefully builds the conditions in which circulation may be brought into the analysis and add positively to its development.

5   Conclusion

This essay has shown that Marx's transformation of values into prices of production includes two stages. In the first, Marx abstracts from (differences in) the value of the means of production, in order to highlight the principle that value is produced by labour alone or, alternatively, that the greater the quantity of living labour put in motion, the more surplus value is produced. Distribution of the surplus value according to the size of each capital forms prices different from values. In the second stage, the economy is analysed at the level of prices of production; all commodities are sold at their prices, and the input prices are taken into account. The role of transformation is to allow a greater determination in the form of social labour, and to explain the distribution of labour and surplus value across the economy.

The use of the organic composition of capital is essential in order to distinguish these stages, because it helps to identify the cause of the transformation and to explain the relationship between prices and values. In addition, the OCC shows that Marx's interest lies in the conceptual relationship between labour, price and profit, rather than the algebraic calculation of prices or the rate of profit. Finally, it indicates that equilibrium (or simple reproduction) assumptions are unwarranted in this case. This reading of the transformation shows that the presentation in *Capital 3* is consistent with Marx's method, and is part of his reconstruction of the main categories of the capitalist economy.

Most of the literature has, instead, investigated the transformation through the VCC. Whilst this is not in itself wrong, and may lead to valuable theoretical developments, this approach has no bearing upon Marx's problem. The solutions to which this approach leads can be distinguished from each other by the structures that they contemplate, the processes at the forefront, and the treatment which is given to them (in other words, the nature of the normalisation condition, the use of interactions or simultaneous equations, and so on). Most transformation procedures found in the literature are alternative to Marx's. They cannot claim to 'correct' the latter, because they address different issues and include a conception of the price-value relationship at odds with Marx's. Inadequate understanding of Marx's transformation has often led to the complaint that he unwarrantedly omitted the specification of the technologies of production or, more often, that he did not transform the value of the inputs. This essay has demonstrated that these objections are misplaced, because they emphasize issues that are not the primary object of Marx's concern in the transformation, and may obscure, rather than help to explain, the subject of his inquiry.

More generally, the TVPP shows that values and prices can be analysed at distinct levels. At the most abstract level, value is a social relation of production. Value can also be seen, at increasingly complex levels, as the labour time socially necessary to reproduce each kind of commodity, direct price, price of production, price of production in the presence of commercial capital, and market price. The value form is transformed at each one of these levels of analysis; as it becomes increasingly concrete, it encompasses more complex determinations of the value relations of capitalism. The development and implications of these analytical shifts comprise a large part of Marx's work in

Capital. In the TVPP, Marx is not addressing the Ricardian (and neoclassical) problem of calculating equilibrium prices from labour magnitudes in the presence of capital and time; rather, Marx is attempting to capture conceptually a relatively complex form of social labour. This approach explains why market exchanges are not directly regulated by labour time; shows that price is a relatively complex form of social labour; allows a more complex understanding of the forms of value, and explains the distribution of labour and surplus value across the economy. Even though it was left incomplete, Marx's procedure is important because it develops further his reconstruction of the capitalist economy, and substantiates the claim that living labour alone, and not the dead labour represented by the means of production, creates value and surplus value.

CHAPTER 6

Transforming the Transformation Problem: Why the 'New Interpretation' is a Wrong Turning

The New Interpretation (NI),[1] previously known as the new approach or new solution to the transformation problem, has been the most striking development in Marxist value theory during the last two decades.[2] The NI is inspired by the 'Rubin school';[3] it draws on social rather than technical relations, and maintains that labour becomes abstract (and is socialised) only through the exchange of commodities with money. Therefore, money is the immediate, direct and exclusive expression of abstract labour. The NI takes this view one step further, arguing that such representation of value by money prevails at the level of the aggregate magnitudes of the capitalist economy.

This interpretation is appealing for those committed to value analysis for several reasons. First, it has links with the previous value debates, especially through the Rubin school and the transformation problem. Second, it is supportive of Marx, retaining value as an underlying abstract and, in some respects, causal category. It preserves, with some modification, key properties of Marx's transformation (ever perceived to be the Achilles heel of value theory), especially the aggregate equalities between price and value and between profit and surplus value. Third, it seeks to put value theory on sound technical foundations, which were perceived by many to have been shaken by 'errors' in Marx's transformation. Fourth, it incorporates money into the analysis, where previously for the transformation problem it had been notably absent, other than as a gold sector setting absolute prices. Fifth, it has inspired concrete analyses, forging an empirical connection between Marx's theory of exploitation and profits and wages.

---

1 Originally published as 'Transforming the Transformation Problem: Why the "New Interpretation" is a Wrong Turning', *Review of Radical Political Economics* 36 (1) 2004, pp. 3–19 (with B. Fine and C. Lapavitsas).
2 Seminal contributions include Duménil (1980, 1983–84, 1984) and Foley (1982, 1983, 1986) and, at a later stage, Lipietz (1982, 1983, 1984).
3 Rubin (1927, 1928); see also Aglietta (1979) and de Vroey (1982, 1985). For a critique, see Saad-Filho (2002, ch.2).

This essay reviews the analytical foundations of the NI, in order to clarify its methodological implications in the wider context of alternative approaches to Marx's value theory. This is not simply a disinterested service to the reader. We believe that the NI's intention of re-asserting the social foundations of the labour theory of value, while disposing of the transformation problem and deriving empirical macroeconomic results, is valuable. Nevertheless, the NI is highly questionable from perspectives other than that derived from Rubin. This is demonstrated through detailed criticism of its structure and content, especially its conceptualisation of the value of money and the value of labour power, and the sequencing and dynamics of the capitalist economy.

We show, moreover, that the NI precludes consideration of a range of issues that are vital to radical political economy. That is not to suggest that the complex factors impinging upon value formation, for example through accumulation and technical change, cannot be introduced into the NI. They can, but only after aggregate value and price relations are posited without reference to (the already assumed) value theory. Put differently, the NI collapses the capitalist economy into a simple, two-level dialectic of value and price, mediated by money. Further analytical progress could be achieved, such as developing an account of capital as a structured and dynamic system of accumulation, but only independently of the NI's own contribution. For the latter, one of the most complex outcomes, i.e., price formation, is already pre-determined. Our general conclusion is that the NI is to be welcomed for the issues that it raises, but not for the manner in which it has dealt with them, for which we offer alternatives. In each case, there is a difference in method, with our emphasis being upon the progressive dialectical movement from more abstract to more concrete and complex economic categories, in contrast to the more immediate movement between value and exchange value in the NI.

This essay is structured as follows. Following this introduction, the first section presents a formal summary of the NI demonstrating the significance for it of the labour expression of money (LEM), of reliance on the net product, and of the peculiar definition of the value of labour power. The second criticises the NI concept of the value of money, suggesting that it obscures the real processes underlying determination of prices and the role of money. The third critically reviews the NI concept of the value of labour power, and argues that NI (as well as Sraffian) views are insufficient to explain its determination. The fourth reviews broader methodological issues surrounding the NI, in terms of its capacity to contribute to an understanding of accumulation and crises. Finally, the fifth section offers a conclusion in terms of value theory as an alternative rather than as a complement to the NI.

1   The 'New Interpretation': A Simple Formal Presentation

The NI, by virtue of its origins in the transformation debate, has been heavily associated with elaborating the relationship between values and prices. But, as is now fully recognised, the NI is not concerned with individual values and prices. The point can be simply captured by presenting the NI through a set of equations that are totally independent of individual values and prices, with two exceptions, those of labour power and money.

Assume total profit, P, total net revenue (total revenue minus non-wage costs), R, money wage rate, w, total amount of living labour, L, total surplus value, S, and the ratio L/R (the LEM, symbolised below by m). Three equations follow immediately: profit is net revenue minus wages; surplus value is living labour minus the value represented by wages; and the value of net product equals living labour:

$$P = R - wL \tag{1}$$

$$S = L - wLm \tag{2}$$

$$Rm = L \tag{3}$$

Equation (3) implies that the labour-equivalent of the money value of the net output equals total living labour. Although this equation is a tautology, given the definition of m,[4] it is taken by the NI to be the analogue of Marx's proposition that total value equals total price (though applied to net rather than gross output). Multiplying equation (1) by m, and substituting for Rm from (3) gives:

$$Pm = L - wLm \tag{4}$$

In other words:

$$S = Pm \tag{5}$$

Profit is the money form of surplus value, as claimed by Marx's other proposition. Thus, it appears that value theory has been vindicated, since both of Marx's much-disputed propositions in solving the transformation problem can be made to hold in a completely general framework.

---

4   We thank Gary Mongiovi for pointing this out.

The reason why the above presentation of the NI is simpler than others in the literature (e.g., Lipietz 1982 and Mohun 1994) is that it makes no reference to individual values, prices or production conditions, which are 'an irrelevant detour' in specifying the analytical content of the NI. In other words, first, the NI is compatible with any set of pricing equations, whether based on equalised rate of profit or some other pricing principle, as long as these satisfy (1) to (3). In spite of this, much of the related literature is concerned with different pricing models, and these can be generalisations of the Sraffian approach to take account of, for example, joint production (Ehrbar 1989), imperfect competition (Reati 1986), and value-price ratios for any pricing system (Szumski 1989, 1991).

Second, the NI does not involve a solution to the transformation problem or, to put it another way, it is compatible with any pricing solution. It is simply an 'interpretation' whose formal content is a tautology arising out of the way in which the LEM (or the value of money) and the value of labour power have been defined. Here we appear to be pushing against an open door as far as the proponents of the NI are concerned:

> In the late 1970s Gerard Duménil and I, independently of each other suggested a reconstruction of Marx's labor theory of value emphasizing the relation between money and labor time that preserves the rigorous quantitative relation between paid and unpaid labor on the one hand and the aggregate wage bill and aggregate gross profit ... on the other. This approach was rather uninformatively described as the "New Solution" to the transformation problem, and, after Duménil's observation that it actually abolished the "transformation problem" as such, and thus was not really a solution to anything, equally uninformatively as the "New Interpretation".
>
> Foley (2000, p. 20); see also Duménil (1984, p. 347)

Similarly, Mohun (1994, p. 407), whose article offers a particularly clear presentation of many of the issues, recognises that:

> Clearly there is an infinite number of conceivable price systems compatible with this understanding of theory, each price system being a different redistribution of labour-times, and each a price representation of abstract labour, or a form of value.

Nevertheless, his own exposition descends to the level of individual values and prices (if not production conditions) even though this is entirely unnecessary.

Despite being neutral with respect to pricing, the NI is not without economic content, for it includes an implicit understanding of how the workings of the capitalist economy should be analysed (see below). In fact, our most telling methodological comment upon the NI is its *immediate* identification of production categories (labour and value) with those of exchange (wages, profits and money). This explains why Duménil (1984) has been so savage in rejecting Lipietz's (1984) suggestion that the NI is compatible with the Sraffian solution where the wage is based on a given bundle of goods.[5] As is apparent from equation (2), the value represented by wages is derived from a monetary magnitude (subject to a conversion factor, the LEM or value of money). This is incompatible with the view that the value represented by wages is given by the value of a certain bundle of goods, showing that the NI has important implications for the understanding of the value of labour power. In short, as will be shown below, the NI is not analytically neutral in method and theory. As such, it is open to criticism.

2   Value of Money

The definition of the value of money by the NI (the inverse of the LEM) provides a theoretical instrument for the *ex post* transformation of monetary quantities into value equivalents, especially of wages into the value of labour power. This section shows that, by defining the value of money in this fashion, the NI precludes analysis of the process of determination of the value of money and its interaction with other socioeconomic factors.

Traditionally, in Marxist analysis, a money commodity (e.g., gold) is assumed to exist, whose unit value, λg, is determined by the labour time socially necessary to produce it (other forms of money are discussed below). The value of gold plays an essential role in expressing abstract labour time embodied in the output as price. However, unlike the LEM, the role of gold in price formation is neither immediate nor direct, but rather mediated by several economic factors, two of which are especially important.

First, if we assume homogenised labour across the economy, the value of gold is determined by the material conditions of its production, including the value composition and turnover rate of gold-producing capital.[6] Differences

---

5   The same ferocity is also directed at Szumski (1991) by Duménil and Lévy (1991).
6   For discussion of the content and analytical significance of the differences between homogeneous, abstract and normalised labour, see Saad-Filho (2002).

between the value composition, or turnover rate, of the gold industry and of the averages for the economy create a discrepancy between the 'intrinsic' value of the monetary unit and its expression in circulation. For example, if the value composition or turnover rate of gold-producing capital are above average, commodity values are expressed in prices generally lower than those prevailing when value composition and turnover rate are below average. Therefore, it is wrong to express commodity values directly as price by simply multiplying them individually by $1/\lambda g$ – the value of the money commodity does not operate identically with the LEM.[7]

Second, two attributes of money in the sphere of exchange are fundamental to the way in which it mediates the expression of value as price, its quantity (M) and velocity (V). If we assume that the entire gross output is sold for money (no trade credit or financial transactions), the relationship between the monetary aspects of exchange, the material and value aspects of production, and the price aspects of exchange is given by:[8]

$$MV = \frac{\lambda x}{\lambda^g} = px \qquad (6)$$

where λ and p are the ($1 \times n$) value and price vectors, respectively, and x is the ($n \times 1$) gross output vector.

Any interpretation of value theory must provide an explanation of the relationship between monetary and 'production' factors in the expression of output value as price. Marx, as is well-known, rejects the quantity theory of money (QTM), on the grounds that the material and value characteristics of production determine the monetary and price aspects of exchange. With velocity assumed fixed by institutional, historical, and geographical factors, Marx presumes that the quantity of circulating gold is constantly readjusted, through hoarding and dishoarding and the production of gold, in order to conform to the shifting material and value characteristics of production, the latter also dictating changes in prices. Hoarding and dishoarding are concrete ways in which money mediates the expression of the value of aggregate output as price, and allow it to happen in accordance with the material conditions of production. If, for example, gross output rose, all else equal, the resulting increase in λx would be expressed as an increase in px (p unchanged) through

---

7   This is clearly explained by Foley (1982, pp. 39–40). See also Lapavitsas (2000b) and Saad-Filho (2002, chs.5 and 7).

8   Lapavitsas (1996, 2000b); see also Lavoie (1986).

an increase in M, the latter elicited from hoards. In contrast, for the QTM a rise in x would lead to an increase in λx but there would be a fall in p exactly compensating the rise in x, since M would have remained the same (no hoards supplying an increase).[9]

This simple example shows that money's functions and the institutional framework of the monetary system are concrete ways in which money mediates the expression of value into price for output as a whole. It is misleading to assume that money can express value as price directly and without mediation: the monetary regime matters greatly, even under our extraordinarily simplifying assumptions. In the example used above, if the monetary regime allowed M to be appropriately adjusted, the increased λx would leave individual prices unchanged; if, on the other hand, the monetary regime prevented M from changing, individual prices would fall. The same value of output would be expressed as higher total price in the former case and unchanged in the latter. Had we measured the LEM after the event (assuming that net output behaved identically with gross), it would be unchanged in the former but higher in the latter. But the difference would contribute nothing to our understanding of the process of expressing value into price.

It also follows from equation (6) that there is a complex relationship between, on the one hand, the value of the money commodity, λg, and on the other, the ratio λx/px, that is the value commanded by units of money in exchange (which is exactly analogous to the LEM in this context). Analysing the relationship between these two values depends on assumptions made about money's functions and the monetary regime. In the example above, when the Quantity Theory approach is adopted, the value commanded by gold appears to rise while value embodied in gold remains the same.[10] Such a disparity has important implications for monetary theory. It means, for instance, that capitalists who happen to find themselves in possession of large amounts of the money commodity, as well as capitalists who produce it, make windfall gains, while capitalists with payments obligations make corresponding losses. The characteristic conclusion drawn by the Quantity Theory in this case, namely that there will be imports of the money commodity, can be understood as a

---

9   Readers familiar with the history of economic thought will recognise here Ricardo's (1951) analysis of the price implications of a rise in the volume of commodities in circulation. Since our presentation uses vector terms, there are some inevitable problems of interpretation of expressions such as 'rise in x' or 'rise in p'. The economic conclusions are, however, clear.

10   As Marx (1987, pp. 403–409) pointed out in discussion of Ricardo's analysis of the interaction of gold and commodities in the sphere of exchange.

particular resolution for the disparity between these two values of money.[11] If, on the other hand, the Quantity Theory is rejected, neither the value commanded by gold nor the value embodied in it appears to change. But for that to be the case, a very different functioning of the monetary system and of its articulation with accumulation has to be postulated, one that relies on regular money hoarding.

It is misleading to assume, as the NI does, that money directly expresses the value of output as price and without mediation. As already noted for the above example, had we simply measured the LEM before and after the event (assuming that net output behaved identically with gross), it would be unchanged in one case but higher in the other. This calculation, based on the definition of the value of money simply as the value commanded by money in circulation, detaches both money and its value from the monetary and financial processes that link money to the general movement of capital accumulation. How deeply unsatisfactory that is becomes obvious when non-commodity forms of money are considered, such as credit money and state fiat money. The functions of these forms of money in and out of the sphere of circulation, especially hoarding, cannot be taken for granted but must be analytically elaborated. Analogously, analysis ought to be undertaken of the mechanisms and institutions (the monetary regime) through which the circulating quantity of these forms of money is determined, for which the NI is hardly useful.

The circulating quantity of state fiat money, for instance, retains an arbitrary element to the extent that the state can manipulate it. In contrast, the quantity of credit money is determined largely through the operations of the credit system and their interaction with the process of real capital accumulation (especially the advance and repayment of loans). Furthermore, given the proliferation of the forms of credit money, there could be differences of determination of quantity among banknotes, deposits, bills of exchange, share trust accounts, and so on. Thus, the processes and relations through which non-commodity forms of money come to command value in circulation differ qualitatively for each of these forms, as well as between each of them and commodity money (if one exists).

It is intuitive that such variations in the mediating role of money could have significant implications for the expression of the value of output as price.[12] If the value commanded by money in exchange depends on the functioning

---

11   For a full analysis of this process in terms of the intrinsic and the exchange value of the money commodity, see Lapavitsas (1996 and 2000b).

12   A fuller analysis of these issues along lines suggested here can be found in Itoh and Lapavitsas (1999, ch. 2); see also Lapavitsas (2000b).

of the monetary regime, it is very important to establish its precise relationship with the value embodied in the money commodity (if one exists). Divergences between the value commanded by money and the value embodied in the money commodity, for example, are unlikely to be eliminated by purely monetary processes. Sudden disruptions of exchange, monetary crises, recessions and fully-fledged economic crises, in which the money commodity could play an important role as means of payment and means of hoarding, are some of the turbulent ways in which money in practice mediates the expression of value as price.[13] Political economy ought to be able to account for sudden and forcible realignments of the value of money. If the value of money is defined in aggregate as in the NI, it is a definition that must be discarded as soon as the real processes of capitalist accumulation are addressed rather than set aside.

In this respect, the NI could not be more deficient. Foley (2000, pp. 21–22) states that:

> this definition of the monetary expression of labour time [MELT, the inverse of the LEM] ... does not depend on any assumption about the particular monetary system operating in the economy. In particular, it works well for a commodity money system like the gold standard, or for state-credit based monetary systems like those of the late 20th century. This point underlies the fact that the *definition* of the monetary expression of labor time in this way does not commit us to any particular theory about the *determination* of the MELT ... [the] determining mechanisms are quite different, but in each case money can be viewed as functioning (in part) to express labor time quantitatively.

This does not go beyond tautology, as is revealed to some extent by equations (1)–(3), and is essentially orthogonal to value (as labour) theory. For the value of anything in money can be expressed by the inverse of the unit of the quantity of money with which it is priced. This sharply reveals the NI's exclusion of the real processes that establish the money form of value through hoarding, dishoarding, credit, etc. This separation of definition from determination is completely arbitrary, and the analytical power of the NI, in this respect, is negligible. Moreover, introducing these more complex factors after the NI has already been laid out is equivalent to rubbing it out and starting again with a

---

13   Marx's (1859, pp. 391–417) analysis of pure price inflation can be interpreted in this way. He shows that reconciliation between the value embodied in and the value commanded by money is neither a smooth nor costless process. Moreover, it is a process that may have important distributive implications.

new LEM, and then doing the same as soon as an even more sophisticated approach is taken to the monetary/financial system and its interaction with the accumulation and circulation of both capital and commodities.

3   Value of Labour Power

We have shown, above, that for the NI the value of labour power is given by transforming the monetary payment of wages through the LEM, while surplus value is the value left over from living labour after the deduction of the value represented by wages. Alternatively, the value of labour power is the worker's share of the net product, while the rate of exploitation measures their inability to command the entire net product. This definition diverges from that traditional conception, in which the value of labour power is given by the value of a fixed bundle of wage goods, usually justified by reference to 'social, institutional and historical' factors.

The difference between these two definitions is significant. They are usually seen as being mutually exclusive because they represent different ways of understanding how the workers are remunerated.[14] The fixed bundle of wage goods represents the value of labour power in advance; in this case, the money wage is determined only after prices have been established. This approach can be criticised on three grounds. First, it leaves unexplained where the wage bundle comes from, how it changes with society, history and custom, and what if individual workers do not buy the standard bundle? Second, it implies that labour power is the only commodity to be purchased at its value after the transformation, which is unjustifiable theoretically. Third, it induces a conflation between the workers and the goods they consume. In this case, it is arbitrary to suppose that workers are exploited, because the model leads to identical results if corn, iron or energy are considered to be 'exploited' in place of labour.

---

14   See Bellofiore (1989), Foley (1982), Gleicher (1989), Laibman (1982), Lipietz (1982) and Mohun (1994). For Duménil (1984), the money approach to the value of labour power is essential for the NI, and it is incompatible with the Sraffian solution for prices. Duménil and Lévy (1991, p. 363) assert their position most clearly: 'The rate of exploitation must be assessed in terms of redistribution value. The specific bundle of commodities that workers buy from their wages is irrelevant ... The issue is that of the potential purchasing power of their product, i.e., of the total net product which they created. This is equivalent to saying that the rate of exploitation must be determined in nominal terms, whereas the conventional measure of exploitation refers to labour originally embodied in the bundle of commodities that workers buy'.

In contrast, the NI definition is *ex post*. The value commanded by labour power varies with the price system, only grinding out a corresponding quantity of labour time after production and exchange have been completed, and prices and working class consumption established. This approach is seductive, both because it avoids the limitations of the traditional analysis, and because it corresponds to actual processes in the capitalist economy, specifically, that wage bargaining is undertaken in money terms. However, the NI definition is limited in two important ways. First, no direct account is taken of social and historical elements in the value of labour power, other than the shifting balance of forces between capital and labour; for example, how does the money wage relate to the economic and social reproduction of the workforce, of which the customary standard of living is one component?[15] Second, the value represented by wages bears no relation to the value of the commodities consumed, given that prices and values diverge from one another.[16]

These limitations arise because the NI leaves undefined the relationship between the value of labour power and the value of other commodities. This raises the question of the commodity character of labour power itself, with potentially destructive consequences for value theory. Moreover, the NI cannot probe beyond one of the effects of exploitation, the inability of the workers to purchase the entire net product.[17] This is the same aspect of exploitation emphasized by 'Ricardian socialist' economists in the early 19th Century, and derided by Marx as being an insufficient explanation of capitalist exploitation (Saad-Filho 1993 and Chapter 3).

The analysis above shows that both interpretations are riddled with contradictions because they seek to translate the value of labour power directly into a concrete outcome. They are, in fact, flat mirror-images of one another, each failing in its own way to acknowledge that the notion of value of labour power is not appropriately attached initially either to a quantity of money or to a quantity of goods. The direct relationship between the value of labour power and a quantity of either goods or money, in these approaches, precludes an account of how the value of labour power is determined except by external agency (non-market custom or market wage conflict, for example). The special nature of the commodity labour power – which is neither capitalistically

---

15   See Wells (1992) for the idea that the value of labour power is ground out by a combination of the roles of the state, households and consumerism.

16   Foley (2000, p. 30) concedes this point: 'Saad-Filho [1996] persuades me more by his criticism of the New Interpretation for being excessively reductionist ... I think this criticism has some merit. For example, there may be a real role for a concept of the value of labour power independent of the *ex post* realised wage share in a fully developed Marxist theory'.

17   See Foley (1982, pp. 42–43; 1986, p. 15).

produced nor reproduced directly – allows for both interpretations, but neither for a choice nor a synthesis between them, as they are mutually exclusive.

In our view, the value of labour power should be understood as a simple abstract concept; as a *value* rather than as a use value or exchange value magnitude, whose more complex form as money wages and commodity purchases is constructed out of the historically and socially specific consequences of accumulation. Fine (1998a) has developed this understanding of the value of labour power in some detail in the context of labour market theory. Its constituent elements are reported here insofar as they bear on the positions adopted around the NI.

First, the value of labour power is neither a quantity of money nor goods, but a quantity of *value*. The value of labour power is determined at the aggregate level through the exchange between capital and labour as a whole (i.e., as social classes), prior to the process of production. This is because, at the most abstract level, advancing the value of labour power is a precondition for the production and realisation of surplus value and, subsequently, the performance of labour and exploitation in production. Second, one of the consequences of accumulation is to raise the level of productivity through the production of relative surplus value. This has two effects. It tends to raise the rate of surplus value and lower the value of labour power (through providing wage goods with less value expended), but it also tends to increase the commodities that can be purchased with a given value of labour power as wage goods are cheapened. Thus, the accumulation of capital on the basis of a given value of labour power tends both to redefine (lower) the value of labour power and (increase) the wage bundle.

So far, we might appear to be concerned with elementary propositions concerning the sharing of productivity increases between capital and labour. But this is to jump to an outcome, i.e., more money or more consumption, without examining the processes by which such outcomes are achieved, as is typical of the two unmediated approaches outlined previously. Third, then, there is an issue that cannot be addressed by either of the mutually exclusive standard approaches, namely how do new customary standards become established? A start can be made by recognising that consumption norms are differentiated between distinct sections of the population. They are not an average as such, even with some above and some below the norm. This norm is more appropriately understood in a more complex way; for the levels and incidence of consumption are determined as the outcome of continuing socioeconomic processes which grind out customary patterns of consumption. Fourth, what those patterns are and how they are determined is very different from one commodity to another. Food habits, housing, entertainment, and so on, are not only differentially consumed but the patterns and levels of consumption are the consequences of very different structures and processes of causation.[18] Nonetheless, each of these elements in the wage bundle is subject to change as a consequence of accumulation, with the exact outcome dependent upon the complex determination of the value of labour power across these constituent elements.

The previous paragraph can be seen as a critique of the wage bundle approach to the value of labour power. It has its counterpart in the critique of the money approach. For the value of labour power should not be seen as an average quantity of money, with some workers paid more and some paid less. Rather, corresponding to the structure of employment, there are established patterns of remuneration both within and across enterprises, sectors and occupations. The value of labour power is the basis on which the accumulation of capital interacts with, and influences, such structures and payment systems, and overall levels and incidence of remuneration. Interaction and transformation occur through the socioeconomic processes explained, for example, in *Capital* – deskilling, reskilling, collective labour, formation of trade unions, and so on. The restructuring of labour markets, wages and conditions of service is the other aspect (apart from consumption) of the redefinition of the value of labour power at a more complex level.

In sum, we claim that the value of labour power as a determinant of the price system cannot be legitimately constructed independently of the contradictory tendencies associated with the accumulation of capital, for which a complex analysis ranging over the dynamic structures of both consumption and employment is a precondition. In a nutshell, the value of labour power is an abstract category whose more complex and concrete reworking depends upon addressing the specific nature of different commodities and the differentiation of the workforce. The NI, specifically, excises the mediation between the value of labour power and prices. By posing the value of labour power as a level of wages, the NI is guilty of chaotic abstraction in the ordering of concepts, as analysis moves between the spheres of production and exchange (and from abstract value to differentiated workers, consumers and objects of consumption). This is not a matter of the more complex variation of the value represented by wages around the value of labour power over time in accordance with, for example, balance in the labour market. Rather, it reflects a direct identification of the rate of surplus value with distributive shares between profits and wages rather than the dialectical building up of such distributional shares out of the more abstract categories attached to production and its shifting conditions with the accumulation of capital.

18   For a general argument along these lines, see Fine and Leopold (1993) and Fine (2002), and Fine et al. (1996) and Fine (1998b) in the specific context of food.

4   Structure, Sequence and Dynamics

As is implicit in the analysis of the value of money and labour power, one of the key characteristics of the NI is that it understands the capitalist economy in terms of a definite structure (production of value as opposed to its sale and purchase in exchange) and sequencing of activity across those structures. Whilst this might appear to be an elementary insight, it opens up the important consequence that, in contrast to most equilibrium approaches to the transformation problem, especially the Sraffian, the determination of values and prices does not take place simultaneously. For the NI, as was shown in the third section, the value of labour power is only determined in exchange after production has taken place, and after the money wage and the value of money have also been determined.

In spite of this important development for value analysis, the solution advanced by the NI forces an analytical wedge between variable and constant capital. In the absence of technical change, the NI preserves the value of constant capital in the passage from production to exchange, but the same is not true of variable capital. For the NI, the value of labour power is transformed because it contributes living labour that has to be evaluated after the event within exchange. Moseley (2000a) has made this point the focus of his critique of the NI, claiming that it represents a major logical inconsistency. According to him, if the LEM were used to transform constant as well as variable capital there would be no analytical problem with the NI, and Marx's own transformation procedure in *Capital* would be confirmed as complete and consistent (p. 312).

Foley (2000, p. 24) acknowledges this difficulty, and attempts to bypass it claiming that he is not averse to using the LEM to render 'the money flow of purchases of intermediate outputs ... [into] the labor time equivalent of the flow of constant capital'. However, he admits (pp. 24–25) that there is '[n]o plausible interpretation of the labor time equivalent of the constant capital or invested capital (since these measures will in general be equal neither to the historical labor embodied in the means of production, nor to the labor that would be required to reproduce them with contemporary technology.)'

The issue runs deeper than the (in)consistency of the NI. If only variable capital were transformed through division by the LEM, the homogeneity of the labour expended during production would provide a logical and real foundation for the analytical procedure adopted by the NI. However, the NI would be open to charges of inconsistency. In contrast, if the release of dead labour during the same period were also transformed using the LEM, severe problems would emerge in spite of Foley's conciliatory statements. There is no logical or economic reason for treating labours expended at different periods in the past, in the several vintages of constant capital that have passed into the value of the current output, as immediately, directly and generally equivalent with each other, as well as with labour expended in the current period, via division by the ratio of the flow of living labour to the price of current net output.

Deploying the LEM would completely disregard the real problems of achieving equivalence between dead and living labour. This is one of the most profound problems of capitalist accumulation, and an endless source of disruption, upset and disequilibrium. Different vintages of capital influence the competitiveness of capitalist enterprises and affect their product price. Competition brings technical change, which leads to sudden readjustment of capital values through the cheapening of their elements as well as 'moral depreciation' (Saad-Filho 2002, ch.5). These forcible and violent changes of valuation of capital are left entirely out of account when the value of constant capital is derived through the simple division of the price of constant capital by a value 'transformer'.

The NI's analytical choice of operation on the net rather than gross product is a direct consequence of its treatment of labour power. It claims that using the gross product would involve double-counting of constant capital on each occasion that it was passed through exchange from one producer to another (Duménil and Levy 1991).[19] This is, however, simply a red herring. For the double-counting only becomes an issue because of the need for the NI to define value and price in aggregate and confront them with one another in determining, *ex post*, the value of money and the value of labour power. In that context, preventing double counting requires that only living labour be counted.

Attention to the issue of double counting has, in some respects, been both misplaced and misleading. For, much more important than the technical issue of double counting for unchanged values are the implications for the NI of changes in values during capital accumulation. In this case, the value of each commodity potentially changes in the passage from the purchase of labour power to the sale of output. Both constant and variable capital are devalued as commodities become cheaper: whatever the value with which they enter the production process, they leave with a different value. In this respect, there

---

19   'What is redistributed in the economy is the value created during each period, i.e. the value of the net product of the period. In the aggregate, productive workers expend in a given period of time a certain amount of labour which defines the added value during the period. This value is embodied in the net product of the period. The redistribution of value ... must be interpreted on this basis, and not on that of the gross product of the period which leads to double-countings for inputs produced and consumed productively during the period or inherited from previous periods' (Duménil and Lévy 1991, p. 363).

is no distinction between dead and living labour, although only living labour adds new value.[20]

The misplaced focus upon the choice between net rather than gross product is a symptom of the NI's approach to Marxist political economy. In general terms, the NI seeks to confront problems in economic theory in order to carry out empirical work. In contrast, we claim that political economy ought to confront real processes in order to appropriate them in thought. At a more specific level, the NI's methodological stance has implications for the analysis of the contradictions of accumulation. For the NI, structured and sequential re-evaluation is already incorporated within what is effectively a static economy. Consequently, the dynamics of accumulation can only be added by superimposition of transformed production conditions. The result is liable to be either a form of dynamic Sraffianism or a resort to post-Keynesianism: take one static model on the basis of given technology, confront it with another and speculate about their differences. Alternatively, take one model and change the distribution of income, the state of expectations or the structure of the banking system, and imagine the consequences. Analyses of this type are insufficient to explain the complex and contradictory tendencies attached to the accumulation of capital and how these are represented in and through exchange.[21]

Finally, the NI accepts that price is a relatively concrete expression of value. This carries the implication that analysis is pitched at the level of many capitals in competition (although the NI does not specify the nature of that competition). Nevertheless, across the NI there is a chaotic mixture of levels of abstraction. Some are pitched at the most concrete level since they hold for each individual capital, while others are derived at the level of capital as a whole, but often for the totality of exchanges, which only exists at the most complex level.

These points can also be addressed from the perspective of appropriate abstraction in the context of sequencing or moving over the circuit of capital. Equation (1) seems to imply that, for the NI, all forms of payment – sales, profits and wages – can legitimately be treated as if they were simultaneous (see below). This assumption may appear realistic for an individual capital,

---

20   See Marx (1981, pp. 259–261). In other words, neither double counting nor the divergence of input values from their prices can be used legitimately either for or against the NI. Proponents of the latter tend, however, to seize the evidence that Marx recognised these issues as signifying his unwitting support (despite his unambiguous and frequently repeated stance to the contrary).

21   For contributions in this vein, see Ernst (1982), Bellofiore (1989) and Naples (1989) whose sequenced disequilibria, however, arise on the basis of given production conditions.

although the treatment of wage payments as simultaneous with commodity sales is peculiar.[22] In addressing capital as a whole, however, the situation is more complicated, because the revenues of all sectors of the economy should not, in general, be treated as if they were simultaneous. This assumption would, of course, involve a violent abstraction, since individual industrial cycles are necessarily sequenced relative to one another. Similarly, equation (3) not only splits out living labour alone as defining the value represented by money, but it does so by collapsing what are necessarily sequenced labours into being simultaneous. In the case of living labour, further abstraction is required to strip away the constant capital that is also realised when commodities confront money.

The use of abstraction to render sequenced activities simultaneous is inevitable in any theory and, as such, is not objectionable. However, the NI involves chaotic abstraction. It moves seamlessly between value and price, and surplus value and profit, without regard to whether this conforms to the simultaneous movement from capital as a whole to individual capitals. Specifically, capital as a whole is restored at the level of the price system whenever this is convenient, even though the analysis has already moved to the more concrete level of individual capitals. The method of abstraction is also highly simplified with direct mediation between value and price, without the filling in of the intervening processes of determination. It is precisely such chaotic leapfrogging in abstraction that leads to the absence of the other considerations that we have brought to the fore – accumulation, technical change, the complex forms and functions of money, and the social and historical determination of the value of labour power (Gleicher 1989).

In sum, the NI brings macroeconomic processes to an abrupt halt once the value of labour power has been defined through the wage revenue. In a capitalist economy, the value represented by wage revenue is transformed once again after it has been spent. In other words, the economy starts with production and ends with exchange before, presumably, starting with production again. However, the NI disregards this transition. The problems this creates are glossed over through reliance on aggregate static conditions, as in equations (1) and (3), and in the lack of concern with the complexity of how values are transformed into prices. As with other assumptions about what values get transformed, how and when, the exclusive focus of the NI upon the passage from production to exchange is arbitrary. While collapsing levels of abstraction

---

22   Note that the timing of payment is not so much at issue as the timing of the exchange. The purchase of labour power must precede production even if payment is made with a lag (although only accidentally at the time of selling the commodities produced).

across the value/price relationship, the NI fixes its sights on a sociology of exploitation in which selective aspects of Marx's procedure of transformation are subject to piecemeal (and arbitrary) survival.

5   Conclusion

Two important features of the NI have endeared it to its supporters. First, it appears to offer support to Marx, albeit in a modified way given the direct mediation between value and price and the substitution of net for gross product in the aggregate identity between value and price. This only goes to show that appeal to Marx embodies a slippery rationale and needs to be handled with considerable caution. Second, because of its understanding of the value of labour power and the value of money, the NI allows, subject to data and conceptual refinement, for the immediate empirical measurement of Marxist categories not least because the rate of surplus value is construed to be identical to the ratio of profits and wages. However, once these measurements have taken place, it is far from clear what significance they have, since they omit the contradictory processes by which the complex categories give rise to the data.

This limitation arises because the NI deploys a notion of abstract and concrete, or essence and form, which has only two layers – value as the essence, and price as the form. Translation between them is immediate and unproblematic, since using the LEM assumes that money represents value in a direct, unmediated, and ideally abstract manner, thus allowing the derivation of macroeconomic relationships. The neutrality of equations (1) to (3) with respect to price formation shows that the material structures, processes and relations through which value becomes price are largely irrelevant for the NI, except as far as quantitative outcomes are concerned. It is as if the simple elaboration of the commodity form at the beginning of *Capital* is sufficient to address wages and profits, without prior attention to the production, distribution and circulation of (surplus) value, technological change, conflicts over the labour process and their influence on accumulation. In effect, the NI seems to imply that the bulk of the three volumes of *Capital* are only marginally (and unsystematically) relevant for the analysis of how the social relations attached to labour become translated into price relations between commodities. However, to collapse the mediated expression of value as price into the simple division of the total hours worked over the price of the total net product is to dissociate the formation of wages and profits from the complexity and significance of the real processes involved. In a sense, the NI is a theory of the commodity form applied directly to the wage-profit relationship, without otherwise elaborating the laws of capitalist production.

The way in which prices are built up out of abstract labour is extremely complex and requires a theory that appropriates that complexity. Constructing such a theory is not simply a matter of gathering together all the factors involved. For they have to be ordered in relation to one another, and the abstractions employed should be justified by demonstrating that they correspond to material relations, structures and processes, rather than being ideal abstractions speculatively constructed in the mind. Consistency requires that the more complex categories of thought reproduce the simpler categories at a more concrete level, rather than undermining them.

For, what is the point of a theory of value and price that takes no account of accumulation and of shifting productivity? How do we know that the NI, with its emphasis on redistribution as the means by which value becomes price, is compatible with what are, arguably, much more fundamental structures and processes within the capitalist system? Whilst some contributors to the NI literature seem to be uninterested in such questions, others tend to presume that their approach is compatible with a full analysis of accumulation although such compatibility is rarely, if ever, demonstrated in practice. Such a conclusion is strikingly illustrated by Duménil and Lévy (1993). Consideration of value theory is confined to an appendix of just two pages that bears no relationship to the remainder of their book, despite the coverage suggested by the title. In particular, their work includes the most abrupt and peculiar of dialectics:

> The transformation problem is not a problem of the derivation of prices of production from values. The knowledge of values is not helpful in the computation of prices of production. Actually, the relationship between values and prices is fully independent from the fact that profit rates are equalized (p. 48).

In this case, Marx's value theory is merely a sociology of exploitation:

> This does not mean, however, that the labour theory of value is irrelevant to the analysis of capitalism. On the contrary, it is crucial to the theory of exploitation ... The capitalist mode of production is simply a new variant of a class society based on the appropriation of surplus labour ... The concept of value is, thus, a necessary component of the theory of exploitation under capitalism, whose analysis was a primary purpose of Marx's work in *Capital* (pp. 48–49).

No other purpose is demonstrated for value theory.[23] Instead, as in other works within the NI, the dialectical mediation between value and price, which has been excised at the outset, is re-introduced after the event. That can take the form of Sraffianism or the presumption that institutional and historical factors or state policy determine the price vector or other economic variables. The essentially exogenous nature of price determination allows more or less arbitrary attachment of a variety of economic principles, on the one hand, and the more or less direct estimation of Marx's aggregate value categories through national income statistics and input-output data, on the other.

Although the NI represents an important advance over Sraffianism, in which price and value are simultaneous concepts derived from conditions of production and distribution, whatever advance has been made carries a very heavy cost. Whilst raising crucial issues for value theory around the form of value, the value of labour power, the value of money, and the structure, sequencing and dynamics of the capitalist economy, the NI resolves none of them. Rather, it proceeds only by setting value theory aside and confining it to a (static) theory of exploitation.

---

23   The same emphasis on value theory as confined to a theory of exploitation is explicitly
      revealed in Duménil and Levy (2000).

CHAPTER 7

The Supply of Credit Money and Capital Accumulation: A Critical View of Post-Keynesian Analysis

Radical monetary theory has made considerable headway in recent years, resulting in work with a distinct flavour produced by Post-Keynesian, Institutionalist, Kaleckian, and Marxist economists.[1] While the components of this work may not always be fully compatible with each other, it could still develop into a cogent alternative to neoclassical monetary theory. The present essay contributes to the development of such an alternative from a Marxist perspective by critically examining the Post-Keynesian theory of endogenous creation of money and credit. The main focus of the essay is the horizontalist current of Post-Keynesian theory, originally associated with Kaldor (1970, 1982, 1985). This current offered a powerful challenge to neoclassical monetary theory, most famously in Kaldor's well-known clash with Friedman. Equally important has been its elaboration of a clear theoretical framework of credit money supply, which captures many of the essentials of Post-Keynesian monetary theory. Precisely because of its importance, and the clarity of several presentations, horizontalism allows identification of critical deficiencies of the Post-Keynesian conception of what money is and of the process of creation of credit money. These deficiencies become increasingly troublesome in the theoretical study of inflation. In this light, it is necessary to strengthen the links between the theory of money and credit, on the one hand, and the theory of production and circulation of capital, on the other. As shall be seen below, the monetary and financial sphere is partly autonomous from the sphere of production but also constrained by the latter. Marxist theory and the work of Marx himself provide powerful insights on this issue.

Our critical discussion of the Post-Keynesian monetary theory focuses closely on the work of Basil Moore (1988) and Marc Lavoie (1992). Moore's is perhaps the most rigorous and clear presentation of the Post-Keynesian theory of endogenous money supply. Lavoie's introduction to what he terms 'post-classical economic theory' is a carefully constructed, comprehensive, and easily

---

1 Originally published as: 'The Supply of Credit Money and Capital Accumulation: A Critical View of Post-Keynesian Analysis', *Research in Political Economy* 18, 2000, pp. 309–334 (with C. Lapavitsas).

accessible synthesis of many strands of thought (especially Post-Keynesianism and the French 'circuitists'.) The first section of this essay focuses on Moore's and Lavoie's analysis of the process of endogenous money and credit creation; the second reviews their critique of the theory of exogenous money supply; the third summarises their analysis of inflation. Section four advances a critique of Post-Keynesian analysis of the origin and role of money in economic activity, endogeneity of the money supply, and the relation between credit money and inflation. The last section draws the several strands of the argument together and suggests directions of development for radical monetary theory.

1   The Fundamental Process of Endogenous Money Creation

Lavoie's 'post-classical' synthesis draws on two main sources, Kaldor and Moore's horizontalist approach, and the 'circuitist' perspective advanced by Schmitt and Parguez, among others (Lavoie 1992, pp. 152–157, 161–169). Lavoie summarizes the process of endogenous money and credit creation as follows:

1   Firms make production plans according to their expectations.
2   Firms demand advances from the banks to purchase capital goods and other inputs, and to pay workers, dividends and interest on their debt. By satisfying firms' demands, banks create credit money *ex nihilo*.
3   The supply of loans generates income flows, as firms distribute revenues to households and purchase goods and services from other firms.
4   Households decide how much money to spend, and how much to hoard and save as bank deposits, bonds and shares. Their consumption expenditures and purchases of bonds and shares eventually reach firms' bank accounts.
5   Firms repay part of their outstanding debt, destroying credit money.
6   The central bank provides base money corresponding to the outstanding money stock at the price of its choice. The net increase in the money supply at the end of the circuit is equal to the net increase in firms' outstanding debt, plus households' net hoards and purchases of financial assets such as bonds and shares. This residual has no causal significance.[2]

---

2   In this light, when the government runs a budget deficit it normally sells treasury bills for credit money, then purchases goods and services from firms and households. As this money circulates, it eventually finds its way into firms' bank accounts, where it may be used to reduce their outstanding debt (this usually being the most economical use for extra money balances, since firms are by assumption always in debt). It follows that (a) government deficits increase firms' internal funds, and (b) the concession of credit to the government does not restrict the amount of loans that the banks can make to capitalist businesses (since credit

The advance of credit and the sale of output determine (endogenously) the money supply. There are three junctures at which such determination takes place. The first juncture lies in the relationship of firms to banks. Banks create money because firms demand credit, a process that generally occurs automatically as firms draw on pre-arranged but previously unused credit lines (such as overdraft facilities), or as individuals use their credit cards. The cost of borrowing is constant and set in advance, although it can vary with firm size and perceived risk. In general, banks cannot reduce their outstanding loans (which are generally non-marketable), except by raising interest rates and collateral requirements, or by refusing to renew old loans. Thus, banks are price-setters and quantity takers in the retail markets for deposits and loans. Any increase in aggregate demand must be preceded by additional credit money creation, and is conditional on the increased indebtedness of some agents.[3] Because the business sector is continually deficit-spending, firms as a whole cannot get back more revenue than they throw into the circuit, and cannot pay interest on their outstanding debt, unless they receive additional loans (Lavoie 1992, pp. 170, 175–178).

The second juncture lies in the relationship between banks and the central bank. After passively responding to loan requests, banks take steps to sustain their reserves. Moore (1986, 1988, pp. x–xiii, chs.2, 5) argues that, for some time, liability management (especially borrowing in the interbank market) could provide banks with reserves independently of the central bank. Banks borrow from the central bank when their ability to procure reserves through liability management reaches its limits. Given that loans have already been extended by the banks, the central bank cannot refuse to accommodate reserve requests if it wishes to maintain orderly conditions throughout the financial system. If the central bank refuses to provide reserves in the open market, it will have to do so through the discount window. Consequently, the central bank cannot control the quantity of base money. However, it can impose quantitative restrictions on new loans and, more importantly, determine the price at which it supplies reserves, i.e. the discount rate.[4] The discount rate is the benchmark

---

money is created *ex nihilo* in all cases). There is crowding in, rather than crowding out, as government deficits generate additional profits and relax the financial constraints on production and growth.

3   The same result may be obtained through dishoarding, government budget deficits, or balance of payments surpluses. However, Moore (1988, pp. 223–224, 291, 295–297) argues that, since the ratio of broad money to income is stable in the long run, new financial assets (mainly credit money) finance most of the increase in aggregate demand. He concludes that the rate of growth of credit money governs aggregate demand growth.

4   Moore (1988, pp. 15–17, 23, 38, 87–88) argues that there is an asymmetry in the power of the central bank: it cannot constrain bank reserves through open market operations, since banks

for the determination of other rates of interest in the economy, thus also an important determinant of the level of economic activity (see also Lavoie 1992, pp. 169–170, 180).

The third and final juncture lies in the relationship between households and banks. That is also the plainest: banks inevitably accommodate households' residual demand for money (net hoards), as already noted in point 6 above.

Five important implications follow from the Post-Keynesian approach to money supply. First, loans make deposits, deposits make reserves, and credit money determines base money. The total amount of credit money increases as loans are advanced and deposits are created, and the central bank supports this expansion by providing reserves. Some deposits remain with the lending bank, and some drain away as borrowers use the funds to make payments. As long as all banks advance loans at a similar rate, deposit losses are cancelled out and all individual banks have sufficient reserves.[5] Money supply is horizontal in money-interest space at the level of interest determined by the central bank. At the same time, demand for money and the rate of interest are negatively related because higher interest rates tend to reduce the profitability of production. For Moore and Lavoie, the demand for money cannot be independent of the supply: there can never be excess supply of money because money settles debts and can always be held for 'convenience' reasons, i.e. for the advantages provided by money's liquidity.[6]

Second, credit money allows businesses to finance their expenditures before the value of their output is realised in sales. For Moore, this inverts the saving-investment link of commodity money economies; in modern credit money economies, investment creates (and quantitatively determines) saving through the finance process. As long as there is unemployment, the necessary savings will always become available without any need to adjust the rate of interest (Moore 1988, pp. 258, 312, 314–315).

Third, profits are invested before they are created. They fall if firms reduce their level of investment, or if households increase liquid savings, given their revenues.

---

cannot quickly reduce their loan assets, but it can expand bank reserves either through open market operations or by lending to commercial banks.

5 Citing Le Bourva, Lavoie (1992, p. 201) argues that '[t]here is no theoretical limit to the amount of credit money which, overall, the banking system can create to satisfy the requirements of increased activity'. See also Moore (1988, pp. 13–14, 19, 93, 211–212, 295).

6 'Any increase in the nominal supply of money will always be demanded. The quantity of nominal money demanded is thus always and necessarily equal to the quantity of nominal money supplied. The quantity of credit money supplied in turn responds to changes in the demand for bank credit, and the demand for credit is simply the demand by borrowers for additional money balances' (Moore, 1988, p. xiii).

Fourth, the composition of banks' asset portfolio is not a matter of (liquidity) preference, because it derives from underlying macroeconomic laws. In particular, reserves are a fraction of bank liabilities that is derived as a residual and does not function as a base for the generation of bank money, contrary to neoclassical presentations of the money multiplier (Moore 1988, p. 89). All monetary claims to output are created before output. The causal elements in the chain of money creation are firms' production and investment plans and the advance of bank loans (Lavoie 1992, pp. 157–161, 169–174).

Fifth, the rate of interest is a distributive variable whose level is politically determined by the central bank; it is not a market-determined price. Moore (1988, p. 257) agrees with the neoclassical view that the rate of interest allots scarce resources to production processes with the highest returns, and induces agents to abstain from consumption in order to increase their stock of capital or wealth. Nevertheless, for Moore, interest rates are a purely monetary phenomenon, largely independent of such real variables as the marginal productivity of capital. There is, of course, no such thing as a natural rate of interest that ensures the full employment of labour or capital (Moore 1988, pp. 254, 258–260, 264). The level of the interest rate is limited by the rate of inflation (otherwise it may become profitable to borrow in order to buy now and resell later) and by the mass of profit (otherwise creditors and rentiers could command the entire surplus). In spite of this indeterminacy, a *fair* real interest rate can be defined as being equal to the rate of growth of labour productivity in the economy. At this level, interest payments do not shift net resources from industrial to financial capital or vice-versa (Lavoie 1992, pp. 193–195).[7]

2 Commodity and Credit Money Systems

Post-Keynesians sharply differentiate themselves from neoclassical monetary analysis. Writers such as Moore (1988, pp. ix–x, 45, 71–72, 252) argue that the latter is ultimately based on the assumption of a commodity (or fully convertible) money system, which is no longer relevant and may never have been. Post-Keynesians usually presume that the point of departure of neoclassical monetary analysis is the following sequence: the stock of base money is determined by the central bank, the multiplier is stable, and banks increase loans only after deposits have increased. Thus, the supply of loans depends on the

---

7 To call this level 'fair' is odd, given that there is no intrinsic fairness in the current distribution of income. Keynes's well-known remarks about the euthanasia of the rentier have more radical implications regarding 'fairness' and the rate of interest.

existence of free reserves. It follows that the money supply is exogenous and vertical in money-interest rate space. The central bank can initiate changes in the money supply by changing the monetary base (currency plus bank reserves), and it can (loosely and imperfectly) control the stock of outstanding loans by influencing the multiplier. By the same token, the central bank cannot autonomously determine the level of the rate of interest rates, which is the price that clears the market for loanable funds. Moreover, for neoclassical theory, typically, the availability of savings limits investment, and aggregate demand growth is constrained by the money supply.[8] Thus, Moore (1988, pp. 10, 13, 20, 241, 302–303) concludes that the neoclassical view of the monetary system corresponds to an economy where products are ultimately bought with products, in which case Say's law holds. Inevitably, the quantity theory of money exercises considerable residual influence on neoclassical monetary theory. Most clearly, the rate of increase of the money supply is normally taken as the main determinant of inflation, and changes in the price level (or in the exchange value of money) bring actual and demanded real money balances in line with each other.

Post-Keynesian writers argue strongly that neoclassical monetary theory is irrelevant for contemporary credit money economies, though it may be valid for commodity money systems. For Moore (1988, pp. 46, 82, 85), the neoclassical approach is invalid for credit money economies for the following three reasons: first, it wrongly assumes that the central bank can control the monetary base simply because that is a central bank liability; second, it incorrectly presumes that commercial banks wait for excess reserves and, when they become available, take the initiative in supplying new loans; third, it falsely attributes causal and behavioural content to the multiplier, which is merely a descriptive identity. For Moore, such theory is implicitly based on attributes of commodity money, which are invalid for credit money. Commodity money is a material thing, while credit money is a financial claim. Even though both are assets of their holders, commodity money is produced out of real resources, it is no-one's liability, it does not carry price or credit risks, it pays no interest, and it is perfectly liquid and capital-certain.[9] The opposite holds for credit

---

8   In neoclassical analysis the supply of money responds not only to central bank decisions but also to changes in private hoards, in velocity of circulation, and to disequilibria in the balance of payments. However, the latter are generally disregarded, and the monetisation of government budget deficits becomes, in practice, the single most important determinant of changes in the money supply.

9   It is important to point out at this point that there is error in this argument, quite apart from its broader significance for theory. Proponents of the labour theory of value from Ricardo onwards have claimed that a change in the productivity of labour in the money-commodity

money, which is created whenever the central bank or the commercial banks purchase assets in exchange for their own monetary liabilities (Moore 1988, pp. xii, 10). Credit money is valuable because of its ability to function as means of payment and to discharge contracts. Its ability to perform the role of money depends on loan performance and collateral (which explains why debt failures may trigger a monetary crisis, see Moore 1988, pp. 50, 243, 294).

Moreover, in credit money economies there is no binding scarcity in the monetary and financial spheres. Neither Say's nor Walras' law hold, and there is no real balance (or Pigou) effect. Money is non-neutral because the central bank and the commercial banks can determine its price (the interest rate), the level of which affects the volume and composition of savings and investment (Moore 1988, pp. 18–20, 290–291). It follows that the aggregate demand curve is vertical (rather than downward sloping) in the price-income space and inflation is not caused by excess money supply (Moore 1988, pp. 4, 241, 298, 316–317, 327, 330, see also the next section). Finally, the neoclassical view that interest rates are determined by the supply and demand for loanable funds is irrelevant for credit money systems, where money can be produced without costs. The supply price of money does not rise with the amount of bank lending, and there is no necessary relationship between the volume of credit and the prevailing interest rate (Moore 1988, pp. 258, 296).

3   Money and Inflation

In neoclassical monetary theory, the quantity theory of money retains considerable influence, which relies on a complex set of underlying assumptions. The most important are: first, that markets are fully flexible; second, that (commodity) money is neutral and the only financial asset in the economy; and third, that money is only a means of circulation, in which case hoarding can be ignored. Given these constraints, any excess supply of money (presumably caused by the monetisation of government budget deficits or unsterilised balance of payments surpluses) necessarily spills over into goods markets and leads to inflation (Moore 1988, pp. 6, 11, 18, 287, 290).

In contrast, Post-Keynesians have provided two distinct analyses of inflation, both of which are substantively different from the neoclassical one

---

industry (e.g., gold mining), *ceteris paribus*, will change the value of money and, consequently, its price relative to all other commodities. Similarly, Foley (1994) has shown that, since commodity money (gold) is a durable asset, its current value could change because of speculation with respect to the prospective efficiency of mining technology.

because they presume that there can never be excess supply of credit money. The best known of the two holds that (cost) inflation is the outcome of a distributive conflict between capitalists, workers, the state, rentiers, and the rest of the world (see Dalziel 1990, Lavoie 1992, ch.7, and Moore 1979, 1983; for a critical analysis, see Saad-Filho 2000a). Put simply, it is usually assumed that money wages are determined exogenously, they are inflexible downwards, and the wage bill determines firm demand for finance. If the wage rate rises, commercial banks must accommodate the additional requests for bank loans, and the central bank must sustain the concomitant increase in the money supply in order to maintain the level of economic activity. If the central bank validates incompatible demands for shares of the national income through monetary accommodation (attempting to preserve orderly financial markets and levels of output), distributive conflict could lead to inflation.

Moore (1988, pp. 268, 287, 346–348, ch.14) has advanced a further explanation of (demand) inflation. In a closed economy, if the central bank sets interest rates too low, demand for money and credit creation will be stimulated, and spending out of previously accumulated money balances will be encouraged. If the rate of increase of aggregate demand exceeds the economy's rate of growth of output at stable prices, demand inflation inevitably follows. Some support for this claim could be provided through analysis of hyperinflation, which, for Moore, is characterised by sharply negative *ex ante* real interest rates.[10] Thus, an important *caveat* is introduced into Moore's theory of endogenous money: if real interest rates are too low, real lending by the banking system is constrained by real lending to the banking system; in contrast, if real interest rates are too high, the volume of bank intermediation is constrained by real credit demand (Moore 1988, pp. 341, 348).

The distributive conflict approach implies that incomes policies are the most effective way to reduce inflation to acceptable levels. In contrast, Moore's analysis implies that possibly lengthy negotiations between social partners are unnecessary. A sharp rise in interest rates can discourage deficit spending and bring demand inflation under control quickly and effectively (however, it would be misguided to use high interest rate policies to control cost inflation, because these may lead to stagflation; see Moore 1988, p. 346).[11] In sum, even

---

10   Moore does not dwell on the difference between *ex ante* and *ex post* real interest rates but, since that difference depends on expected inflation, his analysis appears to rest on such factors as individual assessments of the probability distribution of future inflation. This is awkward because it is a typically neoclassical approach, spurned by all shades of Post-Keynesianism.

11   Moore's argument implies that, if the central bank is concerned only with price stability, there is bias towards high interest rates, unless institutional mechanisms exist that reduce

though the central bank must accommodate the demand for reserves (even if inflationary) in order to preserve financial market solvency, it can choose the price at which liquidity is available (Moore 1988, p. 83). Hence, the central bank has considerable freedom to determine the rate of inflation, and possesses substantial influence over the level of activity in the economy.

4   Two Steps Forward – One Step Back

There are important weaknesses in the Post-Keynesian theory of endogenous money and credit. These are identified below in the following areas: first, in the conception of the origin and role of money in the economy, which underpins the analysis of endogenous money supply as that was outlined above; second, in the (internal) debate about the shape of the money supply curve; and finally, in its theory of inflation. The title of this section can be understood in two related ways. First, we believe that in important respects Post-Keynesian monetary theory is deficient compared with monetary theory based on the work of Marx – without denying that considerable progress has also been made relative to neoclassical theory. Second, we claim that only by critically reassessing some of the key claims of Post-Keynesian theory can further progress be made toward a cogent radical monetary theory.

4.1   *The Origin and Role of Money in the Economy*
In her careful outline of Post-Keynesian theory, Sheila Dow (1984) argues that its starting point comprises three related features of the real world: irreversible historical rather than logical time, formation of expectations under uncertainty, and money as store of wealth. Historical time creates uncertainty because time is unidirectional, the past is unchangeable, and the future is unknowable. Uncertainty heavily constrains production, investment, and consumption plans of entrepreneurs and households. For Post-Keynesianism, as Davidson (1972a chs.2, 3, 1972b, 1978, and 1982 ch.2) has argued in detail, the best way to bridge the unalterable past and the unknowable future is through monetary contracts. These are made possible by money's function as store of value. Thus, for Post-Keynesians, money appears to be an elemental aspect of all human economic activity. This view, even if not directly and openly articulated, underpins Moore's and Lavoie's analysis of credit money. For these writers, capitalist reproduction is impossible without regular supplies of credit money, and not

interest rates in the presence of high unemployment. Moore does not address this question, in spite of its importance to his argument.

only in the trivial sense that the circulation of output relies absolutely on money as means of exchange. Rather, expanding supplies of credit money are necessary for further production and accumulation of surplus value to take place.

It is undeniable and trivial that irreversible time and uncertainty are inescapable aspects of the human condition. However, it does not follow that irreversible time and uncertainty are best confronted by society instituting money contracts. Every society has customs, religious beliefs, laws, and hierarchies that help reduce uncertainty and ensure social reproduction in the course of humanity's constant struggle with nature. Many non-commodity-producing societies have been extraordinarily resilient, and have lasted for far longer than their capitalist counterparts. The presumption that money is the best (or the only) way to reduce uncertainty in material reproduction is an exaggeration without any historical basis. It turns money into an indispensable component of the interaction of human beings with nature, and assumes that past historical societies conformed to a model that does not correspond to their actual experience.[12]

In addition to this, Post-Keynesian monetary theory fails to see that the use of money can increase the uncertainty surrounding economic activity. That money does so can be readily seen in the following two ways. First, in commodity economies the indirect nexus of money replaces the direct (personal and customary) link between producers. The relative certainty of distribution along religious, hierarchical, familial, and other lines is replaced by the uncertainty of distribution founded on money incomes drawn from the prior sale of commodities or from money transfers, which cannot be taken for granted. Uncertainty becomes even greater when trading in money itself takes place creating a class of money-dealers unconnected to production and trade. Trading in money and money-related instruments is further likely to lead to destabilising speculation and fraud, creating further uncertainty even for those not directly involved in such activities.

---

12   Wray (1990) is an extreme proponent of this view. He claims that credit money was the first form of money, created as a unit of account and instituted simultaneously with private property. Only later, with the development of markets, was money used as a medium of exchange (ibid., 54). This claim is unreasonable, and unsupported by historical evidence (see Itoh and Lapavitsas, ch.10). Wray does not recognize that private property is historically specific, and that capitalist property is based on the ownership of the means of production by a class not directly engaged in production. This type of property is completely different from feudal, slave or tributary forms of property. It is meaningless to claim, as he does, that the holders of all these types of property enter similar relations generated by an undifferentiated 'advance' of their property. Private property is a very complex notion that cannot be the theoretical foundation for the derivation of money.

Second, in capitalist economies a distinctive type of uncertainty arises because of the extraction of surplus value. This is necessarily a monetary process, which involves production, circulation and distribution simultaneously and continually creates conflicts at the shop-floor and in society at large. Surplus value is extracted under competitive conditions leading to continuous productivity-enhancing technical change under capitalism. Credit (both trade credit advanced among firms and banking credit advanced by financial institutions) plays a particularly important role in a capitalist economy because it intensifies the ability of a given volume of total social capital to produce surplus value. It does so by mobilising temporarily idle parts of the total social capital and by allowing individual capitalists to anticipate their future returns. However, the repayment of credit (with interest added), hence its fresh advance, cannot be guaranteed at the outset. To say that this is because the future is unknowable is to make a trivially true statement. For the concept of uncertainty to have a more than trivial role in social science, it has to be rooted in social and economic conditions. Economics ought to identify social factors which impart precariousness to credit relations, and which reflect the character of capitalist production and circulation of surplus value. Consider the following.

At a fairly abstract level, continuous technical change (and the ensuing reorganisation of production) destabilises work practices and exacerbates antagonistic relations at the shop-floor, and in society at large. Technical change can lead to redundancy of workers (and managers), sudden devaluation of skills, technologies, machines and infrastructure, substantial price changes, the introduction of new product lines and the discontinuing of others. At the same time, material production must continually meet investment and consumption demands, both individual and social. These demands can be met only through the sale of commodities produced under constantly changing production conditions, whilst ensuring the accrual of surplus value as money profit. Thus, scope is inevitably created for the further exacerbation of antagonistic relations across society as coalitions among similarly placed economic agents are constantly formed and reformed, increasing uncertainty.

At a less abstract level, reliance upon the resources of the financial system in order to expand the production of surplus value can lead to the overexpansion of accumulation, creating conditions of financial and economic crisis. The availability of credit could mislead industrial capitalists into anticipating, and relying upon, favourable returns when none is forthcoming. Moreover, when fresh credit is increasingly used to pay for maturing obligations, over-expansion of accumulation could create conditions of economic crisis. This is particularly true when a climate of optimism is fostered by rises in the prices of financial assets, which feed upon ongoing optimism and increase it even further. Extended use of money and money-related credit under capitalist conditions can lead to forms and levels of economic instability and uncertainty unprecedented in the history of human societies.

Radical monetary theory needs an explanation of the origin and role of money in commodity societies that avoids the drawbacks of Post-Keynesianism. In our view, it should be based on Marx's insights in Chapter 1 of the first volume of *Capital*. For Marx, money has a special place in economic reproduction because it has a special property relative to other goods, which arises from the relations of commodities to each other in the process of exchange. In contrast, neoclassical theory assumes at the outset that commodities are directly exchangeable, and then attempts to derive money as a medium of exchange. This is logically weak because, if commodities are directly exchangeable, it is impossible for money to have special exchangeability relative to the rest. For Marx, the special exchangeability of money derives from the essential aspect of each commodity to request exchange with another commodity possessing a specific use value. This transforms the other commodity into the equivalent form of value: the equivalent receives the property of direct exchangeability from the commodity that requests exchange. The development and generalisation of this relationship allows Marx to explain the appropriation of direct exchangeability with other commodities by one among them, money. Thus, money is a special commodity that can always buy other commodities. The money commodity is typically taken to be gold, but money does not have to be a precious metal: 'In their money-form all commodities look alike. Hence money may be dirt, although dirt is not money' (Marx 1976, p. 204.)

Marx's derivation of money from commodity exchange does not presuppose the historical existence of barter. Rather, it rests on the view that exchange was marginal to pre-capitalist societies, while money also had ritual, ceremonial, and customary uses in these societies. For Marxist political economy, money and exchange are inseparable. However, this does not imply that money emerges when hunter-gatherers meet in a state of nature, or that it is introduced into exchange as a conscious decision to reduce transaction costs. Furthermore, as long as commodity exchange is not fundamental to the reproduction of human society, neither is money; indeed, in a profound sense, money is a veil on human intercourse with nature. General equilibrium analysis makes a similar point, since it assumes direct exchange of goods, but it does so in a crass way that ignores money's influence on economic reproduction.

In contrast, the Post-Keynesian attempt to explain why commodity exchange must use money rests on the presumption that money and credit necessarily mediate all economic activity. This embeds money and credit into the fabric of all human society, and it is an ahistorical and fallacious assertion. It is a better foundation for non-neoclassical monetary theory, and for radical theory in particular, to recognise that money's existence (both logical and historical) is an inevitable by-product of the world of commodities, and to stress that money has a special position in commodity exchange. Money as the bearer of direct exchangeability functions as means of exchange but also as a reserve of value, as means of payment, and general representative of wealth. Under historically specific circumstances, money can also become capital. Only then is it possible for credit to become a pervasive and powerful force underpinning accumulation and dictating the pace of economic reproduction.

4.2   Horizontal Money Supply

The hypothesis of horizontal money supply is not universally accepted by Post-Keynesians. It has been criticised by, for example, Rousseas (1986 chs.3–4, 1989), for whom: (i) unused overdraft facilities are not significant because they are stable in size, (ii) the central bank often rations loans by restricting the availability of reserves, and (iii) an increase in demand for money can be met through a rise in velocity resulting from economy in the use of transactions funds, mobilisation of idle funds and financial innovation, rather than being fully accommodated by the central bank. For Rousseas, when banks need reserves they issue such liabilities as CDs, and alter the composition of their balance sheets away from deposits. This pushes interest rates up in order to entice asset-holders toward less liquid instruments. As a result, although money supply is endogenous in the sense that demand for money creates its own supply, the money supply curve is upward sloping.

Pollin (1991, 1993) has a similar view, but approaches this issue from another angle. For him, banks can raise the liquidity of financial assets in order to increase their reserves at given interest rates. In the process, they change the structure of the financial system. The money supply curve can remain horizontal until the effect of the financial innovations is exhausted; then interest rates rise. Thus, financial innovation results in an upward-sloping money supply curve. If, however, the spontaneous generation of reserves is not successful, a liquidity (and possibly financial) crisis could ensue.

Wray (1990, chs.3, 6) and Dow (1996) have stressed the importance of banks' liquidity preference for the determination of the slope of the money supply curve. Liquidity preference is the desire to hold short-term assets, which varies with the cycle and the state of expectations and can affect demand for money as well as supply. For Dow, the money supply curve is not generally horizontal because, in the downswing, increased risks associated with lending lead to a rise in banks' liquidity preference and so to loan rationing. For Wray, in the upswing, firms' balance sheets become increasing illiquid and, unless the central bank provides the requisite liquidity, the money supply curve becomes vertical. The central bank will eventually provide the reserves in order to maintain financial stability, but at a higher interest rate. Consequently, the money supply curve slopes upward in steps.[13]

Disputes about the shape of the money supply curve in essence refer to the constraints faced by the central bank in setting its own interest rate. Post-Keynesian theory would probably have generated more interesting and important results had it concentrated openly on this issue rather than on the shape of a curve. The view adopted in this essay is that, although central bank policy and practices are important for the determination of interest rates, the scope for the central bank's setting of the lending rate depends crucially on broader economic forces. Unless these forces are analysed first it is difficult to explain policy shifts, as well as differences in the results of similar central bank policies applied to different countries. Two critically important factors in this respect are, first, the relationship of the rate of interest to the rate of profit and, second, the place of the central bank in the structure of the capitalist credit system. Below we turn briefly to both of these.

For monetary theory based on Marx's works, the flows of loanable money capital traded by banks and other financial institutions have an objective basis in the turnover of total social capital, and are not related to liquidity preference as individual predilection of capitalists (Itoh and Lapavitsas, 1999, ch.3). To be specific, in the course of its turnover, capital creates pools of idle money that (i) offset the physical and technical depreciation of fixed capital, and pay for its maintenance and repair; (ii) allow accumulation to expand; (iii) guard against price fluctuations, and (iv) help to maintain the continuity of production, given the alternation between production and circulation and the concomitant need to hold precautionary balances (Lapavitsas 2000a). These temporarily idle funds tend to be held as bank deposits, thus providing reserves for the banking system. The regular creation of idle money in the course of economic reproduction is the foundation of the capitalist credit system. Broadly speaking, the credit system is a mechanism for the internal reallocation of spare funds among industrial and commercial capitalists; as such, it can increase the efficiency of the process of capital accumulation, and enlarge its scope.

In the tradition of classical political economy, interest payments are a share of profit. Profit is generated through the investment of money capital that is already in the possession of individual capitalists, or which is created through gathering and subsequent lending of idle money by the banking system. Having borrowed sufficient funds (as well as used their own money capital),

---

13   For a critique of this argument, see Lavoie (1992, pp. 202–203).

capitals can generate fresh flows of value and surplus value, out of which interest payments are made to the owners of loanable capital. At such a highly abstract level of analysis, there is neither need nor scope for referring to central bank intervention in determining the rate of interest. Interest represents a conventional division of profits generated in production; its rate reflects nothing more than the demand for and supply of loanable money capital in the course of accumulation. In contrast, the rate of profit reflects material aspects of production, such as the level of real wages and the composition and the turnover rate of capital.

A unique claim of Marxist monetary theory is that there is no tendency for equalisation of the rate of interest with the rate of profit, though that should not be confused with absence of equalisation of profit rates for banking and industrial capital, which clearly holds (Fine and Saad Filho 2016, ch.12; Itoh and Lapavitsas 1999, chs.3, 6). Absence of equalisation between the two reflects the structural difference between industrial and loanable capital (the former constituting an integral part of the circuit of total social capital, and the latter being formed from idle money, hence lying outside the circuit of the social capital). Moreover, absence of equalisation also reflects the peculiar character of capital migration between and within the financial and the industrial sectors of a capitalist economy. To take advantage of higher interest rates relative to profit rates, for instance, a given industrial capital has to become loanable capital, i.e., abandon generation of surplus value in the first instance. There is no clear and simple argument as to how that would affect rates of profit and the share of profit accruing as interest. In contrast, to take advantage of higher profit rates in a different sector, industrial capital simply has to migrate to the latter. Such a move, *ceteris paribus*, results in changes in opposite directions for the supply of output of the sectors concerned, which leads to opposite changes in prices and tends to equalise rates of profit. Absence of equalisation between the rate of interest and the rate of profit appears as distinct patterns of movement of the two rates in the course of the business cycle, usually in the opposite direction of each other. This might contribute to the outbreak of economic crisis as a distinct phase of the cycle (Itoh and Lapavitsas, 1999, ch.6).[14]

As already mentioned, the credit system is a set of social mechanisms aimed at collecting loanable money capital and channelling it back toward

---

14   In a crisis, the rate of interest may exceed the average rate of profit. Thus, despite generally contributing in a beneficial way to industrial accumulation through mobilising and reallocating spare money funds, financial capital can also destabilise economic activity by forcibly absorbing part of industrial capital. This potentially destructive role is fully in line with finance's relatively autonomous position with respect to the total social capital.

real accumulation. The credit system assumes a pyramid-like form based on inter-firm trade credit and further consisting of banking credit to capitalist firms, inter-bank credit in the money market, and central bank credit (Itoh and Lapavitsas 1999, ch.4). For Marxist monetary theory, the central bank emerges spontaneously as a bank that holds the centralised reserve of the banking system and provides credit money of the highest acceptability that is typically used in clearing operations by financial institutions and others (Lapavitsas 1997). The state adds further acceptability to state bank credit money by elevating it into legal tender and by undertaking its own financial operations through the central bank. The power of the central bank to affect interest rates derives, in the first instance, from its pivotal position in the money market, that is, the market in which banks trade their liabilities with each other. The central bank, as holder of the centralised reserve and issuer of the best-grade credit money (its own liabilities), can materially affect the terms and the price at which loanable capital is traded in the money market, thus influencing interest rates across the economy.

In this light, and returning to the Post-Keynesian debate about the money supply, several factors are important in determining the ability of central banks to influence interest rates. One such factor is convertibility of the central bank's own liabilities into a reserve asset, which broadly affects the relationship between the central bank's liabilities and its reserves. If credit money is freely convertible into a reserve asset, such as gold, it is evident that the central bank's ability to alter the outstanding volume of its liabilities, and to determine the price at which it supplies these to banks and others, depends on the size and fluctuations of its gold hoard. That is not to negate that the central bank still possesses considerable power to manipulate both volume and price of its liabilities; rather, it is to stress the importance of the institutional context within which this power can be exercised. If, for instance, the central bank were confronted with rapid loss of reserves due to a domestic collapse of confidence in credit, it would find it very difficult to maintain interest rates low. Raising interest rates under such circumstances might appear as conscious policy on the part of the central bank, but it would be truer to say that the central bank is forced to do so in order to defend its reserves. What matters for our purposes here is that the central bank's ability to influence interest rates is specific to the institutional structure of the monetary and credit system, and to the manner in which economic pressures are refracted through that institutional structure.

Even if central bank liabilities are not convertible into a reserve asset its own ability to influence interest rates remains limited, above all by the international institutional structure within which a country's financial system operates. Assume for the sake of argument that one type of credit money (the dollar) in practice acts as international means of payment. It is then evident that the central bank that issues dollars is very differently situated from all others, which might find that they have to defend their reserves of dollars in the face of external pressures. Under such conditions, other central banks are subject to far more reserve discipline, and have far less scope for independent setting of interest rates, than the Federal Reserve System. Correspondingly, the US central bank's freedom of action in setting interest rates is likely to be greater.[15] Even for the Federal Reserve, however (as becomes clearer if we further assume freely floating exchange rates that lessen the pressure to defend the reserves of international means of payment for other central banks) its freedom in setting interest rates is not unlimited. Since changes in exchange rates affect the cost of inputs and the revenues from foreign sales, and given that interest rate changes affect exchange rates – particularly when capital mobility is high – no central bank can ignore the foreign sector in setting interest rates. Exchange rate movements and corresponding balance of payments flows impose significant constraints on the ability of central banks to determine interest rates.

Finally, the possibility of economic and financial crisis, endemic to a capitalist economy, also limits the central bank's ability to influence interest rates.[16] This limitation is due to (rather than in spite of) the central bank's responsibility to maintain orderly financial markets and avoid a collapse of credit. Several Post-Keynesian critics of the horizontalist position have paid more than token attention to the possibility of financial crisis, and attempted to incorporate it as a policy constraint. Unfortunately, they have not generally explained why there is a possibility of crisis in the first place. It was argued above that the capitalist economy is intrinsically unstable because of the conflicting forces of extraction, realisation, and accumulation of surplus value under competitive conditions. In that context, the role of the credit system (and of finance more broadly) is considerably more complex than is allowed for by Moore's and Lavoie's accounts of endogenous money and credit creation. Some aspects of this role are briefly indicated below.

Whilst it is true that firms make plans according to their expectations, the terms and availability of credit affect the making of these plans. As banks

---

15   This is highly relevant for the development of Post-Keynesian monetary theory, given that its theoretical generalisations regarding the supply of credit money typically draw upon the US experience.

16   Itoh and Lavapitsas (1999, ch.6) identify two types of financial crisis: those that derive from and exacerbate industrial crises and those that originate purely from the activities of the credit system.

compete with each other, the banking system can make the supply of credit available on easier terms to industrial and commercial capital. It is in the nature of loanable money capital to confront few material constraints in its motion: given volumes of reserves and own capital allow banks to handle vastly different volumes of credit. By the same token, real wages (the living standards of workers) and the composition and turnover of capital (the technical realities of production) exercise only remote influence on the flows of loanable capital. As a result, banks and the financial system could potentially create a climate of optimism that encourages investment by both industrial and commercial capital.[17] The suspicion with which the financial system has historically been treated by many policy-makers and social reformers is ultimately rooted in this potential. The reason is apparent: there is no guarantee that credit supplied by the financial system will generate flows of value and surplus value out of which repayment will take place. That is particularly so when easy availability of credit allows both industrial and commercial capital to overexpand accumulation. Thus, the repayment of old debt by capitalists might become problematic, and so might be the generation of idle money held as deposits with banks, which provides the wherewithal of fresh loans. Both are typical and acute phenomena of capitalist crises.

The role of the central bank in this connection is significantly more complex than providing reserves that allow banks to support the existing volumes of credit money, and simply choosing the price at which this is done. In a financial crisis, central banks find themselves confronted with the need to supply liquidity to the financial system as a whole in order to avoid bankruptcies resulting from the inability to settle old debt. The need to do so goes beyond the normal requirement to support the volume of credit money. Furthermore, should the security of deposits become doubtful, the pressure on the central bank to provide reserves would increase substantially. How central banks deal with such emergencies depends, above all, on whether they face the need to protect their own reserves.

If they do face such a requirement, defending their hoard of reserve assets takes priority for central banks. That leads to a rise in lending rates, but might also lead to refusal to accommodate the demands of desperate borrowers. Generalised bankruptcy is likely to follow along the usual lines of credit advance – a classic experience of financial crises. However, such disorderly conditions in the financial system do not arise from the actions of the central bank. Rather, they are the consequence of the interaction of the financial system with real

---

17   Not under all circumstances, naturally. When and how finance can lead to over-expansion of real accumulation also depends on the forces unfolding within the latter.

accumulation, given the existence of reserve assets (which may be primarily foreign currencies). If they do not face a pressing need to defend their reserves, however, central banks might still raise their lending rates (reflecting tighter supply of loanable capital in the money market), but could exercise greater discretion with respect to providing reserve funds to financial institutions. That is not to say that all requests made to the central bank for loans have to be met. On the one hand, central banks are mindful of the moral hazard problem of allowing lenders and borrowers to escape the ultimate penalty for credit and investment decisions that have not generated the expected surplus value. On the other, the inherent flexibility of loanable capital implies that partial and selective refusals to accommodate need not translate into wholesale destruction of credit. Even if some banks or companies go bankrupt the whole of the financial system need not collapse.[18]

To recap, there can be no abstract theory of central bank interest rate policy. Such policy is contingent on institutional structure, particularly the relationship between the central bank's reserves and its own liabilities. Moreover, setting interest rates by the central bank reflects the interaction between the credit system and real accumulation, which runs in both directions. Post-Keynesian attempts to provide a general theory of central bank interest rate policy can be interpreted as unwarranted generalisation from the experience of large central banks during the last quarter of century, particularly that of the US, which has not been under severe obligation to defend its reserves domestically or internationally. Such generalisations tend to overestimate the ability of central banks to set interest rates autonomously, while underestimating their ability to restrict their liabilities quantitatively.

4.3   *Inflation*

The problem of whether inflation can be generated by credit money (or, more broadly, of the stability of the exchange value of credit money) is much more important than the shape of the money supply curve, but it has been analysed in much less detail by Post-Keynesians. As we have seen, Moore and Lavoie argue that the supply of credit money is endogenous because bank loans, the demand for which is determined by real accumulation, create money. They have not, however, demonstrated convincingly that the credit system produces quantities of the medium of circulation and payment which are compatible

---

18   Thus, lessening the need to defend holdings of a reserve asset reduces the scope for financial disorder in the classic sense. However, this comes at the cost of increased disorder internationally. The absence of a reserve asset with a fixed nominal value (such as gold under the gold standard and, to a certain extent, the Bretton Woods system) removes the fixity of exchange rates and allows them to fluctuate almost without limit.

with the other variables of accumulation, such as the level of prices, the volume of output, and money velocity. That is without even mentioning more dynamic aspects of the issue of generation of inflation, such as uninterrupted production and realisation of surplus value and sustainable international flows of value.

It cannot be overstressed that, even if the money supply is demanded and willingly held in an individualist sense, endogeneity does not imply that the quantity of credit money is in harmony with the above variables. It is one thing to show that credit money is created through the advance of credit, and that the latter is largely determined by the demands of accumulation. The Post-Keynesian approach to this issue, as we have already argued, provides much insight, although we have also offered a very different interpretation of the role and functions of the financial system in a capitalist economy. However, it is logically quite another thing to show that the quantity of credit money generated by the financial system is in harmony with the money required in the sphere of exchange.[19] Indeed, it is arguable that it cannot be shown simply because no such harmony exists (Itoh and Lapavitsas, 1999, ch.9).[20]

---

19   Moore (1991) has effectively denied that showing this is possible. In debate with Goodhart (1989, 1991), Moore has claimed that the demand for credit money is not independent of its supply. Sustaining this view is Moore's concept of 'convenience lending', i.e. the notion that deposits created as a result of lending will always be held due to their potential liquidity services. That is not a very well thought out notion, as Arestis and Howells (1996) have shown. Monetary theory, including the anti-quantity-theory tradition, has always recognised that the individual money demand, as well as the quantity of money necessary in the sphere of exchange, are separate from (and prior concepts to) the demand for credit.

20   Drawing a clear distinction between credit money creation and the money needs of circulation is a necessary aspect of a radical theory of money and credit, if it is to avoid the fallacies associated with the real bills doctrine that have plagued the anti-quantity-theory tradition for two centuries. As is well-known, for Adam Smith, banks that discount only real bills, as opposed to fictitious bills not backed by sales, can be certain that their reserves will never run low since fresh advances of money are regularly counterbalanced by repayments. More by association than reasoning, he also stated that if banks discount only real bills the channel of circulation will never overflow and the quantity of credit money will adjust itself to the needs of circulation. The critique of Smith's distinction between 'real' and 'fictitious' bills by Henry Thornton was decisive in this respect. For Thornton (1802, chs.1–2), it is incorrect to claim that 'real' bills always represent actual property while 'fictitious' bills are imaginary. The sale of one lot of goods may give rise to several 'real' bills as the goods pass from merchant to merchant. Thornton (1802, p. 87) recognised that 'real' bills are more likely to be repaid promptly than 'fictitious' bills, and that actual sales limit the amount of 'real' bills created, but, for him, this was a 'very imperfect' limit. Moreover, the distinction between 'real' and 'fictitious' bills has little relevance to the practice of a bank. To avoid problematic lending, it is much better for the bank to rely on traditional methods, such as ascertaining the creditworthiness of the debtor.

This has a direct bearing on the Post-Keynesian analyses of inflation. As already mentioned, the most widely held view is that, if that nominal wages are determined institutionally and firms subsequently fix prices by mark-up, inflation is caused by collective bargaining over nominal wages, rather than by a rising money supply. The credit system accommodates cost-push inflation by lending to meet the 'needs of trade', while the central bank provides reserves allowing the process to continue. Moreover, the credit system cannot distinguish between loans necessary to sustain expanded activity and loans that simply meet the requirements of higher money wages. Davidson (1989) has called the former 'real' and the latter 'inflationary' bills: a 'healthy' banking system can be subverted into one that systematically conflates the two. Thus, Davidson has advocated a consistent government policy of full employment backed by permanent incomes policies.

However, as long as the demand for credit money (or the necessary amount of it in circulation) is independent of its supply, the operations of the credit system alone cannot guarantee the harmonious balancing of the two. Demand and supply of credit money are determined by different factors and concerns: the former depends on commodity volumes and values, money velocity, and the tendency to hoard; the latter depends on the advance of credit, its success in generating value and surplus value, and the regularity of debt settlement. If banks cannot adequately discriminate among 'real' and 'fictitious' loans, and if they cannot guarantee the generation of (surplus) value by money capital lent, credit processes alone are not sufficient to establish harmony between the demand and supply of credit money. Instability in the exchange value of credit money for purely monetary reasons could easily arise.

An anchor could be found for the exchange value of credit money if a degree of convertibility were instituted between credit money and a reserve asset held by banks (above all, the central bank). The anchor would operate both through the reserve discipline exercised on banks (restraining their advances of credit and so the generation of credit money), and through the simple fact of convertibility (preventing persistent discounts or premia for credit money relative to the reserve asset). That is not to imply that there would be no significant fluctuations in the exchange value of credit money – it is simply to state that a reserve asset could provide an automatically operating stabilising mechanism. It is also to imply that the removal of convertibility with a reserve asset creates the possibility of frequent disturbances in the exchange value of credit money for purely monetary reasons.

The collapse of the Bretton Woods system can be interpreted in these terms. Removal of convertibility into gold has removed the anchor from the exchange value of credit money, and that at a time when rapid technological change appears to have increased the autonomy of the financial sector relative to real accumulation. Reserve discipline on central banks and the commercial banks has been substantially reduced and convertibility into gold no longer exercises a restraining influence. Put differently, the scope for financial expansion is much greater precisely at a time when the ability of the credit system to bring the supply of credit money in line with its demand has been reduced; hence increased potential instability in the exchange value of credit money. In the post-Bretton Woods era there can be inflation purely due to monetary reasons (as well as speculative bubbles involving housing, the stock exchange and other assets, all of which can harm real accumulation). In this respect, incomes policies can be irrelevant to the prevention of inflation, and can become inimical to workers interests as they prevent the readjustment of nominal (hence real) wages.

Nor is the alternative theory of inflation proposed by Moore (1988) above criticism. Although he recognizes the possibility of excess supply of credit money, responsibility for inflation is placed squarely on the central bank for having set interest rates too low. However, it is incorrect to presume that there is at all times a 'correct' level of interest rates, which the central bank should discover and unflinchingly impose on the markets. Whereas low interest rates facilitate the adoption of speculative and unsustainable investment projects, and may be inflationary in Moore's sense, they also cheapen the adoption of new technology, facilitate the modernisation of the capital stock, and promote capital restructuring through mergers and acquisitions. In contrast, high interest rates prevent inflation because they constrain sales, nominal wages, the creation of new jobs, and real accumulation. In doing so, they reduce capital's ability to restructure itself through the adoption of new technologies (high interest rates facilitate restructuring through bankruptcy, which can waste real resources). Finally, as argued earlier, the actual results of changes in production may be very different from those planned. Changes may be resisted because of their asymmetric (or 'unfair') social impact, or they may be thwarted by competition, changes in tastes, or simply by a flawed judgement of the market.

5   Conclusion: What is Important for the Way Ahead?

In sum, the critical examination of Post-Keynesianism offered in this essay suggests that there are three prerequisites for a radical theory of endogenous money and credit, all of which draw upon Marxist monetary thought. First, monetary theory should be historically specific and based on the distinguishing features of capitalist production (especially competition, wage labour, and the extraction of surplus value). In this context, money's functions as means of payment and store of value are essential. Equally, the specific character of money as monopolist of exchangeability, and the nature of its relationship to commodities, should be understood clearly. The point here is not to lose sight of the historically exceptional role of capitalist money – in itself a reflection of the fact that this economy is based on value and exchange value. It is a very misleading to generalise from this (historically limited) experience and attribute to money a role in human economic activity that it inherently does not possess. It is not impossible for human society to organise itself without using money as the universal preserver of wealth and employer of the human capacity to work, even if it still uses money widely as means of account and means of exchange.

Second, credit money is an advanced form of money, created mostly as liabilities of banks and other financial institutions. Its supply is endogenous in a more complex and profound sense than Post-Keynesian analysis allows. Banking credit involves collecting and advancing loanable capital, and results in creation of credit money as a by-product. The sources of loanable capital comprise idle money created in the turnover of the total social capital. The systematic repayment of loanable capital (plus interest) critically depends on whether fresh flows of value and surplus value are successfully created in the process of accumulation. Post-Keynesians are right to stress that the supply of credit money is credit-driven, but wrong to claim that the supply of credit itself responds passively to its demand. Even when financial institution liabilities are created without idle funds having first accrued from real accumulation, as happens when these institutions anticipate future returns, the inherent uncertainty of accumulation and the crises it generates impose limits on their ability to extend credit. In that context, though the central bank possesses and utilises elements of aggregate rationality in the operations of the credit system, it also faces clear limits on the extent to which it can manipulate the rate of interest and its own liabilities.

Third, though credit money is endogenous, the quantity of it supplied is not always and necessarily compatible with the monetary needs of the sphere of circulation. The needs of circulation, or the social demand for money, depend on commodity values and volume, money's velocity, and the tendency to hoard; the supply of credit money depends on the demand for credit, the generation of loanable capital, and the regular repayment of old debt. It is simply a statement of faith to claim that the operations of the credit system harmoniously balance the two. In this connection, convertibility of credit money into a reserve asset with its own value is one method of providing some stability for the exchange value of credit money. The reserve asset can act as anchor both through its role as reserve of banks and through the simple fact of convertibility of one type of money into another. In the absence of a reserve asset, and despite the endogeneity of the supply of credit money, there is no guarantee of stability in the exchange value of credit money. Pronounced instability, such as inflation, is possible for purely monetary reasons.

CHAPTER 8

Inflation Theory: A Critical Literature Review and a New Research Agenda

The social and economic upheavals associated with the collapse of the 'golden age' of capitalism stimulated important developments in the Marxian analyses of inflation.[1,2] However, the interest of Marxian researchers in developing the insights of the 1970s and 1980s has declined sharply recently, along with their numbers and influence.[3] This is largely due to the shift of the economic debate towards the mainstream, especially since the mid-1970s, the changing interests some of the best-known non-mainstream researchers, and the long-term decline in inflation since the 1980s, which is often presented as one of the most remarkable achievements of the neoliberal (or neomonetarist) economic policies (Arestis and Sawyer 1998).

This essay claims that Marxian inflation theory deserves to be rediscovered, and investigated more fully, for three reasons. First, inflation poses an intriguing theoretical challenge. Analyses inspired by the quantity theory of money usually have unacceptably weak foundations (especially perfect competition, full employment, and costless adjustment between static equilibria), while non-mainstream (especially Marxian) contributions are promising, but remain relatively undeveloped. Second, advances in the understanding of inflation can easily be extended to the study of deflation, and both are very important at this point in time (Moseley 1999). Third, inflation *and* conventional anti-inflation policies usually have high economic and social costs. They often lead to higher unemployment, lower real wages, higher rates of exploitation and to a shift the income distribution and the balance of social forces towards capital and, especially, towards financial interests. It would clearly be important to develop alternative analyses, in order to help to increase the left's ability to confront inflation and the consequences of conventional anti-inflation policies.

---

1 Originally published as: 'Inflation Theory: a Review of the Literature and a New Research Agenda', *Research in Political Economy* 18, 2000, pp. 335–362.
2 The concepts of theory, analysis and approach will be used interchangeably in what follows.
3 Fine (1997) and Lee and Harley (1998) analyse the decline of non-mainstream economics. In spite of the substantial differences in scope and method, these papers reach similarly pessimistic conclusions.

The essay includes this introduction, three substantive sections, and the conclusion. The substantive sections critically review the best known Marxian analyses of inflation, the conflict theory, the monopoly capital-underconsumption analyses, and the extra money approach. This review is limited in many ways. It does not include all Marxian (or, more broadly, radical) approaches, none of the approaches studied here is exclusively Marxian, and they are not surveyed exhaustively. Moreover, in order to simplify the analysis, inflation is identified with a sustained increase of the price level with changes in relative prices. This definition is insufficient for many reasons, among them because it ignores 'hidden' inflation (for example, when technical progress fails to reduce prices, given the quality of the goods). In spite of these shortcomings, this essay achieves two important objectives. First, it shows why attempts to explain inflation in inconvertible monetary systems, drawing on the anti-quantity theory tradition of Steuart, Tooke, Marx, Kalecki, and most Post-Keynesians, are fraught with problems (Mollo 1999). To put it simply, it is very difficult to develop a cogent theory of inflation whilst, simultaneously, preserving the claim that the needs of production and trade call money into circulation (endogeneity) and admitting that money may influence 'real' variables (non-neutrality). This exercise becomes even more complex when it involves different forms of money, issued by the state and by the commercial banks, each of them with a specific type of relationship with the circuit of capital. Despite these difficulties, this essay shows that it is possible to outline the general conditions for inflation from a Marxian perspective.

Second, this essay critically discusses three important Marxian analyses of inflation that are often indistinguishable from non-Marxian views, which makes the analysis applicable across a broad range of theories. For example, conflict theories are endorsed across the radical spectrum, the monopoly capital analysis owes much to Kalecki and Steindl, and certain aspects of the extra money approach are close to Post-Keynesian and circuitist analyses. The critique in the three substantive sections focuses on the agencies causing inflation and the linkages underlying the inflationary process (Fine and Rustomjee 1996). Agencies can be identified from the theories of class, production, the state, and the ensuing analysis of the social conflicts expressed in and through inflation. Linkages include the institutional context of inflation (especially the relationship between the state, industry, finance, the workers, and the foreign sector), and the propagation mechanisms that lead economic instability and social conflict to surface as inflation. This involves, in particular, the money supply and price-setting mechanisms, and the power of monetary and fiscal policy.

1   Conflict and Inflation

Non-mainstream economists of very different persuasions, including many
Marxists and most Post-Keynesians and neo-structuralists, argue that distributive conflicts are usually the most important cause of inflation (this approach
is especially appealing to some Marxists because it apparently vindicates the
notion of class struggle).[4] This section is divided into two parts, the first outlines the conflict theories of inflation, and the second criticises their assumptions and internal structure.

1.1   *Conflict Theories*
Conflict analyses are inspired by cost-push theories, which were very popular in the 1950s-70s. They usually start from equilibrium, and assume that the
money supply is fully endogenous, that fiscal and monetary policies are passive, and that key agents (especially the monopoly capitalists and unionised
workers) have market power and can set the price of their goods or services
largely independently of demand. Inflation arises because the sum of claims
over the national product (which can depend on target real income levels,
shares of the national product, or income growth rates) is greater than the real
income available. If the demand for money and credit is always satisfied, inflation necessarily follows by purely quantitative processes. The rate of inflation is
a positive function of the size of the overlapping claims, the frequency of price
and wage changes and the utilisation of capacity, and a negative function of
the rate of productivity growth. Inflation rates can become downwardly rigid
(inertia) if some agents index-link their prices or incomes, in which case each
negative shock leads to permanently higher inflation rates. In sum, there is
inflation because the central bank validates, directly or through its support for
the financial system, incompatible demands for shares of the national income
through monetary accommodation, in an attempt to protect the financial
institutions and ensure the continuity of production.

---

4   Conflict theories are superbly surveyed by Dalziel (1990); see also Lavoie (1992, ch.7), and
    Sawyer (1989, pp. 359–372). Burdekin and Burkett (1996) provide an outstanding theoretical
    and empirical investigation, but see also Boddy and Crotty (1975, 1976), Glyn and Sutcliffe
    (1972), Green and Sutcliffe (1987), Marglin and Schor (1990), Palley (1996), Rosenberg and
    Weisskopf (1981), Rowthorn (1980, chs.5–6) and Weintraub (1981). For a critique, see de
    Brunhoff (1982), Fine and Murfin (1984, ch.7), Kotz (1987), and Weeks (1979). Obviously infla-
    tion, however caused, can create distributive conflicts, but this will be ignored here.

This argument can be presented very simply as follows (see Kotz 1987 and Lavoie 1992, ch.7). The value of the current output Y is:

$$Y = Py = kwL$$

where P is the price level, y is the real output, w is the money wage rate, L is the volume of employment, and k is the mark-up on wages (presumably the largest cost component). The price level is:

$$P = \frac{kwL}{y}$$

where L/y is the inverse of the average physical productivity of labour, v. It follows that:

$$P = \frac{kw}{v}$$

If a hat denotes growth rates (the rate of inflation is $\hat{P} = \frac{P_1 - P_0}{P_0}$), then:

$$\hat{P} = \hat{k} + \hat{w} - \hat{v}$$

This model indicates that inflation is due to increases in the mark up or in the wage rate in excess of the rate of productivity growth. The model can be refined endlessly by incorporating target income levels, expectations, reaction functions, and limits on the wage claims because of unemployment, or on the mark up because of competition. It naturally follows that, when inflation is anticipated, the process of income transfer becomes less efficient and inflation rates must increase in order to achieve the same results. Eventually, the costs of inflation may become so high that the state must intervene, usually on behalf of (monopoly) capital.

The conflict approach has been used to explain two types of inflation: cyclical or structural. In the first case, inflation is relatively low in the upswing because of the substantial spare capacity, high unemployment, and high productivity growth. Inflation tends to rise towards the end of the boom, when the slack has been absorbed and worker militancy tends to increase (Boddy and Crotty 1976). Cyclical conflict inflation declines with the onset of the recession, which can be engineered by the state in order to 'restore the balance of industrial relations', 'preserve financial stability', 'restore international competitivity'

or, in plain English, to discipline the workers under the threat of unemployment or worse. In the depression, the monopoly sector may increase its prices
in spite of the low demand, either because new entry is more difficult or in
order to preserve its profit mass. If the workers try to defend their standard of
living, long-term stagflation becomes possible. Inflation falls, and growth can
resume, when the workers or the competitive sector, defeated, back down on
their previously 'excessive' claims or concede an additional share of income to
the monopolies.

Structural inflation is not very different, and it was used most famously to
explain rising inflation in the 1970s. Very briefly, rising structural inflation and
the slowdown in productivity growth since the late 1960s were, in part, due
to the workers' growing resistance on the shopfloor. These features allegedly
played a major part in the collapse of the 'golden age' (Devine 1974, Gordon
1981). In the post-war era, the state systematically validated low or 'creeping'
inflation because it helped to stabilise the economy and ensure the continuous
growth of output and productivity, with high levels of investment and employment, and rising incomes. Implementation of these policies was facilitated
by the loosening of the nominal anchors under the Bretton Woods System
and, eventually, their abolition when it became economically necessary and
politically expedient. Between the late 1960s and the late 1970s declining rates
of productivity growth, growing worker militancy and increased competition
due to greater international trade reduced the rate of profit sharply.[5] Capital's
initial response was through price increases, which led to higher levels of inflation (many described inflation as a new form of the crisis, replacing deflation
and unemployment, e.g., Cleaver 1989, Jacobi et al. 1975). As Morris (1973, p. 6)
succinctly put it,

> When unemployment ... was reduced to a level which threatened the
> capitalist power of exploitation of the working class ... inflation provided
> for a time ... a substitute for the industrial reserve army as capitalism's
> way of maintaining its power of exploitation. Eventually, working-class
> reaction to the inflationary substitute for unemployment helped produce
> a rapid acceleration in the rate of inflation.

When capital's reaction proved to be insufficient, the capitalists raised the
stakes by reducing the aggregate level of domestic investment, usually through

---

5 See Glyn and Sutcliffe (1972) and Morris (1973). Howard and King (1990) consider this approach to be merely a variant of Kalecki's (1990a) political business cycle. For a contemporary
   analysis, see Brenner (1998), the critiques by Duménil and Lévy (2000b), Fine, Lapavitsas and
   Milonakis (1999) and the special issue of Historical Materialism (1999).

migration abroad or a shift towards financial investment and real estate at home and abroad, shifts in the technology of production towards labour-saving technology (relative surplus value), and straightforward 'downsizing' (absolute surplus value). The net result of the decline in productive investment, and the shift of the remaining investment towards technologies associated with an increasing technical composition of capital, was higher unemployment and deindustrialisation in several OECD countries (the case of Sweden was especially dramatic, see Glyn 1995). At the same time, monopoly capital and the state attacked the workers politically, reducing their entitlements through sharp recessions legitimated ideologically by monetarism and neoliberalism, and by the use of 'globalisation' as a scarecrow. The defeat of the working class in the 1980s allowed profit rates to rise and inflation to decline simultaneously and almost continually in the following years (Armstrong et al. 1991, Marglin and Schor 1990, Weisskopf et al. 1985; for a critique of this argument, see Clarke 1988 and Weeks 1979).

In order to reduce structural conflict inflation, the state can use recessions, incomes policies, or heterodox shocks. Radical economists usually rightly criticise contractionary monetary and fiscal policies because they are costly, exploitative and distributionally regressive. They reduce inflation only at the expense of long periods of high unemployment, lower wages and substantial output loss, tend to privilege the financial interests at the expense of productive capital and the workers, and may contribute to high unemployment in the long term. Incomes policies are favoured by some Post-Keynesians, who argue that negotiations and carefully chosen policies can help to co-ordinate claims over the national product and reduce inflation, whilst simultaneously preserving growth and (full) employment (Kotz 1987, Davidson 1994). Neostructuralist writers tend to highlight the importance of heterodox shocks. These shocks are a type of incomes policy imposed by the state, rather than being negotiated between the social partners. A shock may become necessary if indexation makes inflation rates high and rigid downwards, in which case agents who accept a reduction in the growth rate of their prices will incur substantial real income losses. The policy implication of this non-co-operative game approach is that the best way to reduce high inflation is through a shock that freezes wages and prices around their real, long-term averages, and institutionally breaks with the dynamic influence of past inflation (Cardoso and Dornbusch 1987, Dornbusch and Simonsen 1983; for a critical analysis, see Saad Filho and Mollo 2002).

1.2   Assessment

Widely different theories of value, production and class are compatible with the conflict approach. Classes are sometimes seen as partners, in which case it is relatively easy to achieve economic stability through negotiated incomes policies. Alternatively, a theory of exploitation may be used; in this case, economic stability can be obtained only through the subordination of the workers by force. This potential ambiguity makes the conflict approach potentially appealing to a wide audience. However, it also opens up possible charges of arbitrariness and lack of analytical rigour. In particular, inflation generally starts from a dislocation that shifts the economy away from a Pareto-optimal equilibrium. 'Apportioning blame' is, therefore, implicitly at issue, and alternative economic policies are usually assessed in terms of their ability to make the economy return to the initial equilibrium. It is not usually explained how that equilibrium was originally determined, or why it merits return. In sum, the conflict approach lacks a clear internal structure, and it is compatible with many alternative theories of employment, demand, income and its initial distribution, and with widely different rules of determination of the target income levels. Some of these rules are problematic; for example, the assumption that workers and capitalists bargain over income shares is inadequate because, in reality, the shares are determined *ex post* rather than being the subject of dispute. The presumption that the capitalists have a target income level is also misplaced because, as a class, they aim for maximum profit (or profit rates). As Kotz (1982, p. 4) rightly put it, '[t]he basic problem with the current versions of conflict theory is ... their lack of clarity concerning the profit-seeking behaviour of capital' (see also Guttmann 1994, p. 124).

Indeterminacies such as these can be eliminated only through the establishment of an organic relationship between the conflict approach and a broader economic theory. Unfortunately, many such connections are possible, and none is necessary. In other words, conflict theories, as they are usually presented, are typically 'middle range' (Fine and Leopold 1993). They derive from a set of stylised empirical observations (e.g., agents exercise claims over the national product through the sale of their goods), and transform these observations into structures that are used to explain these stylised facts (e.g., distributive conflict leading to inflation). This approach borders on a tautology, and it is scientifically unsound because the analysis is not grounded by a broader structure that supports its elementary concepts and contextualises its conclusions. The lack of a theory of production implies that the state cannot be adequately grounded either, and it is usually arbitrarily superimposed to the conflict. The state's role and policies are derived from a further set of stylised facts, and the rationale for, and the power of, economic policies are left unexplained and depend heavily on the analyst's preferences (e.g., the extent to which they are influenced by monetarism, as de Brunhoff (1982) rightly argues in her critique of Rowthorn's (1980) model of inflation). Quite obviously, state policies are important, and the translation of distributive conflicts into inflation is heavily dependent on the monetary policy stance (Isaac 1991).

Regardless of these heavy criticisms, the conflict approach is intuitively sensible and clearly relevant. Distributive conflicts must surely be an essential aspect of any Marxian theory of inflation, for inflation would not persist in the absence of widespread dissatisfaction about the level and/or distribution of the national income, and the monetisation of those incompatible claims (Burdekin and Burkett 1996, p. 13).

2   Monopolies, Underconsumption, and Inflation

In radical economic theory, inflation is often associated with the increasing market power of large corporations. Many radicals, especially some Marxists, believe that their growing influence derives from the tendency towards the concentration and centralisation of capital (Marx 1976, ch.25). Although this is not accepted across the radical spectrum, it is often argued that the process of monopolisation has been reinforced by the interventionist policies of the 'Keynesian State'. This view is often accompanied by underconsumptionism, most clearly in the writings of the monopoly capital school, where expansionary state policies are essential in order to avoid the crisis.[6] This section is divided into two parts; the first outlines the underconsumption-monopoly power analysis of inflation, and the second criticises its internal structure and conclusions.

2.1   *Inflation Theory*
The monopoly power approach argues that state support for the monopolies is essential for economic stability and growth, because the monopoly sector includes the most dynamic firms and the largest investors, employers, producers and exporters. For this reason, the state provides cheap infrastructure to the monopolies, offers tax breaks, finances directly or indirectly part of their R&D costs, and supports their foreign ventures. More broadly, the state spends huge sums in civil servants' wages, consumables, and public investment, funds health, education and defence, and makes large transfers associated with social security. These expenditures support monopoly profits directly through purchases, and indirectly through transfers to their customers. The interventionist policies of the welfare state delivered unprecedented economic stability, high employment and rapid growth, especially between the late 1940s and the late

---

6   The classic example of this synthesis is Baran and Sweezy (1966). Clarke (1988) dissects the 'Keynesian State', and Bleaney (1976) critically examines theories of underconsumption. Paradoxically, in some of their works Sweezy and Magdoff (1970) defend the 'price rigidity' theory of inflation (see de Vroey 1984). In this view, demand shifts can lead to inflation and unemployment, if prices are sticky elsewhere in the economy (Howard and King 1990).

1960s. However, they also contributed to persistent budget deficits, rising public debt, and creeping inflation.

The relative economic stability in the post-war era simplified economic calculation and facilitated the credit financing of investment by the monopolies. At this point, two stories are possible. On the one hand, it can be argued that the exceptionally large credit supply led to overaccumulation of capital and to record levels of excess capacity. The excessively high costs associated with the overaccumulation of capital induced a severe profit squeeze which badly affected the monopoly sector and, therefore, the economy as a whole (Dowd 1976, Sweezy and Magdoff 1983 (drawing on Steindl 1952), Zarifian 1975; for alternative interpretations of the profit squeeze, see the first section of this essay). On the other hand, it has been argued that the excess demand created by government deficit spending (including, in the US, the costs of the Vietnam War) eventually led to inflation. For example, Morris (1972, pp. 18–19) argues that rising inflation was due to the 'endless stimulation of the moribund monopoly capitalist system by even stronger injections of monetary and fiscal anti-depressant drugs' (see also Gamble and Walton 1976).

In either case, the monopolies responded by increasing their prices rapidly, which led to profit-push inflation and falling real wages from the mid-1960s (Dollars and Sense 1978, Sherman 1972, 1976a, 1976b, Spero 1969, Sweezy and Magdoff 1979, Szymanski 1984). It quickly became clear that the state could no longer simultaneously support the monopolies and finance the welfare state, while maintaining low inflation and unemployment. In other words, inflation could be reduced only through the sacrifice of the 'Keynesian consensus'.

2.2   *Assessment*

Two agencies are responsible for inflation, monopolies and the state. Let us deal with the monopolies first. The monopoly power-underconsumption approach argues that the concentration and centralisation of capital are fundamental processes within capitalism, leading inexorably to monopolisation. In spite of its important (but insufficiently grounded) theoretical stature, there is no attempt to develop a distinctly Marxian theory of monopoly power and, even if we assume that monopoly power is generally increasing, the theory fails to identify the correct level of analysis. It is unclear how monopoly power affects the circuit of capital, the circulation of money and the distribution of income, whether or not it can be avoided, and to what extent it makes inflation inevitable. (In particular, it is left unclear why monopoly should lead to *inflation* rather than to one-off changes in relative prices.) The theory of monopoly pricing is particularly weak, although it is essential for the analysis of inflation. It relies on a simple collation of the ideas in Hilferding (1981, ch.15), for whom monopolies impose prices above the prices of production in order to reap extra profits, and Kalecki, for whom monopoly power is a stylised fact and monopolies reap extra profits because of their market power.[7] It is argued that monopoly prices are determined strategically, in order to maximise firm growth, market share or long-run profits, subject to the need to prevent new entries, and are sticky downwards. In Marxist garb, they capture superprofits because of their market power, which may be transfers from the competitive sector or from the workers (in which case the wages fall below the value of labour power). Unfortunately, these potential developments of Marx's theory of price are not pursued systematically. Moreover, there is scant empirical evidence to support the analysis, in spite of the strong assumptions involved (e.g., that monopolies can raise prices almost at will but that, in spite of this power, they often wait for a recession before doing so – yet, they fail to reduce prices in the upturn). Moreover, important theoretical objections to the 'Hilferding-Kalecki synthesis' are not addressed adequately (for example, the threat of entry of domestic and foreign producers may be sufficient to force monopolistic firms to follow competitive pricing strategies, Baumol 1982; see, however, Kotz 1982, 1987). The role of demand and other limits to monopoly power are also often neglected, as are the counter-tendencies to the concentration and centralisation of capital.

The theory of the state is also left unclear, and what is said is potentially contradictory. On the one hand, the state manages the economy relatively autonomously in order to ensure the reproduction of capital as a whole, which requires the accommodation of the interests of different fractions of capital and of the workers, and is best achieved in a democracy (O'Connor 1973). On the other hand, the state has also been seen as little more than a tool of powerful (monopoly) interests, and its policies are limited by the need to obtain their consent, in which case fascism is a clear possibility (Morris 1974).[8]

The workers have no autonomous role, but there seems to be an underlying possibility of social conflict in production and distribution, which is partly responsible for the activist state policies. There is an uneasy relationship between the presumably fundamental opposition between workers and capitalists, and the analytical neglect of the working class, which is generally a spectator of the unfolding events. It is curious that the workers are, apparently, strong enough to prevent the extraction of additional surplus value in

---

7   See Kalecki (1990c) and Sawyer (1985, ch.2); for a Marxian critique, see Fine and Murfin (1984). Bleaney (1976, pp. 225–226) rightly argues that it is 'a severe problem, in writing about modern underconsumption theories, that their influence seems to have far exceeded the extent of their theoretical exposition'. In spite of this, underconsumption theories obviously underestimate the importance of competition (Mandel 1968, p. 363).

8   Marxist theories of the state are discussed by Cammack (1989), Fine and Harris (1979, ch.6) and Holloway and Picciotto (1978).

production, but not to avoid transfers in circulation through monopoly pricing
– even when unemployment is low. The role of the financial system is not analysed in detail, and the balance of payments constraint is generally neglected
(which may be explained by the focus on the relatively closed US economy).
Essentially, inflation is the result of interventionist economic policies trying
to ensure full employment and social stability, in an economy constrained by
monopoly power and pricing strategies (Best 1972).

The linkages connecting monopoly power, state policies and inflation are
left mostly unexplained. There is no clear theory of money, credit or finance,
except for the presumption that money supply responds passively to monopoly demand or to state command, and that (largely unexplained) financial developments are contributory factors. How this leads to inflation is often left
unclear.[9] More generally, the causes of inflation shift between monopoly pricing decisions and excess demand induced by the state (which is the paradoxical result of the state's attempt to avoid underconsumption).[10] The distributive
impact of inflation is not analysed, except to argue that monopolies benefit
at the expense of the workers and other groups receiving nominally fixed revenues. It is unclear how this relates with a theory of wages or of exploitation.[11]
Finally, there is not much empirical research showing that growing monopoly
power leads to higher inflation and to a declining wage share in the national
income.

3   Credit, Extra Money, and Inflation

In the mid-1970s an alternative analysis was outlined, in which inflation is the
result of a permanent upward shift in the relationship between commodity
prices and values. This shift is caused by an increase in the quantity of circulating money, which fails to elicit a corresponding increase in commodity supply

---

9   See, however, Mandel (1968, p. 527) and Sweezy (1974). Sweezy claims that Baran (1973) had
      identified the inflationary danger in Keynesian economics: government deficit financing
      is not sustainable in the long run because most government spending is unproductive
      (e.g., military expenditures). These expenditures are potentially inflationary because they
      increase the ratio between money and commodities, which leads to inflation (see below).
10   See Sherman (1972); for a critique, see Weisskopf et al. (1985). Sweezy and Magdoff (1979,
      p. 9) tautologically claim that 'while monopoly capital may not be the direct cause of
      major upward movements of prices, it is nevertheless the necessary condition for their
      occurrence ... If monopoly is not the motor, it is nonetheless the *sine qua non* of the ex-
      traordinary inflation of the current decade as well as of the preceding upward spirals'.
11   The monopoly capital school has been havily criticised by most Marxists for its use of the
      concept of economic surplus and rejection of surplus value; see Weeks (1977, 1982).

(or, alternatively, by supply cuts unaccompanied by sufficient reductions in the quantity of circulating money). Alternatively, if the quantity of monetary units which, on average, is added to the value of the output per hour of labour increases, in spite of the constant technology and skill of the labour force, the ensuing increase in the price level (which, in practice, is usually accompanied by relative price changes) is inflationary. These systematic changes can be captured only *ex post*. In principle, they are compatible with any type of monetary system but, for reasons that will be explained below, persistent inflation is most likely to happen only in contemporary monetary systems dominated by bank-created credit money and state-created fiat money.[12]

The extra money approach indicates that the relationship between production, which comprises the main variables of the 'real economy', and circulation, including the monetary and credit systems, is essential. However, the precise *type* of relationship which exists between these economic domains is often left unclear. For example, some proponents of the extra money approach (e.g., de Brunhoff) argue that this approach is part of the labour theory of value (Saad Filho 1997). In contrast, others see it as the grounds for the integration between Marx's work and Keynes's (e.g., de Vroey). In spite of its shortcomings (to be indicated below), this section argues that the extra money approach can provide the basis for the systematic development of Marxian theories of inflation and it can incorporate, when this is warranted, the best insights of the other approaches.

3.1   *Money and Credit*

Contemporary monetary systems include primarily two forms of money, inconvertible paper currency issued by the central bank (which is legal tender and discharges all debts) and credit money produced by the commercial banks (liabilities of private financial institutions, offering a potential claim on another form of money). Trade credits, financial assets such as certificates of deposit and treasury bills, and foreign currency, can also fulfil certain functions of money.[13] Non-mainstream writers of widely distinct persuasions share the

---

12   Aglietta (1979), Brunhoff and Cartelier (1974), Fine (1980, ch.4), Lipietz (1983) and de Vroey (1984); see also Loranger (1982a), Mandel (1975, ch.13), Mattick (1978), Orléan (1982) and

Weeks (1981). Many Post-Keynesian writers (e.g., Moore 1988) argue that if the money supply is endogenous there cannot be excess supply of money. For a counter-argument, see Hilferding (1981, ch.5) and Chapter 6 in this volume, drawing upon Lapavitsas and Saad-Filho (2000).

13   Marx's theory of money is reviewed by Arnon (1984), Brunhoff (1976), Itoh and Lapavitsas (1999) and Saad-Filho (1993, see also Chapter 3). The approaches discussed in this essay presume that money has no direct relationship to any 'special' commodity such as gold.

conviction that the quantity of circulating money is determined by the output volume, commodity prices, the value of money and the broader institutional framework (the velocity of circulation will be assumed constant for simplicity). Changes in any of the latter eventually (though *not* instantaneously) elicit changes in the quantity of circulating money primarily through changes in hoards (which may include all manner of financial assets), the volume of bank loans, and the monetary base. It follows that the money supply is endogenous in two senses; first, qualitatively and more generally, because money is necessary for, and a necessary aspect of, capitalist production (in other words, a 'real' economy independent of 'monetary' variables, or a 'capitalist barter economy', is impossible and theoretically meaningless, regardless of mainstream assumptions to the contrary). Second, quantitatively and more specifically, the money supply is endogenous because the circulating quantity of money is ultimately determined by 'the needs of trade'.[14]

Temporary discrepancies between money supply and demand are inevitable. These discrepancies correspond to fluctuations of the relationship between prices and values, and of the monetary expression of labour. These shifts are generally inconsequential because they tend to be associated with financial or productive changes which gradually eliminate the discrepancy spontaneously. (These fluctuations are not generally noticed because the circuits of capital are staggered rather than simultaneous, and fluctuations in one direction tend to be cancelled out by fluctuations in the opposite direction.) In sum, endogeneity does not imply that money supply never deviates from demand, for two reasons. First, and more generally, because the empirical determinacy of the quantity and velocity of money declines as the analysis becomes more concrete. They depend on social conventions, including the financial rules and regulations, the structure of the financial system and its relationship with production, the international relations, the property relations in the economy, the degree of concentration of capital, and other variables that make the 'supply' and 'demand' for money extremely difficult to estimate. Second, and more specifically, even though the supply of credit money necessarily corresponds to *individual* demand (credit money is always created in response to a loan

---

The conditions underlying the existence of inconvertible paper money are examined in Saad-Filho (1997), where it is argued that inconvertible paper money is compatible with Marx's derivation of money in *Capital 1*. This essay also suggests that commodity money and inconvertible paper money are equally suited to fulfil the function of measure of value.

14   Lapavitsas and Saad-Filho (2000) and Mollo (1999) show that Marx's notion of endogeneity is broader than the better known Post-Keynesian approaches outlined in Minsky (1975, 1986) and Moore (1988).

request), the *total* credit supply may not reflect the needs of the economy as a whole. This is clearly the case when speculative loans help to inflate a real estate or stock market bubble, or when banks unwittingly finance the production of unprofitable or unsaleable goods (Itoh and Lapavitsas 1999, Lapavitsas 1991; see also Mandel 1968, pp. 254–259).

3.2   *Extra Money Inflation*

In order to show how discrepancies between money supply and demand can lead to inflation, the extra money approach starts from the circuit of capital. The productive circuit begins when a capitalist draws on previously accumulated funds or borrows newly created credit money in order to finance production. The injection of these funds into the economy increases the ratio between money and output value. If more output is eventually produced and sold at its normal price (the price of production), the initial increase in the ratio between money and value is cancelled out by the output growth. The sale of the output creates additional income, which is used to repay debts, to finance accumulation by the firm, or it may be distributed as profit or dividends.

However, if the output cannot be not sold, or is sold only at a discount, the firm suffers a loss which may be absorbed in two ways. Very simply, if the 'market rules' are strictly respected, a well-defined agent, or set of agents, bears the cost, usually the firm (through a decline in the value of its assets), or its bank (if the firm goes bankrupt). At a further remove, the firm may try to offset their losses through transfers from other agents, for example its workers (if the rate of exploitation increases, perhaps only temporarily), or its customers (if the firm has unused monopoly power and raises prices in other lines). 'Market' solutions such as these can be destabilising, because they may systematically lead to unemployment, capacity underutilisation, the deterioration of the working conditions, and financial fragility. They may also lead to inflation (if the firm increases prices to cover its losses, possibly inducing other firms to respond in kind) or deflation (if the firm reduces prices in order to boost sales, or if demand declines because of unemployment or a financial crisis).

Alternatively, the loss may be socialised if the 'market rules' are violated. This may happen in two different ways. The bank may refinance the firm's debt, or the firm may receive a state subsidy (in the extreme, it may be nationalised and 'restructured' with public funds). In either case, there is an injection of purchasing power into the economy that perpetuates the initial discrepancy between the circulating money and the output; in other words, the initial (presumably transitory) increase in the monetary equivalent of labour becomes permanent. Following de Vroey (1984), the money injected into the economy through a violation of market rules is called *extra money*.

Let us summarise the analysis above. The discrepancy between circulating money and output value was originally created when the firm borrowed money (or dissaved) in order to expand its output. If the additional output had been sold at the usual price the discrepancy would have been eliminated 'spontaneously'. However, if the output is not sold at the usual price the discrepancy persists. It may be eliminated through 'market processes' if the firm dissaves in order to repay its debts, or if the bank uses its own assets to cover the bad loan. Alternatively, the bank or the state may refinance the firms' debt, usually through the creation of new credit money or new fiat money. This (extra) money prevents the reduction of the monetary equivalent of labour back to its original level, in spite of the failure of the output to increase as had been originally anticipated.

It was shown above that banks or the state may create extra money in order to cover production losses. Extra money may also be created in other circumstances, for example if the central bank assists the banking system through the discount window in response to losses unrelated to bad loans (which was the case discussed above), if the country runs a non-sterilised surplus in its balance of payments, for example as a result of a favourable turn in the terms of trade, or if firms or households dissave or borrow in order to speculate with shares, real estate or works of art (for a similar argument, see Kalecki 1997 and de Vroey 1984). Obviously, the reverse operations can destroy extra money (depreciation allowances are the opposite of new investment). A reduction in the velocity of circulation can neutralise the extra money and cancel its effects, while an increase in V can multiply the potential impact of a given sum of (extra) money.

In each of these cases the extra money increases the nominal income or the liquid wealth of the consolidated non-financial sector (i.e., the potential money and financial capital available in the economy increases), in spite of the constant value of the output, and regardless of the existence of equilibrium, currently or in the past. (The creation of extra money is not usually meant to relieve temporary liquidity constraints of industrial of financial capitalists, because other mechanisms are available to eliminate this potential bottleneck (e.g., bank loans, overdrafts and trade credit.)

If the extra money is spent rather than being saved elsewhere in the economy, or destroyed in the repayment of loans, it may induce a (potentially multiplied) quantity response in those sectors operating with substantial spare capacity (the 'Keynesian' scenario). In this case, eventually there will be more money and more commodities in circulation, which cancels the extra money and may restore the previous relationship between value and money at a higher level of income and output, regardless of equilibrium assumptions. However, if the extra money increases demand in a sector without spare capacity, and if additional imports are not available (the 'monetarist' case), the monetary expression of labour rises. This increase is established through an increase in prices in this market, ostensibly because of excess demand. This is *extra money inflation*. (If the economy is highly unbalanced, with bottlenecks in some sectors and substantial spare capacity in other sectors, it is likely that high inflation and high unemployment will coexist. This is the 'structuralist' scenario.)

Extra money inflation can happen regardless of monopoly power or distributive conflicts, although it is usually a reflex of one or both of them. It may be due to state intervention, but the state cannot be generally 'blamed' for it because extra money is routinely and necessarily created by private decisions that are not subject to state control (as was shown above). Moreover, even if the extra money is created by the state it is impossible to know in advance where it will go, and whether it will have a quantity or price effect, or both (targeting is possible, but necessarily imprecise). In due course, discrepancies between the quantity of circulating money and demand (determined by the 'needs of trade') will tend to be eliminated by changes in output, velocity or hoards. However, these adjustments take time, and they may create additional instability through their effects on prices, the exchange rate, the balance of payments or the interest rate.[15] If the monetary discrepancies outlined above are continually renewed, they can lead to persistent inflation, severe balance of payments disequilibria and prolonged economic stagnation, which demonstrate the non-neutrality of money and its potential influence over production. This analysis implies that the coexistence of inflation and unemployment is natural, because inflation is due to the propagation of localised devaluations of money. Finally, it may be inferred that the changes in relative prices that necessarily coexist with inflation are a reflex of the structural differences between systems of provision.[16]

The extra money approach does *not* imply that governments should try to eliminate extra money in order to control inflation. The regular creation

---

15 Some horizontalist Post-Keynesians, following Kaldor (1982), argue that 'excessive' bank loans will be passed around until they reach someone with an outstanding loan, who will use the funds to repay the loan; in this sense, there can be no excess money. This argument overlooks the fact that the money increases demand across many sectors of the economy until it is destroyed, and that it may be used, for example, to inflate a speculative bubble. I owe this insight to Malcolm Sawyer.

16 Systems of provision are described by Fine and Leopold (1993) and Saad-Filho (2000b). Indexation violates this tendency, because sectors not directly affected by a given price increase will respond automatically. Indexation accelerates the devaluation of money, because it perpetuates the successive rounds of price increases across the economy.

and destruction of extra money is *necessarily* part and parcel of the circuit of capital. Contractionary monetary policies usually reduce the quantity of extra money being injected into the economy, but even the most draconian policies cannot eliminate extra money completely, for two reasons. First, because the economic and social costs of higher unemployment, lower investment and economic stagnation eventually becomes excessively high. Second, because the state cannot control all the potential sources of extra money, including the private financial system, the foreign sector, the savings behaviour of the workers and capitalists, and so on. In other words, the regular operation of the financial system, state economic policies and the economy's international relations *inevitably* involve the regular creation and destruction of extra money, and they may lead to inflation or deflation whatever policies the state pursues (in spite of these limitations, persistent inflation is clearly more likely if the state intervenes extensively in the economy and if its policies are expansionary).

In spite of their apparent similarity, the theory of extra money inflation is incompatible with the quantity theory of money. The quantity theory's assumptions that money supply is exogenous, that money is only a medium of exchange and that money is not hoarded, are wrong and unacceptable from the perspective of the extra money approach. First, this approach argues that extra money is regularly and spontaneously created by the interaction between the central bank, commercial banks, firms and workers, and that its quantity cannot be controlled, or even known precisely, by the state. In contrast, the quantity theory presumes that the banking system is always fully loaned up, and that the central bank can determine autonomously the supply of money directly (through the monetisation of government budget deficits or purchases of government securities) or indirectly (through changes in compulsory bank reserves, which should lead unproblematically to changes in the outstanding stock of loans). Other sources of changes in the supply of money are usually ignored, and the possibility that changes initiated by the central bank will be neutralised by hoarding, the repayment of bank loans or by a compensatory change in bank loans are generally neglected by the quantity theory.

Second, extra money is non-neutral in the short and in the long run; it may change irreversibly the level and composition of the national product and the structure of demand, depending on how it is created and how it circulates. In contrast, the quantity theory presumes that money is neutral in the long and, in extreme cases, even the short run. Third, the effects of extra money (whether quantity, price, or both) cannot be anticipated. All that one can say is that high rates of capacity utilisation and activist state policies increase the probability of extra money inflation, but there is never likely to be a simple relationship between them. In contrast, for the quantity theory the relationship between money supply and inflation is usually straightforward. Because of the underlying assumptions of perfect competition, full employment, and money neutrality, a change in the supply of money (initiated by the central bank and automatically propagated by the commercial banks through the money multiplier) unproblematically leads to a predictable change in the price level.

3.3   Inconvertibility and Inflation

If the domestic currency is legally and easily convertible into a reserve asset such as gold at a fixed price, there is a strong reserve discipline limiting the creation of extra money by the commercial banks and the central bank. At the same time, arbitrage makes it impossible for commodity prices to deviate permanently from their gold prices of production, although cyclical fluctuations are inevitable. At the risk of oversimplifying the problem, in the boom demand increases steadily (partly for speculative purposes) and prices tend to increase, until the rapidly growing mass of debt can no longer be serviced by the existing income flows. At this point the need for gold as the means of payment increases rapidly. In order to avoid a potentially catastrophic gold drain, the central bank must raise the discount rate, in spite of the high degree of market vulnerability. The high discount rate increases the distress of both borrowers and lenders, and the scramble for gold by firms and banks leads to price deflation and rising unemployment. The economy contracts rapidly.[17]

This blind and wasteful mechanism can operate relatively smoothly only if prices and wages are highly flexible. If they are not (e.g., because of monopoly power or workers' resistance against nominal wage cuts), the costs of convertibility may become excessively high because of the distortions which are continually introduced into the relative price system, and the social and economic instability which is created by the crises. The elimination of the nominal anchor allows the central bank to reduce the discount rate and simplify the access to the discount window at the trough, in order to support industry and the financial sector. In sum, currency inconvertibility facilitates the creation of extra money by the state, and may stimulate its creation by the private sector, which may reduce both the constraints on growth and the contractionary impact of the crisis. However, currency inconvertibility may also lead to extra money inflation instead or in spite of the crisis, because it reduces the constraints imposed by convertibility upon speculative booms, and because inconvertibility allows the mismatch between the structure of supply and the

---

17   See Aglietta (1979), Itoh and Lapavitsas (1999) and Weeks (1981). This analysis can explain cycles under contemporary currency board systems with only minor changes.

composition of demand to increase sharply, which can be an important cause of the crisis.

Currency inconvertibility allows the state (and the banks) to smooth out the cycles, through the manipulation of the supply of extra money in order to alleviate temporary cash flow problems and, more controversially, through direct support to failing companies or banks (Guttman 1994). However, this is not likely to eliminate the crisis entirely, and it may lead to permanent inflation (Aglietta 1980, Clarke 1994, Grou 1977, Mattick 1978, Perelman 1996). The lack of *a priori* co-ordination in capitalist economies implies that only crises can reduce a substantial mismatch between supply and demand and curtail flawed financial strategies. Moreover, if crises are avoided for long periods the threat of failure declines, which reduces the stimulus for technical innovation and for the adoption of the most profitable management strategies. This is likely to reduce the rate of productivity growth, lead to wasteful investment practices and reduce economic efficiency (Fine 1980). At the same time, the workers tend to become increasingly strong because of the high level of employment.

In sum, long term inflation may derive from the attempt by the state to deliver continuous economic growth, and from its attempt to avoid deflation when growth falters. This requires the constant injection of extra money into the economy. In the upswing, the extra money is provided mainly by the private sector with the support of the central bank, in order to finance consumption and new investment. Therefore, growth necessarily breaches the established relationship between value and money, and it is always potentially inflationary (depending on the supply and import responses). As the economy grows, disproportions and bottlenecks inevitably develop, financial structures become more fragile and, unless cheap imports are readily available, prices (and, possibly, wages) tend to increase. At this stage, the crisis erupts either spontaneously or because contractionary policies have been adopted.[18] If the crisis becomes acute and deflation looms, the state will usually intervene and deliberately inject (or facilitate the private creation of) extra money.[19]

---

18   The possibility that the state may deliberately engineer a recession shows that the state has a certain discretionary power with respect to the determination of the interest rates and the nominal supply of money and, therefore, that it influences the level of economic activity. This does not imply that the money supply is exogenous. It was shown above that the supply of money is determined by the interaction between the central bank, the commercial banking and financial system, the exporters, producers, workers and other sectors of the economy. None of them has complete control over the supply of money, although each of them can influence it in a certain (possibly conflicting) direction.

19   This conclusion is very similar to that of Minsky (1986), which reinforces de Vroey's (1984) argument about the potential compatibility between the extra money approach and (Post-) Keynesian analyses.

This analysis does not imply that capitalism must face either permanently rising inflation or continually declining growth rates. Distributive conflict inflation (analysed above) can be thwarted by a 'change in the balance of industrial relations' (i.e., high unemployment and increased repression against the workers), while monopoly price increases can be contained by trade, industrial and exchange rate policy measures. The creation of private extra money can be checked by direct regulation or high interest rates, and their inflationary impact can be reduced through fiscal policy shifts or the greater availability of competing imports. Finally, the injection of extra money by the state can be reduced by the curtailment of welfare expenditures or by privatisation. This shows that the relationship between extra money and inflation is complex, and it is liable to change depending on the broader circumstances surrounding production and exchange.

3.4   *Assessment*

The extra money approach offers a reasonably well grounded analysis, which can provide the basis for the development of a theory of inflation which incorporates the main claims of the labour theory of value and the most important insights of the previous analyses of inflation. However, the extra money approach is still undeveloped at critical points, and it suffers from deficiencies and ambiguities which need to be addressed urgently. Let us start with its deficiencies. The analysis of the supply of central bank and credit money is usually very weak and simplistic, and it would benefit from greater exposure to, and confrontation against, recent Post-Keynesian developments (for a taste of the vast literature, see Arestis and Howells 1996, Cottrell 1994, and Dow 1996; for a critique, see Lapavitsas and Saad Filho 2000), circuitist contributions (Loranger 1982b, Nell and Deleplace 1996), and the work of Kalecki (1990b, 1997, see also Messori 1991). At a more concrete level of analysis, the valuable contributions of Minsky (1975, 1986) and Dymski and Pollin (1994) on the intrinsic financial instability of modern capitalism need to be evaluated in detail and, when this is warranted, their contribution should be incorporated into the analysis.

This is relatively easy to achieve. However, much work remains to be done in order to make the structures and categories employed in the extra money approach fully compatible with those of Marx's theory of value. For example, the relationship between the supply of money and the monetary expression of labour (Duménil 1980, Dymski 1990, Foley 1982) is usually left very unclear. It is not obvious how newly created (credit or fiat) money is related to value production and its realisation through sale, and how the monetary expression of labour fluctuates during the circuit of capital. Moreover, the extra money approach often shifts arbitrarily between levels of analysis, especially between capital in general and many capitals; consequently, the role of competition is left unclear. Finally, further work is necessary to distinguish between price increases caused by extra money, and those caused by other types of money supply growth. This would go a long way to clarify the remaining ambiguity between the extra money approach and the quantity theory of money, especially with respect to the role of excess demand as the main trigger of inflation.

Addressing these problems in a systematic manner will make it possible to link the extra money and conflict theories and, at a later stage, to incorporate systematically the inflationary impact of the concentration of capital and other important contemporary phenomena such as financial development and financial and capital account liberalisation. It will also make it possible to analyse concrete problems such as the potentially inflationary impact of the public debt overhang, whose increasing liquidity is synonymous with the injection of extra money into the economy (Grou 1977, Marazzi 1977, Mattick 1978).

4   Conclusion

This essay has analysed critically the three best known Marxian theories of inflation. They are closely related to one another, and to non-Marxian analyses such as the Post-Keynesian, circuitist, Kaleckian and institutionalist. They argue, in different ways, that inflation is a historically specific phenomenon, but its form can be abstractly determined from the broad features of modern capitalism. However, beyond a certain point concrete studies become necessary in order to contextualise the analysis. Different alternatives are proposed in order to overcome the difficult dilemmas imposed by the attempt to explain inflation in inconvertible money systems, while preserving the endogeneity and non-neutrality of money. They are also heavily dependent on the context of the analysis.

These approaches agree that inflation is potentially functional to modern capitalism, in many different ways. For example, inflation generally leads to transfers to corporations, banks or the state, which may foster accumulation through forced savings or by giving a 'second chance' to firms which have made mistakes in the past. These functional elements were predominant under creeping inflation, between the late-1940s and the mid-1960s (Aglietta 1979, Grou 1977, Jacobi et al. 1975). There is disagreement about the causes of the subsequent acceleration of inflation, and they have been reviewed in this essay. There is considerable scope for the further development of Marxian analyses of inflation, as well as for substantial cross-fertilisation with other political economy theories.

The conflict and the monopoly capital-underconsumption theories are especially close to one another. Whilst the latter claims that inflation (and, more generally, the crisis) is largely a consequence of the excessive strength of the capitalist class, the former argues that they are due to the excessive strength of the workers. This can help to explain why one was relatively popular in the weakly unionised USA, whilst the other became better known in Europe (Howard and King 1990, Weisskopf et al. 1985; in contrast, the extra money approach has been developed mostly by Francophone writers). The extra money approach is different in its aims and scope and, in my view, it provides the basis for further theoretical work on the monetary aspect of inflation, that may encompass the valuable insights of the other approaches. The extra money approach argues that inflation is necessarily a monetary phenomenon, and it analyses the monetary aspect of inflation explicitly (though often unsatisfactorily), whilst at the same time demonstrating that the quantity theory is sterile as a starting point. It shows that extra money can lead to higher output, employment and increased productivity, to inflation, or to any combination of them. In sum, it preserves valuable insights of the anti-quantity theory tradition, and develops them further in the context of contemporary monetary and financial systems.

The analysis in this essay needs to be developed much further, but some of its policy implications are already clear. First, inflation can be functional (as explained above), but its dysfunctional aspects gradually tend to become predominant when inflation becomes permanent. Indexation reduces the positive implications of inflation for growth, economic calculus becomes increasingly complex, and capital restructuring becomes more difficult because inefficient capitals and productive processes are preserved, rather than being annihilated by 'market' processes. Second, inflation leads to financial crisis by its cumulative character, through the formation of increasingly unstable debt structures. Crises may be postponed almost indefinitely by increasing the supply of extra money, but this may lead to hyperinflation (as in some Latin American and former socialist states). Third, there can be inflation purely for monetary reasons, usually associated with speculative bubbles involving housing, the stock exchange and other assets, which can harm real accumulation by draining it of funds. In this respect, incomes policies can be irrelevant to the prevention of inflation, and they can become inimical to the workers' interests as they prevent the readjustment of nominal (hence real) wages (Lapavitsas and Saad Filho 2000). Fourth, inflation is not inevitable, whatever the power of the banks, monopolies or the workers. However, financial deepening, the concentration of capital, the reduction of trade flows, and worker militancy increase the vulnerability of the economy to inflation, and the difficulty to reverse the process once it is under way.

PART 2

Essays on Contemporary Capitalism

..

CHAPTER 9

Anti-Capitalism: A Marxist Introduction

The need of a constantly expanding market ... chases the bourgeoisie over the whole surface of the globe ... All old-established national industries ... are dislodged by new industries ... that no longer work up indigenous raw material, but raw material drawn from the remotest zones; industries whose products are consumed, not only at home, but in every quarter of the globe. In place of the old wants, satisfied by the productions of the country, we find new wants, requiring for their satisfaction the products of distant lands and climes ... The bourgeoisie, by the rapid improvement of all instruments of production, by the immensely facilitated means of communication, draws all ... nations into civilisation ... It compels all nations, on pain of extinction, to adopt the bourgeois mode of production; it compels them to introduce what it calls civilisation into their midst, i.e., to become bourgeois themselves. In one word, it creates a world after its own image.

> Marx and Engels (1998, pp. 13–14), emphasis added

1 Capitalism and Anti-Capitalism[1]

The Communist Manifesto rings even truer today than in 1848. Key features of nineteenth-century capitalism are clearly recognisable, and even more strongly developed, in the early twenty-first century. They include the internationalisation of trade, production and finance, the growth of transnational corporations (TNCs), the communications revolution, the diffusion of Western culture and consumption patterns across the world, and so on.

Other traits of our age can also be found in the *Manifesto*. In the early twenty-first century, powerful nations still rule the world by political, economic and military means, and their gospel is zealously preached by today's missionaries of neoliberalism. They follow on the footsteps of their ancestors, who drew strength from the holy trinity of Victorian imperialism: God, British capital and the Royal Navy. Today's evangelists pay lip service to human rights and the elimination of poverty, but their faith lies elsewhere, in the sacred

---

1 Originally published as: 'Introduction', in A. Saad Filho (ed.) *Anti-Capitalism: A Marxist Introduction*. London: Pluto Press, 2003, pp. 1–23.

Tablets of copyright law and in the charter of the IMF. They travel to all corners of the globe and, despite untold hardship in anonymous five-star hotels, tirelessly preach submission to Wall Street and the US government. They will never take no for an answer. Native obduracy is initially explained away by ignorance or corruption, and then ridiculed. However, even saintly patience has its limits. Eventually, economic, diplomatic and other forms of pressure may become necessary. In extreme circumstances, the White House may be forced to bomb the enemy into submission, thus rendering another country safe for McDonalds.

It seems that, in spite of our fast cars, mobile phones and the internet, the world has not, after all, changed beyond recognition over the past hundred and fifty years. However, even if Marx can offer important insights to understanding modern capitalism, what about his claim that communism is the future of humanity? Surely the collapse of the Soviet bloc, China's economic reforms, and the implosion of left organisations across the world prove that Marx was wrong?

Contributors to this book beg to differ. *Anti-Capitalism: A Marxist Introduction* explains the structural features and the main shortcomings of modern capitalism, in order to substantiate our case against capitalism as a *system*. Chapters 1, 2 and 3 show that Marx's value theory provides important insights for understanding the modern world, including the exploitation of the workers, the sources of corporate power and the sickening extremes of overconsumption and widespread poverty. Chapters 5, 10 and 17 claim that classes exist, and that class struggle is, literally, alive and kicking around us. Chapters 4 and 6 show that technical change is not primarily driven by the urge to produce cheaper, better or more useful goods, but by the imperatives of profit-making and social control. Chapter 8 reviews the driving forces of capitalism across history, and Chapter 7 shows that capitalism is inimical to the Earth's ecological balance. Whereas environmental sustainability demands very long-term calculus of costs and benefits, capitalism is based on short-term rationality and profit maximisation. *This social system must to be confronted, in order to preserve the possibility of human life on this planet.*

Chapters 9 to 16 challenge other idols of contemporary thought, including the claims that capitalism promotes democracy, world peace and equality within and between nations, that every debt must be paid, that globalisation is unavoidable and unambiguously good, that national states are powerless, and that economic crises can be eliminated. Finally, Chapters 18 and 19 argue that capitalism is both unsustainable and undesirable. In our view, communism is justified not only on material but, especially, on human grounds. Much of what we argue is obvious. Yet, often the obvious must be demonstrated over and over again, until it becomes self-evident to the majority.

This book also challenges the knee-jerk reaction against critiques of contemporary capitalism, the trite motto that 'there is no alternative' (TINA). Leading proponents of TINA include rapacious free-marketeers, prematurely aged philosophers of the 'Third Way', delusional economists, opportunistic politicians, corrupt bureaucrats, bankrupt journalists and other desperados. They claim that human beings are genetically programmed to be greedy, that capitalism is the law of nature, that transnational capital is usually right, and that non-intrusive regulation is possible when it goes wrong. They argue that capitalist societies, even though historically recent, will last forever, and that the triumph of the market should be embraced because it is both unavoidable and advantageous to all. They reassure us that massive improvements in living standards are just around the corner, and that only a little bit more belt-tightening will suffice.

Deceptions such as these have helped to legitimise the growing marketisation of most spheres of life in the last twenty years. In rich countries, this has taken place primarily through the assault on the social safety nets built after World War 2. Low paid and insecure jobs have been imposed on millions of workers, the provision of public services has been curtailed, and the distribution of income and wealth has shifted against the poor. In poor countries, national development strategies have collapsed nearly everywhere. Under Washington's guidance, a bleak 'era of adjustment' has taken hold across the so-called developing world. In these countries, low expectations and policy conformity are enforced by usurious foreign debts and neoliberal policy despotism monitored by the IMF, the World Bank and the US Treasury Department. Recent experience abundantly shows that neoliberalism tramples upon the achievements, lives and hopes of the poor everywhere, and that it often leads to disastrous outcomes (see below).[2]

In spite of the much-repeated claim that history is dead or, more precisely, that significant social and political changes are no longer possible, the neoliberal-globalist project has been facing difficult challenges. It has suffered legitimacy problems in the US because of falling wages in spite of rising national income, in Western Europe because of simmering social conflicts triggered by high unemployment and stagnant living standards, and in Japan because of the protracted economic crisis. It has had to contend with the social and economic collapse of the former Soviet bloc, and with repeated financial and balance of payments crises in Southeast Asia and Latin America. It has also had to explain away the economic and political meltdown in sub-Saharan Africa, and to face frequent wars and unprecedented levels of terrorist activity across the world. Last but not least, neoliberal globalism has been confronted

---

2 Resistance against IMF policies in poor countries is documented in WDM (2000).

by profound disillusion everywhere, and by vibrant protests and mass resistance, especially in Argentina, Ecuador, Indonesia, Mexico, Occupied Palestine, and South Korea.

In this context, the recent 'anti-globalisation' or 'anti-capitalist' protest movements are important for two reasons. First, they are global in scope, combining campaigns that were previously waged separately. In doing so, they have raised questions about the *systemic* features of capitalism for the first time in a generation. Second, they have shed a powerful light upon the dismal track record of contemporary capitalism. Although initially marginalised, these movements shot to prominence in the wake of the Zapatista rebellion, the Jubilee 2000 campaign and the confrontations that brought to a halt the Seattle WTO meeting. The new movements have joined vigorous mass demonstrations in several continents, and they have showed their opposition to the monopolistic practices of the TNCs, including pharmaceutical giants and corporations attempting to force-feed the world with genetically modified crops. They have challenged patent laws and clashed against other forms of 'corporate greed', leading to boycotts against Shell, Nike and other companies. These movements have also targeted repressive regimes, such as Myanmar's military dictatorship, and shown international solidarity, for example, with the Zapatistas and the Brazilian landless peasants.

In spite of their rapid growth, these movements remain fragmented. Different organisations pursue widely distinct objectives in diverse ways, and occasionally come into conflict with one another. The lack of a common agenda can hamper their ability to challenge established institutions and practices. Several pressure groups, including the environmental, peace, women's, gay, lesbian, anti-racist and animal liberation movements, international solidarity organisations, trade unions, leftist parties and other groups defend their autonomy vigorously, sometimes allowing sectional interests to cloud their mutual complementarity. Despite these limitations, political maturity, organisational flexibility and heavy use of the internet have allowed the new movements to expand. Moreover, they have often been able to transcend the rules, habits and conventions that constrain the NGOs, trade unions, political parties and other institutions on the left. Their recent successes show that there is widespread discontent and fertile ground for the discussion of alternatives, at different levels, around the world.

Continuing confrontation against the neoliberal-globalist project and its destructive implications is inevitable. Perhaps more significantly, it is likely that the anti-capitalist feeling previously channelled through trade unions and political parties of the left has found new outlets. If true, this shift will have important implications for the political landscape.

2   September 11 and Beyond

The growing opposition against the neoliberal-globalist project was temporarily checked by the tragic events of September 11, 2001. In response to those terrorist atrocities, the US government unleashed a loosely targeted state terrorist campaign against millions of people, both at home and abroad. The most important thrust of this strategy has been the so-called 'infinite war' against elusive (but always carefully selected) adversaries. Rather than helping to resolve existing grievances, US state terrorism has provided further excuses for private terrorists around the world to target the United States and its citizens. In our view, all forms of terrorism – whether private, state-sponsored or state-led – are reactionary, repulsive, destructive, criminal and utterly unacceptable.

The so-called 'war on terror' has been rationalised by the naked conflation between the neoliberal-globalist agenda and US imperialism. The global elite (the Washington-based 'international community') has brazenly subordinated international law to US foreign policy interests. It has granted itself a licence to apply unlimited force against unfriendly regimes ('rogue states') or social movements ('terrorist organisations'), either for so-called humanitarian reasons or in order to defeat whatever they decide to call 'terrorism'.[3]

The overwhelming military superiority of the United States allows its government to pound foreign adversaries anywhere, secure in the knowledge that its own casualties will be small and that the damage to the other side will eventually crack the opposition. The wars unleashed by the US and its vassal states against Iraq, in 1990–91, and further military action in Afghanistan, Bosnia, Kosovo, Palestine, Panama, Sierra Leone, Somalia, Sudan and elsewhere have brought important gains to the global elite, not least unprecedented security guarantees for its business interests. However, the cost of these operations is incalculable. Conveniently, the victims are almost invariably dark-skinned and poor. They speak incomprehensible languages and worship lesser gods. They live in intractable troublespots, which they are rarely allowed to leave because (in contrast with their money and goods) they are not welcome abroad. Their fate is of little concern, as long as they ultimately comply with Western geopolitical designs.

The tragedy of September 11 has revealed unexpected limits of neoliberal globalism. The depth of dissatisfaction with Washington's political and economic rule has been exposed, and the claim that trade and financial liberalisation can resolve the world's most pressing problems has suffered a severe blow. The argument that states are powerless against the forces of globalisation has

---

3 See German (2001, pp. 126–127).

been demoralised by the expansionary economic policies adopted in the wake of the attacks, and by the co-ordinated wave of repression unleashed across the world. Repression included not only the restriction of civil liberties, but also refined controls against capital flows and the limitation of property rights, for example, against pharmaceutical patents in the US at the height of the anthrax threat. Finally, important anti-war movements emerged in several countries, especially the UK and – courageously – the US.

In the wake of the tragedy of September 11, the global elite seized the opportunity to open its batteries against all forms of dissent. Amid a rising tide of xenophobia and racism, rabid journalists cried out that anti-corporate protests were also anti-American, and scorned principled objections against the 'war on terror'. Colourful politicians on both sides of the Atlantic, eager to please their masters, even claimed that the new protest movements share the same objectives as Osama Bin Laden.[4]

Difficulties such as these bring to the fore the need for clarity of objectives and careful selection of targets when campaigning against important features or consequences of modern capitalism. Unless our objectives are clear and the instruments appropriate, we will be unable to achieve our goals, at great cost to ourselves and the world.

Four issues play critical roles in the analysis of contemporary capitalism and, consequently, in the search for alternatives: neoliberalism, globalisation, corporate power and democracy. It is to them that we now turn.

3   Four Pressing Issues

3.1   *Neoliberalism*

In the last twenty years, for the first time in history, there has been a concerted attempt to implement a single worldwide economic policy, under the guise of neoliberalism. The IMF, the World Bank, the US Treasury Department and, more recently, the European Central Bank, have strongly campaigned for neo-liberalism, and they have sternly advised countries everywhere to abide by their commands. In this endeavour, they have been supported by the main-stream media, prestigious intellectuals, bankers, industrialists, landowners, speculators and opportunists vying for profits in every corner of the globe.

---

4 'G7 activists no better than Bin Laden' (*London Evening Standard,* November 5, 2001). Similar claims were reportedly made by US Representative Don Young, US Trade Representative
   Robert Zoellick and Italian Prime Minister Berlusconi, among others (Karliner 2001).

The spread of neoliberalism is due to several factors. They include the rise of conservative political forces in the US, UK and other countries, and the growing influence of mainstream theory within economics, both in its traditional form and through new institutionalism.[5] The forward march of neoliberalism was facilitated by the perceived failure of Keynesianism in the rich countries, developmentalism in poor ones, and the collapse of the Soviet bloc. Finally, the US government has leaned heavily on the IMF, the World Bank, the United Nations and the WTO to promote neoliberal policies everywhere. Pressure by these organisations has validated the increasing use of aid, debt relief and foreign investment as tools with which to extract policy reforms from foreign governments.

Neoliberal policies are based on three premises. First, the dichotomy between markets and the state. Neoliberalism presumes that the state and the market are distinct and mutually exclusive institutions, and that one expands only at the expense of the other. Second, it claims that markets are efficient, whereas states are wasteful and economically inefficient. Third, it argues that state intervention creates systemic economic problems, especially resource misallocation, rent-seeking behaviour and technological backwardness.

These premises imply that certain economic policies are 'naturally' desirable. They include, first, rolling back the state in order to institute 'free markets', for example, through privatisation and deregulation of economic activity. Second, tight fiscal and monetary policies, including tax reforms and expenditure cuts, in order to control inflation and limit the scope for state intervention. Third, import liberalisation and devaluation of the exchange rate, to promote specialisation according to comparative advantage, stimulate exports and increase competition in the domestic market. Fourth, liberalisation of capital flows, to attract foreign capital and increase domestic capacity to consume and invest. Fifth, liberalisation of the domestic financial system, to increase savings and the rate of return on investment. Sixth, labour market flexibility, to increase the level of employment. Seventh, overhauling the legal system, in order to create or protect property rights. Eighth, political democracy, not in order to safeguard freedom and human rights but, primarily, to dilute state power and reduce the ability of the majority to influence economic policy.

It has been obvious for many years that these policies are successful only exceptionally, even in their own terms. Economic performance during the last twenty years, in rich and poor countries alike, has been disappointing, with growth rates usually lagging behind those in the preceding (Keynesian) period. Poverty levels have not declined significantly, if at all; inequality within and

---

5   See Fine, Lapavitsas and Pincus (2001).

between countries has increased substantially; large capital flows have been associated with currency crises, and the fêted economic transition in the former Soviet bloc has been an abysmal failure (at least for the majority). Neoliberals invariably claim that these disasters show the need for further reform. However, it is equally logical, and more reasonable, to conclude that the neoliberal reforms share much of the blame for the dismal economic performance in rich as well as poor countries.

The above conclusion is reinforced by five theoretical arguments.[6] First, neoliberal reforms introduce policies that destroy large numbers of jobs and entire industries, tautologically deemed to be 'inefficient', whilst relying on the battered patient to generate healthy alternatives through the presumed efficacy of market forces. This strategy rarely works. The depressive impact of the elimination of traditional industries is generally not compensated by the rapid development of new ones, leading to structural unemployment, growing poverty and marginalisation, and to a tighter balance of payments constraint in the afflicted countries.

Second, neoliberal faith on the market contradicts even elementary principles of neoclassical economic theory. For example, in their 'second best analysis', developed half a century ago, Lipsey and Lancaster demonstrate that, if an economy departs from the perfectly competitive ideal on several counts (as all economies invariably do), the removal of one 'imperfection' may not make it more efficient. Therefore, even mainstream economic theory can explain why neoliberal reforms can be worse than useless.

Third, the presumption that the market is virtuous while the state is wasteful, corrupt and inefficient is simply wrong. This false dichotomy is often employed in order to justify state intervention on behalf of capital (for example, privatisation and the curtailment of trade union rights facilitate capitalist abuse, consumer 'fleecing' and the increased exploitation of the workforce). In fact, states and markets are both imperfect and inseparable. They include many different types of institutions, whose borders cannot always be clearly distinguished. For example, the inland revenue service, financial services regulatory agencies, accounting and consultancy firms and state-owned and private banks are inextricably linked to one another, but the precise nature of their relationship is necessarily circumstantial.

Fourth, economic policies normally do not involve unambiguous choices between state and markets but, rather, choices between different forms of interaction between institutions in both spheres. Privatisation, for example,

---

6   See Arestis and Sawyer (1998) and Fine and Stoneman (1996), on which this section draws, and the references therein.

may not imply a retreat of the state or even increased efficiency. The outcome depends on the firm, its output, management and strategy, the form of privatisation, the regulatory framework, the strength and form of competition, and other factors.

Fifth, developed markets arise *only* through state intervention. The state establishes the institutional and regulatory framework for market transactions, including property rights and law enforcement. It regulates the provision of infrastructure, ensures that a healthy, trained and pliant workforce is available, and controls social conflict. The state establishes and regulates professional qualifications and the accounting conventions, and develops a system of tax collection, transfers and expenditures that influences the development of markets, firm performance, and employment patterns. Since capitalist economies rely heavily and necessarily on state institutions, attempts to measure the degree of state intervention are simply misguided. What *really* matters is the gains and losses for each type of state policy, and the implementation of purposeful and co-ordinated policies.

This approach to markets and states does not deny the Marxian claim that the state is 'a committee for managing the common affairs of the whole bourgeoisie'[7] or that it is 'an essentially capitalist machine ... the state of the capitalists, the ideal collective body of all capitalists'.[8] The reasons are easy to understand. First, the state is *constitutionally* committed to capitalism by custom and law, and state institutions are geared towards, and have been historically shaped by the development of markets, wage employment and profit-making activities. Second, the staffing and policy priorities of the state institutions are heavily influenced by the interest groups represented in and through them, where capital tends to be hegemonic. Third, the reproduction of the state relies heavily on the fortunes of capital, because state revenue depends upon the profitability of enterprise and the level of employment. Fourth, the economic and political power of the capitalists, and their influence upon culture, language and habits, is overwhelming, especially in democratic societies. Although the commodification of votes, state control of the media and the imposition of openly ideological selection criteria for state officials are usually associated with the strong-arm tactics of African chiefs and Latin American landlords, they are nowhere more prominent than in the United States.

In conclusion, economic policy and its effects are both context-dependent *and* structured by the needs of capital. On the one hand, pressure for or against specific policies *can be effective*, and the ensuing policy choices *can* improve

---

7   Marx and Engels (1998, p. 12).

8   Engels (1998, p. 352).

significantly the living conditions of the majority. On the other hand, these potential successes are limited. When faced with 'unacceptable' policies, the capitalists will refuse to invest, employ, produce and pay taxes; they will trigger balance of payments crises, cripple the government, paralyse the state and hold the workers to ransom. And they will not hesitate to resort to violence to defend their power and privileges. History abundantly shows that most state institutions, including the police and the armed forces, will rally around the moneyed interests and seek to protect them against challenges from below.

3.2   *Globalisation*

'Hyper-globalism' is the international face of neoliberalism. During the 1990s, analysts and pundits stridently claimed that developments in technology, communications, culture, ideology, finance, production, migration and the environment have modified the world beyond recognition. Drawing on these superficial insights, the 'hyper-globalists' argue that globalisation entails the supremacy of international over domestic institutions, the decline of state power, and the relentless domination of social life by global markets.[9]

Neoliberals have been at the forefront of the hyper-globalist assault. Most neoliberals proclaim both the virtues and the inevitability of the coming world market for everything (except labour, to be kept caged behind borders). They argue that markets ought to reign unimpeded by national legislation and meddling international organisations and, implausibly, claim that policy subordination to *global* imperatives is essential for *national* welfare.

Hyper-globalist views have been discredited by a range of critical studies. These studies show, first, that global integration builds upon, rather than denies, the existence of nation states, which remain the seat of legitimacy and political and economic power. Rather than withering away because of the penetration of TNCs, vast international capital flows and the weight of international treaties, the critics have argued that powerful states promote international integration in pursuit of their own agendas, especially improved competitive positions for home capital in key business areas. Second, global neoliberalism has been associated with undesirable outcomes, including increasing poverty and inequality, the debasement of democracy and the erosion of the welfare state, to the benefit of powerful corporations and financial interests. Third, the critical literature claims that globalisation is neither new nor overwhelming. It was preceded by similar episodes, especially before World War 1; it is not truly 'global', being largely restricted to trade and investment flows between developed countries and, even in this restricted sphere, capital is not 'free' to

---

9   This section draws on the critical surveys by Radice (2000) and Fine (2001a).

move at will; finally, in spite of appearances to the contrary, the net macroeconomic effect of trade and financial liberalisation is often very small. Fourth, the critics argue that the hyper-globalists conflate 'global' markets with the theoretical construct of perfect competition, characterised by perfect information and costless capital mobility. This confusion provides ideological cover for pro-business policies and for aggressive state intervention to foster private capital accumulation.

These critiques of hyper-globalism have led to three policy conclusions, which may or may not be mutually compatible. Some have argued for 'localisation', or the decentralisation of the world economy with increasing reliance on local production and exchange. Others have emphasised the need to democratise policy-making, including an increased role for sector-specific trade and industrial policy and national controls on capital flows. Yet others have pursued 'internationalisation', or the reform and revitalisation of international institutions (the UN, IMF, World Bank, WTO, EU, ECB, and so on), in order to promote the positive aspects of globalisation.[10]

Unfortunately, there are severe problems with each of these alternatives. 'Localisation' promotes small capital vis-à-vis large capital, represented by TNCs. This can be analytically misguided, because it ignores the close relationship that often exists between large and small firms. For example, small firms often cluster around and supply parts and other inputs to large firms, provide cleaning and maintenance services, and so on. Their relationship can be so close as to render 'separation' between these firms impossible. Moreover, small firms tend to be financially fragile, lack the resources for technical innovation and the adoption of new technologies developed elsewhere, cannot supply large markets, and often treat their workforce more harshly than large firms. Finally, curbing the TNCs will inevitably reduce the availability of important commodities across the globe, including foodstuffs, electronic appliances and industrial machinery.

Attempts to 'recover' industrial policy for progressive ends can be successful; however, misguided policies can be useless and even counter-productive. Finally, 'internationalisation' is utopian. Most international institutions are firmly under the grip of the neoliberal-globalist elites, and it is unrealistic to expect that control can be wrestled from them. In most cases, these institutions ought to be abolished, to be replaced, when necessary, by alternatives designed from scratch.

The insufficiencies of these critiques of hyper-globalism are often due to the misguided opposition between the global, national and local spheres.

---

10   For a similar analysis, see Callinicos (2001).

This separation mirrors that between markets and states, discussed above. In general, those spheres should not be contrasted as if they were mutually exclusive, because they constitute one another and can be understood only through their mutual relationship.

Specifically, the presumption that the local and national economies are the building blocs of the global economy is misguided. The so-called 'global' economy is nothing but the commuters daily going to the Manhattan financial district and the City of London, manual workers clocking into position in the Ruhr, English-speaking call-centre workers cycling to their jobs in Mumbai, stevedores working in Maputo, and hundreds of millions of workers producing for people living in distant lands, and consuming not only locally produced goods but also commodities produced elsewhere. In this sense, there is little difference between domestic and cross-border economic transactions, and economic growth necessarily encompasses the simultaneous development of the local, national *and* global economies. In fact, there are reasons to believe, first, that important aspects of production and finance have always been 'international'. Second, long-distance trade has been *more* important for social and economic development than exchanges between neighbours. Third, capitalism originally developed neither in a single country nor in discrete regions, but locally, regionally and internationally *at the same time*.

Terms like 'globalisation' or the 'internationalisation of production and finance', on their own, are simply *devoid of meaning*. Capital is neither national nor international; it is a relationship between people that appears as things or money. Consequently, there is nothing intrinsically national *or* international about capitalist institutions, production or practices. Detailed studies have shown, for example, that 'globalisation' is not a homogeneous, unidirectional and inevitable process taking place between neatly separated national economies. Globalisation does not tend to 'eliminate' the nation state, and recent developments in production, finance, culture, the environment and so on are profoundly different from one another and must be analysed separately. What is often called 'globalisation' is, in fact, a set of more or less interlocking processes, some of which articulated systemically and others largely contingent, moving in different speeds and directions across different areas of the world economy. Some of these processes tend to erode national states and local identities, while other reinforce them.

Wholesale support *or* challenges to 'globalisation' are profoundly misguided (for example, it makes no sense for a *global* protest movement to be called 'anti-globalisation'). What matters, at the local, national *and* global levels, is what is produced and how, by whom, and for whose benefit. In the early twenty-first century, as in the mid-nineteenth century, the distances between people matter less than the relationships between them. Similarly, geography remains less important than the social structures of control and exploitation that bind people together within cities, between regions, and across the world.

3.3   *Corporate Power*

The new 'anti-capitalist' movements are famously critical of the large corporations, especially TNCs. This section argues that the market power and political influence of TNCs raise important ethical and economic questions. However, TNCs are not new, and their recent expansion is not the harbinger of fundamental changes in the economic and political landscape. Therefore, it would be misguided to try to turn them into the main focus of resistance.

Several commentators sympathetic to the new movements claim that one of the most important problems of contemporary capitalism is the excessive tilting of power towards the large corporations. The causes and implications of this process are usually left unexamined, although they are presumably related to neoliberalism and globalisation. It is also left unclear what should be done about it, other than imposing unspecified curbs against corporate power.

This is clearly insufficient. Arguments along those lines are often fruitless because they are not based on a consistent theory of the state and its relationship to the corporations, and on a theory of monopoly power and capitalist behaviour, without which corporate practices cannot be understood. For example, although it is right to claim that the state is controlled by capitalist interests and forces (see above), it is wrong to ascribe boundless power to specific groups or interests, such as the TNCs, financiers, landlords or foreign capitalists. No social group can exist in isolation, and none exercises unlimited power.

Let us analyse in more detail the claim that 'large firms' control production, exchange, distribution and the political process. This view is incorrect for four reasons. First, it artificially disassembles capital into 'large' and 'small' units (see above). Second, it suggests that small firms, such as tiny grocery stores, family-owned newsagents and small farms conform more closely to local interests, as if they were independent of the large firms which they represent and that provide them with inputs and markets, and as if small firms were renowned for their promotion of employee interests. Third, it erroneously implies that the evils of capitalism are due to the large firms only, and that these wrongs can be put right by anti-monopoly legislation and domestic market protection against foreign firms. Fourth, this view misrepresents 'competitive capitalism', as if it had actually existed at some idyllic point in the past. In this idealised image of Victorian capitalism, unsightly features such as poverty, imperialism, slavery, genocide and the forces that transformed 'competitive' into 'monopoly' capitalism are arbitrarily expunged.

Sleights of hand such as these, and the lack of a theory of capital, the state, competition and monopoly power, explain the coexistence of critiques of corporate practices with pathetic apologias of capitalism. For example, in the words of a well-known critic of 'globalisation':

> My argument is not intended to be anti-capitalist. Capitalism is clearly the best system for generating wealth, and free trade and open capital markets have brought unprecedented economic growth for most if not all of the world. Nor is ... [it] anti-business ... [U]nder certain market conditions, business is more able and willing than government to take on many of the world's problems ... I mean to question the moral justification for a brand of capitalism ... in which we cannot trust governments to look after our interests in which unelected powers – big corporations – are taking over governments' roles.
>
> HERTZ (2001, p. 10)

This approach is profoundly misguided. The outrageous behaviour of large corporations, from the East India Company to Microsoft, and from ITT to Monsanto, is not primarily due to their size, greed, or the support of states that they have hijacked at some mysterious point in time. Corporate practices and monopoly power are due to the forces of *competition*. By the same token, our collective addiction to McChickens and corporate logos is not simply due to the crude manipulation of our desires by brutish TNCs. Corporate behaviour, and its welfare implications, is ultimately rooted in the dominance of a system of production geared towards *private profit* rather than *collective need*.

3.4   Democracy

Several critics have recently highlighted the increasing emasculation of democracy, the erosion of citizenship and the declining accountability of the state even in 'advanced' democratic societies. These processes are often blamed on the capture of the state by corporate and other interest groups. However, this view is misleading, and the explanation is inadequate.

This section briefly reviews the relationship between the state, capital, the political regime and economic policy. Along with most of the literature, it claims that political freedom is immensely valuable, and that the spread of democracy across the world has been possible only through the diffusion of capitalism. However, this section also shows that *capitalism necessarily limits democracy*, and that the expansion of democracy into critically important areas of life requires the *abolition* of capitalism.[11]

---

11   For a detailed analysis, see Wood (1981).

A remarkable distinction between pre-capitalist and capitalist societies is the separation, in the latter, between the 'economic' and 'political' spheres. This separation means that, under capitalism, 'economic' processes – including the production, exchange and distribution of goods and services, the compulsion to work and the exploitation of the workers – are generally carried out 'impersonally', through market mechanisms. It is completely different in pre-capitalist societies. In these societies, economic processes are directly subordinated to political authority, including both personal command and state power, and they generally follow rules based on hierarchy, tradition and religious duty.

The separation between the economic and political spheres has three important implications. First, it constitutes a separate 'political' sphere. For the first time in history, the owners of the means of production are relieved from public duty, which becomes the preserve of state officials. The separation of the political sphere establishes the potential and limits of state intervention in the economy, including the scope of economic policy and the possibility of 'autonomous' political change, with no direct implication for the 'economic' order. The substance and degree of democracy is a case in point (see below).

Second, separation entrenches capitalist power within the 'economic' sphere. Manifestations of economic power include the ownership and control of means of production (the factories, buildings, land, machines, tools and other equipment and materials necessary for the production of goods and services), the right to control the production process and discipline the workforce, and the ability to exploit the workers.

Third, the separation between the economic and political spheres is relative rather than absolute. On the one hand, the 'political' power of the state and the 'economic' power of the capitalists may lead to conflict, for example, over the conditions of work, the minimum wage, pension provisions and environmental regulations. On the other hand, we have already seen that modern states are essentially *capitalist*. Experience shows that the state will intervene directly both in 'political' conflicts (e.g., the scope of democratic rights) and in purely 'economic' disputes (for example, pay and conditions in large industries), if state officials believe that their own rule or the reproduction of capital are being unduly challenged. When intervening, the state relies on the power of the law, the police and, *in extremis*, the armed forces.

The existence of a separate political sphere, explained above, implies that capitalism is compatible with political (formal or procedural) democracy. Political democracy includes the rule of law, party-political pluralism, free and regular elections, freedom of the press, respect for human rights, and other institutions and practices that are essential for the consolidation of human freedom.

However, capitalism *necessarily* limits the scope for freedom because it is inimical to *economic* (substantive) democracy. These limits are imposed by the capitalist monopoly over the economic sphere, explained above. For example, the franchise and political debate are not generally allowed to 'interfere' with the ownership and management of the production units and, often, even with the composition of output and the patterns and conditions of employment, in spite of their enormous importance for social welfare. In other words, even though political campaigns can achieve important transformations in the property rights and work practices, the scope for democratic intervention in the economic sphere is always limited.

The limits of capitalist democracy come into view, for example, when attempts to expand political control over the social affairs are constrained by the lack of economic democracy – typically, when governments or mass movements attempt to modify property rights by constitutional means. The resulting clashes were among the main causes of the defeat of the Spanish Republic, the overthrow of Chilean president Salvador Allende and, less conspicuously but equally significantly, the failure of attempted land reforms across Latin America. Mass movements attempting to shift property rights by legal means but against the interests of the state have also been crushed repeatedly, in many countries. In these clashes, the success of the conservative forces often depends upon the arbitrary limitation of political democracy. This implies that political democracy is rarely able to challenge successfully the economic power of the capitalist class (embodied in their 'core' property rights). This is not a matter of choice: *the advance of political democracy is permanently limited by the lack of economic democracy.*

Tensions between economic and political democracy generally surface through the ebb and flow of political democracy and civil rights. These tensions are nowhere more visible than in the 'developing' countries. In recent years, multi-party democracy and universal suffrage have been extended across the world, the repressive powers of the state have been curtailed by the UN and the International Court of Justice, and by the precedents established by the Pinochet affair and the prosecution of officials of the former Rwandan government.

In spite of these important advances, the forward march of political democracy has been severely hampered by the exclusion of economic matters from legitimate debate. The imposition of neoliberalism across the world is the most important cause of these limitations. Because of neoliberalism, worldwide policy-making capacity has been increasingly concentrated in Washington and in Wall Street, leaving only matters of relatively minor importance open for debate, both in 'developing' and developed countries.

Specifically, in the 'newly democratic' states of Latin America, sub-Saharan Africa and Southeast Asia the transitions towards political democracy were generally conditional upon compromises that ruled out substantive shifts in social and economic power. Even more perversely, in these countries *the imposition of neoliberal policies often depended upon the democratic transition.* After several decades attempting to subvert democratic governments and shore up dictatorships across the globe, the US government and most local elites have realised that *democratic* states can follow diktats from Washington and impose policies inimical to economic democracy more easily and reliably than most dictatorships. This is due to the greater *political legitimacy* of formally democratic governments.

This argument can be put in another way. Repression is often necessary in order to extract the resources required to service the foreign debt, shift development towards narrow comparative advantage and support parasitical industrial and financial systems. However, dictatorships can rarely impose the level of repression necessary to implement neoliberal policies. This is something that only democratic states can do successfully, because *their greater legitimacy allows them to ignore popular pressure for longer* (however, the recent upheavals in Argentina show that this strategy is also limited).

In this sense, the neoliberal-globalist project involves a fundamental inconsistency: it requires *inclusive* political systems to enforce *excluding* economic policies. These policies demand states hostile to the majority, even though democratic states are supposedly responsive to democratic pressure. As a result, we see across the world the diffusion of *formally democratic* but *highly repressive* states. We also see the perpetuation of social exclusion and injustice, in spite of political pluralism and the consolidation of democratic institutions in many countries.

'Democratic neoliberalism' has consolidated *economic apartheid* both within and between countries. Economic apartheid includes the increasing concentration of income and wealth, the segregation of the upper classes in residential, work and leisure enclosures, their unwillingness and inability to interact with the poor in most spheres of social and civic life, the diffusion of organised and heavily armed criminal gangs, and unbridled corruption in state institutions.

Economic apartheid and the evacuation of economic democracy can be at least partly reversed through successful mass struggles. These struggles can limit the power of industrial and financial interests, and open the possibility of policy alternatives leading to improvements in the living conditions of the majority. However, democracy can be extended into critically important spheres of life *only* if the capitalist monopoly over the economic sphere is abolished.

In this sense, the success of the struggle depends on the extent to which the democratic movement becomes *anti-capitalist*.

4   The Way Ahead

The previous section has shown that we should not expect significant transformations of contemporary capitalism through appeals for the restoration of state power, the reform of international institutions, campaigns for corporate responsibility or the expansion of formal democracy. Reforms are certainly possible in these and in other areas, and they can increase greatly the power and influence of the majority. However, these reforms are always limited and, even if successful, they will be permanently at risk because they fail to address the root cause of the problems of contemporary capitalism.

Strategic success depends on four conditions. First, *holism*. Successful challenges against different forms of discrimination, 'shallow' democracy, the inequities of debt, the destructive effects of trade and capital flows, environmental degradation, corporate irresponsibility, and so on, require the consolidation of sectoral struggles into a single mass movement against the global rule of capital – the root cause of these wrongs.

Second, whilst the movement ought to remain *international*, it should focus its energies in the *national* terrain. This is only partly because the potential efficacy of the struggle is maximised at this level (it is much harder to mobilise successfully in the international sphere). It is also because national states play an essential role in the choice and implementation of economic policy, the operation of markets and the limitation of corporate power. Moreover, 'global capitalism' is organised primarily nationally, and its actors (TNCs, international organisations, global markets, and so on) depend heavily upon state promotion and regulation.

It was shown above that *there is no such thing as global capitalism* independently of national states and local workers and capitalists. By the same token, the most effective means of influencing 'global' developments is by exercising pressure upon national states. In fact, it is because the national states are the critical and, at the same time, the weakest link in the 'global economy' that capital endlessly repeats the myth that globalisation renders the state powerless and irrelevant.[12]

Third, the movement should develop further the *ability to mobilise large numbers of people by non-traditional means*, and pursue innovative forms of struggle.

---

12   See Wood (2002).

Fourth, the growth of the movement depends heavily upon its ability to *incorporate the immediate concerns* of the majority. They includes issues related to unemployment and overwork, low pay, lack of employment security and rights in the workplace, the degradation of heavily populated environments, the provision of public health, sanitation and clean and efficient transport and energy, and so on. Success also requires closer attention to the *workplace*, which is the basis of capitalist domination and economic power. Unity between economic and political struggles, and challenges against both capital and the state, especially through mass confrontation against *state economic policy* and its consequences, are important conditions for growth and victory.[13]

Fifth, given the limits of political democracy and state power, the achievement of equality and the elimination of poverty and exploitation within and between countries demands *transcendence*, or the abolition of capitalism. These conclusions are explained and substantiated by every essay in this book.

5   Leaving Capitalism Behind

Social reformers, utopian socialists, anarchists, social democrats, Marxists and many others have questioned the legitimacy and desirability of capitalism for at least two centuries. However, it is beyond dispute that Marxism provides the basis for the most comprehensive and critique of this social and economic system, including the development of the radical alternative to capitalism: communism. The Marxist analysis of transcendence can be divided into two areas, the critique of capitalism and the importance of communism.

Several problems of contemporary capitalism have been discussed above and, in each case, the root cause of these problems and the limits to their potential solution under capitalism were highlighted. Some of these problems can be remedied within the current system, for example, the erosion of political democracy, lack of corporate responsibility, and absolute poverty. In contrast, other problems cannot be resolved, because they are *features* of capitalism; among them, unemployment, exploitation of the workforce, economic

---

13   Barker (2001, p. 333) rightly argues that 'Putting a brick through the window of Starbucks is a moral gesture, but an ineffective one. Organising Starbucks workers is harder, but more effective – and hurts the Starbucks bosses more ... We need to focus on people's lives as producers and not simply as consumers – for there is a power in producers' hands that consumer boycotts can never match. In any case, many consumers can't afford to "choose"'. Isaac Deutscher made a similar point to student activists in the mid-1960s: 'You are effervescently active on the margin of social life, and the workers are passive right at the core of it. That is the tragedy of our society. If you do not deal with this contrast, you will be defeated' (cited in Wood 1988, p. 4).

inequality, the encroachment of work upon free time, systematic environmental degradation, the lack of economic democracy, and production for profit rather than need. Problems such as these can be, at best, concealed by propaganda and mitigated by economic prosperity.

Marxists claim that the limitations of capitalism can be eliminated only through the institution of another form of social organisation, communism. The misrepresentation of communism in the past two centuries cannot be put right in this book. However, three comments are in order. First, communism should not be confused with the political system associated with the USSR or China.[14] Second, communism is neither inexorable nor unavoidable. Capitalism will change and, ultimately, be displaced, only if overwhelming pressure is applied by the majority. Failing that, capitalism may persist indefinitely, in spite of its rising human and environmental costs. Third, communism is neither an earthly version of paradise, nor the 'end of history'. Quite the contrary: communism marks the end of the *prehistory* of human society. Communism will eliminate the socially created constraints of poverty, drudgery, exploitation, environmental degradation, and other limitations currently caused by the manic search for profit. Removal of these constraints will allow history to *begin*, because human beings will, finally, free themselves from the dictatorship of moneyed interests, destitution due to large-scale property, and inequality engendered by wealth and privileged upbringing. *Economic equality is essential for political equality*, thus allowing everyone to become a valued member of a truly open society.

The struggle against capitalism is part and parcel of the struggle for democracy in society and in the workplace, against profit and privilege, and for equality of opportunity for everyone. These are the struggles that define the new movements, but taken to their logical consequence.

---

14   See Chattopadhyay (1994).

CHAPTER 10

Neoliberalism

Neoliberalism[1] (also spelled neo-liberalism) defies simple definition. In the Marxian literature, it has been understood in four closely related ways: as a set of *ideas* inspired by the Austrian and Chicago schools of economics and German Ordoliberalism and elaborated under the umbrella of the Mont Pèlerin Society; as a set of *policies, institutions and practices* inspired and/or validated by those ideas; as a *class offensive against the workers and the poor*, led by the state on behalf of the bourgeoisie in general or finance in particular; and as a *material structure of social, economic and political reproduction*, in which case neoliberalism is the mode of existence of contemporary capitalism or a system of accumulation.

The differences between these understandings of neoliberalism are symptomatic of the distinct methodologies and viewpoints within contemporary Marxism, their relationship with influential non-Marxist approaches in the social sciences, and the complexity of neoliberalism itself. From a Marxian perspective, these analytical tensions can be felt at three closely related levels.

First, all neoliberal experiences share significant commonalities; some are relatively abstract and universal, for example the growing power of finance and the curtailment of political democracy, while others are relatively concrete and (country-)specific, such as privatisation and the spread of non-governmental organisations into areas that, previously, were the domain of state institutions. While these commonalities imply that neoliberalism cannot be adequately described in purely contextual terms, they are also insufficiently general or historically distinctive to define a new mode of production. Inevitably, then, analyses of neoliberalism straddle across levels of abstraction within capitalism, including (some understanding of) such basic concepts in Marxist theory as the commodity, value and labor power all the way to conjunctural description, by way of specific understandings of exploitation, class, competition, price formation, finance, the state and international trade.

Second, Marxist analyses are by definition systemic, and seek to encompass the economic, sociological, institutional, political, legal, cultural, ideological and other aspects of neoliberalism. This necessarily includes how, why and to what extent the neoliberal 'reforms' have transformed economic and social

---

1   Originally published as: 'Neoliberalism', in D.M. Brennan, D. Kristjanson-Gural, C. Mulder, E. Olsen (eds.) *The Routledge Handbook of Marxian Economics*. London: Routledge, 2017.

reproduction after the disarticulation of the Keynesian-social democratic compact in the leading capitalist economies, the paralysis of developmentalism, the implosion of the Soviet bloc, the dramatic transformations in China and the crises in the European periphery. This historically grounded and interdisciplinary approach is both superior to and incompatible with the narrow focus provided by most traditional disciplines in the social sciences. Among its many advantages, it allows Marxist explanations to offer more comprehensive and logically coherent explanations of the origins of neoliberalism and its recurrent crises than rival interpretations can provide. Nevertheless, the contributions of those social science disciplines inevitably remain influential in the background. This helps to explain the distinct conceptualisations of the key features of neoliberalism observed in the Marxist literature and the diverse understandings of their articulation and relations of determination. It follows that Marxist analyses can more or less legitimately reach very different conclusions about the vitality of contemporary capitalism, its vulnerability to crisis, the scope for electoral politics, the feasibility of radical alternatives, and so on.

Third, while the schematic depiction of the key ideas underpinning neoliberalism can plausibly eschew the domain of the 'international' by focusing, instead, on the realm of ideas or the description of stylised institutions, actually existing neoliberal experiences are completely inseparable from highly complex global processes, especially imperialism and globalisation. From this angle, too, neoliberalism cannot be encapsulated into a soundbite: it can neither be defined purely conceptually, nor captured inductively through the description of historical experiences.

Identification of these analytical difficulties can help to contextualise the Marxist understandings of neoliberalism identified above; it can also support claims for the potential superiority of Marxist views over rival explanations of neoliberalism. For example, while Marxist analyses are necessarily systemic, class-based and nested on a grand theory (in the sense of Mills 1959), competing interpretations tend to be either middle-range or descriptive, unsystematic and (sometimes despite appearances to the contrary, as in many varieties of Keynesianism) methodologically individualist.

1   Neoliberal Ideas

As a system of ideas, neoliberalism draws upon the contributions of a wide spectrum of variously talented, frequently inconsistent and sometimes spectacularly cantankerous writers, including Friedrich von Hayek, Ludwig von Mises, Wilhelm Röpke, Ludwig Erhard, Milton Friedman, James Buchanan,

Gary Becker and Ayn Rand (Burgin 2012; Cahill 2014; Dardot and Laval 2013; Mirowski and Plehwe 2009; Stedman Jones 2012).

They argue, in profoundly dissimilar ways, that differently endowed property-owning individuals exchanging goods, services and (in certain cases) information in minimally regulated markets can allocate resources more efficiently than either democratic processes or state guidance. Their arguments seek to legitimise extreme versions of free-market capitalism, and they have frequently promoted US geopolitical interests either directly or indirectly. Unsurprisingly, they were welcomed by powerful interests. Many contributors to the neoliberal literature benefitted from substantial economic, political and institutional support received from private as well as public sources, which unquestionably enhanced the public visibility and political impact of their interventions (Birch and Mykhnenko 2010).

This propitious milieu nurtured several lines of criticism of Soviet-style socialism, Keynesianism, developmentalism and 'excessive' democracy since the mid-twentieth century. They were loosely co-ordinated through the Mont Pèlerin Society and the extensive networks of academic institutions, think tanks and *faux* 'grassroots' associations established by the neoliberal lobby (Mirowski 2009). Some of those views were precariously articulated with a rapidly expanding body of neoclassical economic theory in the 1950s-60s through monetarism. After the disintegration of monetarism in the 1980s, in the wake of the failure of Friedmanite ideas to inspire effective policy-making in several advanced economies, and the inability of monetarist writers to address the criticisms addressed to them, neoliberal ideas were strapped more or less awkwardly to different versions of 'supply-side' and new classical economics, new Keynesianism and new institutionalism (Fine, Lapavitsas and Pincus 2001; Fine and Milonakis 2009; Milonakis and Fine 2009). In the late 1990s, similar ideas were recycled in social democratic garb through the so-called Third Way, which was described in the Marxist literature as a position akin to 'neoliberalism with a human face'.

Closer examination reveals considerable tensions between the theories underpinning neoliberalism. For example, while the Austrian school emphasises the inventive and transformative subjectivity of the individual and the spontaneous emergence of an increasingly efficient order beyond individual reason through market processes, neoclassical economics focuses on the efficiency properties of a static equilibrium achieved entirely in the logical domain on the basis of unchanging individuals, resources and technologies. Neither captures the political economy and moral philosophy associated with Adam Smith, despite an obsessive recourse to (different interpretations of) the 'invisible hand' (see Fine and Saad-Filho 2014 and Chapter 14). In turn, the inconsistencies of

monetarism had been exposed in merciless detail by Marxist and other heterodox economists even before 'early' neoliberal policymakers admitted their
inability to identify or control the money supply and deliver macroeconomic
stability and growth in the 1980s. Finally, the Third Way was analytically vacu-
ous, and its fleeting renown was predicated on political opportunism and the
wilful abandonment of intellectual integrity. It dissolved into irrelevance faster
than one could spell 'triangulation' (a badge of political expediency rendered
temporarily famous by US President Bill Clinton and UK Prime Minister Tony
Blair) (Callinicos 2001).

The inconsistencies and policy failures associated with neoliberalism
would swiftly have condemned rival heterodoxies to oblivion. In sharp contrast, the institutional sources of support available to the neoliberal literature
ensured that it would expand relentlessly from its strongest base in economics
to claim hegemony across a whole spectrum of neighbouring social sciences.
This literature has also promoted a populist understanding of 'competitiveness' and 'democracy' that has been deployed repeatedly, if incoherently, in
order to validate selected policy reforms and repression against the opposition.
In this discourse, competition is presented in the short-termist (Chicagoan)
sense associated with the operation of financial markets (the closest real-
world equivalent to 'perfect competition'), while democracy is circumscribed
to the (Hayekian) view of competition between shades of neoliberalism in the
political markets. The significance of these ideas in the legitimation of the status quo and the neoliberal policy reforms has reinforced an idealist conception
of neoliberalism both within and outside Marxism, in which social organisation essentially derives from pre-existing ideologies. It incorrectly follows (see
below) that social and economic transformation must be driven by ideational
change (Cahill 2013).

2   Policy Shifts and Institutional Changes

Marxist studies have shown that the neoliberal policies implemented through
Reaganism, Thatcherism and the (post-)Washington Consensus are largely
inspired by the Chicago School, and they are supported by five ontological
planks (Saad-Filho and Johnston 2005). First, the dichotomy between markets
and the state, implying that these are rival and mutually exclusive institutions
(significantly, this dichotomy is rejected by the Ordoliberals). Second, the assumption that markets are efficient while state intervention is by definition
wasteful because it distorts prices and misallocates resources (in comparison
with what an ideal market would have done), induces rent-seeking behaviour

and fosters technological backwardness. Third, the belief that technological progress, the liberalisation of finance and capital movements, the systematic pursuit of 'shareholder value' and successive transitions to neoliberalism around the world have created a global economy characterised by rapid capital mobility within and between countries and (an ill-defined process of) 'globalisation'. Where they are embraced, rapid growth ensues through the prosperity of local enterprise and the attraction of foreign capital; in contrast, reluctance or 'excessive' state intervention (however it may be determined) drives capital, employment and economic growth elsewhere (Kiely 2005). Fourth, the presumption that allocative efficiency, macroeconomic stability and output growth are conditional upon low inflation, which is best secured by monetary policy at the expense of fiscal, exchange rate and industrial policy tools. Fifth, the realisation that the operation of key neoliberal macroeconomic policies, including 'liberalised' trade, financial and labor markets, inflation targeting, central bank independence, floating exchange rates and tight fiscal rules is conditional upon the provision of potentially unlimited state guarantees to the financial system, since the latter remains structurally unable to support itself despite its escalating control of social resources under neoliberalism.

Marxist analyses have also shown that the neoliberal policy reforms are usually implemented through a two-stage process (see Fine and Saad-Filho 2014 and Chapter 14). The first (transition or shock) phase of neoliberalism requires forceful state intervention to contain labor, disorganise the left, promote the transnational integration of domestic capital and put in place the new institutional framework. The second (mature) phase focuses on the stabilisation of the social relations imposed in the earlier period, the consolidation of financial sector control of resource allocation, state management of the new modality of international integration of production, and the introduction of specifically neoliberal social policies both to manage the deprivation created by neoliberalism and to reconstitute society along neoliberal lines (see below). All of them require extensive regulation, despite the rhetorical insistence of all manner of neoliberals on the need to 'roll back' the state.

Marxist critiques of these policies and their institutional framework have offered rich insights about the features and repercussions of the neoliberal transition in various countries. However, neoliberalism cannot be reduced to a collection of policies, which would suggest that a multiplicity of discrete policy initiatives might be sufficient to reverse or even transcend neoliberalism. Policy changes are certainly essential, but the scope for such changes can be questioned in the light of the political means available to the left, the strength of the coalitions potentially committed to them, and the scope to drive the required distributional, regulatory and policy reforms given the neoliberal transformation of the state in recent decades. None of these can be adequately assessed without a prior understanding of the systemic features of neoliberalism and the transformations that it has wrought on class relations and institutions and the processes of economic and social reproduction.

3   Classes and Class Struggle

Marxism is intimately wedded to class analysis through its logical structure, historical development and unique commitment to the abolition of capitalism by means of communist revolutions led by the working class. Class analysis has informed Marxian interpretations of neoliberalism in two ways.

On the one hand, Marxian studies of neoliberalism are overtly informed by a class perspective. This explains their focus on the modalities of exploitation emerging through financialisation, globalisation and the neoliberal reforms, including the 'flexibilisation' and intensification of labor, the limitation of wage growth, the rollback of collective bargaining and the changes in the welfare regime and how they have affected the workers, women, minorities, immigrants, and so on. Marxian and closely related analyses have also examined the effects of privatisation and the appropriation of the 'commons' (i.e., areas where property rights were either absent or vested upon the state) (Harvey 2005), and the destructive consequences of the financialisation of social reproduction for the working class (Krippner 2011; Montgomerie 2009). And Marxian analyses have illuminated the destabilising implications of neoliberalism and its propensity to generate macroeconomic crises that penalise disproportionately the working class and the poor (Duménil and Lévy 2011; McNally 2014).

On the other hand, Marxist political economy directly informs political activism by shedding light on the limitations and contradictions of neoliberalism and suggesting how mass action can disrupt the reproduction of neoliberal societies. In doing this, Marxism supports the search for an alternative future in which the vast majority can realise their potential beyond the systemic constraints imposed by the contemporary form of capitalism.

In both cases, Marxian approaches rightly show that analyses of neoliberalism and the conditions for transcendence must take into account the power relations embodied in the structure of society, the state, production, technology, trade and finance. However, taken to the extreme this approach might suggest that neoliberalism is a 'capitalist conspiracy' against the workers, in which case there would be nothing systemic or historically specific about it (since capitalists and the state have always conspired against the workers). Alternatively, they could also be read as implying that 'things were much better' under previous systems of accumulation (Keynesian, developmentalist, and so on), in which case they should, in principle, be restored.

These conclusions would be illegitimate. First, the Marxist literature demonstrates that the key features of neoliberalism are articulated systemically; they were not designed arbitrarily by right-wing political parties, libertarian think tanks or more or less secretive debating societies (Mont Pèlerin, Bilderberg and Davos, among others) and they cannot be unpicked or reversed at will. Second, even if the superiority of previous systems of accumulation in terms of growth, employment or distribution could be demonstrated, this does not imply that they could be revived. After all, there were material reasons behind their decline; moreover, if they were so obviously superior from the point of view of capital the capitalists themselves – currently enjoying much greater power than before – would already have prompted the reversal of history. This implies that neoliberalism offers distinctive advantages to capital beyond reformist demands for growth, full employment or distributional improvements. Finally, and more interesting from a Marxist perspective, there is no reason why the aspirations of the working class should be circumscribed by those earlier systems of accumulation, as if they represented the best of all possible worlds.

4   Neoliberalism, Financialisation and Globalisation

Most Marxist analyses have insisted that financialisation is the defining feature of accumulation under neoliberalism and that it has driven the restructuring of the global economy since the 1970s. Financialisation has been described in different ways, but in essence it expresses the control of interest-bearing capital (IBC) upon the allocation of social resources and social reproduction more generally, through distinct forms of fictitious capital (Fine 2013–14). These processes have been buttressed by extensive institutional transformations expanding and intensifying the influence of finance over the economy, ideology, politics and the state (Duménil and Lévy 2004; Panitch and Gindin 2012).

The prominence of finance under neoliberalism cannot be attributed to a 'distortion' of pre-existing competitive or industrial capitalism or to a financial sector 'coup' against productive capital, as if finance were an independent sector that, in the late 1970s, managed to wriggle itself into a lording position over capitals which it must, ultimately, also be parasitical upon. For finance is not merely the pool of liquid capital held by the financial institutions, standing in opposition to the 'real' (productive) capital metaphorically stuck to the ground.

In neoliberal economies, transnationally integrated finance controls the allocation of resources, including the volume and composition of output and investment, the structure of demand, the level and structure of employment, the financing of the state, the exchange rate and the pattern of international specialisation, and it restructures capital, labor, society and the state accordingly. As such, *finance has become the mode of existence of capital in general*, and its prominence expresses the subsumption of sectoral capitals by (the interests of) capital as a whole. These are both expressed and imposed through the regular operation of the financial markets, and through the institutions, rules and ideas attached to them. In policy terms, the prominence of finance implies that accumulation is not regulated by contingent sectoral coalitions but by the capitalist *class*. It also follows that there is no 'antagonism' between production and finance under neoliberalism, and there should be no expectation that industrial capital might 'rebel' against finance and push for the restoration of old systems of accumulation. Quite the opposite: industrial capital has become structurally embedded into IBC, and it reproduces itself according to the financial logic of the system of accumulation (Rude 2005; Panitch and Konings 2008; Saad-Filho 2008 and 2011).

The structurally dominant position of finance under neoliberalism has supported the development of a whole array of instruments of fictitious capital, the expansion of purely speculative activities and the explosive growth of rewards to high-ranking capitalists and managers in every sector, especially finance itself, funded by a rising rate of exploitation. Financialisation has also driven the restructuring of production through the transnationalisation of circuits of accumulation, which is commonly described as 'globalisation'.

These developments have recomposed the previous 'national' systems of provision at a higher level of productivity at firm level, created new global(ised) production chains connected through transnational patterns of ownership, finance and circulation of the output, reshaped the country-level integration of the world economy, and facilitated the introduction of new technologies and labor processes while compressing real wages. Finally, financialisation has also supported the reconstitution of US imperialism in the wake of the collapse of the Bretton Woods System, US defeat in the Vietnam War and the Iranian revolution (Gowan 1999, Kotz 2015). As a result, corporate power has increased almost everywhere, a globalised and US-led financial system has acquired unmatched policy influence, the political spectrum has shifted to the right, social democracy has imploded, left parties and mass organisations have shrivelled, and the trade unions have been largely muzzled or disabled by legal and behavioural changes and shifting patterns of employment. Neoliberalism has also created an income-concentrating dynamics of accumulation that can be limited, but not reversed, by marginal (Keynesian) interventions.

In summary, while financialisation expresses IBC control of the main sources of capital and the levers of economic policy in most countries, globalisation reflects the centralisation of those levers in US-led financial institutions and their regulation by US-controlled international organisations. These relations of mutual determination have established the material basis of neoliberalism (Albo 2008; Saad-Filho and Johnston 2005).

The structures of accumulation outlined above imply that neoliberalism cannot be adequately described simply through libertarian ideas or fanciful notions concerning the 'withdrawal' of the state or the 'expansion' of markets in general or finance specifically. Neoliberalism draws upon the power of the state to impose, under the ideological veil of non-intervention, the hegemony of globalised finance in each area of social life, not least in production itself, and it requires the state to drive, underwrite and manage the internationalisation of production and finance in each territory. The ensuing – typically *neoliberal* – modality of social reproduction is the historically specific mode of existence of contemporary capitalism, or the dominant system of accumulation. It encompasses the currently dominant forms of production and employment, international exchanges, the state, ideology and the mode of reproduction of the working class.

Furthermore, neoliberalism has redefined the relationship between the economy, the state, society and the individuals. It has constrained the latter to give their lives an entrepreneurial form, subordinating social intercourse to economic criteria, and has nullified the previous structures of political representation. The ideology of self-responsibility has been especially significant since it is antagonic with any form of working class agency or culture: it deprives the citizens of their collective capacities, values consumption above all else, places the merit of success and the burden of failure on isolated individuals, and suggests that the resolution of every social problem requires the further individualisation and financialisation of social intercourse.

5   Contradictions and Limitations

Neoliberal ideology is too fragmented to provide a coherent representation of society. It offers, instead, a populist discourse drawing upon poorly defined notions of 'individual freedom', 'competition' and 'democracy' that justify a set of loosely articulated finance- (i.e., capital in general-) friendly state policies and practices giving neoliberalism a semblance of purpose in the realm of ideas and considerable resilience in practice. Those policies cannot be contested easily, since the neoliberal restructuring of the economy and society drastically narrows the scope for debates about economic policy.

Despite these strengths, neoliberalism remains limited by five contradictions identified in different strands of the Marxist literature.

First, the neoliberal restructuring of production introduces mutually reinforcing policies that dismantle the systems of provision established previously (which are defined, often *ex post*, as being 'inefficient'), reduce the degree of co-ordination of economic activity, create socially undesirable employment patterns, feed the concentration of income and wealth, preclude the use of industrial policy instruments for the implementation of socially determined priorities, and make the balance of payments structurally dependent on international flows of capital. In doing this, neoliberalism fuels unsustainable patterns of production, employment, distribution, consumption, state finance and global integration, and it increases economic uncertainty, volatility and vulnerability to (financial) crisis.

Second, financial sector control of economic resources and the main sources of capital allows it to drain resources away from production; at the same time, neoliberalism systematically favours large capital at the expense of small capital and the workers, belying its claims to foster competition and 'level the playing field'. As a result, accumulation in neoliberal economies tends to take the form of bubbles that eventually collapse with destructive implications and require extraordinarily expensive state-sponsored bailouts. These cycles include the international debt crisis of the early 1980s, the US savings and loan crisis of the 1980s, the stock market crashes of the 1980s and 1990s, the Japanese crisis dragging on since the late 1980s, the crises in several middle income countries at the end of the twentieth century, and the dotcom, financial and housing bubbles of the 2000s, culminating with the global meltdown that started in 2007.

Third, neoliberal policies are justified ideologically through the imperatives of 'business confidence' and 'competitivity'. This is misleading, because confidence is elusive, ungrounded in reality, self-referential and volatile, and it systematically leads to the over-estimation of the levels of investment that will ensue from the pursuit of finance-friendly policies. In turn, the pursuit of competitivity amounts to the self-infliction of capital's imperatives ('flexibility', conformity, low wages, and so on), usually for someone else's profit.

Fourth, neoliberal policies are not self-correcting. Instead of leading to a change of course, failure to achieve their stated aims normally leads to the

deepening and extension of the 'reforms' with the excuse of ensuring implementation and the promise of imminent success this time around.

Fifth, neoliberalism is inimical to economic democracy and it hollows out
political democracy. The neoliberal discourse and practice of TINA (There Is
No Alternative) blocks the political expression of dissent and feeds apathy,
populism and the far right. This is the outcome of a neoliberal political project
including a modality of democracy that isolates the political from the socio-
economic sphere, restricts democracy to the former, and limits democracy to
voting in elections while, simultaneously, imposing a strongly illiberal agenda towards civil liberties and collective action. The crisis of this modality of
democracy has become evident through increasing global instability and the
proliferation of 'pseudo-' or 'illiberal' democracies and 'electoral authoritarian'
regimes, 'failed states', civil wars and 'terrorism', especially in the post-colonial
world. The limitations of conventional democracy have also raised concerns
in the 'advanced' West, where large numbers of people now reject ritualistic
elections leading to power scarcely distinguishable political parties as a means
of addressing their economic and political concerns. Despite their limitations,
the 'Arab Spring' and the emerging popular movements in crisis-hit Western
economies have reiterated their aspiration for a substantive form of democracy, encompassing the 'economic' domain that has been insulated by neoliberalism – that is, including substantive choices about the nature of social
provision, the structure of employment, and the distribution of income (Ayers
and Saad-Filho 2015; see also Chapter 12).

The economic contradictions of neoliberalism, the incremental sclerosis of
the political institutions regulating its metabolism and the inevitable corrosion of its ideological foundations make this system of accumulation vulnerable to *political* challenges. This does not imply that electoral strategies are
sufficient (after all, the electoral system has been thoroughly contaminated by
neoliberal capitalism), or that changes in social, industrial, financial or monetary policies can fulfil radical expectations. Quite the contrary: neoliberalism
has repeatedly demonstrated its resilience both in practice and in the realm
of ideas. But the demand for *the expansion and radicalisation of political and
economic democracy* can integrate widely different struggles, delegitimise neoliberalism and support the emergence of alternatives.

CHAPTER 11

Thirteen Things You Need to Know About Neoliberalism

Oh no, not another piece on neoliberalism,[1] synthesising what has gone before, adding its own particular angle, and thereby compounding the confusion as much as clarifying what has gone before.[2] And, what's more, written with a popular title along the lines of Ha-Joon Chang's (2011) 23 *Things They Don't Tell You About Capitalism*. But appearances can be deceptive. For, whilst this is a stocktaking exercise, delivered to some degree in popular and stark form, it gains depth from three sources. One is longstanding scholarship on neoliberalism itself.[3] Another is being able to view, and to present, neoliberalism in light of the global crisis. The third is to have illustrated the nature of neoliberalism through comparative case studies around housing, health, pensions and water, themselves situated in the broader context of study of the impact of financialisation on economic and social functioning.[4]

This intellectual exercise is both significant and timely because the current 'age of neoliberalism' has already lasted beyond one generation – exceeding the lifetime of the preceding Keynesian 'golden age' – and there are no signs that it is about to give way. The solidity of neoliberalism, its continuing ability to renew itself and intensify its hold on governments and societies despite economic volatility and the depth of the current crisis, warrants recognition and detailed investigation. We offer our contribution in what follows.

---

1 Originally published as: 'Thirteen Things You Need to Know About Neoliberalism', *Critical Sociology* 43 (4–5), pp. 685–706, 2016 (with B. Fine). Minor editing added.

2 Much of the neoliberal conundrum is neatly illustrated by Wacquant (2009, p. 306): 'Neoliberalism is an elusive and contested notion, a hybrid term awkwardly suspended between the lay idiom of political debate and the technical terminology of social science, which moreover is often invoked without clear referent. For some, it designates a hard-wired reality... while others view it as a doctrine ... It is alternately depicted as a tight, fixed, and monolithic set of principles and programs that tend to homogenize societies, or as a loose, mobile, and plastic constellation of concepts and institutions adaptable to variegated strands of capitalism'.

3 See, for example, Ayers and Saad-Filho (2015, and Chapter 12), Bayliss et al. (2011), Chang, Fine and Weiss (2012), Fine (2010a, 2010b), Fine and Hall (2012), Fine and Saad-Filho (2014), Saad-Filho (2003 and Chapter 9, 2007a and Chapter 13, 2008, 2011 and Chapter 15), Saad-Filho and Johnston (2005) and Saad-Filho and Yalman (2010).

4 This essay does not draw upon material from those case studies, but relevant contributions are included in Work Packages 5 and 8 of the Fessud project, http://fessud.eu/

1   A New Stage

The first thing you need to know about neoliberalism is that it represents a new stage in the development of capitalism emerging in the wake of the post-war boom.

In the social sciences literature, neoliberalism has generally been understood in four closely-related and not always easily separable ways: (a) as a *set of economic and political ideas* inspired, unevenly and often inconsistently, by the (neo-)Austrian School and monetarism;[5] (b) as a set of *policies, institutions and practices* inspired and/or validated by those ideas;[6] (c) as a *class offensive against the workers and the poor* led by the state on behalf of capital in general and finance in particular (this attack is normally justified by recourse to neoliberal ideas and carried out through so-called economic 'adjustment', especially in developing but increasingly in developed countries in crisis),[7] and (d) as a *material structure of social, economic and political reproduction* underpinned by financialisation, in which case neoliberalism is the current phase, stage, or mode of existence of capitalism. Each conceptualisation of neoliberalism necessarily involves a further issue: does this concept offer anything of substance or coherence in understanding the contemporary world as opposed to 'free market' capitalism, post-Fordism (underpinning post-modernism), the 'knowledge economy', the ever popular consumer society, or whatever?[8]

Our own starting point is to characterise neoliberalism in light of approach (d). This immediately raises three further questions. First is how do we define a stage of capitalism. This is done through the distinctive ways in which economic reproduction (the accumulation, distribution and exchange of value) is organised and reorganised *and* its implications for social reproduction (the structures, relations, processes and agents that are not directly or predominantly economic, including the political and the ideological). As Dardot and Laval (2013, p. 14) rightly put it, 'the originality of neoliberalism is precisely its creation of a new set of rules defining not only a *different* "regime of accumulation", but, more broadly, a *different* society'.

---

5   See Chapter 10, and Dardot and Laval (2013), Mirowski and Plehwe (2009) and Stedman Jones (2012).

6   Thus, for Dardot and Laval (2013, p. 7), 'Since the late 1970s and early 1980s, neo-liberalism has generally been interpreted both as an *ideology* and as an *economic policy* directly informed by that ideology'.

7   See, for example, Duménil and Lévy (2004) and the works reviewed in Cahill (2014).

8   Similar, if not identical, questions might be asked of 'globalisation' which is the most prominent way of characterising the contemporary world, not necessarily as a stage of development, but with multiple, competing, contested and not always consistent interpretations (Kiely, 2005; Kozul-Wright, 2006; Labica, 2007; Rosenberg, 2000, 2005).

Second is how do we characterise previous stages of capitalism. This is to some degree academic, as there tends to be uniformity over the periodisation of capitalism into separate stages even if slightly different criteria from ours are used to do so.[9] Some sort of laissez-faire period in the nineteenth century is presumed to give way to a more monopolistic stage in the first half of the twentieth century which then passes to a stage in which state intervention is significant, conventionally termed the Keynesian or Fordist period.[10] More significantly, stages of capitalism are distinguished by global and not merely a collection of national conditions, so it would be inappropriate to start inductively from the classification of countries into those that are more or less (neo) liberal, Keynesian or whatever. Rather, different countries exist within, and influence, the dominant stages of global capitalism in different ways, and the same is true of the economic, the political and the ideological more generally at different levels and in different arenas.

The third issue is why should neoliberalism be considered a new and separate stage of capitalism. Our answer is to be found throughout what follows but is fundamentally based upon the insight that the most salient feature of neoliberalism is financialisation. As is shown in the *fifth thing*, the rise of financialisation over the past thirty years, defined as the intensive and extensive accumulation of interest-bearing capital, has transformed profoundly the organisation of economic and social reproduction. These transformations include not only outcomes but the structures, processes, agencies and relations through which those outcomes are determined across production, employment, international integration, the state and ideology. The term financialisation, then, encapsulates the increasing role of globalised finance in ever more areas of economic and social life. In turn, financialisation underpins a neoliberal system of accumulation that is articulated through the power of the state to impose, drive, underwrite and manage the internationalisation of production and finance in each territory, often under the perverse ideological veil of promoting non-interventionism.

Our favoured approach, then, not only claims that neoliberalism is the current stage, phase or mode of existence of capitalism but also explains how it should be understood as such. It also implies that the starting point in specifying neoliberalism must have both logical and historical content. The former

---

9   Of course, there may be exceptions if periodising by relatively disconnected criteria such as political systems, wars and technologies.

10   This leaves open how to characterise the stage after Keynesianism if not neoliberalism, with post-Fordism also having proven incapable of delivering anything other than a temporary and unsatisfactory answer.

concerns the nature of economic reproduction under neoliberalism, while the latter focuses on the (uneven) ways in which neoliberalism exists across different countries including both social and economic reproduction. For, as will be seen under the *tenth thing*, neoliberalism is distinctive but not homogenising. Instead, it fosters diversity and differentiation underpinned by common aspects. It is the latter that have to be identified in the first instance, together with their internal contradictions, tensions and sources of dynamics and, consequently, potential to realise uneven outcomes and the mechanisms and determinants through which they do so in specific instances. In contrast, the commonly held presumption that neoliberalism is homogenising is grounded at an excessively concrete level and in a selective manner, either missing out on the diverse consequences of the common drivers of neoliberalism, or inevitably concluding that it is an incoherent specification of contemporary capitalism in light of this diversity.[11]

This approach to neoliberalism informs a specific understanding of two key features of the contemporary political economy. These are, first, that financialisation has transformed the global patterns of growth. The rates of investment and GDP growth in the advanced economies have tended to decline since the crisis of the so-called Keynesian, Fordist and social democratic 'golden age', regardless of the unprecedentedly favourable conditions for capital accumulation, in part imposed through neoliberalism itself. These conditions include the West's victory in the Cold War and the collapse of most nationalist movements in the Global South, and the closely related liberalisation of trade, finance and capital movements, the provision of unparalleled support to accumulation by competing states, the containing of taxation, transfers and welfare provision in most countries, the secular decline in the power of trade unions, peasant movements, left parties and social movements (the traditional sources of resistance within previous forms of capitalism), and the unprecedented ideological hegemony of a bogus but vociferous 'free market' capitalism. Finally, the unprecedented availability of new technologies serves as a potential source of productivity increase, alongside significant increases in the global capitalist labour force, not least with China's integration into the capitalist world economy. Instead of thriving on the basis of these conditions, global accumulation in the core countries has been hampered by continuing instability and, since 2007, by the deepest and longest economic crisis since the Great Depression.

The second key feature is that neoliberal patterns of production, employment, finance and consumption have simultaneously sustained impressive

---

11   See Castree (2006) and Ferguson (2007) but also, on the contrary, Hart (2002, 2008) for
       neoliberalism's contingent diversities as opposed to incoherencies.

rates of investment and GDP growth in particular regions, with Northeast and Southeast Asia to the fore and, more recently, the transformation of China into the assembly hub of the world.[12] This is far from suggesting that neoliberalism fosters an unproblematic 'global convergence'. Rather, it creates new patterns of uneven and combined development, in which unparalleled prosperity within and across countries and regions, and for specific social strata (possibly identified as financial or other elites or oligarchs, the top 1%, the top 0.01% or whatever), both, coexist with new patterns of poverty as well as its reproduction in areas where it already prevailed.

2   An Ideology?

The second thing you need to know about neoliberalism is that it is not reducible to a cogent ideology, but it is attached to a wide spectrum of ideas. These ideas display a changing relevance in rationalising current conditions and selected policies, quite apart from their leverage over state policy and in confining and steering the political and other contestations.

Neoliberalism draws heavily, if at times indirectly, upon the Austrian tradition of Ludwig von Mises, Friedrich von Hayek and their neo-Austrian successors, and the US monetarist school associated with the Department of Economics, University of Chicago in general and with Milton Friedman in particular. They argue, albeit in sharply dissimilar and logically incompatible ways, that differently endowed property-owning individuals exchanging goods, services and information in minimally regulated markets constitute the most desirable form for allocating resources and should prevail over an interventionist role of the state and, even if less apparent in popular discourse, democratic processes: the neoliberal ideology of free markets can never entirely part company with its antithesis in some respects, the authoritarian state.[13]

Despite their shared purposes and conclusions, even casual examination reveals considerable tensions between these scholarly underpinnings of neoliberalism. For example, while the (neo-)Austrians emphasise the inventive and transformative subjectivity of the individual and the spontaneous emergence of an increasingly efficient order through market processes,

---

12   Bellamy Foster and McChesney (2012).

13   See Ayers and Saad-Filho (2015 or Chapter 12), and note the putative 'de-politicisation through economisation' (Madra and Adaman, 2014). The neoliberal dilemma across freedom of, and yet control over, individual choice is neatly addressed in scholarship, ideology and, increasingly, policy in practice, by the notion of 'nudging' behaviour (Fine et al. 2016).

neoclassical economics focuses on the efficiency properties of a static equilibrium achieved entirely in the logical domain on the basis of unchanging individuals, resources and technologies and, possibly, mediated by the semi-divine intervention of the 'auctioneer'. Nor does either capture the political economy and moral philosophy associated with Adam Smith, despite their obsessive rhetorical recourse to the 'invisible hand', with its meaning and rationale subject to varieties of (mis)interpretations.[14]

The analytical inconsistencies and policy failures of monetarism have been exposed in merciless detail by Keynesian and heterodox economists, but these shortcomings have been largely ignored by mainstream economists, policy-makers and the media.[15] They promoted, instead, a populist understanding of 'competitiveness', 'individual freedom' and 'democracy' that has validated neoliberal policy reforms and repression of opposition in country after country, while also providing reassurance that the neoliberal reforms spawn the best of all possible worlds.

Despite, or because of, its impressive strengths, neoliberal ideology remains too fragmented to provide a coherent representation of society. It offers, instead, an individualist, formally egalitarian, meliorist and universalist conception of self and society. This worldview justifies a set of loosely articulated finance-friendly state policies and practices giving neoliberalism a semblance of coherence in the realm of ideas, and considerable resilience in practice: these policies cannot be contested easily, for the neoliberal restructuring of the economy and society not only narrows drastically the scope for, and directions of, debate, but also hollows out the institutional channels from which alternatives could emerge. These limitations are notable, for example, in stridently defended privatisations that are habitually awarded to, or create, monopolies, and in decentralisation of state provision, in which a leading thrust is to 'devolve' responsibility for delivery to lower levels of administration (claiming also to democratise), whilst not providing sufficient resources to allow for provision to meet requirements whether formal or otherwise, and imposing the requirement to rely on private suppliers (see *ninth thing*).

---

14   See Hands (2010) and Witztum (2013) for the poverty of the attempted socialisation of the individual in mainstream economics relative to Smith. Medema (2009) demonstrates the tension between appealing to pursuit of self-interest as a rationale both favouring and opposing state intervention.

15   Following the decline of Friedman's monetarism in the 1980s, the emerging neoliberal ideas were strapped more or less awkwardly to different versions of 'supply-side' and new classical economics, new Keynesianism and new institutionalism, depending on how imperfectly working markets were conceptualised and incorporated into macroeconomic analysis (see Fine, Lapavitsas and Pincus 2001, Fine and Milonakis 2009, Milonakis and Fine 2009 and Fine and Dimakou 2016).

3   A Reaction?

The third thing you need to know about neoliberalism is that it is not fully nor appropriately understood as the mirror image of, or a reaction against, Keynesianism, itself often inadequately seen as the explanation for the post-war boom.

Although almost every area of economic and social reproduction has been reconfigured under neoliberalism (see *first* and *second things*), neoliberal ideology tends to induce a shallow opposition between neoliberalism and Keynesianism, as if the former could be reduced to the rollback of the latter. In turn, Keynesianism is often described through 'state intervention' and collectivised forms of provision, including the short-run macroeconomic manipulation of effective demand, the welfare state, nationalised industries, some measure of planning and social contracts, which might progress to socialism through incremental reform.

It may be appealing to see neoliberalism as the counterpart to this conception of Keynesianism, offering a swing in the balance between market and state provision (see *fourth thing*). Even acknowledging that Keynesianism is associated with more or less progressive forms of state expenditure and intervention, the post-war boom was not driven by a bland and presumably incremental socialism but by economic and social restructuring with internationalisation of all forms of capital to the fore, especially that of productive capital, supported by (mainly US-dominated) finance, with a heavy role for the state in promoting such restructuring through both national and international corporate champions.[16] In turn, Keynesianism was driven to collapse because of the economic and social transformations that it engendered and supported, and the contradictions embodied in its own policies.[17] The simplistic dualism between Keynesianism and neoliberalism fails to acknowledge the broadly spread and deeply rooted transformations in economic and social reproduction and their reflection in the profound changes across each of scholarship, ideology and policy in practice.[18]

This failure to recognise the complex relationship between neoliberalism and Keynesianism has fed two additional illusions. One strand of thought, especially within Marxism, sees the emergence of neoliberalism in general and financialisation in particular as either the epiphenomenal consequence of,

---

16   See Duménil and Lévy (2004), Fine and Harris (1985) and, especially, Panitch and Gindin (2012).
17   See Gowan (1999) and Saad-Filho (2007a and Chapter 13).
18   See Fine and Milonakis (2009 and 2011).

or the functionalist response to, the *still* unresolved crisis of Keynesianism.[19] Such reductionism is insufficient because it simply sets aside three decades of global restructuring of production, employment, trade, finance, ideology, state and society, and overlooks the role of financialisation (see *fifth thing*) in promoting and supporting the contemporary (neoliberal) forms of accumulation and the social reproduction that accompanies it.[20]

The antithetical illusion, associated with social democracy, is that a return to Keynesianism can restore more favourable economic and social conditions today. Even though higher taxes, controls on trade, domestic finance and capital flows, expanded social provision and the fine-tuning of aggregate demand can help to address competing short-term macroeconomic objectives and promote short-term improvements in economic performance and social welfare, these policies would have only limited bearing on the long-term performance and underlying dynamics of the global economy and, even if achievable today, would remain hostages to neoliberal imperatives. Highlighting the contradictions of neoliberalism by contrast with (the strengths and virtues of) what existed before is an important analytical task in its own right, but it will neither reveal alternatives to neoliberalism nor make the limitations of Keynesianism disappear in practice.

It follows that neoliberalism and the potential for overcoming it cannot be encapsulated in conventional debates in macroeconomics, which express the rivalry between more or less sophisticated versions of monetarism and Keynesianism over whether and how to manipulate effective demand and other macroeconomic variables in order to deliver rapid and stable accumulation.[21] This bypasses almost entirely the problems of economic and social restructuring

---

19   Most recently, see Kliman and Williams (2015).

20   The most prominent example of this sort of reasoning is the Brenner hypothesis of investment overhang involving competitiveness between nations and large national capitals discouraging new investment. See, however, Fine et al. (2005) for a critique focusing on the extraordinary restructuring in the steel industry. Hypotheses of lack of movement since the 1970s rarely can provide evidence from particular sectors of the economy for which, of course, little has remained the same.

21   It is part and parcel of the inheritance from Keynesianism and its debate with monetarism that health, education, welfare, industrial policy, finance for investment, and so on, as opposed to effective demand, are sidelined alongside the focus on the short run as if it were independent from the long run. In this respect, monetarism only completed what Keynesianism started, finishing with the failure to acknowledge financialisation, itself merely the tip of the iceberg in the neglect of the other determinants of economic policy and performance. Hence the insights from and limitations of Crouch's (2009) notion of privatised Keynesianism, that neoliberalism is based upon demand management through private credit rather than state expenditure.

and reproduction. Even if alternative policies are appropriately identified, the means to secure them against neoliberal imperatives remains unaddressed as neoliberals themselves would suggest in terms of the imperatives of the market, globalisation and so on.

4   Markets and States

The fourth thing you need to know about neoliberalism is that it is not primarily about a (possibly pendular) shift in the relationship between the state (or the Polanyian social or collective) and the market.

Market-state dualism is insufficient because neoliberalism is not defined by the withdrawal of the state from social and economic reproduction.[22] As Wacquant (2009, p. 307) suggests:

> A central ideological tenet of neoliberalism is that it entails the coming of 'small government': the shrinking of the allegedly flaccid and overgrown Keynesian welfare state and its makeover into a lean and nimble workfare state ... stressing self-reliance, commitment to paid work, and managerialism ... [But] the neoliberal state turns out to be quite different *in actuality*.

Under neoliberalism, state institutions intervene upon and through markets and other institutions in specific ways that tend to extend and/or reproduce neoliberalism itself.[23] Exactly the same is true of other systems of accumulation, not least those attached to the Keynesian, developmental or Soviet-type states that are presumed to have been more interventionist.[24] In all these cases, the roles of 'the state' and 'the market' (unduly undifferentiated) cannot be usefully identified through their simplistic opposition. Instead, the relevant patterns of accumulation, restructuring and social and economic reproduction can be understood only through relatively concrete and historically specific analyses. These must include the interaction, contestation and co-operation among specific institutions within, across and beyond that putative divide. Those processes are themselves heavily influenced by, but not reducible to, the

---

22   As Wade (2013, p. 7) rightly puts it, '[t]he "market" is the polite way of referring to "the owners of capital", especially financial capital'.
23   See, for example, Lemke (2001).
24   See Fine et al. (2013) in the context of the developmental state paradigm that accepts the analytical agenda of state versus market.

underlying economic, political and ideological (class) interests that act upon and through such institutions.

In practice, then, first, much has been achieved through state provision in the past, and this has itself become the basis for privatisation, for example, in terms of availability of productive facilities. The scope for such achievements can only have been enhanced over time through improved technological capabilities and new management techniques. Yet, these successes are rarely if ever recognised, while public provision is invariably and arbitrarily deemed to be inferior to private provision often on the basis of casual or flawed studies, that rarely even consider firm and market structure, finance, degree of monopoly and so on.[25]

Second, state intervention has been transformed rather than simply 'reduced' under neoliberalism (see *sixth thing*). Currently, while the overall logic of state policies and interventions remains to promote economic and social reproduction and the restructuring of capital, the interests and role of finance have increasingly come to the fore either directly or indirectly. Such is evident, for example, from the policy responses to the global crisis and the continuing recession; but it is equally characteristic of the policies implemented over the entire neoliberal period, as the interests of private capital in general and of finance in particular have been favoured by the state (see *eighth thing*).

5   Financialisation

The fifth thing you need to know about neoliberalism is that it is underpinned by, although not reducible to, financialisation.[26]

Whilst seeing neoliberalism as tied to financialisation is pushing against an open door, especially in the wake of the current global crisis, financialisation itself has often been imprecisely defined and variously understood across a burgeoning literature. In much of this literature, financialisation is merely a buzzword reflecting the greater significance of finance in economic and social reproduction in recent decades, and the (closely related) growth and proliferation of financial assets. However, if financialisation is defined as the increasing presence and influence of finance, then, given its remarkable rise over the last thirty years, it is tautological to define neoliberalism as attached to financialisation. This leaves open the question of the drivers and contradictions of

---

25   See Bayliss and Fine (2008).
26   See *first thing* and Fine (2013).

financialisation and neoliberalism, and how they should be addressed in terms of analytical content and their effects.

Our more specific view of financialisation focuses, instead, on the role of finance as (interest-bearing) *capital* and not just as financial or credit relations in general. It is precisely in this respect that financialisation marks a departure from the past both in the scale and in scope of financial activity in pursuit of financial returns at the expense of production. In this sense, a mortgage, for example, remains a simple (transhistoric) credit relation between borrower and lender. However, it becomes embroiled in financialisation once that mortgage obligation is sold on as part of some other asset, which becomes routinized only under neoliberalism. With such financialisation spread more generally, so grows the influence of finance over the control of resource allocation – including the flows of money, credit and foreign exchange and, correspondingly, the level and composition of output, employment, investment and trade, and the financing of the state – by money-capital embodied in an array of (more or less esoteric) financial assets.[27] Those assets are created, held, traded and regulated by specialist institutions that, under neoliberalism, are integrated in a distinctly US-led global financial system.[28]

---

27   Quoting at length from Ashman and Fine (2013, pp. 156–57): '[F]inancialisation has involved: the phenomenal expansion of financial assets relative to real activity; ... the proliferation of types of assets, from derivatives through to futures markets with a corresponding explosion of acronyms; the absolute and relative expansion of speculative as opposed to or at the expense of real investment; a shift in the balance of productive to financial imperatives within the private sector whether financial or not; increasing inequality in income arising out of weight of financial rewards; consumer-led booms based on credit; the penetration of finance into ever more areas of economic and social life such as pensions, education, health, and provision of economic and social infrastructure; the emergence of a neoliberal culture of reliance upon markets and private capital and corresponding anti-statism despite the extent to which the rewards to private finance have ... derived from state finance itself. Financialisation is also associated with the continued role of the US dollar as world money despite ... its deficits in trade, capital account, the fiscus, and consumer spending, and minimal rates of interest ... [H]owever financialisation is defined, its consequences have been perceived to be: reductions in overall levels and efficacy of real investment as financial instruments and activities expand at its expense even if excessive investment does take place in particular sectors at particular times; ... prioritising shareholder value, or financial worth, over other economic and social values; pushing of policies towards conservatism and commercialisation in all respects; extending influence of finance more broadly, both directly and indirectly, over economic *and* social policy; placing more aspects of economic and social life at the risk of volatility from financial instability and, conversely, placing the economy and social life at risk of crisis from triggers within particular markets ...Whilst, then, financialisation is a single word, it is attached to a wide variety of different forms and effects of finance.'

28   Panitch and Konings (2008), Panitch and Gindin (2012) and Rude (2005).

The creation and circulation of these financial assets is an intrinsically speculative activity that tends to become unmoored from the constraints of production, even though this autonomy can never be complete.[29] The ensuing tensions and limitations lead to a number of outcomes that characterise financialised accumulation. These include the diffusion of a peculiar form of short-termism in economic decisions (e.g., not only through purely speculative activities but also through securitisable long-term investment, with pursuit of immediate profitability at the expense of productivity growth);[30] the imperative for generating and appropriating surplus out of finance; and the explosive growth of rewards to high-ranking capitalists and managers in every sector, especially finance itself, fuelling the concentration of income under neoliberalism. These financialised forms of accumulation are mutually reinforcing, but they can also dysfunctionally diverge (see *twelfth thing*).

The relations of mutual determination between finance and economic and social reproduction, identified above, establish the material basis of neoliberalism as a system of accumulation, described in the *first thing*.[31] In turn, financialisation has supported the global restructuring of production, that has become known as 'globalisation', and the reconstitution of US imperialism in the wake of the collapse of the Bretton Woods System, the US defeat in the Vietnam War and the Iranian revolution.[32]

This understanding of financialisation has four significant implications. First, financialisation underpins neoliberalism analytically, economically, politically and ideologically, and it has been one of the main drivers of the restructuring of the global economy since the 1970s; financialisation is, then, the defining feature of the forms taken today by accumulation and economic and social reproduction. Second, financialisation has been buttressed by institutional transformations expanding and intensifying the influence of finance over the economy, ideology, politics and the state. Third, contemporary financialisation derives both from the post-war boom and from its collapse into the stagflation of the 1970s.[33] Fourth, financialisation has been closely associated with the increasing role of speculative finance in economic and social reproduction, not least through privatisation of public utilities and,

---

29   Fine (2013–14), Fine and Saad-Filho (2016, ch.12).
30   Note that reducing wages in pursuit of profit is by no means unique to neoliberalism. But, for the latter, the pressure is that much greater in view of financial imperatives (also explaining why rewards within or linked to that sector have become so disproportionate).
31   Albo (2008) and Saad-Filho and Johnston (2005).
32   See, *inter alia*, Duménil and Lévy (2004), Gowan (1999) and Kotz (2015).
33   For a historical overview see Panitch and Gindin (2012), Rude (2005) and Saad-Filho (2007a and Chapter 13).

more recently, public-private partnerships in provision of economic and social infrastructure.

6   Policy Changes

The sixth thing you need to know about neoliberalism is that it does not merely involve a change in policies that, in principle, could be readily reversed.

The neoliberal 'policy reforms' implemented through Reaganism, Thatcherism and the (post-)Washington Consensus are supported by five ontological planks.[34] First is the dichotomy between markets and the state, implying that these are rival and mutually exclusive institutions. Second is the assumption that markets are effective if not efficient while state intervention is wasteful because it distorts prices and misallocates resources in comparison with what an ideal market would have done, induces rent-seeking behaviour and fosters technological backwardness. Third, the belief that technological progress, the liberalisation of finance and capital movements, the systematic pursuit of 'shareholder value' and successive transitions to neoliberalism around the world have created a global economy characterised by rapid capital mobility within and between countries and (an ill-defined process of) 'globalisation'. Where they are embraced, rapid growth ensues through the prosperity of local enterprise and the attraction of foreign capital; in contrast, reluctance or 'excessive' state intervention (however it may be determined) drives capital, employment and economic growth elsewhere. Fourth, the presumption that allocative efficiency, macroeconomic stability and output growth are conditional upon low inflation, which is best secured by monetary policy at the expense of fiscal, exchange rate and industrial policy tools. Fifth, the realisation that the operation of key neoliberal macroeconomic policies, including 'liberalised' trade, financial and labour markets, inflation targeting, central bank independence, floating exchange rates and tight fiscal rules is conditional upon the provision of potentially unlimited state guarantees to the financial system, since the latter remains structurally unable to support itself despite its escalating control of social resources under neoliberalism.

Neoliberalism has not only changed the policies adopted by governments but also the conditions within which policy is conceived, formulated, implemented, monitored and responded to. This has been recognised clearly, if partially, in the literatures that seek to distinguish different types of capitalism.[35]

---

34   Saad-Filho and Johnston (2005).
35   Thus, for example, the social structures of accumulation approach has been modified to suggest that neoliberalism is a particularly dysfunctional articulation of social structures (Kotz et al., 2010).

For example, the Varieties of Capitalism (VoC) approach perceives differences in the institutional construction of policy and, in the case of social policy, the Welfare Regimes Approach (WRA) focuses on the balance of power and resources between capital and labour and how they are mediated through (influence upon) the state. Presumably, each of these approaches would emphasise the encroaching gains of neoliberal capitalism, although neither was originally grounded upon the changing role of finance in specifying the varieties and regimes, respectively, and their evolving fortunes.[36] Instead, these approaches are caught on the intellectual cusp between the post-war boom and neoliberalism, seeking to defend or promote what is perceived to be the best of the past (boom) against the worst of what was yet to come, itself extrapolated from the past as a less successful liberal form of post-war capitalism.

That neoliberalism is not reducible to changes in macroeconomic policy is not a novel insight, as neoliberalism has, often, been defined instead by microeconomic shifts, not least through privatisation and commercialisation as symptomatic of the presumed withdrawal of state intervention. However, such distinctions between the microeconomic and the macroeconomic cannot generally be sustained not least as, for example, the provision of economic and social infrastructure straddles both, as do trade, industrial, commercial and, not least, financial policy. Our interpretation of neoliberalism as grounded upon finance-driven economic and social restructuring can encompass both (admittedly parodied) extremes of micro and macro shifts, integrate them and develop their insights further.

7   The Balance of Power

The seventh thing you need to know about neoliberalism is that it represents more than a shift in the balance of power, primarily against labour and in favour of capital in general and of finance in particular, undoubtedly true though this is.

Neoliberalism invariably has a significant impact on class relations and the distributional balance between them, for example, through financialisation, globalisation and neoliberal reforms. This includes the 'flexibilisation' and intensification of labour, the limitation of wage growth, the rollback of collective bargaining and the adverse changes in the welfare regime, and how each of them has affected workers, women, minorities, immigrants, and so on. Neoliberalism has also affected social relations through privatisation and

---

36   See, in this light, Ashman and Fine (2013) and Fine (2014b) for critiques of VoC and WRA, respectively. Note that each approach to different types of (parts of) capitalism is grounded in methodological nationalism in which the global as such is just one factor amongst many.

the appropriation of the 'commons' (i.e., areas where property rights were either absent or vested upon the state),[37] and through the financialisation of social reproduction (see *eleventh thing*). Finally, neoliberalism has triggered macroeconomic crises that penalise the poor disproportionately (see *twelfth thing*).[38] In these ways, neoliberalism has both expanded the power of capital and created an income-concentrating dynamics of accumulation that can be limited, but not reversed, by marginal (Keynesian) interventions.

These shifts in the balance of power are both symbolic of the establishment of neoliberalism and fundamental to its reproduction, with the anti-labour policies and assaults of Reaganism and Thatcherism to the fore. These are so significant that, especially in US political economy literature, they are often taken to be the defining characteristic of neoliberalism, with financialisation as its consequence.[39] This argument follows from an analysis of neoliberalism primarily in distributional terms, suggesting that lower economic and social wages cause high inequality as well as deficient demand, to which speculative finance is a corollary through both investment by the wealthy and the expansion of credit to the poor (for consumption, mortgages, and other short-term responses to wage compression). This is, however, to reduce economic and social restructuring in general, and neoliberalism specifically, to the spheres of circulation (effective demand) and distribution (between wages and profits). In the context of specifying both the balance and the nature of power under neoliberalism, this is too limited, and it extrapolates unduly from US (and, to some extent, UK) conditions.

This point can be made by reference to what might be termed the social compacting paradigm (SCP), which has been deployed to characterise economic and social 'settlements' over the post-war boom, typically in order to explain comparative national performance: for example, why did West Germany and Japan grow faster than the USA or the UK.[40] SCP suggests that formal and

---

37   Harvey (2005) calls this process 'accumulation by dispossession', an umbrella term for an extremely diverse range of phenomena that at most and only occasionally has a limited connection to primitive accumulation in the classical Marxist sense and, more often than not, are underpinned by financialisation (as, for example, in futures carbon trading, which is probably the most fetishised form of dispossession).

38   See, for example, Duménil and Lévy (2011) and McNally (2014).

39   Thus, for the monopoly capital school, US capitalism has been chronically beset, even during the post-war boom, by deficient demand, in this case deriving from the underconsumption deriving from high monopoly prices, and correspondingly low real wages and output. For Polanyi Levitt (2013, p. 164): 'The objective of the neoliberal counterrevolution was to restore the discipline of capital over labour, and the principal means of achieving it were deregulation, liberalization, privatization and explicit attacks on trade unions'.

40   For a critical review, see Fine (2014a).

institutionalised negotiation between capital and labour offered fuller and stronger labour representation in policymaking, and that the social partnership agreement around wage restraint in return for expanding social wages induced higher investment and faster productivity growth than the Anglo-Saxon paradigm.

Irrespective of the extent to which differential performance across countries can be explained primarily by industrial relations,[41] however broadly conceived, the contrast with the neoliberal period is striking. The weakening power of labour has led to, and been reflected by, its systematic exclusion from policymaking. Consequently, social compacting has itself been widely dismantled and, where it has survived, it has shrivelled into a tokenistic ritual or illusory role of legitimation of neoliberal policies addressing the implications of faltering growth, rather than negotiating the distribution of gains due to productivity, output and income growth. Most importantly, financial policy and the functioning of the financial system invariably remain outside the scope of any social compacting.[42]

Such considerations are well-illustrated by examples in Eastern Europe and South Africa where, with the collapse of the Soviet regime and apartheid, respectively, in the early nineties, neoliberalism both arrived late and sought to make up for lost time. Necessarily, the forms taken by policymaking and the powers underpinning and exercised through the transition to neoliberalism were subject to considerable variation across countries and over time, and were hardly reducible to a shift from the state to the market (see *fourth thing*). For example, whilst forms of tripartism flourished in post-Soviet Eastern Europe, their content was eviscerated as they were used to ease the emergence of new elites and consolidate the old in new circumstances. Consequently, in these neoliberal experiences reliance upon, or marginalisation, of tripartism has been a matter of convenience, leading to an 'illusory corporatism' that bears little relationship either to the post-war boom social corporatism in the West or to the influence of, and support for, labour characteristic of the Soviet period.[43]

---

41   Significantly for what was to come, germane to comparative performance during the post-war boom were debates about different financial systems (typically, bank-based vs market-based) and how conducive they were for economic and social restructuring, in both generating finance for investment and interacting with the policymaking processes (Ashman and Fine, 2013; Fine and Harris, 1985; Zysman, 1983).

42   The leading example is provided by the Irish Republic, not least in the wake of the global crisis; see Doherty (2011) and Regan (2009).

43   For example, in Hungary, '[c]ommitted to introducing new fiscal discipline and to cutting real wages, the Socialist government unilaterally imposed it austerity budged and reinstituted wage controls, bypassing the IRC [Industrial Relations Code] while continuing to

A similar account can be told of South Africa, where the form taken by social corporatism is the Triple Alliance of the ANC, the South African Communist Party and COSATU, the confederation of trade unions. Yet, the ANC Government is generally recognised as having taken a neoliberal turn in the mid-1990s, not least with the adoption of the Growth, Employment and Redistribution (GEAR) policy framework. As the economy was thoroughly restructured through financialisation during the post-apartheid period, the main forum for tripartite policymaking, the National Economic Development and Labour Council (NEDLAC), became increasingly ineffective because of the non-participation of the most powerful businesses and lack of influence over major policies and issues, especially those involving finance.[44] In short, social compacting under neoliberalism, if and when it occurs, actually undermines the labour movement, and much the same is liable to be so of new social movements, in and of themselves, in the absence of strong and supportive left movements and organisations.

8   Scholarship, Policy and Practice

The eighth thing you need to know about neoliberalism is that it involves varied and shifting combinations of scholarship, ideology, policy and practice, with connections but not necessarily coherence across and within these elements.[45]

The tensions across these domains can be illustrated at three levels. First, the meaning and significance of neoliberal scholarship, the ensuing ideology and their policy implications have shifted across time, place and issue, and there can be inconsistencies across their component parts. These are, often, due to tensions between the rhetorical and policy worlds built by the advocates of neoliberalism, and the realities of social and economic reproduction. The most striking example is provided by the shift from privatisation to public-private

---

claim commitment to the tripartite process' (Ost 2000, p. 510). In Poland, 'the main task of ... [the] tripartite commission has been to secure labor's consent to its own marginalization' (p. 515). In sum, 'the best that can be said is that tripartism means formal negotiations over very broad issues, with no guarantees that the agreements will become law or be respected by employers ... equally likely are tripartite sessions where the government simply informs "social partners" of its intentions and seeks labor assent to *fait accompli*' (Ost 2000, p. 515).

44   See Webster et al. (2013).
45   See, especially in the context of 'development', Bayliss et al. (2011), Fine (2010a) and Fine and Saad-Filho (2014).

partnerships, especially where large-scale state support for private provision of economic and social infrastructure is concerned.[46]

Second, even the most ardent supporter of freedom of the individual in general, and market freedom in particular, concedes that those freedoms can only be guaranteed through state provision of, and coercion for, a core set of functions and institutions, ranging over fiscal and monetary policy to law and order and property rights, through to military intervention to secure the 'market economy' when this becomes necessary. In practice, then, neoliberalism can be closely associated with authoritarianism, while its attachment to classical liberalism and political democracy is hedged and heavily conditional in practice (see *second thing*).[47]

Third, the tensions and inconsistencies across scholarship, ideology, policy and practice were sharply revealed by the policy responses to the current crisis, with the ideology of free markets, especially those of finance, smoothly giving way to heavy intervention on its behalf, what has been dubbed socialism for the bankers and capitalism for the rest of us, followed by a bewildered response from the discipline of economics to events that were not so much unpredicted as deemed to be either impossible or subject to policy control. Paradoxically, while unlimited resources have been made available to salvage finance, no concession has been offered at the level of ideology or scholarship, where the intolerant hegemony of mainstream economics remains virtually unscathed.

9   Two Phases

The ninth thing you need to know about neoliberalism is that it has been subject to two phases, loosely divided by the early 1990s.

The first phase of neoliberalism is aptly characterised as the transition or shock phase, in which the promotion of private capital proceeded in country after country without regard to the consequences. This phase requires forceful state intervention to contain labour, disorganise the left, promote the transnational integration of domestic capital and finance and put in place new institutional frameworks (see *first* and *third things*).

The second (mature) phase has been, if only in part, a reaction to the dysfunctions and adverse social consequences of the first phase, not least in social welfare provision. This ('third wayist') phase focuses on the stabilisation of the

---

46   See Bayliss and Fine (2008).
47   See, for example, Barber (1995) and Bresnahan (2003).

social relations imposed in the earlier period, the consolidation and continued expansion of the financial sector's interventions in economic and social reproduction, state management of the new modalities of international economic integration, and the introduction of specifically neoliberal social policies both to manage the deprivations and dysfunctions created by neoliberalism and to consolidate and reconstitute social and individual agents along neoliberal lines (see *tenth thing*).

Both phases require extensive (re-)regulation, despite the rhetorical insistence of all manner of neoliberals on the need to 'roll back' the state, interpreted, in the first phase of neoliberalism, as 'hollowing out', followed by the 'rolling out' of new and, occasionally, more explicit forms of intervention on that foundation in the second phase (see *fourth thing*). Inevitably, these phases are more logical than chronological, as they can be sequenced, delayed, accelerated, or even overlain in specific ways depending on country, region and economic and political circumstances.

10 Variegated Neoliberalism

The tenth thing you need to know about neoliberalism is that it is highly variegated in its features, impact and outcomes.

Although neoliberalism has an identifiable material and ideational core (see *first, second* and *fifth things*), and neoliberal policies share readily recognisable features, neoliberal experiences take a wide variety of forms in different countries and over time (see *ninth thing*). There are three reasons for this. First, despite its common core, neoliberalism can be associated with significant differences in the forms, degrees and impact of financialisation, the depth and modalities of internationalisation of production and dependence on external trade, societal changes, ideology, structures of political representation, and so on.

Second, these variegated relationships interact among themselves and with specific aspects of economic and social reproduction in historically contingent ways. Thus, for example, the more or less universal expansion of mortgage markets has interacted with the pre-existing housing systems in different ways across countries.

Third, whilst financialisation is a core aspect of neoliberalism, it remains not only uneven but also confined in its direct grasp over economic and social reproduction – not everything is financialised even where finance or even just the market is present. Thus, many public services are not commercialised, let alone financialised. As a result, even though financial institutions may not directly dictate how these services are provided, this does not mean that financialisation exerts no influence. The result is to create space for diversity in deviating not only from exclusive reliance upon financial imperatives where they do apply (such as the extent and level of user charges, for example) but also, and inevitably, where they do not.[48]

In sum, while the secular rise of financialisation and its extended reach across both economic and social reproduction is what motivates our understanding of neoliberalism as the current stage of capitalism (see *first* and *fifth things*), the impact of financialisation is variegated across industrial production and other types of enterprise, and so on.[49] Concretely, whilst financialisation feeds in part by transforming economic and social activity in ways in which the associated revenues can be packaged into corresponding assets), the extent and influence of financialisation across the various elements of economic and social reproduction are highly contingent, reinforcing the variegated nature of outcomes. In short, economic and social reproduction cannot be reduced to financialisation, but nor is the latter entirely absent of influence where it is not present.[50]

With the increasing role of financialisation, whether directly or indirectly, there will remain dysfunctions and dissonances where the logic of the market does not prevail, most obviously with the hard to employ, house, educate, provide for in old age, raise out of poverty, provide for health, and so on. This is to raise the issue for neoliberalism of how to intervene where the market fails or is absented and which, in practice, is necessarily contingent upon how markets and the non-market are formed and contested. Such issues are obvious in case of social policy but by no means confined to it where for example, neoliberal ideology of (un)deserving poor dovetails with support for those in or into work. Precisely because dysfunctions in the hard to serve through the market are multi-dimensional and uneven in their incidence, individual anomalies are liable to be created across them either in the form of 'undue' benefits (to be cut) or 'undue' harshness (to be alleviated). In the context of chronic increases

---

48   See Gingrich (2015) for variability in institutional forms of social provision in light of what is provided and how and corresponding implications for 'cost' of neoliberal change.

49   Note that beyond the pursuit of the eponymous stakeholder value, study of the relationship between financialisation and the restructuring of productive capital remains seriously underdeveloped, partly because it is limited to drawing upon macroeconomic generalisations in terms of low investment. For a telling illustration in the context of financialisation of global production networks, see Coe et al. (2014).

50   See, for example, Graeber (2014) on the neoliberalisation of the university.

in inequality and the acute impact of crisis and recession,[51] there are inevitable pressures both to reduce individual and overall benefits and to protect the most vulnerable, even if this contest can be highly uneven. How these and other tensions within neoliberalism are resolved is not pre-determined.

Somewhat different considerations apply where the forms taken by neoliberal economic and social reproduction are of more direct interest to the various fractions of capital than moderating social conflict and dysfunction in general. The state has long intervened to represent the interests of particular capitals, against the interests of others and, in some respects, for capital as a whole against the potentially destructive impact of competition between capitals. This remains the case under neoliberalism and implies that the state does not privatise everything, does not rely exclusively on private finance, and can even exclude such in order to pursue other interests and dynamics not least those of productive capital (on which financialisation in other spheres may heavily depend). Nonetheless, such interventions tend to be marked by the neoliberal condition, especially where private and/or international finance is involved, whether directly or indirectly, or even where it is absent because, for example, of continuing state provision (itself to be contingently explained and related to the broader role of finance, not least in funding the state and influencing its policies).

Whilst the current grip of neoliberalism raises doubts about the strength and viability of social resistance against the commodification of 'sacred' types of provision (including public goods and the environment), our perspective is distinctive in two respects. On the one hand, there is a social content to all objects of provision, including commodities, and each is open to particular types of reaction against market forms as is evident, for example, in the differences between housing, water, transport and health, and the wide variety of the targets of charity, from food banks to woodlands to opera. On the other hand, the dualism between neoliberal (re-)commodification and decommodification under, despite or against neoliberalism, is too crude. In other words, simply focusing on market forms is insufficient because these are far from homogeneous,[52] as they can reflect everything from production for profit to user charges with (more or less targeted) subsidies, and obliterating the ways in which commodities serve provision along the chains of activities that attach production to the market.

---

51   For the capacity of the top 10% of the income distribution to grow at the expense of the bottom 40%, see Palma (2009) on the 'neoliberal art of democracy'.

52   See Fine (2013)

11   Everyday Life

The eleventh thing you need to know about neoliberalism is that its economic and social reproduction is attached to particular material cultures that give rise to what might be termed the (variegated) neoliberalisation of everyday life.

It was consistently shown by *the previous things* that neoliberalism has redefined the relationship between the economy, the state, society and individuals. It has constrained the latter to give their lives an entrepreneurial form, subordinated social intercourse to economic criteria, and neutered the previous structures and institutions of political representation. The ideology of self-responsibility has been especially significant since it deprives the citizens of their collective capacities, agency and culture, values consumption above all else, places the merit of success and the burden of failure on isolated individuals, and suggests that the resolution of every social problem requires the further individualisation and financialisation of social provision and intercourse.

The scholarly literature has pinpointed these features of neoliberalism in different ways, for example, through the idea that finance 'exploits us all'.[53] This notion draws upon, first, the intuition that low and stagnant wages, high unemployment, privatisation of basic services and the introduction of user charges have undermined the ability of many to sustain customary or desired living standards in the absence of credit, so that exploitative indebtedness results by way of (strictly temporary) remedy. Second, it is seemingly validated by the proliferation of financial relationships and institutions into daily life under neoliberalism. Such a perspective contains an element of truth in that financialisation has been associated with increasing inequalities of access and with volatility and insecurity in the provision of many aspects of economic and social life, with the potential for deprivation to be mutually compounding and multi-dimensional. But the nature and incidence of such deprivations are far from uniform across different social strata, age groups and areas of provision, and it is doubtful that the financialisation of everyday life is primarily characterised by exploitative indebtedness.

A broader approach suggests that the financialisation of daily life is better understood in terms of the subjection (which may or may not include relations of exploitation) of households to financial markets and processes. For example:[54]

---

53   See especially Lapavitsas (2013) and Fine (2010c and 2013–14) for wide-ranging critique with alternatives.

54   Bryan and Rafferty (2014, p. 404).

> [H]ouseholds have become a frontier of capital accumulation, not just as producers and consumers, but also as financial traders ... The requirements of this emergent financial citizenship for the house and households extend beyond just honouring payments on a home purchase, it is requiring a culture of financial calculation that becomes absorbed as part of the daily norms and dispositions of social being.

However, this framing immediately begs the question of which activities attached to the household are subject to a culture of (financial) calculation, why and how, and whether (in the absence of profit as the bottom line) they cohere into an integral system including both calculation and stable trade-offs. In turn, the corresponding social norms of financial behaviour are highly contingent upon the extent to which financialised forms of provision are prevalent, and what are the norms for provision of what is not financialised.[55] Inevitably, then, across commodity consumption, housing, education, health, transport and so on, the impact of financialisation will be highly uneven and differentiated and far from reducible to, nor even primarily influenced by, an increasing presence of financial calculation.

A more promising approach can be rooted in the work of Foucault in seeing the neoliberalisation of everyday life – including the financialisation of social intercourse – as the subjective, if resisted and reflexive, internalisation of specifically neoliberal norms and dispositions.[56] For Dardot and Laval (2013, p. 8):

> Neoliberalism is not merely destructive of rules, institutions and rights. It is also *productive* of certain kinds of social relations, certain ways of living, certain subjectivities ... This norm enjoins everyone to live in a world of generalized competition; it calls upon wage-earning classes and populations to engage in economic struggle against one another; it aligns social relations with the model of the market; it promotes the justification of ever greater inequalities; it even transforms the individual, now called on to conceive and conduct him- or herself as an enterprise. For more than a third of a century, this existential norm has presided over public policy, governed global economic relations, transformed society, and reshaped subjectivity. The circumstances of its triumph have often been described – in its political aspect (the conquest of power by neoliberal forces), its

---

55 Such financialisation of everyday life directly leads to the notion that the over-indebted are in need of financial literacy programmes as a result of being irrational (see Santos, 2014).

56 See, for example, Langley (2008) and Kear (2013).

economic aspect (the expansion of globalized financial capitalism), its social aspect (the individualization of social relations to the detriment of collective solidarities, the extreme polarization between rich and poor), and its subjective aspect.

Even though this is more than an agenda of what needs to be discovered than discovery itself it suggests, once again, that the content of, and pathways to, neoliberalisation and the responses to it are highly diverse.

12   Growth, Volatility and Crises

The twelfth thing you need to know about neoliberalism is that it is associated with specific modalities of economic growth, volatility and crisis.

The neoliberal restructuring of economic reproduction introduces mutually reinforcing policies that dismantle the systems of provisioning established previously (which are defined, often *ex post*, as being 'inefficient'), reduce the degree of coordination of economic activity, create socially undesirable employment patterns, feed the concentration of income and wealth, preclude the use of industrial policy instruments for the implementation of socially determined priorities, and make the balance of payments structurally dependent on international flows of capital. In doing this, and despite ideological claims to the contrary, neoliberalism fuels unsustainable patterns of production, employment, distribution, consumption, state finance and global integration, and it increases economic uncertainty, volatility and vulnerability to (financial) crisis.

In particular, financial sector control of economic resources and the main sources of capital allows it to drain capital from production; at the same time, neoliberalism systematically, if unevenly, favours large capital at the expense of small capital and the workers, belying its claims to foster competition and 'level the playing field'. As a result, accumulation in neoliberal economies tends to take the form of bubbles that eventually collapse with destructive implications and requiring expensive state-sponsored bailouts. These cycles include the international debt crisis of the early 1980s, the US savings and loan crisis of the 1980s, the stock market crashes of the 1980s and 1990s, the Japanese crisis dragging on since the late 1980s, the crises in several middle-income countries at the end of the twentieth century, and the dotcom, financial and housing bubbles of the 2000s, culminating with the global meltdown starting in 2007.

In turn, neoliberal policies are justified ideologically through the imperatives of 'business confidence' and 'competitiveness'. This is misleading, because confidence is elusive, materially ungrounded, self-referential and volatile, and it systematically leads to the over-estimation of the levels and effectiveness of investments that will ensue from the pursuit of finance-friendly policies. Moreover, those policies are not self-correcting. Instead of leading to a change of course, failure to achieve their stated aims normally leads to the deepening and extension of the 'reforms' with the excuse of ensuring implementation and the promise of imminent success the next time around.[57]

Unsurprisingly, then, however we interpret the differences between the post-war boom (including Keynesianism, developmentalism, Soviet regimes and their variants) and the neoliberal period, economic performance for the latter in terms of growth and volatility has been generally worse and, ultimately, led to a global crisis driven by finance and financialisation, despite unambiguously and unprecedentedly favourable conditions for capitalism worldwide (see *first thing*).

13   Alternatives

The thirteenth thing you need to know about neoliberalism is that there are alternatives, both within and beyond neoliberalism itself.

It was shown in the *sixth thing* that neoliberalism cannot be reduced to a collection of policies, which would suggest that alternative policy initiatives can reverse the neoliberal reforms and even transcend neoliberalism. Policy changes are certainly essential, but the scope for such changes can be questioned in the light of the political means available to the opposition, the strength of the coalitions potentially committed to them, and the scope to drive the required distributional, regulatory and policy reforms given the neoliberal transformation of production, international integration, the state, ideology and society itself. None of these can be adequately assessed without a prior understanding of the systemic features of neoliberalism and the transformations that it has wrought on class relations and institutions and the processes of economic and social reproduction.

It was also shown in the *seventh thing* that neoliberalism is not a 'capitalist conspiracy' against the workers, in which case there would be nothing systemic or historically-specific about it, since capitalists and the state have always readily conspired against the workers.[58] Conversely, in this case neoliberalism

---

57   This is evident in the 'evaluatory trap' associated with privatisation (Bayliss and Fine, 2008) and in the hype surrounding private sector funding of the public sector.

58   In Adam Smith's (2009) famous words, 'People of the same trade seldom meet together, even for merriment and diversion, but the conversation ends in a conspiracy against the public, or in some contrivance to raise prices'.

could be dislocated through a counter-conspiracy, or even by changes in the law. Alternatively, this approach can also be read as implying that 'things were much better' under previous systems of accumulation (Keynesian, developmentalist, and so on), which, in principle, should be restored.

The latter goals are laudable but implausible. For, while neoliberalism is incompatible with economic democracy, it simultaneously hollows out political democracy (see Chapter 12). On the one hand, the discourse and practice of TINA (*There Is No Alternative*), often now muted and implicit, under neoliberalism blocks the political expression of dissent even in moderate forms and feeds apathy, populism and the far right, courting destabilising implications for neoliberalism itself. On the other hand, the institutional shifts, the changes in the structures of political representation, and the social and economic transformations wrought by neoliberalism systematically reduce the scope for the expression of collective interests, the emergence of transformative programmes, and even the aspiration to change society beyond neoliberalism.

In short, the post-war consensus inspired a political contest over whether collectivism in the forms of (Keynesian) reformism or socialist revolution would be capable of continuing to deliver progressive outcomes. Neither now is on the agenda, not least as the dominant form taken by collective economic and social reproduction has been appropriated by finance. Nevertheless, the economic contradictions of neoliberalism, the incremental sclerosis of the political institutions regulating its metabolism and the cumulative corrosion of its ideological foundations make this system of accumulation resistant to economic change, but also vulnerable to a multiplicity of political challenges.

This does not imply that electoral strategies are sufficient, nor that changes in social, industrial, financial or monetary policies can fulfil radical expectations. Quite the contrary: neoliberalism has repeatedly demonstrated its resilience both in practice and in the realm of ideas. But the demand for the expansion and radicalisation of political and economic democracy can integrate widely different struggles, delegitimise neoliberalism and support the emergence of alternatives. These are now urgently needed.

CHAPTER 12

Democracy against Neoliberalism

A democratic republic is the best possible political shell for capitalism.

V.I. LENIN 1917

Democracy is an essentially contested concept.[1,2] Nevertheless, a specific model of democracy currently dominates political thought and practice in most countries. Since before the collapse of the USSR, Western states have systematically enforced this model across several – though not all – parts of the post-colonial (or 'developing') world and the former 'Socialist' states (see Ayers 2009, Cammack 1997, Robinson 1996), to the extent that 'democracy promotion' has been considered 'the essence of post-Cold War politics' (Smith 2000, pp. xi–xii).[3]

According to the conventional model, democracy comprises the rule of law, a specific conception of human rights, the periodic election of political representatives via credible multiparty elections, 'good governance', a 'market economy', and a pluralist civil society. This model embodies an individualist, formally egalitarian, capitalist, meliorist and universalist conception of self and society. Political community is understood in terms of nation-states, constituted by three domains – the neoliberal 'minimal' and 'neutral' state, the neoliberal public sphere ('civil society'), and the neoliberal individual ('self') (Ayers 2008, Kurki 2010). This view conceptualises a restrictive Weberian-Schumpeterian procedural model of democracy, where the latter is 'not a kind

---

1 Originally published as: 'Democracy Against Neoliberalism: Paradoxes, Limitations, Transcendence', *Critical Sociology*, 41 (4–5), 2015, pp. 597–618 (with A. Ayers).

2 Gallie (1956); see also Connolly (1993) and Diamond (2008). As Kurki (2010, p.372) has noted, mainstream scholars 'make fleeting references to the essential contestability of the idea of democracy ... before speedily returning to the liberal consensus view of democracy'.

3 Western powers have been selective in their approach to democratic reforms in the post-colonial world, ignoring gross violations of human rights and 'governance failures' in, for example, Algeria, Colombia, Indonesia, Niger, Pakistan, Sri Lanka, Uzbekistan and much of the Middle East. Western agencies have also routinely prioritised economic liberalisation over democratic sensitivities, as in the former Soviet Bloc. Finally, Western intervention has regularly throttled autonomous democratic processes, as in Angola, Brazil, Chile, Iran, Mozambique, Nicaragua and across the Middle East. More recently, interventions have been justified by the imperative to secure countries for democracy and human rights, as in Afghanistan, Bosnia-Herzegovina, Côte d'Ivoire, Iraq, Kosovo, Libya and Mali (see Fasenfest 2011).

of society nor a set of moral ends', but merely 'a mechanism for choosing and authorizing governments' whereby 'two or more self-chosen sets of politicians (élites), arrayed in political parties [compete] for the votes which will entitle them to rule until the next election' (Macpherson 1977, pp. 77–78; see Schumpeter 1976 and Weber 1972, 1978). This approach was synthesised in Dahl's (1972, 1989) work, which identified the procedural criteria for an elitist mode of governance that have guided the democratisation project.[4]

The rise of the Weber-Schumpeter-Dahl model has been closely associated with the ascendancy of neoliberalism. Neoliberalism fuses distinct political tendencies, including those oriented to the market (expressed under the ideological guise of *laissez-faire*), and illiberal policies towards personal and civil liberties, including growing restrictions to privacy and collective action, which have become especially prominent since 2001 (Cassel 2004, Ewing 2010, Herman 2011, Hoover and Plant 1989, Larner 2000). The rise of neoliberalism has transformed the 'mature' democracies (Dean 1999), and shaped the constitution of democratic polities across the post-colonial world (Ayers 2009, Tully 2006, 2008).

The crisis of this project has become evident through increasing global instability and the proliferation of so-called 'pseudo-' or 'illiberal' democracies and 'electoral authoritarian' regimes, 'failed states', civil wars and 'terrorism', especially in the post-colonial world (Brooker 2009, Diamond 2002, Zacharia 1997, 2004; see also EIU 2011 and HDR 2002). The limitations of conventional democracy have also raised concerns in the 'advanced' West, where large numbers of people now reject ritualistic elections leading to power scarcely distinguishable political parties as a means of addressing their economic and political concerns.[5] In many countries, policy convergence around the tenets of neoliberalism belies the appearance of 'free' choice in the political market, leading to anomie, the growth of the far-right, and a sense that politicians are 'there only for the taking' (Chomsky 2010, Crouch 2004, Ghosh 2012, Kulish 2011, Munck 2005, Olshansky 2007, Tamás 2011, Wolin 2008).

The erosion of democracy has facilitated the recent replacement of elected governments in the Eurozone by so-called non-party technocrats, when hard choices became necessary. These coups d'état under a democratic veneer have highlighted concerns about the meaning and vitality of political democracy

---

4 For notable critiques of polyarchy see Cammack (1997, ch.1), Macpherson (1977), and Robinson (1996).
5 In this essay, the terms 'conventional', 'political', 'liberal', 'procedural', 'formal', 'capitalist' and 'bourgeois' democracy are used interchangeably.

under neoliberalism. In contrast, the 'Arab Spring' and the emerging popular movements in crisis-hit Western economies have reiterated longstanding aspirations for a democracy transcending electoral rituals. Echoing Mészáros (2006, p.43), these developments concern not 'the more or less frequent crises *in* politics' but 'the crisis *of* the established modality of politics itself'.

Critics often attribute the crisis of democracy to the capture of states by selfish interests under neoliberalism, which has, presumably, corrupted the traditional mechanisms of representation and public administration (Lemke 2002, p.6). These views are misguided in positing an ontological autonomy of the state and an external relationship between capitalism and democracy. Such an approach misunderstands democracy, the state, and the structures of representation and political rule under neoliberalism. This essay offers a Marxist critique of current forms of democracy, highlighting the continuing appropriateness of Lenin's aphorism regarding 'the best political shell for capitalism'. Currently, this can be encapsulated in the concept of *neoliberal democracy*.

Despite its uncompromising critique of the limitations of neoliberal democracy, this essay does *not* claim that it should be dismissed as a mere cloak or a 'show' staged by the ruling elites in order to pacify the masses. We affirm the immense value of political freedom, and recognise that the diffusion of political democracy has been made possible by the expansion of capitalism. However, we stress that capitalism necessarily limits democracy because the 'very conditions that made liberal democracy possible also narrowly limit the scope of democratic accountability' (Wood 1995, p.234). We also emphasise that the democratic achievements in most societies are, almost invariably, the outcome of costly mass struggles for a more equitable politico-economic order. Democracy, and the associated restrictions to political freedom, take specific forms under neoliberalism. These are examined in detail below, leading to the conclusion that neoliberalism is incompatible with the expansion of democracy into critically important areas of social life. Conversely, the expansion of democracy can provide the most effective lever for the abolition of neoliberalism, the contemporary form of capitalism.

These abstract and conceptual – rather than descriptive or anecdotal – arguments are developed in five sections. The first examines the paradoxical relationship between democracy and capitalism. The second focuses on the specific features of democracy in the age of neoliberalism. The third interrogates the limitations of neoliberal democracy. The fourth argues that the expansion and radicalisation of democracy is the most promising way to destabilise neoliberal capitalism. The fifth concludes the essay.

1 Capitalism and Democracy

The voluminous literature on democracy in the post-Cold War period has generally upheld an abstract and class-neutral notion of 'democracy in general'. In contrast, left analysts advocate a class analysis of democracy, drawing on Lenin's (2001, p.41) aphorism that: 'It is natural for a liberal to speak of 'democracy' in general; but a Marxist will never forget to ask: "for what class?"'

Lenin's insight suggests that there are historically specific relationships between social (typically, class) domination, modalities of state rule and forms of political representation. These relationships are neither direct nor unchanging over time: they can be understood historically but not prescribed *ex ante*. For example, under each modality of state rule 'political freedom' supports the domination of some classes or groups, whilst securing the subordination of others. The examples of 'democratic' slave polities in antiquity are both illustrative and uncontroversial (Wood 2008). Yet, this literature tends to elide the specific problem posited by democracy under capitalism, that is, 'the inclusion *within* the democratic framework of the dominated classes' (Hunt 1980, p.9).

Crucial to a class analysis of capitalist democracy is the separation between the political and economic aspects of the relations of exploitation, which is specific to this mode of production (Wood 1981, 1995). This separation derives from the fact that, while production takes place in privately-owned workplaces where the capitalists or their agents control the labour process, the exploitative relationship between the class of wage workers and the class of owners of the means of production is mediated by anonymous (impersonal, or market-based) economic compulsions. These encompass the compulsion to work, the recruitment of labour, the purchase of means of production, finance, and the exchange and distribution of goods and services. It is different in non-capitalist societies, where economic processes are normally directly and visibly subordinated to political authority, and follow rules based on hierarchy, tradition and religious duty which make the relations of exploitation transparent.

The separation between the economic and the political in capitalism has six paradoxical implications. First, *it reveals two levels of the capitalist relations of exploitation*: the firm as the economic locus of the rule of the bourgeoisie, and the state as its political locus, with the responsibility for legitimising and managing the social relations of class, property, currency, contract and markets (Panitch and Gindin 2004). In capitalist states, public office is ostensibly autonomous from the ownership of the means of production and the control of the conditions of employment. A stratum of officials takes charge of the day-to-day affairs of the state, just as a professional cadre of managers and administrators controls the capitalist enterprises. Political activity revolves around contrasting strategies for the administration of public affairs (that is, class relations in their broadest sense), which seem to be only indirectly related to the extraction of surplus value. In order to prosper, capitalist states must be committed to the expanded reproduction of the dominant social relations, and they must have adequate revenue-generating and coercive powers to secure their own operations (Harvey 2003, Saad-Filho 2003 and Chapter 9). For these reasons, states must intervene both in 'political' conflicts (e.g., concerning the scope of democratic rights) and in 'economic' disputes (for example, around pay and conditions in large industries), if state officials consider that their strategies for the reproduction of capital-in-general are being challenged in significant ways. When intervening, the state relies on the power of law, the media, finance, domestic and international public opinion, the police and, *in extremis*, the armed forces.

Second, *the 'separation' splinters the political process, and the state itself,* across a large set of interlocking institutions, structures, agencies and processes, whose fragmentation is intensified by the process of economic development. Correspondingly, there is a growing disconnect between localised conflicts around working conditions, sectoral struggles around state policies, and general disputes about the (increasingly intangible) political rule of the capitalist class. These disjunctions ultimately help to entrench capitalist power in the workplace, hugely expand the scope for the accommodation of class struggles within capitalism, and dilute their systemic (transformative) implications.

Third, *the 'separation' opens the possibility of shifts in the modalities of class rule – including the potential for political democracy –* while protecting the economic processes of exploitation. Historically, the rule of capital has been compatible with distinct political regimes, among them monarchy, fascism and parliamentary democracy, and with diverse modalities of transition of power across rival parties and regimes. However, even in the most liberal cases political democracy remains limited because capitalist states cannot manage politically the exploitation of the majority while, simultaneously, implementing an emancipatory programme. The structural limits of capitalist democracy come into view when attempts to expand political control over the economic affairs are blocked, regardless of their popular backing or even legitimacy within the established order. Examples include the destruction of the Spanish Republic, the overthrow of Iranian prime minister Mohammad Mossadegh and Chilean president Salvador Allende, the political genocides in Indonesia, Argentina and in several Central American countries and, equally significantly, the systematic failure to achieve meaningful land reforms and greater economic equality in the post-colonial world. These episodes starkly demonstrate that political democracy was never meant to reach the economic realm.

These limitations help to explain why the expansion of democracy has rarely been a gift bestowed by the privileged or the direct outcome of the diffusion of capitalist relations of production. Democratisation has been achieved almost invariably through mass mobilisations, sometimes against significant resistance from powerful economic interests.[6] Democratic movements have also been closely associated with demands for redistribution of assets and income, implying that, from the point of view of the majority, political and economic demands are inseparable. This also suggests that mainstream claims that Western democracy is the 'natural' outcome of economic development and that it offers a template for the organisation of all societies (the 'end of history') are hollow. Evidence from China, Germany, Japan, the UK, US and elsewhere indicates that economic growth and the rising complexity of the social division of labour play, at best, a marginal role in the expansion of democracy. The diversity of historical paths across these and other countries suggests that democracy emerges from specific processes of struggle around the privileges of the ruling class while, simultaneously, helping to accommodate the interests of conflicting social groups, especially the workers (Eley 2002, Therborn 1977).

Fourth, *political democracy systematically promotes the interests of capital*. Democracy legitimises capitalist exploitation because political equality veils the structures and processes perpetuating economic inequality. Conversely, it is widely recognised that the smooth accumulation of capital ('economic prosperity') is essential for social welfare, and accepted that political stability helps to achieve this goal. This materially-grounded perception of the common good is validated by direct experience ('common sense'), and through the media, the schools and other means of (in)forming public opinion. Thus, in normal circumstances the capitalists can confidently expect the poor to vote for their own exploitation. At a further remove, the asymmetry of economic power and the proliferation of sectoral conflicts warp the majority-based structures of democratic representation under capitalism. Democracy fosters an array of squabbling political parties, lobbies, NGOs, movements, trade unions and interest groups with limited horizons, a strident rhetoric (essential to be heard among the cacophony), and no grand vision for society. The formulation, implementation and monitoring of state policy in democratic societies requires the accommodation of overwhelming (capitalist) interests as well as the management of countless sectional demands, which can be achieved only through

---

6   See Eley (2002). Wood (1995, p.211) rightly argues that '[t]he devaluation of citizenship entailed by capitalist social relations is an essential attribute of modern democracy. For that reason, the tendency ... to represent the historical developments which produced formal citizenship as nothing other than an enhancement of individual liberty – the freeing of the individual from an arbitrary state ... – is inexcusably one-sided'.

political compromises. While these are essential for democratic governance, these compromises systematically protect the power of propertied interests against transformative forces. The ensuing gyration of the main political parties around the centre, and their need to demonstrate administrative 'competence' and play a constructive role in the management of sectional disputes in order to remain electable tends to evacuate substantive debates and disenfranchise groups with radical ambitions.

Fifth, in a democracy the legal system is meant to guarantee social stability and the predictability of the rules of the game. Since the rule of law is predicated on the reproduction of the pre-existing balance of social forces *the judiciary has an inherently conservative bias*, regardless of its formal independence. In turn, 'legality' offers powerful, avaricious or conservative interests ample opportunity to block transformative agendas in the courts, whether because they infringe upon existing rights or because they fail on a technicality (progressive decisions may be possible in the courts in exceptional circumstances, usually as part of a last-ditch effort to contain explosive social conflicts). In sum, the strength of the legal system normally expresses the degree to which the state and social reproduction are controlled by the propertied interests.[7]

Sixth, during periods of relatively stable accumulation *the greater legitimacy of democratic regimes*, due to their inclusive political rights and attachment to constitutional rules, *allows them to impose exclusionary economic policies and insulate elite interests from mass pressures more efficiently than most dictatorships*. Nevertheless, in times of crisis or when the established order is thought to be threatened, naked force will be deployed. Hence, '[t]he [bourgeois] commitment to democracy ... emerges to be not axiomatic and eternal, but pragmatic and ephemeral. Since it is the economic system itself which is now at stake, all political measures needed to save it, including dictatorship, become legitimate' (Knei-Paz 1978, p.355).

The paradoxes examined above show that the separation between the economic and the political plays a structurally determinant role in the possibility, historical emergence, scope and limitations of bourgeois democracy. This approach contradicts the mainstream view that representative democracies channel, express and respond to popular pressure. We claim, instead, that although capitalism opens the possibility of political democracy, it is inherently incompatible with economic democracy, and that the economic asymmetries

---

7 '[W]e are citizens ... For the poor it consists in sustaining and preserving the wealthy in their power and their laziness. The poor must work for this, in presence of the majestic quality of the law which prohibits the wealthy as well as the poor from sleeping under the bridges, from begging in the streets, and from stealing bread' (France 2009, Kindle Locations 1044–1047).

which constitute capitalism limit the scope of political democracy, subvert its principles, and turn it into an ancillary mechanism for the reproduction of bourgeois privileges.[8]

The reproduction of capitalist societies requires the constant management of class conflicts between capitalists and workers, including attempts to transform them into narrowly focused demands or into sectional, corporatist, competitive, religious or cultural disputes. These are managed by overtly neutral state institutions and processes of conflict resolution, including laws, contracts, ombudsmen, shareholder meetings, trade unions, markets, lobbies, political parties, parliamentary debates, the judicial system and the press. As it systematically morphs class conflict into morsels of limited disagreement, capitalist democracy stabilises bourgeois rule and becomes structurally hostile to majority interests, especially with regard to the economic issues which play a determining role in social welfare: property rights, employment law, work practices, welfare provision, and the distribution of income. Aware of these limitations of democracy, Wood (1981, p.95) rightly argues that:

> battles ... over the power to govern and rule ... remain unfinished until they implicate not only the institutions of the state but the political powers that have been ... transferred to the economic sphere. In this sense, the very *differentiation* of the 'economic' and the 'political' in capitalism – the symbiotic division of labour between class and state – is precisely what makes the *unity* of 'economic' and 'political' struggles essential.

The critical literature has long recognised the narrow limits of political democracy, leading many radicals to question its value. For example, Therborn (1977, p.3) asked: 'How has it come about that, in the major and most advanced capitalist countries, a tiny majority class – the bourgeoisie – rules by means of democratic forms?' Between the 1960s and the 1980s, Parenti claimed that bourgeois democracy was a charade to mislead the people into thinking that they were free and self-governing.[9] Political democracy certainly can be illusory; for example, Western political systems are generally defined as democratic despite their sponsorship of discrimination, electoral fraud, political repression, illegal interception of communications, infiltration into lawful organisations,

---

8   For a similar argument, see Roper (2013).

9   Parenti revised his views in the late 1980s, arguing that democracy is not merely a 'subterfuge' or 'cloak' created by ruling elites, although it can serve that purpose; see Parenti (2011). As Therborn (1977, p.3) argues, '[t]he bitter experiences of Fascism and Stalinism ... have taught the firmest revolutionary opponents of capitalism that bourgeois democracy cannot be dismissed as a mere sham'.

disinformation, and imprisonment, torture and execution of dissenters at both home and abroad. But democracy is not always or necessarily so limited, and it can offer a vitally important platform for the promotion of the interests of the majority (see below).

The mismatch between political freedom and economic exploitation was also observed, implicitly, by advocates of bourgeois rule. At one level, concern that extension of the franchise would allow a proletarian majority to undo the existing social system was evident in writings by Locke, Madison, Mill and de Tocqueville. Conversely, the possibility that the majority might choose a tyrant was noted in Popper (1945). This concern also underpinned Samuel Huntington's (1991) 'paradox of democracy', whereby democratic experiments often brought in their wake nationalistic populist movements (for example, in Latin America) or fundamentalist movements (for example, in Muslim countries). At another level, in *The Road to Serfdom*, Hayek (1944, p.70) argued that '[d]emocracy is essentially a means' for safeguarding individual freedom, and that it is not 'the fountainhead of justice', since majorities must recognise 'proper limits to their just power'. In *The Constitution of Liberty*, he claims tellingly that the 'limits [of democracy] must be determined in the light of the purpose we want it to serve' (Hayek 1960, p.108). These are, firstly, a method of non-violent social change; secondly, a 'safeguard of individual liberty' and, thirdly, 'a process of forming opinion ... [with regards to] some general conception of the social order desired' (pp. 107–109, 114). This approach was further elaborated in Milton Friedman's *Capitalism and Freedom*, which lauded competitive capitalism 'as a system of economic freedom and a necessary condition for political freedom' (Friedman 2002, p.4, 7–10). Such approaches eventually led to public choice theory's claim that there is no such thing as public interest or even an autonomous state. Every interest is private, and bureaucrats are only trying to maximise their own welfare by manipulating political power. At this point, the mainstream theory of democracy reaches its limits.

2   Democracy in the Age of Neoliberalism

Neoliberalism is the contemporary mode of existence of capitalism. This global system of accumulation emerged gradually, since the mid-1970s, through successive attempts to stabilise the global economy, reduce the power of labour, recompose capitalist rule and restore profitability after the disarticulation of the Keynesian-social democratic consensus, the paralysis of developmentalism and the implosion of the Soviet bloc (Duménil and Lévy 2004, O'Connor 2010, Saad-Filho 2003 and Chapter 9, 2007a and Chapter 13, Saad-Filho and

Johnston 2005). Neoliberalism is based on the systematic use of state power, under a 'free market' cloak, to transform the material basis of accumulation at five levels: the allocation of resources, international economic integration, the role of the state, ideology, and the reproduction of the working class (Jessop 1991).

Critically important for the purposes of this essay, under neoliberalism the state's influence upon the allocation of resources (the level and composition of output, employment, investment and consumption, the structure of demand, state finance, the exchange rate and the patterns of international specialisation) has been systematically transferred to a globalised financial sector dominated by US institutions. Neoliberalism also redefines the relationship between individuals, society, state and the economy, encouraging individuals to give their lives an entrepreneurial form, and subordinating social intercourse to economic criteria.[10]

The roll-out of neoliberalism has been closely associated with the defeat of the left and the organised working class, and the spread of formal democracy in Latin America, Eastern Europe, 'sub-Saharan' Africa and, more recently, in parts of North Africa and the Middle East. This coincidence of events, in concert with the expansion of a rationality centred around 'individual freedom and initiative' (Held 1996, p.253), has elicited comments about the supposed 'natural fit' between market forces and political democracy. This section examines why and how formal democracy has come to constitute the political form of neoliberalism.

Such a claim may seem inapposite, since neoliberalism has often been 'productive of authoritarian, despotic, paramilitaristic, and/or corrupt state forms and agents within civil society' (Brown 2003), and transitions to neoliberalism have often been effected by authoritarian regimes, typically, in the Southern Cone of Latin America in the 1970s (Díaz-Alejandro 1985, Klein 2007). Nevertheless, first, *most neoliberal economies are democratic* in the limited sense examined above. Second, *most non-democratic countries are not neoliberal* and, third, *most transitions to democracy* in the last thirty years, whether from military dictatorship, single-party rule, autocracy or Soviet-style socialism, *have been coeval with transitions to neoliberalism.*

Theories of democratisation since the nineteenth century generally held that democracy was incompatible with the early stages of economic development. Even in the 1980s it was commonly argued that authoritarian regimes could more easily force through the shock therapy associated with the

---

10 See Lemcke (2001, pp. 198, 202). For a neoliberal argument about the restructuring of the state, see Osborne and Gaebler (1992).

neoliberal reforms, because their greater capacity for coercion allowed them to enforce the unpopular policies required to achieve long-term economic gains (Abrahamsen 2000). Similarly, the Trilateral Commission's 1975 *Crisis of Democracy* report famously alerted to the need to moderate the *'excess* of democracy' achieved in the West during the previous decade. It noted that 'Truman had been able to govern the [United States] with the cooperation of a relatively small number of Wall Street lawyers and bankers'. However, by the mid-1960s this was no longer possible, since 'the sources of power in society had diversified tremendously' and governability was threatened by 'previously passive or unorganized groups' including 'blacks, Indians, Chicanos, white ethnic groups, students and women – all of whom had became organized and mobilized in new ways to achieve what they considered to be their appropriate share of the action and of the rewards'. Their 'concerted efforts' to 'establish their claims' and 'control over ... institutions' violated the proper 'balance between power and liberty, authority and democracy, government and society', because '[t]he effective operation of a democratic political system usually requires some measure of apathy and non-involvement on the part of some individuals and groups'.[11] The report pointed to the importance of reducing the demands on government and restoring 'a more equitable relationship between government authority and popular control', while alerting that 'a decline in governability of democracy at home means a decline in the influence of democracy abroad' (Trilateral Commission 1975).

This report was prescient. For the political project of neoliberalism includes a modality of democracy which 'explicitly isolates the political from the socioeconomic sphere and restricts democracy to the political sphere. And even then, it limits democratic participation to voting in elections' (Robinson 2006, p.100; see also Gills and Rocamora 1992, Gills, Rocamora and Wilson 1993 and Jessop 1991). This project is predicated on a concept of citizenship springing from *consumption*. Individuals are regularly invited to make a token visit to the polling booths, where they consume the freedom to vote by registering their preferences in much the same way as they express their identities by choosing soft drinks, clothes, schools and hospitals. Meanwhile, the substantive choices about the nature of social provision, the structure of employment and the

---

11   A further threat was posed by 'the intellectuals and related groups who assert their disgust with the corruption, materialism, and inefficiency of democracy and with the subservience of democratic government to "monopoly capitalism"'. They constitute a threat to democracy by their 'unmasking and delegitimization of established institutions' causing 'a breakdown of traditional means of social control'. They 'challenge the existing structures of authority' and even the effectiveness of 'those institutions which have played the major role in the indoctrination of the young' (Trilateral Commission 1975).

distribution of income are made elsewhere. This sterilisation of the political process, through its insulation from radically different perspectives, strategies and goals, amounts to the *depoliticisation of politics* (Munck 2005). Unsurprisingly, in neoliberal democracies political parties increasingly comprise 'a self-reproducing inner elite, remote from its mass movement, but nested squarely within a number of corporations, which will in turn fund the opinion polling, policy-advice and vote-gathering services' in exchange for political influence (Crouch 2004, p.74; see also Leys 2008). While

> elections exist and can change governments, public electoral debate is a tightly controlled spectacle, managed by rival teams of professionals expert in the techniques of persuasion, and considering a small range of issues selected by those teams. The mass of citizens plays a passive, quiescent, even apathetic part, responding only to the signals given them. Behind this spectacle of the electoral game, politics is really shaped in private by interaction between elected governments and elites that overwhelmingly represent business interests.
>
> CROUCH 2004, p.4

Only once democracy has been suitably atrophied can it be claimed that capitalism flourishes best under a democracy, or that democratic values can be protected only in a market economy (Lipset 1994). This new orthodoxy became established gradually (van der Pijl 2011). The simultaneous spread of formal democracy and neoliberalism since the early 1980s demonstrated that political openness was compatible with 'economic responsibility',[12] allaying fears that political openness would feed unruly populism in the South. At the same time, the perceived threat of undependable ('rogue') dictatorships increased, helping to shift the balance of risks for the global neoliberal elite (Kiely 2007, Robinson 2006). The new democracies repeatedly proved their mettle by imposing unpopular economic reforms, while successfully channelling disaffection into electoral politics rather than revolutionary struggle. By the early 1990s, a positive correlation between democracy and development was proclaimed. Thus, democracy could be 'instituted at almost any stage of the developmental process of any society ... irrespective of its social structure, economic condition, political traditions and external relations, and ... it [would] enhance development'. Democratic governance was no longer considered the 'outcome

---

12   Sachs (2000) argued that Bolivia 'showed that you could combine political liberalization and democracy with economic liberalization. That's an extremely important lesson, to have both of those working in parallel and each one reinforcing the other'.

or consequence of [capitalist] development, as was the old orthodoxy, but a necessary condition of development' (Leftwich 1996, p.4).

These analytical and policy shifts were validated by the new academic discipline of 'transitology'. Its principles were outlined by Dankwart Rustow in the 1970s, and developed further by Linz and Stepan (1978), O'Donnell, Schmitter and Whitehead (1986), Diamond, Linz and Lipset (1988–89) and Huntington (1991). Transitology elides high theory and supports a narrowly procedural notion of democracy. It privileges (political) 'choice' against (economic) 'structure', attributes great significance to leadership and the role of political elites, and endorses the withdrawal of the state from direct economic intervention (Cammack 1997). Such thinking also accorded with the emergence of the post-Washington consensus in the 1990s, inspired by new institutionalist economic theory (Fine, Lapavitsas and Pincus 2001). The new 'consensus' shares with the democratisation project a concern with a broad set of policy recommendations, rather than a narrowly focused shock therapy agenda, and it aims to create a government apparatus which can enable a market-based modality of development that is, simultaneously, socially inclusive (see CGD 2008, in contrast with the previous 'consensus' sketched in Williamson 1993). The promotion of formal democracy in the developing countries has also been embraced by the development industry: the Washington institutions could finally establish a dialogue with the aid agencies, NGOs and political movements which, in the not-too-distant past, had criticised the human cost of the Washington consensus and its close links with political repression (Bracking 2009).

The neoliberal reforms have imposed (financial) market imperatives and transferred to finance the responsibility for allocating social resources, while political democracy has sustained these reforms through a widely respected constitutional order, independent central banks, and the conditionalities imposed in exchange for debt relief and aid. Significantly, once the neoliberal reforms have been introduced formal democracy makes it *harder* to reverse them, because it embeds the logic of financial policy discipline into the country's institutional fabric. In doing this, neoliberalism aims to foreclose the possibility of constituting – or even imagining – democracy in any other terms (Ayers 2009).

3   The Limitations of Neoliberal Democracy

Neoliberalism has intensified the evacuation of capitalist democracy, and turned it into a tool supporting the neoliberal restructuring of social reproduction. In turn, neoliberal democracy has contributed to the fragmentation of the working class and other potential sources of opposition, helping to stabilise both neoliberalism and its modality of democracy. These processes have stretched the contradictions of democracy (outlined above), suggesting fundamental limitations to neoliberalism itself.

The contradictions of neoliberal democracy can be located at three levels. First, neoliberalism fosters accumulation through the reconstitution of capitalist class supremacy and the intensification of the exploitation of the majority, while decomposing the opposition, in part, through an increasingly debased form of democracy. However, the enforcement of a mutually supporting relationship between the economic and the political domains of the capitalist relations of reproduction implies that tensions in one of them can contaminate the other. Second, the social and economic depredations wrought by neoliberalism have aggravated the tensions between global capitalism and national states, including the impossibility of finding stable configurations of national (popular) sovereignty and international integration, the fluctuating scope for foreign intervention in case of deviations from neoliberal governmentality, and the intensification of religious, nationalist and xenophobic political programmes. Third, neoliberalism has bred a (largely constitutional) new authoritarianism, both through its own political development in the 'heartlands' and as an alternative to neoliberal democracy in the 'periphery'.

4 Economic and Political Imbalances

Neoliberalism has circumscribed political democracy through the incremental exclusion of key economic matters from legitimate debate and the concentration of worldwide policy-making capacity in Wall Street and Washington D.C., leaving only matters of relatively minor importance open for debate. The evacuation of democracy was partly due to the material realities of this system of accumulation; for example, neoliberalism is driven by the global integration of production and finance, which has created the need for international policy harmony through negotiation, conditionalities and competition between countries. The evacuation of democracy was also, partly, engineered to protect neoliberalism (see the second section of this essay). The diffusion of a limited form of democracy has been accompanied by the imposition of specific modalities of social discipline upon the key social agents. Neoliberal states are compelled to enforce contractionary monetary and fiscal policies and restrictive welfare policies, which systematically benefit finance, under the continuing threat of fiscal, balance of payments and exchange rate crises. Industrial capital is disciplined by global competition promoted by the state and facilitated by a globalised financial system, and the financial sector is disciplined through its competitive international integration under a US-led regulatory umbrella. However, unquestionably the most stringent forms of economic repression have been imposed upon the working class, sometimes just as their political rights expanded.

Hundreds of millions of workers have been incorporated into transnational capital accumulation through the globalisation of production, trade liberalisation and financial integration. These have greatly increased competition between capitals and between (and within) national working classes. The global restructuring of production and regressive legal, regulatory and political changes have transformed the patterns of employment in most countries, reduced the efficacy of established modes of organisation of the working class, and facilitated the imposition of restrictions to the wages, subsidies, benefits, entitlements systems and other non-market protections introduced in previous systems of accumulation. These technological, economic, legal and political shifts have sterilised the political institutions of the state, and severely limited the scope for constitutional resistance against neoliberal capitalism.

Social discipline has also been imposed through the financialisation of the reproduction of the working class, most remarkably through the housing market boom and the expansion of personal credit in the last two decades, affecting particularly the US and UK. Under their straitened circumstances – partly because of the disappearance of relatively well-paid skilled jobs and, partly, because of the retrenchment of the welfare state – many working class households were drawn into systematic borrowing and chronic reliance on asset price inflation, through serial remortgaging, in order to meet their reproduction needs[13] Pressures for repayment based on the threat of losing homes, cars and reputations helped to push many debtors into financial difficulties, including the need for long working hours in multiple precarious jobs, rising stress levels, and a declining propensity to engage in industrial or political militancy.[14]

This process is, ultimately, untenable. It has engendered chronic deficiencies of aggregate demand in parallel with the build-up of manufacturing overcapacity, especially in East Asia, and fed a diseased financial system which has generated the greatest economic crisis since 1929 and, subsequently, has choked the economic recovery (McNally 2012, Saad-Filho 2011 and Chapter 15). These economic constraints have created severe political tensions. In some

---

13   For detailed studies of the financialisation of the reproduction of the US working class, see Kotz (2009), Krippner (2005) and Montgomerie (2009).

14   See Collini (2010), Kotz (2009, p.310) and UNCTAD (2012).

countries, electorates have been coerced into backing neoliberal adjustment programmes under the impending threat of economic meltdown driven by the financial markets and their agents ensconced in the central banks. In others, elected leaders have been swept aside by constitutional coups d'état, and replaced by alleged non-party 'technocrats' – in reality, right-wing operators with no electoral track record but extensive experience running the government machinery. In both cases, the neutered political systems in the West have demonstrated their inability to respond to the ongoing crisis, while their democratic veneer has been seriously corroded.

5 Globalism and (Nation-)States

Neoliberalism has internationalised the rule of capital across the domains of the economy, culture, ideology, politics and society. These processes have often been summarised under the term 'globalisation'. Despite the significance of these processes, and the corresponding shrinkage of domestic policy space, (nation-)states remain the linchpin of social reproduction. Formally exclusive sovereign territorial states, involved in complex relations of integration, cooperation, conflict, domination and subordination, provide the essential conditions of accumulation in each country, not least the separation of the workers into rival national groups. They also drive, underwrite and administer the internationalisation of production and finance, and articulate global capital with, and through, the domestic political economy, often justifying their policies through the imperative of 'national competitivity' (Ahmad 2004, Cammack 2006).

This system of accumulation is fraught with contradictions. At its most abstract level, capitalism's separation between the political and the economic is expressed through a territorially-fragmented space, heightening the disjuncture between the two moments of exploitation: the coercive and localised process of extraction of surplus value, and its conflict-ridden and, increasingly, globalised appropriation through a range of economic and political processes. These contradictions surface through tensions between and within states, and through the drift into dysfunctionality of the neoliberal system of global governance. Examples include the proliferation of 'failed states', the multiplication of 'humanitarian' interventions to secure the space for globalised accumulation, disputes over the remit of international institutions and the limits of foreign oversight of domestic policy, and the creeping paralysis of the WTO, the UN Security Council, the World Bank, the IMF and the European Union (Akyüz 2010, Ayers 2012, Khor 2010).

The mainstream did not expect to face these difficulties so soon after its proclamation of 'the end of history'. They have been accompanied by the emergence of a new generation of proto – and neo-fascist movements in the West, growing scepticism about the international institutions, and the decay of national political systems, which have become ill-equipped to address local economic difficulties.

6   New Authoritarianism

Under neoliberalism, overtly market-driven imperatives coexist somewhat uneasily with a distinctly illiberal agenda towards civil liberties and collective action. The conflict between these economic and political imperatives has re-configured political democracy. While it remains formally inclusionary, neo-liberal democracy is substantively exclusionary at the levels of the economy (concentration of income, unemployment) and human freedom (political re-pression, intolerance of dissent). The ideology of self-responsibility has been spectacularly successful on both counts. It deprives the citizens of their collective capacities, and places the merit of success and the burden of failure on isolated individuals (see Worrell 2013). Self-responsibility renders the neo-liberal social order immune to social dissent, because it 'interprets any extant and prospective *social* issue as a *private* concern' (Bauman 1991, p.189). It also suggests that the solution to every social problem requires the state to 'retreat' further.

Neoliberal democracy has also built upon the trend towards paramilitary policing which emerged in most Western countries since the 1960s. By the 1980s, repression had become part and parcel of the neoliberal rollback of social programmes. As poverty and homelessness increased, financially straight-ened states directed increasing sums to social control, building prisons and giving the police military-grade weapons which, in the US, have bred a 'prison-industrial complex'. The other components of the law-and-order agenda were put in place gradually: public hysteria about drugs, crime and terrorism, the imperative of social cleansing through urban regeneration initiatives, mount-ing repression against immigrants and refugees, the creeping closure of le-gal avenues for dissent, and the systematic monitoring of social intercourse (Gordon 2006, McNally 2006). This process has tied in seamlessly with the post-2001 'national security' agenda spreading across North America, Europe and Australasia, which discriminates heavily against (poor) people from the South, Muslims, and other potentially dissenting groups (Herman 2011).

The attacks on September 11, 2001 have ushered in a brand of political the-ology in the US not dissimilar to that of Nazi legal philosopher Carl Schmitt.

According to such models of political authoritarianism, 'exceptional historical moments ... require a suspension of norms, e.g., curtailment of civil liberties and other deprivations and necessary sacrifices, and that the executive (the President) is justified in exercising what amounts to dictatorial and unconstitutional powers' (Worrell 2013 p.16). This model also underpins the resurgent binary opposition of either 'with us' or 'for the terrorists' that has characterised American geopolitics since 9/11. Even prior to the collapse of the USSR, 'terrorism' had been seized upon as a potential threat that could

> legitimate a more-of-the-same posture that would continue to plow trillions of dollars into the military industrial complex, augment the state security apparatus, and demand further austerity for Americans and subjugated nations in order to fund yet another wave of military adventurism.
>
> WORRELL 2013 p.18; see also Worrell 2011

The unfolding of neoliberalism has severely degraded political freedoms while, simultaneously, corroding the political structures which provide essential support to the reproduction of this system of accumulation. Neoliberalism has concentrated income and power back to levels last seen in the 1930s, diluted the accountability of the state, and ratcheted up state-sponsored intolerance against collective action and against racial, national, religious, political and other minorities.[15] Each success has consolidated the hegemony of neoliberalism while, simultaneously, eroding its political legitimacy and demonstrating that individual initiatives cannot counteract its socially regressive logic. *The triumph of neoliberalism has posited the need for collective action against it.* Whilst mass initiatives have achieved only limited successes so far (see Section 4), failure has also triggered continuing experimentation with new modalities of resistance. Effective ones will eventually be found, not least in the face of continuing macroeconomic crisis, providing a strong incentive for the mobilisation of larger numbers of people. Accommodation will gradually become impossible, while enhancing repression will threaten the political foundations on which neoliberalism currently stands.

7   Transcending Neoliberalism through Radical Democracy

Neoliberalism has transformed the political landscape. The political spectrum has shifted to the right; left parties, trade unions and mass organisations have

---

15   Bourdieu (1998, p.4) alluded to 'the destruction of all the collective institutions capable of counteracting the effects of the infernal machine'.

imploded in most countries, and domestic politics is now driven by the need to insulate 'the market' from popular demands – that is, the imperative of labour control to secure international competitiveness. Job security has declined and unemployment has risen almost everywhere. Experience shows that these income-concentrating dynamics of accumulation can be limited, but not reversed, by marginal (Keynesian) interventions.

These economic, political and social transformations are mutually reinforcing and, to-date, they have secured the stability of the neoliberal system of accumulation. This section reviews the strengths and the main contradictions of neoliberalism, examining the vulnerabilities which may play a role in the construction of an alternative system of accumulation. It will be argued that, since neoliberalism has reshaped social relations and transformed the material basis of social reproduction, it cannot be dislocated primarily through the ballot box. Yet, the main lever of transcendence of neoliberalism must be political, and based on the *expansion and radicalisation of democracy*. Five areas of vulnerability of neoliberalism are especially relevant.

First, 'economic deregulation' and 'globalisation' have dismantled the established systems of production, reduced the degree of coordination of economic activity, created undesirable employment patterns, fed the concentration of income and wealth, and precluded the use of industrial policy instruments for the implementation of socially determined priorities. In doing this, and despite claims that it delivers macroeconomic stability, sustained growth and improvements in living standards, neoliberalism has sapped growth and social welfare, fuelled unsustainable patterns of production and consumption, and increased economic uncertainty, volatility and vulnerability to (financial) crisis.

Second, financial sector control of the main sources of capital has systematically favoured large capital at the expense of small capital and the workers, belying neoliberal claims to level the playing field and foster competition. Because of its strategic economic position, mediating payments, savings, investment flows and international transactions, finance can drain capital from production, and its activities have often created economic volatility and balance of payments instability. At a further remove, the globalisation of financial markets 'is essentially an *Americanization of financial institutions*' as the specific institutional structure and speculative dynamism unique to American finance displaces other financial systems (Krier 2008, p.131). As such, American-style transactional finance is attaining a global hegemony with virtually every economy in the world ... moving toward the adoption of American-style financial institutions' (Krier 2005, p.266). This institutional structure underpins the essentially speculative character of contemporary

US finance, which shapes other aspects of economic life, especially the stock-market driven restructuring of industry.[16] This modality of speculative man-agement has been highly destructive, as speculators' drive for short-term share price has resulted in the devaluation of constant capital and the wholesale elimination of jobs. In finance-driven economies, accumulation has tended to take the form of bubbles which eventually collapse with destructive implica-tions and requiring state-sponsored bailouts. These cycles have included the international debt crisis of the early 1980s, the US savings and loan crisis of the 1980s, the stock market crashes of the 1980s and 1990s, the Japanese crisis drag-ging on since the late 1980s, the crises in several middle income countries at the end of the twentieth century, and the dotcom, financial and housing bub-bles of the 2000s, culminating with the current global meltdown. At this level, too, neoliberal claims to promote stability and growth have no basis in reality.

Third, neoliberal policies are justified ideologically through the impera-tives of 'business confidence' and 'competitivity'. This is misleading, because confidence is intangible, self-referential and volatile, while the pursuit of competitivity amounts to the self-infliction of capital's imperatives, usually for someone else's profit. It is, then, unsurprising that the mainstream sys-tematically overestimates the investment and growth rates ensuing from the neoliberal policy prescriptions, while sweeping under the carpet the inevitable spread of fraud and criminality in economic life.

Fourth, the neoliberal policies are not self-correcting. Instead of leading to a change of course, failure to achieve their stated aims generally leads to the deepening and extension of the reforms, with the excuse of ensuring imple-mentation and the promise of 'imminent' success this time around.

Fifth, as detailed above, neoliberalism is inimical to economic democracy, and it hollows out political democracy.

The ongoing global crisis has exposed these contradictions of global neo-liberalism, and disrupted its reproduction to an unprecedented extent. The crisis has also shaken the political legitimacy of neoliberalism, and raised the

---

16   As Krier details, the key dimensions that underpin the inherently speculative charac-ter of American securities markets include mass participation in financial markets, the structure of financial intermediation (and the privileging of *market* intermediation), the relative dominance of secondary markets, the accommodation of extensive specula-tion relative to investment, the emphasising and predominance of equity (as opposed to debentures), the preponderance of 'private associations' as the principal organisational form of financial securities markets, and the form of financial accounting and extensive-ness of financial information available to market participants. Collectively, these seven dimensions underpin the analysis 'of corporate reorganization for speculative gain in contemporary America' (Krier 2008, p.136; see also Panitch and Gindin 2012).

imperative to change the system of accumulation. This is not a straightforward demand. Despite its contradictions, outlined in previous sections, the material basis of neoliberalism – the patterns of production, employment, trade and finance developed during the last 30 years – remains firmly in place, and has even been reinforced with each successive crisis (Saad-Filho 2011 and Chapter 15). In contrast, *neoliberalism is increasingly vulnerable at the political level*, where repeated mismatches between promises and reality, structural contradictions and successive crises have sapped its legitimacy. At the same time, the hollowing out of democracy blocks the political expression of dissent and feeds apathy, populism and the far right (Mair 2009).

The economic strengths of neoliberalism, the corrosion of its ideological foundations, the sclerosis of the political institutions regulating its metabolism and the loss of credibility of the political process suggest that electoral strategies to replace this system of accumulation are limited, while attempts to do so primarily through changes in social, industrial, financial and monetary policies will invariably fall short of expectations. Neoliberalism cannot be challenged effectively through the political institutions and modalities of dissent which neoliberalism itself has put into place.

The implications of this approach can be gleaned by analogy with the experience of another system of accumulation. In his perceptive critique of the former Soviet Bloc states, Bauman (1991, pp. 189–190, 192) argues that the:

> dictatorship over needs and monopoly over the means and procedures of needs-satisfaction [made] the communist state an obvious target of individual disaffection, but it cannot but collectivize individual frustrations in the same way it collectivized the vehicles of gratification ... [Thus, although opposition] came from diverse quarters and [was] motivated by diverse reasons ... the ... concentration of ... discontents, through their convergence on one well defined, undisguised and obvious target, added considerably to their collective strength and assured them of the effectiveness that they would not necessarily possess in another sociopolitical framework.

The metamorphosis of the defining features and the key sources of strength of Soviet-type regimes into their fatal weaknesses suggests that the capture of the political process by neoliberalism might bring similar consequences. On the one hand, the loss of democratic legitimacy can shred the political cloak sheltering the formulation, implementation and monitoring of neoliberal policies from majority influence. On the other hand, neoliberalism may not survive the recovery of the democratic rights lost in the last 30 years, and it is certainly incompatible with the extension of democracy into the economic domain.

A left strategy to build a democratic system of accumulation can focus on mass mobilisations to transform existing neoliberal states and processes of socio-economic reproduction and political representation. The new social movements ('anti-globalisation', 'Stop the War', 'anti-capitalism', 'Indignados', 'Occupy' and so on) have challenged the legitimacy of neoliberalism and demanded the expansion of democracy, but they have not yet offered a systemic alternative including a new material basis of social reproduction. The demand for the *expansion and radicalisation of political and economic democracy* can integrate a wide variety of struggles and support the emergence of these alternatives, while simultaneously destabilising neoliberalism (Albo 1997, Cairns and Sears 2012, Ghosh 2012, Rooksby 2011, Roper 2013 and the *Socialist Register 2013*, among a vast literature).

The economic democracy being advocated here can be defined at two levels. At the microeconomic level, it is determined by the influence of the workers in their place of employment. This type of democracy was significant in former socialist countries, especially Yugoslavia and the USSR, and it can reduce alienation in production and empower people in an important sphere of their lives. However, it can also reduce the degree of macroeconomic co-ordination, prevent the reorganisation of the labour process, and sap the incentives for technical change (Campbell 2011, Gunn 2011). At the macroeconomic level economic democracy is determined by the degree of influence of the citizens upon the material conditions of social reproduction. This includes the economic policies and strategies of the state, the level and composition of the national product, the structure of demand and employment, the conditions of work, the level, structure and distribution of income, assets, transfers and taxes. Evidently, this essay focuses upon the latter, while recognising the significance of the former as well as the specific problems it posits, which cannot be examined here.

In suggesting this course of action – focusing upon the expansion and radicalisation of macroeconomic democracy – social analysis must, first, recognise that each historical epoch, and each system of accumulation, brings with it a specific configuration of class and other relations, which correspond to definite modes of political representation and particular forms of struggle.[17] Second, socialism is not currently on the agenda and, while the left ought to reiterate its continuing relevance, this aspiration should not cloud the mass mobilisations which can take place today. Third, the consolidation of the new

---

17   See McNally (2012) for a contemporary survey. For an earlier period: 'history ... has not merely dispelled the erroneous notions we then held; it has also completely transformed the conditions under which the proletariat has to fight. *The mode of struggle of 1848 is today obsolete in every respect*' (Engels 1998, p.10, emphasis added).

mass movements requires a renewal of the sense of *collectivity* which has been systematically dismantled by neoliberalism. Previously, collectivity drew upon a shared working class culture, trade unions, left parties, nationalist campaigns and, in some countries, populist movements. These have been largely wiped out. New forms of organisation will need to be experimented with, until some of them show traction. Fourth, while broad political alliances are indispensable, there should be no presumption that there is an antagonic relationship between production and finance under neoliberalism, and no expectation that industrial capital will support (and, much less, lead) the emergence of alternatives to neoliberalism. The internationalisation of accumulation and financial market control of state funding have made the realisation of profits strictly dependent on the interests of global capital, making attempts to decouple from the neoliberal compact simply too costly for most capitalists.

The economic and political platforms against neoliberalism, and the aspiration for democracy, can be integrated through demands for *redistributive, democratic and sustainable economic policies*. These demands are, simultaneously, fundamental conditions for a substantive democracy, and incompatible with neoliberalism. They also reflect the notion that the most promising lever for challenging neoliberalism is *political*, both because neoliberalism's key vulnerabilities are in the political domain, and because political mass movements are essential for effecting meaningful social and economic changes.

Building alternatives to the dominant system of accumulation requires, then, the integration of economic and political demands. These directly bring to light the complementarities between democracy and socialism while, at the same time, demonstrating the incompatibility between capitalism and democracy. It is at this point that practical questions can be raised about transcending *capitalism*, rather than merely one of its modes of existence. These demands can be driven forward only by a politically re-articulated working class, as one of the main levers for its own economic recomposition. The difficulty is that this virtuous circle cannot be wished into being. It requires the development of new structures of political representation corresponding to the current mode of existence of this class and, in turn, supporting the emergence of new modalities of social reproduction.

8   Conclusion

Advocates of neoliberalism have often drawn upon Friedrich von Hayek's notions of individual rights and freedoms to argue that markets provide a more efficient mechanism of resource allocation and conflict resolution than democratic processes. Market processes can address certain categories of conflict efficiently, but they are limited because they are predicated upon the social inequalities which structure social reproduction under capitalism. Market processes can also undermine popular sovereignty because they atomise society and dislocate the institutions protecting collective rights and providing public goods.

The incompatibility between (capitalist) market relations and the democratisation of social relations is expressed, at different levels, by the paradoxes of democracy identified in this essay. They also suggest that political democracy is a necessary but insufficient condition for economic democracy. Moreover, capitalism can accommodate only a limited political democracy, because the latter is based upon universal inclusion and equal rights, while market processes (the nature of capital posited as external necessity) are predicated upon minority control of the means of production and class-based disparities of influence over the conditions of social reproduction. Finally, competition and the spread of market relations generate inequalities of income and wealth that can limit both political and economic democracy. For example, the concentration of economic power facilitates the domination of the political process by the rich, and limits the capacity of the majority to influence the economic policies.

This essay has also shown that neoliberalism has captured the political process and placed it at the service of capital. This capture has weakened conventional democracy beyond repair. On the one hand, pre-neoliberal civil liberties will not be restored easily. On the other hand, authoritarian modalities of governance have emerged both within and outside neoliberalism. However, the weakening of democratic structures of representation is, increasingly, blocking the political processes which help to secure the smooth accumulation of capital. The erosion of democracy is a direct product of neoliberalism where it is hegemonic, and it contaminates the alternatives currently in existence. It also undermines the stability of the global system of accumulation.

Recognition of the limitations of democracy under capitalism raises a final paradox: why should collectivities fight for the expansion of democracy if it is bound to be limited? This paradox can be addressed at three levels. First, democracy is valuable in itself, because it facilitates the expression of social preferences and can offer a platform for the improvement of the living and working conditions of the vast majority of people. Second, the contradictions between (substantive) economic and (formal) political democracy illuminate the limitations of neoliberalism, as the contemporary form of capitalism. Third, the expansion of economic and political democracy requires the extension of the political sphere. Specifically, political struggles about the nature and content of democracy bring together individual and social motivations, and they can throw into question the class relations and the ultimate limits of capitalism. For example, they can show that democracy can become more than an institutional shell, acquire transformative content, and include critically important spheres of life *only* if the capitalist monopoly of economic power is abolished. In this sense, struggles against neoliberalism can be supported by mobilisations around *democracy*. In turn, success depends on the extent to which these democratic movements become *anti-capitalist*. The expansion of democracy operates, then, as a synthesis of many determinations in the mobilisation against neoliberalism.

CHAPTER 13

Monetary Policy and Neoliberalism

This essay[1] reviews the monetary policy framework associated with neoliberalism which, as a general rule, is based on the so-called New Monetary Policy Consensus (NMPC),[2] which includes both inflation targeting (IT) and Central Bank independence (CBI). The NMPC became the dominant ('best practice') monetary policy paradigm in several advanced, middle-income and, increasingly, poor countries, gradually, since the late 1980s.[3] The popularity of the NMPC among mainstream economists and policymakers is based on the theoretical strengths of the NMPC (from the point of view of neoclassical economics), and the alleged successes of countries implementing this policy compact.

From this point of view, the NMPC is meant to address a key policy problem: how to anchor domestic monetary systems in the age of neoliberalism, with societies fractured by incompatible political and economic demands, where working classes are under continuing attack, and with economies based on inconvertible credit money and with bloated and liberalised financial systems. In this sense, the NMPC helps to underpin neoliberalism. The manner in which it does so, examined below, makes the NMPC the most appropriate monetary policy strategy for the age of neoliberalism.[4] In this sense, the NMPC is hegemonic: it incorporates the most refined policy conclusions drawing upon mainstream economic theory; it is attractively packaged, and its policy recommendations draw upon the 'common sense' of the neoliberal age;

---

1   This essay is original; it is based on 'Monetary Policy in the Neoliberal Transition: A Political Economy Review of Keynesianism, Monetarism and Inflation Targeting', in R. Albritton, B. Jessop and R. Westra (eds.), Political Economy and Global Capitalism: The 21st Century, Present and Future, London, Anthem Press, 2007, pp.89–119, and 'Monetary Policy and Neoliberalism', in D. Cahill, M. Cooper and M. Konings (eds.) SAGE Handbook of Neoliberalism. London: Sage, 2018, pp. 335–346.
2   The term NMPC is suggested by Arestis and Sawyer (2005) and Fontana (2006); for a review, see Chapter 13.
3   An incomplete list includes Australia, Brazil, Canada, Chile, Colombia, Czech Republic, Ghana, Guatemala, Hungary, Iceland, Indonesia, Israel, Mexico, New Zealand, Norway, Peru, Philippines, Poland, Serbia, South Africa, South Korea, Sweden, Thailand, Turkey and the United Kingdom (see Hammond, 2012 and Roger, 2010). Countries following similar strategies include Argentina, Japan, Singapore, Switzerland and the United States plus the Eurozone.
4   '[C]entral banks appear to have learned how to maintain inflation at a low level. For many Central Banks, this new era has been characterised by Central Banks adopting implicit or explicit inflation targets' (Bordo et al. 2003, p.1).

consequently, they are easy to understand and justify. These policies also promote powerful (finance-driven) interests that are presented as expressions of the 'common good'.

The success of this monetary policy paradigm is not simply the outcome of reasoned academic debate and enlightened policymaking. It is, primarily, due to the reorganisation of social relations and the transformation of economic policies in country after country under neoliberalism. It was only in this context that the mainstream could address important shortcomings of the anti-inflation strategies attempted after the collapse of the Bretton Woods System, that were generally based either on 'social accords', or money supply or exchange rate targeting. Despite the achievements of the NMPC in policy practice, this essay shows that the theoretical foundations of IT and CBI are both eclectic (including insights from the monetarist, new classical and new Keynesian schools of thought) and analytically flawed. They cannot represent reality adequately and, consequently, fail to deploy policy instruments consistently in order to maintain economic stability, especially in challenging times, when sensible monetary policies are most needed. In difficult times, countries must resort to pragmatic policies outside the NMPC.

The essay includes eight sections. After this introduction, the first substantive section reviews the development of the mainstream theory and policy practice of inflation control, focusing on IT and CBI. The second describes the analytical underpinnings of the NMPC and the third focuses on its institutional features and modalities of operation in practice. The fourth considers its outcomes, and explains why they are difficult to assess. The fifth focuses on the costs of the NMPC, including high interest rates, conflicts between IT and balance of payments equilibrium, financial instability and the costs of CBI. The sixth examines the implications for the NMPC of the global financial crisis, starting in 2007. The conclusion summarises the main lessons from this essay, and outlines the challenges ahead.

1   Monetary Policy for Mature Neoliberalism

In the post-war (Keynesian-social democratic) 'golden age' of capitalism, inflation was generally assumed to be due to cost pressures, especially rising wages and balance of payments difficulties. Policy recommendations included, then, incomes policies and exchange rate adjustments within the Bretton Woods System, to allow persistent differences in rates of productivity growth to be absorbed through the exchange rate rather than through changes in employment. Perceptions shifted between the late 1960s and the early 1980s, when inflationary pressures were assumed to result from adverse supply shocks, excess money supply growth and unreasonably optimistic assumptions about the stability of the Phillips curve. In this period, many mainstream economists leaned towards monetarism, and suggested that governments should control inflation through labour market reforms to increase 'flexibility' and cut employment costs, and impose money supply (or, alternatively, exchange rate) targets in order to secure fiscal discipline and anchor private sector expectations.

The monetarist experiences in Germany, Switzerland, the UK, the US and elsewhere during the 1980s did not vindicate the claims that money supply targeting was either feasible or conducive to inflation stabilisation; in turn, exchange rate anchors failed catastrophically in Argentina, Chile and Uruguay (Díaz-Alejandro 1985). In addition to those difficulties of implementation, monetarist theory was badly damaged by the criticisms inflicted by new classical, Keynesian and radical political economists.[5] Briefly, Keynesians and radical political economists argued, first, that since the velocity of money and the money demand function are unstable, the relationship between money supply and nominal income is unpredictable. Therefore, even if money supply targeting were feasible (which it is not), it would be insufficient to control inflation. Second, although in a monetary economy there must be some relationship between changes in the stock of money and changes in the price level, this does not imply that the growth of the money stock *determines* the rate of inflation. It follows that, even if money supply targeting can help to squeeze inflation out of the economy, it does so slowly and unreliably, and potentially at a high cost. Third, government attempts in the 1970s and 1980s to control the money supply while, at the same time, liberalising the financial system and the capital account of the balance of payments were self-defeating. Liberalisation modified the monetary transmission process and the linkages between money, finance and output. It also created incentives for the development of financial instruments that blurred the definition of the monetary aggregates and bypassed existing controls over the supply of money, throwing the entire exercise into confusion. Even the radically mainstream new classical economists criticised the monetarist experiment. In spite of their general agreement with the monetarist analysis of inflation, the new classicals claimed that the policy shift towards money supply targeting induced changes in private sector behaviour that invalidated the predictions of existing econometric models. Consequently, the monetarist policy recommendations were doubtful analytically, and potentially unhelpful in practice.

---

5   For an overview of these debates, see Carlin and Soskice (1990), Levacic and Rebmann (1982) and Sawyer (1989).

The shortcomings of monetarism and the heavy criticisms levelled by its opponents contributed to the emergence of a vast literature on inflation and stabilisation in the 1980s. In the absence of significant wage pressures or major supply shocks during the period of consolidation of neoliberalism in the leading economies, inflation was associated with fiscal deficits, adverse expectations, and lack of government policy credibility.[6] This diagnosis directly led to policy recommendations focusing on the need for greater 'policy credibility', supported by some kind of nominal anchor, especially exchange rate or inflation targets. These anchors were ostensibly designed to 'discipline the politicians' and remove the inflation bias. These policy recommendations were followed by pressures for CBI and trade and capital account liberalisation, in order to dismantle selected features of the Welfare State, further increase labour market flexibility, curtail the remaining sources of potential labour unrest, and impose finance-friendly policy discipline on presumably reluctant governments (see Gowan 1999, Panitch and Gindin 2005, and Rude 2005).

By the mid-1990s, the NMPC had already become the hegemonic framework for anti-inflation policy. This policy regime was perceived to be the most conducive to the consolidation of the low inflation regime recently achieved in the advanced economies, and it spread rapidly from pioneering New Zealand, which first adopted it in 1989. The NMPC also seemed to have something to offer to the middle-income and poor countries, even though their Central Banks generally lack experience supervising complex, liberalised and internationally integrated financial systems (which, nevertheless, were imposed by external as well as internal pressures, as part of the neoliberal transitions in these countries). In those countries, the NMPC could, allegedly, deliver greater economic stability, institutional transparency, objective monetary policy rules, standardised channels for the diffusion of information and, hopefully, reduce the costs of international financial integration.

2   Inflation Targeting and Central Bank Independence

For mainstream economic theory, price stability is the most important contribution that monetary policy can give to social welfare. Attempts to use monetary policy to achieve other goals, such as higher output, employment or productivity growth, should be avoided because they tend to reduce economic efficiency and introduce an inflationary bias into the economy. In order to achieve that desirable outcome, the government should signal its

---

6   For a review of the transition to neoliberalism in the USA, and the role of finance, see Panitch and Gindin (2012) and Konings (2018).

'explicit acknowledgement that low and stable inflation is the overriding goal of monetary policy' (Bernanke and Mishkin 1997, p.97), by setting a legally binding target for the rate of inflation. The IT is usually defined as a low positive interval, including a small tolerance margin. This should be the only nominal anchor in the economy, as IT cannot be pursued simultaneously with money supply, wages, employment or exchange rate targets (in other words, IT tends to require at the very least a 'dirty' floating exchange rate regime; see Agénor 2001).

The inflation-targeting regime (ITR) presumably operates at multiple levels. It institutionalises 'good' (i.e., mainstream) monetary policies, increases the 'transparency' of Central Bank policies and provides a trend for the inflation expectations of the private sector, which should reduce uncertainty and facilitate economic planning and co-ordination. The transition costs to the new policy regime depend on the credibility of the government's commitment to IT and the reputation of the Central Bank. The higher they are, the faster expectations will converge to the IT, and the lower the output costs of reducing inflation (the 'sacrifice ratio'). Once established, ITR should bring several benefits, including lower and more stable inflation, higher economic growth rates, and a permanently lower sacrifice ratio. These potential benefits suggest that other policy objectives such as employment generation, economic growth and income distribution are subordinated to the IT (Carare et al. 2002, p.5).

In turn, CBI institutionalises the primary responsibility of the Central Bank for achieving the IT, which presumably limits the influence of politicians over economic policy-making, greatly reducing uncertainty and eliminating time-inconsistency, the political business cycle and the inflation bias. Therefore, CBI should also contribute to the improvement of economic performance. CBI can include two types of independence. Political or administrative independence involves the appointment of Central Bank directors for fixed terms (preferably not coinciding with the mandate of the country's President or the legislators, in order to ensure policy continuity), and the regular assessment of the Bank's performance through the trajectory of inflation and regular Bank reports to the government, Parliament and the media. In contrast, instrument independence involves the Bank's autonomy to conduct monetary policy, essentially calibrating the interest rates in order to fine-tune the level of economic activity and, therefore, the rate of inflation. The institutional arrangements underpinning CBI regimes vary between countries and over time. Differences may include the precise duties of the Bank, the policy instruments that it controls, its degree of autonomy, the relationship between the Central Bank and other government departments, the procedure for appointing Bank directors, and the limits on government borrowing from the Bank. In spite of their practical significance, these details will be ignored in what follows.

The NMPC is a monetary policy paradigm for *mature neoliberalism*. In contrast with exchange rate targeting, for example, IT is not an inflation stabilisation strategy (it can be introduced only when inflation is already low), and it operates optimally when the financial markets have already been liberalised. Despite these limitations, IT is the policy regime most conducive to the consolidation of low inflation under neoliberalism, because there is little scope for the deviation of the goals of monetary policy from the preservation of value of money. Moreover, in contrast with exchange rate targeting, that is very rigid, IT allows monetary policy to respond flexibly to adverse shocks, reducing the vulnerability of the policy regime to speculation, instability and crisis. Even more significantly, IT locks government policy into the neoliberal framework institutionally. For these reasons, IT is potentially a durable monetary policy regime, and it is singularly appropriate for those countries completing the transition to neoliberalism. These features help to explain the adoption of ITR in a rapidly rising number of countries.

Supporters of ITR claim that it can 'deliver as much price level stability as a commodity [gold] standard' (Bordo et al. 2003, p.1). Despite these considerable strengths, even the mainstream cautions that ITR is not appropriate for all countries and circumstances, and that five conditions must be satisfied to secure the viability of this policy regime. First, the monetary authorities need effective policy tools and autonomy to deploy them. Second, the absence of fiscal dominance; that is, fiscal policy considerations cannot play a determining role in macroeconomic policy decisions. This requires strict limits on government borrowing from the Central Bank, while public sector funding should rely on a broad tax base and efficient tax system, rather than seignorage. Third, the rate of inflation should be low enough at the start to ensure a reasonable degree of Central Bank control of the monetary aggregates (therefore, and to reiterate, IT is *not* a stabilisation policy). Fourth, the financial markets must be sufficiently developed, deep and efficient to absorb placements of public debt, such as treasury bills or bonds, which could otherwise side-track monetary and fiscal policy. Fifth, the absence of external dominance – in other words, the country's balance of payments should be sufficiently solid to allow monetary policy to focus on inflation control, rather than being constantly diverted by the need to respond to adverse external shocks.

3   The New Monetary Policy Consensus in Practice

The economic model underpinning the NMPC is very simple (see Figure 1). It includes two key parameters: the IT and the inflation expectations; the former

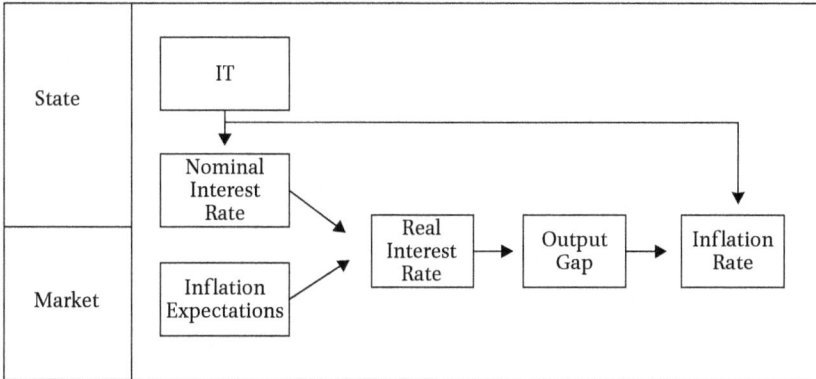

FIGURE 1   Inflation targeting

is set by the government and the latter by 'the market'. The model also includes one discretionary policy instrument, the nominal interest rate.

The government policy objective is to eliminate the inflation gap (the difference between the rate of inflation and the IT) at a specific point in the future (the policy horizon). The model presumes that the rate of inflation is jointly determined by the inflation expectations and the output gap, with the latter fluctuating around a supply-side equilibrium. Alternatively, unemployment fluctuates around either the natural rate of unemployment (NRU) or the non-accelerating inflation rate of unemployment (NAIRU), such that unemployment below (above) the NRU/NAIRU would lead to higher (lower) rates of inflation. The output gap (the difference between the rate of unemployment and the NRU/NAIRU) is determined by the real interest rate. Finally, the real interest rate is, by definition, equal to the nominal interest rate minus expected inflation.

In this model, the Central Bank attempts to hit the IT through the manipulation of the nominal interest rate, in order to influence the state of expectations and, at a further remove, fine-tune aggregate demand. If the Central Bank forecasts a positive inflation gap during the policy horizon, either because aggregate demand is too high or because the market expects that inflation will rise in the future for whatever reason, the Bank will adjust monetary policy, usually by raising nominal (and, *ceteris paribus*, real) interest rates.

The model implies that inflation control is achieved through fluctuations in the output gap. The lower is the government's tolerance to an inflation gap, the shorter is the time-span available to achieve IT. Similarly, the more open is the economy, the larger will be the fluctuations of the output gap and, therefore, the variance of the unemployment rate. Finally, although a wide variety of instruments can be used to achieve IT, in practice Central Banks tend to focus on the manipulation of nominal interest rates. This instrument is especially convenient because it is simple to use; it is also supposedly non-distortionary, because it does not systematically discriminate between economic sectors and, therefore, does not lead to resource misallocation.

In contrast with money supply or exchange rate targeting regimes, the NMPC is flexible at three levels. First, the IT is normally low and positive, rather than zero, and the targets are usually bands, rather than points. Bands are used because of the possibility of misspecification, parameter uncertainty or structural breaks in the Central Bank's economic model, given the uncertainty surrounding the monetary transmission process and the multiple (and uncertain) links between the policy levers and inflation outcomes, and because of the possibility of shocks. All this would make it difficult to hit continuously a single point target for inflation. Even trying to do so might increase the volatility of the interest rates which, in turn, could have destabilising effects.

Second, in exchange rate targeting regimes it is impossible to depart temporarily from the peg without a severe loss of credibility or a currency crisis. In contrast, in ITR the Central Bank normally targets inflation over a policy horizon of one to three years in the future, so it can ignore transitory disturbances that, in and of themselves, would not trigger long-term changes in the rate of inflation. In order to make the ITR even more robust, inflation is usually measured by a 'core' (rather than headline) price index, usually the CPI. This is to minimise the impact of adverse supply shocks, natural disasters, sudden fluctuations in the exchange rate or terms of trade, seasonal variations of food and energy prices, changes in indirect taxes, regulated prices, subsidies and mortgage payments, and even the direct (first-round) impact of interest rate changes.

Third, although interest rate manipulation is the favoured monetary policy instrument under ITR, the Central Bank should ideally deploy all relevant information and a wide variety of tools in order to pursue IT. These tools depend on the institutional structure of the Central Bank, the country's political system and the policymaker's conviction about how best to operate. They could include, for example, changes in banking regulations or the required reserve ratios, the imposition of differential asset requirements, or anything else, as long as it contributes to achieving IT within the policy horizon. In sum, the NMPC allegedly offers the optimal combination of instruments to lock in low inflation and create conditions for sustainable growth, bringing together the virtues of policy simplicity, credibility, legitimacy, sustainability and flexibility. Claims such as these have contributed to the rapid growth of the appeal of the NMPC around the world.

4   The Performance of Inflation-Targeting Regime and Central Bank
       Independence

There is a vast literature assessing the performance of IT and CBI. This section
focuses on evaluations of IT only, for reasons of space.

Several studies have identified gains stemming from IT in such areas as
lower inflation rates, volatility and inertia, improved expectations, faster absorption of adverse shocks, lower sacrifice ratio, output stabilisation, and the
convergence of poorly performing countries toward well performing country
standards.[7] Similar gains have been attributed to CBI.[8] However, other studies
have been less supportive, claiming that there is no evidence that IT and/or
CBI improve economic performance.[9] These conflicting views are partly due
to the use of distinct approaches, datasets and econometric methodologies;
as such, they are no different from the contradictory views in other areas of
macroeconomics. However, there may be four additional reasons for these
diverging views of the efficacy and efficiency of IT and CBI.

First, it is difficult to classify policy regimes rigorously. Countries can be
grouped in different ways according to whether they follow 'explicit' or 'implicit' IT policies, or the extent to which their Central Banks have administrative
and/or instrument independence. If one also controls for the structural differences between the economies being examined, the relevant samples tend
to become very small, making it difficult to make meaningful before-after or
with-without comparisons of performance.

Second, IT and CBI experiences are relatively new, with none starting before 1989, and many being much more recent than that. It is difficult to draw
clear conclusions based on those short and disparate sample periods.

Third, as was shown above, IT is not an inflation stabilisation strategy. Consequently, although high inflation countries may be more inclined to adopt
IT, they can do so only *after* a successful disinflation programme that is, itself,
unrelated to IT. On adoption, the ITR will almost invariably inherit falling inflation rates, growing monetary policy credibility and, quite possibly (if their
economies have been in the doldrums for long periods), above-trend growth

---

7   See, for example, Bernanke et al. (1999), Carvalho-Filho (2010), Debelle et al. (1998), Dot-
    sey (2006), Landerretche et al. (2001), Mishkin (1999), Mishkin and Schmidt-Hebbel (2002),
    Roger (2010) and Svensson (1997a, 1997b, 2007).
8   See, for example, Alesina (1989), Alesina and Summers (1993), Cukierman (1992), Grilli et al.
    (1991) and Hammond (2012).
9   See, for example, Agénor (2001: 43–44), Bibow (2010), Carare et al. (2002), Carare and Stone
    (2003), Cecchetti and Ehrmann (1999), Chang and Grabel (2004: 183–184), Debelle et al.
    (1998), Neumann and von Hagen (2002) and Wray (2014).

rates. These favourable developments are *conditions* for IT rather than outcomes of this policy regime, and they should be factored into the assessment of the performance of ITR.

Fourth, even when the economic performance of IT countries improves *more* than that of non-IT countries by whatever criteria, it cannot be assumed that the difference was *due* to IT. For example, Ball and Sheridan (2003) find evidence that the countries showing the greatest performance improvements during their period of analysis were those with the worst performance in the previous period, and these tend to be IT countries (possibly because underperforming economies are more likely to change policy regimes). However, those improvements could be due simply to their regression to the mean, which helps to explain why performance *also* improved in the non-IT countries. Therefore, the apparent success of IT countries may be due to their having 'high initial inflation and large decreases, but the decrease for a given initial level looks similar for targeters and non-targeters' (Ball and Sheridan 2003, p.16). Once they control for regression towards the mean, Ball and Sheridan find no evidence that IT improves any aspect of economic performance.

In conclusion, IT and CBI seem to have little influence on economic performance. Why, then, does the mainstream discourse place so much emphasis on IT and CBI, and why does even the most cursory perusal of IMF publications reveal such enthusiasm for IT and CBI? Three contributing factors can be readily identified. First, mainstream theory is structurally predisposed to see value in IT and CBI, since they share the same methodological foundations (real-monetary dichotomy, quantitativism, abhorrence of state intervention, and so on). Second, IT and CBI became *fashionable* in the 1990s. They became part of the common sense of the neoliberal age, and these policy recommendations tended to creep unthinkingly into even heterodox discourse. Third, IT and CBI promote the interests of domestic and international finance, ensuring that they will find support among a very powerful constituency (see below).

5   Costs of the New Monetary Policy Consensus

This section examines the potential economic costs of the inflation policies associated with the NMPC. Four types of costs are considered: the cost of using interest rates as the main tool to control inflation, the cost of conflicts between IT and balance of payments equilibrium, the cost of financial instability, and the costs of CBI.

5.1   The Cost of High Interest Rates

It was shown above that, in the NMPC, inflation control is achieved primarily through the manipulation of interest rates. This implies that real interest rates will tend to be higher in this policy regime than under an alternative arrangement in which a wider set of instruments plays a more significant role in (non-targeted) inflation control.

There is no question that high interest rates can reduce inflation, since they increase the costs of production, investment and consumption, and may trigger government spending cuts because of the higher cost of servicing domestic public debt. Weaker aggregate demand tends to compress profit margins, at least in the competitive sector of the economy (oligopolistic firms may be able to increase prices in order to defend their profits, but this will be ignored here). In turn, higher financial costs can force highly leveraged or financially weaker firms into bankruptcy, regardless of their economic prospects, technical efficiency or strategic importance. The remaining firms could respond to these cost and demand pressures by reducing variable costs in different ways. For example, they could seek to evade tax or social security payments, increase the intensity of work, the number of unpaid hours or labour turnover, delay bill payments, and so on.

High interest rates also change the relationship between the tradable and non-tradable sectors, industry and agriculture, and the sub-sectors within them; despite appearances, they are anything but neutral policy tools. The sectoral and distributional impact of higher interest rates cannot be anticipated precisely, since it depends on the structure of the economy, the pattern of demand, the response of the exchange rate and the export and import sectors, and other variables. However, it is widely accepted that higher interest rates tend to bring gains to finance, both in terms of policy influence and through additional shares of national income.[10]

5.2   The Cost of Conflicts between Inflation Targeting and Balance of Payments Equilibrium

ITR may conflict with intertemporal balance of payments equilibrium at two levels. First, there may be conflicting pressures on the rate of interest. In any small open economy with relatively developed currency and financial markets, there are close relationships between the interest rate, the rate of inflation, the fiscal deficit, the rate of unemployment, the exchange rate, and the level and

---

10   See Argitis and Pitelis (2001), Mann (2013), and Rochon (2007). For alternative views, see Brancaccio and Fontana (2013) and Knibbe (2015).

direction of international capital flows. Correspondingly, there is *a priori* no guarantee that a single interest rate can deliver, simultaneously, IT, a sustainable fiscal balance, exchange rate stability, balance of payments equilibrium and low unemployment. Achieving these goals requires a combination of policies in which interest rates should play an important but not necessarily decisive role.

Attributing unwarranted priority to the manipulation of interest rates in economic policymaking implies that these rates will tend to be determined by the higher of two levels: those required achieving IT, and those needed to close the balance of payments, with the rate of unemployment being a residual. If the balance of payments constraint is binding, the exchange rate may be stable but aggregate demand will tend to be too low, potentially leading to a stabilisation trap: a persistent situation of low growth, high unemployment and, potentially, intractable problems of poverty and inequality. Alternatively, if the IT is binding, the interest rate will be too high for balance of payments equilibrium, leading to excessive inflows of foreign capital, especially if international capital movements have been deregulated, as is often the case in countries in transition to neoliberalism. The ensuing increase in external liabilities will tend to be sterilised by a swelling domestic public debt; the inflows may also trigger unsustainable consumption or financial bubbles. The outcome is that the economy becomes more exposed to financial, balance of payments and fiscal crises.[11]

The second set of difficulties is that it may be difficult to pursue IT if the private sector has large liabilities in foreign currency. In this case the financial institutions and their customers may be burdened with currency mismatches, which could become costly should the exchange rate depreciate. These mismatches will create pressures for the Central Bank to provide hedging instruments and to maintain exchange rate stability, even though this is incompatible with ITR (Eichengreen 2002, pp. 38–41). In these circumstances, IT may be an inappropriate policy regime, and a hard exchange rate peg may be more desirable, especially for very small economies.

5.3   *The Cost of Financial Instability*

Although the Central Bank is primarily responsible for achieving IT, it must also be the institution responsible for securing domestic financial stability (see below). These mandates may occasionally clash, especially if the asset and product markets give contradictory signals about inflation, if asset prices are very volatile, or if asset values rise rapidly as a proportion of GDP. For example, if price inflation threatens to escalate, the Central Bank may be compelled to

---

11   See Arestis and Glickman (2002), Jomo (2001), Palma (1998) and Weller (2001).

raise interest rates, which could undermine the stability of the financial system and trigger a costly crisis. Alternatively, if deflation looms, the Central Bank may be forced to lower interest rates, although this might fuel destabilising shifts in asset prices or debt and consumption bubbles.

The close relationship between price inflation, personal and company debt, financial system stability and asset price inflation, and the potentially large cost of financial crises, suggest that the Central Bank ought to monitor asset prices and levels of debt as part of its duty to maintain macroeconomic stability. It follows that the excessive focus of the NMPC on inflation control tends to distract attention away from the financial sector as a major source of *instability*. This is misguided, because the output and employment costs of financial crises can easily exceed the costs of moderate inflation – as was dramatically demonstrated by the global crisis starting in 2007.

Higher interest rates also increase the risks associated with financial activities. This is not only because of the adverse impact of higher interest payments on indebted agents, but also because of the larger size of the liability mismatches in the economy, the emergence of new financial assets and markets requiring distinct (and, generally, more risky and less well regulated) investment strategies, and a more volatile economic environment. In extreme cases, rigid inflation rates (due to cost or balance of payments pressures, or deep social divisions), or excessively ambitious IT, can lead the Central Bank to impose very high real interest rates, which can push the economy into a stabilisation trap. These are only some of the ways in which high interest rates enforce discipline upon industrial capital and finance, and impose regressive changes in the structure of the economy and the distribution of income.

5.4   The Cost of Central Bank 'Independence'

Arguments for CBI are based on the presumably greater transparency, legitimacy and accountability of monetary policy under this institutional arrangement. However, this claim veils the greater scope for (asymmetric) *discretion* in the conduct of monetary policy under CBI. In this policy regime, the board of the Central Bank is expected to consult 'the markets' – only – in order to set the interest rates. In contrast, in previous monetary policy regimes, claims for interest rate changes would be the subject of political argumentation at several levels of government, especially at the Ministry of Finance. There, counter-claims expressing the interests of different social groups could (at least in principle) be heard, and there might be scope for reaching a more balanced decision. This debate should be welcomed, for how 'could it be thought reprehensible for the elected representatives of the people to seek to influence – by persuasive argument perhaps – the central aspects of [economic] policy?' (Forder n.d.; see also Forder 2003).

The insulation of monetary policy from public debate reduces the accountability of the Central Bank and curtails the legitimacy of monetary policy, suggesting that CBI is incompatible with economic democracy. More generally, anti-inflation policies ought to be selected through an assessment of the social and economic costs of inflation, their distributive implications, and the distribution of the gains of stabilisation. It follows that the 'credibility' and 'reputation' of the Central Bank are misnomers. The improved indicators of credibility that usually follow the NMPC reflect the positive sentiment of a narrow circle of powerful individuals, whose material interests are directly affected by the choice of monetary policy. In this sense, 'improved expectations' are due to the much closer relationship between the Central Bank and the financial markets under CBI, as well as the appreciation of the financial market operators of the Central Bank's performance, and their confidence that monetary policy remain subordinate to their interests. That is, 'credibility' measures the *takeover* of monetary policy by the interests of finance in mature neoliberalism.

The institutional rigidities imposed by IT and CBI are, then, part of an attempt to impose a specific form of monetary policy discipline upon the state, industrial capital, the financial institutions and the working class. This is not only regressive, it is also misguided. First, it presumes that the independent Central Bank can deliver the IT if it *really* wants to. This is merely a revamped version of the monetarist claim that money supply targeting is feasible and sufficient to control the rate of inflation, which was proven wrong several decades ago. Second, it ignores the real dilemmas involved in Central Bank policy, especially the potential conflicts between monetary, financial and balance of payments stability. Third, if inflation is determined by contingent combinations of complex factors, it is important to preserve monetary policy flexibility; institutional rigidity is hardly the most efficient way to tackle evolving economic problems.

In summary, IT and CBI lock into place the mainstream theory of inflation and the anti-inflation policies associated with the reproduction of neoliberalism, and serving primarily the interests of finance. These rigidities are bound to create unnecessary costs and political difficulties when the causes of inflation change or when shifts in the correlation of social forces permit the implementation of less regressive policies. Finally, the insulation of monetary policy from public scrutiny and political control can thwart the co-ordination of policies that is essential for the success of *any* relevant government initiative. It is much harder to deliver the outcomes chosen by the electorate if the government can count on only one set of (fiscal policy) instruments, while monetary and exchange rate policy may be pursuing entirely different targets that may even compromise the achievement of other socially desirable objectives.

6   The Impact of the Global Crisis

The NMPC established itself as the typical monetary policy for neoliberalism during the 1990s and the early 2000s. The consolidation of neoliberal economic policies and the NMPC in a growing number of countries supported a fundamental transformation of the role of finance in general, and policymaking specifically. 'Liberalised' financial systems gained increasing control over economic resources and their allocation, and the scope to develop a largely autonomous sphere of speculation based on trading titles of fictitious capital. These developments were fully supported by presumably 'independent' Central Banks.[12]

Because of its strategic position at the hub of social reproduction, including control of the key sources of capital, foreign exchange and state finance, the financial institutions could appropriate a growing share of surplus value. For example, in the USA, the profits of financial companies (that is, excluding profits due to the financial activities of non-financial firms) jumped from below 5 per cent of after-tax corporate profits in 1982, to well over 40 per cent in the early 2000s.[13] Since finance is directly unproductive of value, these profits can only be transfers from the non-financial corporate sector and wage-earners. Their expansion has contributed greatly to the concentration of income under neoliberalism (Mohun 2015, Piketty 2014, UNCTAD 2012).

This period of rapid expansion of finance was dubbed the 'Great Moderation' by mainstream economists and policymakers (Bernanke 2004). That presumably blissful age of rapid and stable GDP growth and low inflation, at least in comparison with the erratic performance of most advanced economies since the late 1960s, is now long forgotten. The moniker serves only as a reminder of the hubris of the spokespeople for neoliberalism, who claimed ownership of a modality of global growth drawing on a conventional set of macroeconomic policies including IT, CBI, and liberalisation of domestic finance and international capital flows. These policies promoted the rapid accumulation of private debt and rising current account deficits in the US, UK, the Eurozone periphery and in leading middle-income countries, and unsustainably large current account surpluses and currency reserves in China, Japan, Germany and several

---

12   For a detailed analysis, from slightly different viewpoints, see Gowan (1999), Lanchester (2010), Norfield (2016), Panitch and Konings (2008), Panitch and Gindin (2012) and Tett (2009a).

13   See 'Financial Sector Profits as a % of All Domestic Corporate Profits', US National Income and Product Accounts, table 6.16A, http://www.bea.gov/iTable/iTable.cfm?ReqID=9#reqid=9&step=3&isuri=1&903=236.

East Asian and oil exporting countries. Both sides were brought together by misaligned currencies, kept at untenable levels by enormous currency flows channeled by a bloated and short-termist financial system.

The dysfunctionality of this model of growth was missed by neoliberal academics, ministers of finance, academics, journalists, and the all-important independent central bankers. Their self-congratulatory mood was rudely dislodged by the deepest crisis of capitalism since the Great Depression, starting in 2007. The crisis revealed that, under neoliberalism and the NMPC, global growth had become structurally unbalanced, consisting primarily of speculative bubble-like episodes taking place *between* increasingly severe finance-driven crises: the neoliberal 'Great Moderation' was a myth driven by indefensible policies backed up by finance-friendly economic dogma. Scandalously, the trajectory of the distribution of income and wealth in most countries shows that neoliberal economies tend to generate inequality when they grow, and to distribute losses inequitably when they contract (Arestis and Sawyer 2010, Saad-Filho 2008, 2011, Tcherneva 2015).

Despite these shortcomings, the strategy of crisis management since 2008 demonstrates the depth and extent of the hegemony of neoliberalism over ideology as well as state policy. First, neoclassical economics dominates the discipline almost entirely, to the extent of treating Keynesian anti-cyclical policies as a set of tools that can be deployed selectively in emergencies, especially to support finance itself, but otherwise beyond the pale as suggesting unacceptable tolerance of inflation and the interests of the poor. Second, the astonishingly skewed finance-friendly strategy of containment of the global crisis received almost universal applause, even though it amounted to a barefaced socialisation of losses in order to salvage the largest financial institutions in particular, and the neoliberal system of accumulation more generally. Third, even though the crisis imposed significant monetary policy changes in several countries, primarily through the generalisation of ZIRP (zero interest rate policies) and quantitative easing (QE) in most advanced economies, it did not lead to the formal abandonment of IT or CBI anywhere. In this sense, both neoliberalism and the NMPC remain unchallenged, while policy implementation has retained as much flexibility as necessary in order to help salvage the system of accumulation by any means necessary.

Despite its success in further consolidating the hegemony of neoliberalism, the attempt to address the crisis in the advanced economies through relaxation of monetary policy, provision of virtually unlimited public support for finance, and fiscal 'austerity' has failed to drive the economic recovery anywhere. In essence, Central Banks in the USA, UK, Japan, Switzerland and the Eurozone reduced interest rates virtually to zero, sometimes even straying into negative territory, which was previously thought to be impossible. Those Central Banks also purchased vast quantities of worthless assets from large financial institutions through QE, in order to buttress private balance sheets.

Those policies required the temporary abandonment of IT, with outcomes ranging from inflation much above the official target band for extended periods, as in the UK, or significantly below target, as in the Eurozone, without *any* analytical, practical or institutional consequences. Given the overwhelming need to save neoliberalism from itself, the supposedly all-important inflation targets became wholly irrelevant. CBI similarly vanished without a trace, as bankers confabulated overtly with governments and the largest financial institutions whenever this became necessary, in order to find the best way to stabilise finance and, presumably, and by implication, the economy. The *political* roots of the NMPC and the irrelevance of its grandiose principles became evident. As former Fed chairman Paul Volcker (2008, pp. 1–2) colourfully summarised it:

> [W]e have moved from a commercial bank centered, highly regulated financial system, to an enormously more complicated and highly engineered system. Today, much of the financial intermediation takes place in markets beyond effective official oversight and supervision, all enveloped in unknown trillions of derivative instruments. It has been a highly profitable business, with finance accounting recently for 35 to 40 percent of all corporate profits ... It is hard to argue that the new system has brought exceptional benefits to the economy generally ... Simply stated, the bright new financial system – for all its talented participants, for all its rich rewards – has failed the test of the market place. To meet the challenge, the Federal Reserve judged it necessary to take actions that extend to the very edge of its lawful and implied powers, transcending certain long embedded Central Banking principles and practices.

Despite those contortions, the neoliberal crisis resolution strategy failed at another level too. Pumping large quantities of money into a dangerously unstable financial system, while offering near-zero interest rates at home, triggered a stampede of capital from advanced economies into the 'emerging' economies, where the economic prospects were, then, much healthier. This took place through carry trade and a 'currency war' in the late 2000s, which led exchange rates to respond pro-cyclically: rising unsustainably in the 'South' and declining in the 'North'. That torrent of taxpayer-funded financial capital was eventually absorbed by the rapid growth of corporate debt in developing countries:

> The corporate debt of nonfinancial firms across major emerging market economies [has] increased from about US$4 trillion in 2004 to well

over US$18 trillion in 2014. The average emerging market corporate debt-to-GDP ratio has also grown by 26 percentage points in the same period.

IMF 2015, p. 84

The resource flows initiated by the attempt to save the banking system in the advanced countries have destabilised exchange rates, current accounts and growth prospects in numerous countries, so far without a plausible form of resolution, and suggesting that the current crisis may remain unresolved for some time.

7   Conclusion

Monetary policy is political. It regulates and disciplines capital accumulation in each country and globally, and helps to perpetuate the inequalities underpinning the production of the material conditions of social reproduction under any system of accumulation.

In the Keynesian era, monetary policy aimed at the maximisation of the rate of accumulation, subject to the constraint of preserving macroeconomic stability. In the 'core' Western economies, rapid growth of output, employment and income helped to contain the lure of communism and supported political stability within a social democratic framework. In the Global South, rapid accumulation was usually accompanied by harsher political regimes; in the meantime, the Bretton Woods System provided the framework for the integration of domestic accumulation within global capitalism, under US hegemony.

The Keynesian compact unravelled between the late 1960s and the early 1970s. The monetarist experiment validated the abandonment of government commitments to social cohesion and full employment, and rationalised the shift of monetary policy away from output growth and towards inflation control. At a further remove, it supported the financialisation of capitalist economies and societies. Monetarism also helped to institutionalise floating exchange rate regimes, which embedded the financial markets into the fabric of macroeconomic policy formulation, implementation and monitoring.

This policy shift contributed to the elimination of high inflation; it also helped to restore US hegemony and impose, in several countries, a harsh and seemingly market-driven (thus, 'neutral') discipline upon a restless working class. However, monetarism was deeply flawed theoretically, money supply targeting was largely ineffective, and monetarist policies did not facilitate the resumption of rapid and stable growth. The subsequent transition to neoliberalism derived from the growing pressures for the imposition of social discipline and the restoration of the conditions for accumulation through the prominence of finance. These trends culminated in the NMPC – the monetary policy framework for mature neoliberalism.

IT and CBI are primarily political rather than 'technical' choices. They supported the social and economic reorganisation associated with the transition to neoliberalism, including the takeover of the state's legitimacy, resources and policy-making capacity by finance, and their deployment to strengthen minority power and promote the interests of capital-in-general dressed up as the general good. These objectives are disguised by the veil of 'technical objectivity', 'rules' and 'policy neutrality' provided by mainstream economics. The NMPC excludes troubling political dilemmas from public scrutiny, entrenches the current balance of social forces into the institutional fabric of the society, and creates rigidities preventing the consideration of alternative economic policy goals. These policy changes are normally introduced in response to domestic political imperatives, and they are validated by the financial markets, the international financial organisations and the US Treasury and State Departments. These institutions monitor the outcomes of their preferred policy framework, and they can supply expertise and resources to assist the implementation of the NMPC. Finally, mainstream economics provides academic credibility for this policy consensus, as it lends theoretical density and depth to the NMPC.

The NMPC can deliver low inflation for long periods, because demand control through the manipulation of interest rates can reduce inflation regardless of its causes. Yet, the NMPC is based on doubtful assumptions, unwarranted generalisations, overly optimistic expectations about convergence to a virtuous circle of prosperity and – importantly – the ability of neoliberal policies and institutions to extricate the economy from finance-driven crises. The NMPC also imposes low inflation targets that can lock the economy into a pattern of low growth, high unemployment and potentially intractable problems of poverty and inequality. In addition, the NMPC offers only blunt and inefficient policies against inflation, grinding it down through potentially long periods of high unemployment that reduce the economy's growth potential while increasing its financial fragility. Finally, hyper-vigilance against inflation, which is built into IT and CBI, is incompatible with rapid or equitable growth, because it fosters the interests of a parasitical financial system at the expense of the majority of the population, and locks countries into economic development strategies that are inimical to the achievement of democratic outcomes.

The vulnerabilities of the NMPC are not due to its theoretical weaknesses, or the inability of IT and CBI to flush out inflation from the economy. The most important vulnerability of the NMPC is the lack of political legitimacy for this policy framework. NMPC policies are blunt, inefficient and costly. They keep inflation low through high unemployment and the reduction of the economy's growth potential, and they increase its vulnerability to financial and balance of payments instability. Those policies are also regressive. They impose harsh modalities of social control, facilitate the transfer of income and political power to the minority, and lock rich and poor countries into development strategies that are intrinsically undemocratic. The potential lack of legitimacy of the NMPC and the neoliberal system of accumulation more generally render them vulnerable to political challenges, especially in the aftermath of the global financial crisis, whose consequences are still unfolding, one decade later.

Neoliberal Development and Its Critics

This essay[1] examines the emergence of neoliberalism in development economics and development studies, and the implications of the neoliberal transition across both scholarship and policy-making. It argues that the meaning and significance of neoliberal theory and its policy implications have shifted over time, place and issue, and that there can be inconsistencies across its component parts. These are, often, due to tensions between the rhetorical and policy worlds built by the advocates of neoliberalism and the realities of social and economic reproduction in the so-called 'developing' countries. Examination of these tensions can help to illuminate the weaknesses of the Washington consensus, the reasons for its displacement by the post-Washington consensus led by Joseph Stiglitz, and the ensuing disputes between the post-Washington consensus and its predecessor around the shortcomings of 'deregulation', and the desirability and optimal extent of state intervention in the economy. The essay concludes that the differences between the Washington consensus and the post-Washington consensus have been overblown and, in particular, that they share much the same conception of development and attachment to neoliberalism, and the same limited commitment to democracy. However, because of its greater plasticity the post-Washington consensus is better positioned to weather the criticisms levelled against the Washington consensus, especially after the impact of the economic crisis starting in 2007.

1 Neoliberalism and Its Critics

Over the last few years, doubts have been expressed over whether neoliberalism is a concept that can be deployed either validly or even usefully across the social sciences (see, for example, Castree 2006, and Ferguson 2007). This may reflect the continuing throes of discursive critique of concepts in general and would apply equally to other commonly used terms, most notably, globalisation. But, for neoliberalism in particular, there are genuine doubts sown about

---

1 Originally published as: 'Politics of Neoliberal Development: Washington Consensus and post-Washington Consensus' in H. Weber (ed.) *The Politics of Development: A Survey*. London: Routledge, 2014 (with B. Fine).

its diversity in both policy and impact and, consequently, over its capacity either to define a distinctive ideology or set of policies, or to specify the nature of contemporary capitalism.

These conundrums are no less pronounced in the case of neoliberalism and development. For the sake of convenience, and as is common across both scholarship and popular discourse, neoliberalism in this context is heavily associated with the Washington consensus (WC) and the practices of the World Bank, the IMF and other international organisations, including the WTO, the European Commission and the European Central Bank. But, in the last years of the millennium, the WC gave birth, if not way, to the so-called post-Washington consensus (PWC; see Fine, Lapavitsas and Pincus 2001). The PWC has emphasised that markets (and institutions) work imperfectly and so provides the rationale for state intervention. For some, this shift from WC to PWC represents a distinct break between the two, at least to the extent that the PWC is implemented in practice. This is certainly how proponents of the PWC see matters (for example, Stiglitz 1998), as they associate neoliberalism narrowly with the WC and the dogmatic belief in the virtues of the free market by way of their own critical point of departure. For others, though, the PWC is essentially the WC (and the continuation of neoliberalism itself) by other means. Adding to the confusion is the stance of John Williamson, who first coined the phrase, WC, in the late 1980s. He both disassociates it from neoliberalism as such *and* considers that differences between the WC and PWC are minor and exaggerated for polemical purposes by proponents of the PWC relative to core principles that it shares in common with the WC around the virtues of 'sound' macroeconomic policy (that is, restrictive fiscal and monetary policy, 'flexible' labour markets, 'free' trade and capital flows, privatisations, the absence of government intervention on prices, and so on), and maximal, though not exclusive, reliance upon (global) market forces (see below, Marangos 2007, 2008, and Williamson 2007).

This essay argues that neoliberalism is a valid and useful concept, both in general and in the context of development, but it has to be reconstructed carefully across three dimensions (see Fine 2009a). The *first* is conceptual. Neoliberal thought incorporates a complex construct of rhetorical (ideological), intellectual (scholarly) and policy elements. There is a shifting combination of these across time, place and issue, and the notion of neoliberalism is not always deployed consistently in distinct contexts or over time. There is also a tension across these elements and the material reality that they purport to represent and project: a virtual world made up of more or less thwarted market forces, and one which should be remade as far as possible to conform to the image conjured by neoclassical economic theory (Carrier and Miller 1998).

There can be inconsistencies within each of these elements. The scholarly justification for the virtues of the market has been supported both by the neo-Austrianism closely associated with Friedrich von Hayek and the general equilibrium theory of mainstream economics, which is based on neoclassical orthodoxy and is absolutely intolerant of alternatives (see Denis 2004, 2006, and Mirowski 2007). But these are at odds with one another, with the former emphasising the inventive and transformative subjectivity of the individual and the spontaneous emergence of an increasingly efficient order through market processes, whereas the other is preoccupied with the efficiency properties of a static equilibrium achieved entirely in the logical domain, on the basis of unchanging individuals, resources and technologies. Despite their claims to the contrary, neither captures the political economy and moral philosophy that underpins the invisible hand associated with Adam Smith (see Milonakis and Fine 2009).

Moreover, in the rhetorical and policy worlds, even the most ardent supporter of freedom of the individual in general, and through the market in particular, concedes that those freedoms can only be guaranteed through state provision of, and coercion for, a core set of functions and institutions, ranging over fiscal and monetary policy to law and order and property rights, through to military intervention to secure the 'market economy' when this becomes necessary. In practice, then, neoliberalism is often heavily associated with authoritarianism, while its attachment to classical liberalism and political democracy is hedged and heavily conditional in practice (see below, and Chile serves as a classic illustration in view of its dependence after the overthrow of Allende on the monetarist Chicago boys – as it were, we have ways of making markets to be free!; see, for example Barber 1995, Bresnahan 2003, and Chapter 13). The foregoing begins to explain why the term neoliberalism should prove especially elusive across rhetoric, scholarship, policy and realism. As such, it is possibly no harder to pin down than such concepts as globalisation or social capital but, as for these as well as other examples pervasive across the social sciences, this requires that it be critically reconstructed and assessed.

In this respect, the *second* key dimension for the reconstruction of neoliberalism concerns what is distinctive about it over and above its rhetorical emphasis on the freedom of both market and individuals. This is to be found in the distinguishing characteristic of capitalism over the last forty years or so, which has set it apart from what has gone before, and increasingly so over time. This is the role of finance in general and of financialisation in particular (Fine 2009a). These processes include not only the extraordinary proliferation and expansion of financial markets and instruments as such, both within and between countries, but also the penetration of financial processes and imperatives into ever more aspects of economic and social reproduction. The result has been, both directly and indirectly, precisely the economic phenomena that are commonly associated with neoliberalism, and which go far beyond the traditional contrast, within macroeconomics, between monetarism and Keynesianism, or between the new orthodoxy in development economics of relying upon the market as opposed to the old developmentalism based upon modernisation, welfarism and industrialisation. Typically, there has been deregulation of the financial sector itself, accompanied by commercialisation, commodification, privatisation, imposition of user charges, liberalisation of the capital account of the balance of payments, and so on. These were component parts of state strategies to transfer capacity to allocate resources intertemporally (the balance between investment and consumption), intersectorally (the composition of output and employment) and internationally towards an increasingly globally integrated financial sector. This is not simply to reduce such systemic developments to the power or imperatives of finance, but to recognise how the promotion of markets in general has underpinned the promotion of financial markets in particular as a key feature of neoliberalism.

Third, apart from reconstructing neoliberalism across its multiple dimensions and highlighting its inextricable connections with financialisation, there is a significant distinction between two phases of neoliberalism. The earlier might be dubbed the transition or shock phase. In the wake of Reaganism/ Thatcherism, states intervened heavily and forcefully to promote the globalised expansion of capital in general and of finance in particular, through contractionary fiscal and monetary policies, privatisation, deregulation, social security cutbacks, the introduction of stiffer rules constraining social protests, and so on. These policies have represented a severe assault on the poor and progressive values, but they also represented a redefinition rather than a withdrawal of the state in which, either by accident or design, the weight and influence of finance in national and international economies have grown by leaps and bounds (see Gowan 1999, Panitch and Konings 2008, and Saad-Filho and Johnston 2005).

By contrast, the later phase of neoliberalism, leading to the financial crisis starting in 2007, was more muted and comprised two aspects. On the one hand, it accommodated the reactions against the extreme inequity and iniquity of outcomes across economic and social provision which were enforced in the transition phase. On the other hand, and of greater weight, is the use of the state to sustain the newly established framework for capital accumulation, especially the prominence of finance, with its most regressive consequences being targeted for regulation or amelioration at the margin. This arrangement was stress-tested most dramatically in the recent financial crisis, when developed countries rapidly committed unprecedented resources to sustaining their collapsing financial systems. Such heavy state intervention was unmistakably neoliberal in substance, not least being introduced by erstwhile President Bush and Prime Minister Gordon Brown in order to shore up failing banks and insurance companies, including the formal nationalisation of key institutions and the absorption of failing banks by their healthier competitors. Despite these occasionally audacious initiatives, no significant structural change has taken place in Western financial systems in the aftermath of the crisis.

2   Neoliberalism and Development

Against this background, our focus can shift to neoliberalism and development more generally. Attention to this can be placed upon the shift between the WC and the PWC. But, before doing so, reference should be made to what might be termed the pre-WC. This is most closely associated with Robert McNamara's Presidency at the World Bank (1968–81). At the level of rhetoric, this period is attached to anti-communism in a context where the Soviet model offered an alternative to the 'developing' countries in the wake of widespread decolonisation and intense left activity in most countries, including armed mass movements in three continents. The notion of development within this orthodoxy was linked to modernisation, and underpinned by Keynesianism and a rudimentary version of welfarism. Methodologically, development economics was both highly inductive and historical in content, grasping the idea that development involved a transition through modernisation to the ideal-type of advanced capitalism, most notably represented by the five stages of economic growth popularised by Rostow (1960) in his appropriately entitled *The Stages of Economic Growth: A Non-Communist Manifesto*.

By the same token, policy was perceived to involve significant state intervention and the provision of social and economic infrastructure for industrialisation, including public ownership of key industries if necessary. These developmental policies and perspectives were posited without reference to the Cold War, the brazen allocation of aid and development finance according to Western policy imperatives and commercial interests, the systemically biased workings of the global economy and the constraints that this imposed on the development strategies of the poor countries. Of course, the pre-WC was also heavily contested. Indicative was the strength of radical alternatives in scholarship, against an orthodoxy that now seems disconcertingly progressive by comparison to that of today. This confrontation was especially prominent in the various forms of dependency theory, which promoted the view that development and underdevelopment constitute two sides of the same coin (see Cardoso and Faletto 1979, Kay 1989, ch.5, Palma 1981 and Saad-Filho 2005).

The WC emerged in the late 1970s and early 1980s as a dramatic right-wing reaction against the perceived weaknesses of the pre-WC developmentalist consensus. Rhetorically, the WC involved a heavy attachment to a universalist neoliberal ideology, with absolute commitment to the free market and the presumption of the state as a source of both inefficiency and corruption, not least through rent-seeking. At the level of scholarship, the WC suppressed the old development economics as a separate and respected field within the discipline, even denying the scope for its existence, and imposed, instead, a rigid adherence to the deductive and formal methods of mainstream, neoclassical economics which, supposedly, only needed to be applied to specific fields, among them economic development. This process provides a striking example of 'economics imperialism' in the form of the so-called new development economics in which not only the economy itself but also social aspects of development should be seen as reducible to the principles of the dismal science of pursuit of self-interest (see Fine and Milonakis 2009, Jomo and Fine 2006, and Fine 2009b).

While the WC claimed to be leaving as much as possible to the market, the previous section has shown that this is better seen as rebuilding the state to intervene on a discretionary basis systematically to promote the expansion of a globalising and heavily financialised capitalism. In effect, the WC comprised three elements: the hegemony of mainstream economics within development theory; the predominance of the World Bank in setting the agenda for the study of development, with the Bank and the IMF imposing the standards of orthodoxy within development economics itself; and the redefinition of development from systemic transformation to a set of policies to achieve development, with limited specification of what this would be. Strikingly, the WC discarded the previous consensus around (domestically financed) capital accumulation as the key to development and, instead, focused almost exclusively on the need for 'appropriate' incentives and the 'correct' economic policies, especially fiscal restraint, privatisation, the abolition of subsidies and government intervention on the prices of goods and services, flexibilisation of the labour market, trade liberalisation, export-led growth and an open capital account of the balance of payments.

Not surprisingly, the WC did not go unchallenged both from within economics and from development studies. But each of these has also experienced a sharp decline in political economy approaches since the early 1980s, under the sustained assault of mainstream economics and right-wing ideology and politics that had become wedded to neoliberalism and wholly intolerant of alternatives. Despite these profound difficulties, by the late 1980s there was considerable momentum behind the critique of the WC both within academia and in the emerging social movements, with two complementary approaches to the fore.

The first of these was inspired by the notion of the developmental state (see Fine 2006, for an overview). With particular emphasis upon industrial policy, the notion of a developmental state was perceived to apply to the successful industrialisations in the East Asian newly industrialising countries (NICs), with Japan as the classic precursor, followed by the four 'tigers' (South Korea, Taiwan, Singapore and Hong Kong) in the 1960s and 1970s. These were followed, in turn, by Malaysia, Thailand, Indonesia, China and Vietnam. In all these cases, it was found that the state had violated the main tenets of the WC, not least through protectionism, directed finance, and other major departures from the free market. The second criticism of the WC focused upon adjustment with a human face. Irrespective of the questionable merits of the WC in bringing stability and growth, the adverse impact of WC policies on those in, or on the borders of, poverty was highlighted. The WC stood accused of being at least oblivious to the issue of who bore the burden of adjustment and stabilisation. It was also criticised for tolerating, and even promoting, rising inequality as a way of reducing the fiscal burden on the state and of enhancing the scope for introduction of market incentives in everything from health and education to agriculture and to the workings of urban labour markets (see Chang 2003 and Chang and Grabel 2004).

The mounting opposition to the WC on these fronts dovetailed with the growing evidence of the 1980s as a 'lost decade' for development across the portfolio of policies and countries that were subject to adjustment through conditionalities imposed by the World Bank and the IMF. As a result, the World Bank in particular sought to defend itself through questionable appeals to the empirical evidence, selective reference to the occasional if invariably temporary (and always carefully promoted) star performers, and the argument that the problem was not with the policies but with lack of their implementation (opening the way to subsequent discourses around corruption, good governance, and the like). This effort culminated in the publication of a major report on the East Asian NICs (World Bank 1993), arguing that government intervention had been extensive but had only succeeded because it had been along the lines of what the market would have done had it been working perfectly – and, in any case, the East Asian experience was not replicable in other countries.

These attempts to defend the WC soon proved to be futile, and the PWC was launched from within the World Bank in the second half of the 1990s. In terms of scholarship, both in intrinsic quality and external recognition, the PWC has been far more powerful than its predecessor, with its pioneer, Joseph Stiglitz, receiving the Nobel Prize for economics in 2001 having just been removed from his position as Chief Economist at the World Bank for reasons that will become apparent below. Substantively, the intellectual thrust of the PWC has been to emphasise the significance of market and institutional imperfections, as opposed to the virtues of the (perfect) market promoted by the WC. Consequently, the PWC rejects the WC for its antipathy to state intervention, and it also questions the conventional macroeconomic stabilisation policies for their severely adverse short- and long-term impacts. Policy-wise, the rhetoric of the PWC was comparatively state-friendly but in a limited and piecemeal way, with intervention only justified on a case-by-case basis, should it be demonstrable that narrow economic benefits would most likely accrue. Despite its obvious limitations, the PWC provided a rationale for discretionary intervention across a much wider range of economic and social policy than the WC. However, it remained fundamentally pro-market, favouring a poorly examined deepening of the process of 'globalisation' but, presumably, with a human face and guiding hand.

Rhetorically, the PWC tended to exaggerate the contrast with the traditional WC concerns (van Waeyenberge 2007), allowing Stiglitz stridently to protest policies imposed by the IMF on Russia and South Korea, in particular, which triggered his enforced departure from office at the World Bank. Significantly, like the WC, the PWC also has no notion of development beyond growth and efficiency, as opposed to an exaggerated emphasis on the means of achieving it. The PWC focuses on the correction of market and institutional imperfections on a piecemeal basis, rather than simply relying upon the market as for the WC, but also presuming that the 'correct' institutional and policy framework is sufficient to secure long-term economic success, understood as a higher growth rate. Further, policy in practice under the PWC has, if anything and despite flagship Poverty Reduction Strategy Papers, promoted by the World Bank and the IMF as part of their external debt relief initiative, tightened on the traditional measures associated with the WC conditionalities in the application of criteria for assessing eligibility for aid or debt forgiveness (van Waeyenberge 2007). The one exception, apparently, is in liberalising the controls on international capital flows, but this is explained by the extent to which this had already been achieved, and is no longer necessary as an imposed policy.

The emergence of the PWC is best seen as deriving from economic orthodoxy or, at least, from trends within it. The market imperfection economics on which it is based, especially the appeal to the notion that *individual* agents are imperfectly coordinated by the market alone, did not evolve in the context of development, but was applied to it after the event, at an opportune moment.

This was as replacement for the discredited WC view that had pioneered the new in place of the old development economics in the context of the rise of neoliberalism, monetarism and supply-side economics, and which also emerged without a thought for development, as was shown above. Further, the PWC itself is indicative of a more general and aggressive phase of economic imperialism, in which the economic and the social are perceived to be reducible to market imperfections and the institutional responses to them (Fine 2009b). Everything from corruption through to civil war and aid-effectiveness is to be explained by reference to imperfectly coordinated pursuit of self-interest, defined by reference either to narrow economic motives or to arbitrary addition of other motives and factors (such as degree of linguistic diversity, tropical climate, and so on).

Thus, despite what appears to be a radical shift from the WC to the PWC, upon closer analysis the PWC only represents a limited break from it. This can be highlighted in two ways. First, despite its rejection in principle of the neoliberal free market ideology and one-model-fits-all WC policies, the PWC remains wholly committed to mainstream economics. This is strikingly brought out by one of the leading proponents of the new (market imperfections) development economics. In his book, appropriately entitled *One Economics, Many Recipes*, Dani Rodrik (2007, p. 3) pronounces:

> This book is strictly grounded in neoclassical economic analysis. At the core of neoclassical economics lies the following methodological predisposition: social phenomena can best be understood by considering them to be an aggregation of purposeful behaviour by individuals – in their roles as consumer, producer, investor, politician, and so on – interacting with each other and acting under the constraints that their environment imposes. This I find to be not just a powerful discipline for organizing our thoughts on economic affairs, but the only sensible way of thinking about them. If I often depart from the consensus that 'mainstream' economists have reached in matters of development policy, this has less to do with different modes of analysis than with different readings of the evidence and with different evaluations of the 'political economy' of developing nations ... [T]he tendency of many economists to offer advice based on simple rules of thumb regardless of context (privatize this, liberalize that), is a derogation rather than a proper application of neoclassical economic principles.

Second, although the developmental state literature played a major role in discrediting the WC since the 1980s, the PWC has proceeded as if this concept, and its more systemic approach to development, does not exist. In part, this reflects the peculiar relationship between mainstream (WC or PWC) development economics and development studies. The latter has always been at least multidisciplinary if not interdisciplinary, was borne out of support for decolonisation and antipathy to modernisation as a unifying framework for addressing (under)development. Significantly, the discipline was housed in newly formed dedicated departments in the UK and several Western European countries, but in non-economics disciplinary departments in the United States. While these arrangements have allowed its radicalism to persist, it was gradually outflanked as well as encroached upon by the rise of the new development economics within and around economics departments, and the increasing influence of the Washington institutions over the entire development agenda since the early 1980s (Fine 2009b).

3   Neoliberalism, Politics and Development

Such considerations are crucial in broaching the politics of the WC and its critics. The IMF and, later, the WC, were notoriously equivocal in their commitment to political democracy. Their casual attachment to political liberalism was driven by an overwhelming commitment to the geopolitical interests of the United States and, later, to the shock therapy associated with the first stage of the neoliberal reforms. If these reforms could be imposed only by an undemocratic state, as was the case in Chile and elsewhere (see above), the Washington institutions would turn a blind eye to human rights and other abuses.

However, as the 1980s progressed the simultaneous spread of democracy *and* neoliberalism demonstrated that political openness was not inimical to economic 'responsibility'. Further evidence supported an even stronger case for democracy within neoliberalism. Mainstream academics and the Washington institutions gradually realised that democratic regimes can more reliably deliver the jurisdictional certainty required for the smooth functioning of the (financial) markets than most dictatorships. This is largely because of the constitutional attachment of the democratic regimes to due process and the rule of law (see, for example, Gill 2002). When neoliberalism achieved worldwide hegemony, after the fall of the Berlin Wall and the implosion of the international left, and in the light of the controlled transitions to democracy in Latin America and South Africa, the dangers of 'rogue' (undependable) dictatorships trumped the Western fears of political openness in the South. These fears were, traditionally, grounded on the supposed propensity of democratic regimes in poor countries to accommodate populist electoral majorities and their inability to contain leftist agitation. These concerns remained in the background, but they were tempered by the realisation that, once the neoliberal reforms had been introduced, it would be *harder* to reverse them in a democracy to the extent that the logic of financial and financialised policy discipline imposed its apparently sacrosanct logic upon the constitutional process and the institutional fabric of the country (see below). The crisis starting in 2007 has exploded the associated myth of TINA (there is no alternative) not least as, in the midst of economic crisis, developed countries with the USA in the lead, have dedicated vast resources to shore up a dysfunctional financial system having previously denied such resources and corresponding interventionist policies to their own populations and to developing countries for health, education, welfare and aid in far more favourable circumstances. In fact, Oxfam has estimated that the financial rescue packages would suffice to eliminate world poverty for the next fifty years.[2]

Retrospectively, it is clear that the WC had stumbled, casually, upon the best of all possible worlds. The neoliberal reforms transferred to the financial markets the responsibility for allocating social resources, while political democracy supported these reforms through the institutionalisation of a *legitimate* state which was, simultaneously, permanently hamstrung by some combination of insufficient administrative capacity (after the 'roll-back' of the state through the neoliberal reforms), fractious multiparty legislatures and bitterly competing sectional interests, which inevitably flourish in a democracy. In these fragmented and structurally weakened states, the balance of power is preserved by an 'independent' judiciary that locks in the neoliberal reforms under the guise of the 'rule of law', an independent central bank, or conditionalities imposed in return for aid.[3]

In contrast, the PWC has always been more sensitive to the non-economic domain than its heavily blinkered predecessor, and it proved to be better adapted to the new circumstances. In the 1990s and 2000s, Stiglitz and his associates rationalised the emerging synthesis between political democracy and neoliberal economic policies under the guise of institution-building and the imperative to limit corruption (which is, presumably, better achieved in

---

2   Oxfam press release, 1 April 2009, https://www.oxfam.org/en/pressroom/pressreleases/2009-04-01/bank-bailout-could-end-poverty-50-years-oxfam-tells-g20 (accessed 7 June 2018).

3   Typically, the limited achievements of the Lula administration in Brazil, despite the high expectations elicited by his presidential election, were mirrored by similar lame improvements in social policies and economic outcomes in most countries caught in the 'pink tide' across Latin America (Argentina, Chile, Nicaragua, Paraguay and Uruguay). Only in those countries where the Constitution was rewritten (Bolivia, Ecuador and Venezuela) were more significant achievements possible. See, for example, ECLAC (2008).

a democracy), in order to support long-term economic growth. The emerging commitment of the Washington institutions with political democracy was supported by the expanded conditionality promoted by the World Bank, which included not only the narrow menu of policy reforms identified by John Williamson as the Washington Consensus,[4] but also a whole raft of, at times, less tangible reforms aiming to consolidate 'good governance'.[5]

These mutually reinforcing reasons to promote democracy in the South were enthusiastically supported by the development industry which preyed upon, and thrived in and around, the aid-dependent countries. The Washington institutions could finally establish a constructive dialogue with the aid agencies and NGOs which, in the not-too-distant past, had criticised heavily the human cost of the WC policies (see, for example, Bracking 2009 and Green 2008).

4   Conclusion

The accretion of conditionalities and policy reforms by the PWC reveals its attachment to the same conception of development previously espoused by the Washington Consensus. That is, development as the natural (financial market-led) outcome of a set of more or less narrow, and sometimes shifting but unambiguously 'correct' policies imposed from above, and under external guidance. Paradoxically, this has been compatible with a significant increase in the degree of legitimacy of the policies associated with the Washington institutions, as they have been embraced, within limits, by some of its erstwhile critics.

This emerging accommodation suffered a grievous blow with the onset of the 2007 financial crisis. As the crisis unfolds, and the mainstream seeks shelter under heavy state intervention while, simultaneously, seeking to blame poor financial sector regulation for the debacle, the rationale for untrammelled

---

4   These included fiscal discipline; redirection of public expenditure priorities toward fields offering both high economic returns and the potential to improve income distribution, such as primary health care, primary education, and infrastructure; tax reform (to lower marginal rates and broaden the tax base); interest rate liberalization; competitive exchange rates; trade liberalisation; liberalization of inflows of foreign direct investment; privatisation; deregulation (to abolish barriers to entry and exit), and secure property rights.

5   The augmented WC includes improvements to corporate governance; anti-corruption; flexible labor markets; WTO agreements; financial codes and standards; 'prudent' capital-account opening; non-intermediate exchange rate regimes; independent central banks/inflation targeting; social safety nets, and targeted poverty reduction.

liberalisation has lost its residual credibility. It is unlikely to disappear completely while capitalism remains, but it may become marginalised for a relatively long period of time. In contrast, the PWC, with its boundless capacity to incorporate policy novelties and refinements while remaining faithful to the tenets of the mainstream, is likely to prosper and to become the hegemonic player in the development field, including the Washington institutions, academia, and many aid agencies.

Although the PWC can more readily accommodate different institutional arrangements, state intervention and pro-poor policies, which is commendable from the point of view of the critics of the WC, the greater plasticity of the PWC could make it extremely difficult to dislodge, although this is not impossible. The need and prospects for alternative development strategies, and for heterodox understandings of the development process, to supplement and support the social movements challenging neoliberalism and regressive economic policies, remain as urgent as they are uncertain in scope, content and appeal.

CHAPTER 15

Crisis *in* Neoliberalism or Crisis *of* Neoliberalism?

The banks are fucked, we're fucked, the country's fucked.
Anonymous British cabinet minister, *The Guardian*, 19 January 2009

This rather perceptive assessment of the implications of the current crisis for the United Kingdom (and a good many other countries) is more candid and insightful than the twaddle of many mainstream journalists, economists and politicians, who proclaim the virtues of the 'free market' while blaming an unholy coalition of unhinged bankers, shifty borrowers and incompetent regulators for the disaster.[1],[2] In order to save neoliberalism from itself, the free marketeers have nationalised some of the largest financial institutions in the world, socialised financial market risks and pumped huge amounts of public money into the economy. The rhetorical gyrations justifying this frenzy have been ideological in the worst possible sense: they are deliberately misleading representations of reality, concocted to confuse the audience and stultify the opposition. In contrast, Marxian assessments of the crisis, being grounded upon the realities of accumulation and located within systemic analyses of the class relations under neoliberalism, suggest that this is not a crisis of (de) regulation but, instead, a *systemic crisis in neoliberal capitalism*. It is not, yet, a crisis *of* neoliberalism.

1   Neoliberalism and Financialisation

Neoliberalism is the mode of existence of contemporary capitalism. This system of accumulation emerged gradually, since the mid-1970s, in response to the transformation of the conditions of accumulation accompanying the

---

1   Originally published as: 'Crisis in Neoliberalism or Crisis of Neoliberalism?', in L. Panitch, G. Albo and V. Chibber (eds.), Socialist Register, London: Merlin Press, 2010, pp.242–259. Minor editing added.

2   For example, George Osborne and Jeffrey Sachs (2010) suggest that: 'Blaming our predicament on financial markets ... ignores the awkward truth that governments have enabled, if not enthusiastically promoted, recklessness, through chronic deficits and lax financial regulation'; see also The Economist (2008).

disarticulation of the Keynesian-social democratic consensus, the paralysis of developmentalism and the implosion of the Soviet bloc.[3] In essence, neoliberalism is based on the systematic use of state power, under the ideological guise of 'non-intervention', to impose a hegemonic project of recomposition of the rule of capital at five levels: domestic resource allocation, international economic integration, the reproduction of the state, ideology, and the reproduction of the working class. These are summarily described below in order to locate the contradictions leading to the current crisis.

Under neoliberalism, state capacity to allocate resources intertemporally (the balance between investment and consumption), intersectorally (the composition of output and investment) and internationally (the articulation of capitalist production and finance across borders) has been systematically transferred to an increasingly globalised financial sector in which US institutions play a dominant role.[4] Resource control has given the financial institutions a determining influence upon the level and composition of investment, output and employment, the structure of demand, the financing of the state, the exchange rate and the patterns of international specialisation in most countries. The extended influence and resourcing of finance has supported the development of a whole array of new instruments, the rapid expansion of purely speculative activities and, inevitably, the explosive growth of rewards to high-ranking financiers.[5]

Financialisation and the restructuring of production are underpinned by the transnationalisation of circuits of accumulation, which is commonly described as 'globalisation'. These developments have recomposed the previous 'national' systems of provision at a higher level of productivity at firm level, created new global production chains, reshaped the country-level integration of the world economy, and facilitated the introduction of new technologies and labour processes, while compressing real wages.[6] Finally, financialisation has also supported the reassertion of US imperialism.[7]

Financialisation is not a distortion of a 'pure capitalism' or the outcome of a financial sector 'coup' against productive capital. It is, rather, a structural feature of accumulation and social reproduction under neoliberalism. In this sense, 'finance' includes not only the banks and institutional investors (pension

---

3 See Saad-Filho (2003 and Chapter 9), Saad-Filho and Johnston (2005), and Saad-Filho and Yalman (2010).
4 See, for example, Panitch and Gindin (2004), Panitch and Konings (2009), and Rude (2005).
5 For a detailed analysis of financialisation in the US, see Krippner (2005).
6 See Kotz (2009) and Watkins (2010).
7 See the *Socialist Register* (2004, 2005).

funds, mutual funds, hedge funds, stockbrokers, insurance companies and other firms dealing primarily with interest-bearing capital), but also the financial
arm of industrial capital, whose profitability increasingly depends on financial
engineering. The constitutive role of finance in the capital relation under neoliberalism has allowed it to appropriate an increasing share of the profits extracted by the non-financial corporate sector. This process has played a major
role in the polarization of incomes under neoliberalism.[8]

Even before the current crisis, the notion that finance mobilises and allo-
cates resources efficiently, drastically reduces systemic risks and brings significant productivity gains for the economy as a whole was untenable.[9] Not only
did the expected acceleration of growth through financial and capital account
liberalisation fail to materialise in most countries but, instead, finance-
induced crises have become more frequent.[10] Conversely, the growth accelera-
tions in the age of neoliberalism have been largely unrelated either to changes
in financial sector regulations or capital account liberalisation. An alternative
interpretation is more plausible: regardless of these limitations, financialisation plays a pivotal role in contemporary capitalism because it supports the
transnationalisation of production, facilitates the concentration of income
and wealth and supports the political hegemony of neoliberalism through continuing threats of capital flight. The power of finance has become especially
evident during the current crisis, when several governments were compelled
to rescue large institutions and, in some cases, entire financial systems at huge
cost to the public. Even more strikingly, these revived institutions immediately
started demanding budget cuts because of the alleged 'unsustainability' of the
fiscal position of states that, nominally, 'own' some of the largest banks in the
land.[11] Never in economic history has so much trouble and expense been rewarded with such effrontery.

---

8   For example, and including only a subset of what has been defined as 'finance': 'In 2002,
the [narrow financial] sector generated an astonishing 41 per cent of US domestic corporate profits ... Average pay in the sector rose from close to the average for all industries
between 1948 and 1982 to 181 per cent of it in 2007' (Wolf 2009a). See also Bellamy Foster
and Holleman (2010) and Kotz (2009).

9   For example, '[It] is hard to argue that the new [financial] system has brought exceptional
benefits to the economy generally. Economic growth and productivity in the last 25 years
has been comparable to that of the 1950's and 60's, but in the earlier years the prosperity
was more widely shared' (Volcker 2010, p.1).

10   See Reinhard and Rogoff (2010); and Stiglitz (2010).

11   For a particularly egregious example, see *Financial Times* (2010, p.17).

2   Financialisation and Social Discipline

Neoliberal financialisation has imposed specific modalities of social discipline upon key social agents. These include the state (the need to enforce restrictive welfare policies and contractionary monetary and fiscal policies under the continuing threat of fiscal, exchange rate or balance of payments crisis), industrial capital (global competition promoted by the state and facilitated by finance), and the financial sector itself (competitive international integration under a US-led regulatory umbrella). However, unquestionably the most stringent forms of discipline have been imposed upon the working class.

Hundreds of millions of workers have been forcibly incorporated into transnational circuits of accumulation during the last three decades, greatly increasing competition between individual capitals and between (and within) national working classes. The global restructuring of production, accompanied by regressive legal, regulatory and political changes, have transformed the patterns of employment in most countries and facilitated the imposition of restrictions to the wages, subsidies, benefits, entitlements systems and other non-market protections that had been introduced under various interventionist regimes. These technological, economic, legal and political shifts have drastically narrowed the scope for resistance against neoliberal capitalism.

At another level, social discipline has been imposed through the financialisation of the reproduction of the working class, most remarkably by means of the housing market boom and the expansion of personal credit in the last two decades. These offered highly profitable lines of business for many financial institutions and became an important mechanism of social integration, especially in the US and UK. Under their chronically straitened circumstances, partly because of the disappearance (or the export) of millions of traditionally relatively well-paid skilled jobs and their replacement by less well-paid service jobs and, partly, because of the retrenchment of the welfare state, many workers were drawn into systematic borrowing while their conditions of employment deteriorated. In these circumstances, it is unsurprising that many households became either chronically indebted or increasingly reliant on asset price inflation, or both, in order to meet their reproduction needs.[12] For example,

---

12   Needless to say, millions of working- and middle-class households have profited from financialisation and asset inflation by refinancing their mortgages under more advantageous conditions or purchasing goods and services that would otherwise have remained beyond their reach. Although no generalisation across the working class is possible, there is incontrovertible evidence that large numbers of workers and members of the

[T]here has been a 74 per cent increase in health insurance premiums for the average US family with health care coverage, which has led to 29 million American adults incurring unsecured consumer loans to make up for the gap between medical coverage and actual costs ... [U]nsecured debt has also become an important contributor in granting access to university education ... [M]iddle-income households are [also] using mortgage debt to supplement the lack of funding for basic education as many families now opt to pay a premium for purchasing houses within a good school catchment area ... In addition to medical bills and education ... a large portion of middle-and low-income households use unsecured debt as a safety net or to fund daily living expenses ... [M]iddle-income households are incurring ever greater levels of debt to maintain the historically constructed notion of the American middle-class standard of living.[13]

Many households reacted to the neoliberal reforms by maxing out their credit cards and turning their homes and retirement pensions into virtual cash machines in order to bypass the stagnation of wages and the retrenchment of public welfare provision.[14] However, pressures for timely repayment based on the threat of losing homes, cars and reputations helped to push many debtors into financial difficulties, including the need for long working hours in multiple jobs with precarious employment rights, rising stress levels and, inevitably, a declining propensity to engage in political or industrial militancy.

Unsurprisingly, financialisation has supported a significant rise in the rate of exploitation foremost seen in a corresponding decline in the wage share of national income in most countries. In the US, for example,

From 1979–2004 the [income] share of the top 5 percent of households rose from 15.3 percent to 20.9 percent while that of the poorest 20 percent fell from 5.5 percent to 4.0 percent ... [I]ncome growth has been particularly concentrated at the very top. In 2000 and again in 2005 the richest hundredth of one percent ... of families in the United States received 5 percent of total income, a level that had been not been reached previously

---

middle-class (however defined) have become chronically financially distressed during the last twenty years (see below).

13   Montgomerie (2009, pp.16–18).

14   'In 2002 ... [the gross equity extracted from housing in the US] leaped up to equal about 8 percent of disposable personal income, and from 2004–06 they were in the range of 9–10 percent of disposable personal income. These huge extractions from home equity, which would not have been possible in the absence of the rapid runup in home prices, represented additional spendable funds beyond households' disposable income' (Kotz 2009, p.312).

since 1929. During the 1950s and 1960s the share received by the top 0.01 percent was between 1 percent and 1.5 percent of total income.

KOTZ 2009, p.310

Similarly, in the UK,

[The] top 0.05 per cent of the population had seen its share of national income decline ... from 1937 till the 1970s ... but by 2000 its share was *higher* than it had been in 1937. And the very rich got richer faster than the merely wealthy. In the 1980s, every group in the top tenth of taxpayers increased their share of national income, but in the 1990s the increase in the share of the top tenth was *all* accounted for by the top 0.1 per cent ... [T]he average ratio of CEO-to-employee pay was 47 in 1999; ten years later it was 128.

COLLINI 2010, p.31

Personal credit was also a key macroeconomic policy tool. Every time the US and UK economies slowed down as, for example, in the late 1990s, after the dotcom bubble and after 9–11, their central banks lowered interest rates and encouraged remortgaging and the accumulation of unsecured debt in order to prop up demand. These policies have been referred to as 'asset price Keynesianism',[15] because, to some extent, private deficits replaced the role of public sector deficits in macroeconomic stabilisation. This policy was temporarily successful, and demand induced by home equity extractions added approximately 1.5 percent per year to the rate of growth of US GDP growth between 2002 and 2007. Suggestively, this was just about the difference between US and Eurozone growth rates during that period (Marazzi 2010, p.35).

The significance of personal debt for social reproduction under neoliberalism does not support the right-wing view that the current crisis was caused by the profligacy of poor US and UK households. Nor does the left-populist claim that the indebted workers were merely victims of structural forces hold up. The analysis above *does*, however, imply that the crisis was the outcome of an unsustainable process of neoliberal financialisation, perverse changes in labour market structures and regressive shifts in the provision of the means of subsistence, underpinned by limited macroeconomic policy tools and propped up by deeply ideological claims about 'competition' and 'individual choice'. The crisis also shows that it is impossible to eliminate poverty by lending to

---

15   See, for example, Brenner (2009) and Marazzi (2010, pp.34–35).

the poor: poverty has many causes, but insufficient access to credit is not one of them.

It is also impossible to stabilise complex economies over long periods through the manipulation of mass credit. Unlike the state, or the banks, the working class cannot employ itself (although some workers can revert to self-employment or informal work, or they can become petty commodity producers), and they cannot devalue their own debts or print money. These material limitations in their ability to repay restrict the working class's borrowing capacity. Consequently, *in extremis*, their debts may have to be nationalised, inflated away or legislated out of existence. But this happens only exceptionally: under normal circumstances, excess debt leads only to individual penury and social degradation.

3   Neoliberalism's Contradictions

The neoliberal system of accumulation is structurally unstable at five levels. First, the sheer weight of finance in the economy, facilitated by technological developments that reinforce financial innovations and speed financial transactions, and by regulatory liberalisation, determines that accumulation under neoliberalism has often taken the form of financial (bubble-like) cycles which eventually collapse with destructive implications and requiring a state-sponsored bailout. These cycles include: the international debt crisis of the early 1980s, the US savings & loan crisis of the 1980s, the stock market crashes of the 1980s and 1990s, the Japanese crisis of the late 1980s, the crises in several middle income countries at the end of the twentieth century, and the dot-com, financial and housing bubbles of the 2000s, culminating with the current global meltdown. It is also striking that the business model of neoliberalism's beacon enterprises is, often, based primarily on plunder and fraud, across a spectrum ranging from Enron to Bernard L. Madoff Investment Securities. Although these crises and a succession of large-scale bankruptcies demonstrate the irrationalities of accumulation under neoliberalism, the illusion of prosperity was supported by the Fed's apparent ability to coordinate the cleanup operations while sustaining growth in the dynamic centre of the world economy.

Second, the latest cycle was predicated on a seemingly bottomless appetite for credit by households and the state, which provided outlets for the commodities and the fictitious capital produced by the global corporations. However, growing household consumption was sustainable only while rising house prices conjured up the equity which could be withdrawn through new loans and remortgages.[16] It would eventually become impossible to service rising debts with stagnant household incomes – especially if interest rates had to rise in order to prick asset bubbles or keep inflation low. Rising house prices also depended on the flow of mortgage credit by the financial institutions, which was, in turn, reliant on US and UK policies to promote speculative capital inflows, buy-to-let swindles (in the UK) and predatory subprime lending (in the US) allegedly in order to 'expand home ownership'.[17] These loans were sliced up and traded repeatedly among the financial institutions, generating staggering fortunes in the process.[18] However, when swelling losses threatened to overwhelm the financial sector, governments swiftly collectivized risks, nationalised the imperilled institutions and plugged the sector's balance sheet with endless quantities of newly minted cash.

Third, the cycle required a continuing flow of financial resources to the US and the UK to buy shares, T-bills, mortgage-based securities and real estate. These funds were converted into tradable financial assets, allowing the intermediaries to extend credit in the domestic economy. Evidently, these transfers are ultimately unsustainable because the US and UK cannot expect to be permanently subsidized by cheap goods *and* cheap finance supplied by the rest of the world. Nevertheless, these resource flows temporarily supported the claim that the finance-driven restructuring of capitalism had been successful, and that the US and UK were consistently doing 'better' than the economies which embraced neoliberalism a little more reluctantly (especially Japan and the Eurozone). These performance differences in the years preceding the crisis helped to legitimize neoliberalism, and to disguise the fact that the so-called 'Great Moderation' was largely founded on unsustainable debt-led growth supported by misaligned exchange rates.[19]

Fourth, macroeconomic stability, predictable central bank policies, hands-off financial regulation, the Basel II framework and 'mark to market' accounting rules increased the economy's vulnerability to swings, shocks and confidence crises. They created incentives for rising leverage and for an increasing reliance

---

16   'By the summer of 2007 housing prices had risen by 70 percent corrected for inflation since 1995. At its peak in 2007, the housing bubble created an estimated $8 trillion in inflated new housing wealth, out of total housing wealth of $20 trillion, or 40 percent of housing wealth' (Kotz 2009, p.311).

17   For a review of Alan Greenspan's ideologically-driven support for the property boom, see *Le Monde Diplomatique* (2009).

18   For a detailed study of remunerations in the financial sector, see Bebchuk, Cohen and Spamann (2009).

19   For a starry-eyed overview of the 'Great Moderation', see Bernanke (2004). For a review of the US experience, see Panitch and Gindin (2009).

by the financial institutions on short-term wholesale funding rather than retail deposits. Leveraging and the creation of liquidity through the transformation of debt into tradable papers boosted asset prices which, in turn, encouraged further leveraging, in a kind of Ponzi process. Conversely, when liquidity fell highly leveraged financial institutions had to cut their balance sheets rapidly, contributing to the severity of the crisis.

Fifth, it was expected that securitization would increase the resilience of accumulation by transferring risk to those better able to hold it. However, in reality the financial institutions lost the incentive to evaluate risk because their papers were being traded immediately, while the buyers relied on meaningless credit ratings to disguise their ignorance.[20] The ensuing flood of securities silently destabilised global finance.[21] In sum, although the trigger for the crisis was the collapse of subprime mortgages in the US, there were several weak links along the chain: the recycling of US and UK current account deficits, the rate of accumulation of personal debt, the relationship between consumption and interest rates, the fragility of the balance sheets of the large financial institutions and their structured investment vehicles, the need for low inflation and predictable changes in interest rates, and so on.

In this sense, the current crisis exposes the limitation of financialisation as the driver of global accumulation. The contradictions underlying the crisis indicate that this is a *systemic crisis in neoliberalism*, but it is *not a crisis of neoliberalism* because, although the reproduction of the system of accumulation has been shaken, it is not currently threatened by a systemic alternative.

4   Not Moving Forward

The financial collapse delivered a stunning blow to the neoliberal consensus, as was aptly illustrated by Alan Greenspan's (2008, p.2) confession of 'shocked disbelief'. *The Economist* (2008) was nothing less than apocalyptic:

> [E]conomic liberty is under attack and capitalism ... is at bay ... but those who believe in it must fight for it ... In the short term defending capitalism means, paradoxically, state intervention. There is a justifiable sense of outrage ... that $2.5 trillion of taxpayers' money now has to be spent

---

20   'The proposition that sophisticated modern finance was able to transfer risk to those best able to manage it has failed. The paradigm is, instead, that risk has been transferred to those least able to understand it' Wolf (2009b).

21   For an engaging account of the transformations of finance during the last two decades, see Tett (2009a).

on a highly rewarded industry. But the global bailout is pragmatic, not ideological ... If confidence and credit continue to dry up, a near-certain recession will become a depression, a calamity for everybody.

For a few weeks in 2008 global capitalism seemed to bleed uncontrollably, as losses reportedly climbed towards US$ 40 trillion or, alternatively, 45 percent of the world's wealth.[22] Several states nationalised key financial institutions, guaranteed deposits and financial investments, cut interest rates and implemented expansionary fiscal policies and so-called 'quantitative easing' to support finance, aggregate demand and employment. It is impossible to calculate the cost of these initiatives. They included central bank purchases of temporarily worthless financial assets, which may gain value as the global economy stabilises, 'Keynesian' initiatives to protect employment, which partly pay for themselves through additional tax revenues and reduced social security transfers, and a significant amount of borrowing to fund regular spending, which became necessary because of the crisis-driven decline in taxation. These measures were unsurprising: they reflect, on the one hand, the post-Great Depression consensus that aggressive expansionary policies can avert a deflationary spiral, and, on the other, the neoliberal claim that financial sector stability is paramount.

Heavy state spending and the socialisation of losses and risks stemmed the haemorrhage of bank capital and postponed the collapse of some large manufacturing conglomerates, especially the old US automakers. However, they did not revive bank credit, and their huge costs have triggered severe fiscal problems especially in the US, UK, peripheral European economies and fragile Gulf states. As Joseph Stiglitz (2010b) put it,

> [T]he very actions that saved the economies of the world have presented a new problem for fiscal policy, as questions are being raised about governments' ability to finance their deficits. There are speculative attacks against the weakest countries, which find themselves caught between a rock and a hard place ... The financial markets that caused the crisis – which in turn caused the deficits – went silent as money was being spent on the bailout; but now they are telling governments they have to cut public spending. Wages are to be cut, even if bank bonuses are to be kept.

Despite their *tactical* proficiency, instantly coming up with trillions of dollars to support the banks and shore up the global economy, the neoliberal

---

22   See Greenspan (2009, p.13), Tett (2009b), and Davies and Siew (2009).

bourgeoisies and their paid economists have demonstrated a staggering lack of *strategic* imagination. Even the most promising recovery scenarios offers only slow growth, a decade of austerity and a wave of unemployment which may last for an entire generation. The neoliberal consensus view is that the system of accumulation can be fixed with a little financial regulation, marginal exchange rate adjustments, a bit more consumption in East Asia and in Germany, and belt-tightening in the US and UK. These cosmetic changes are unlikely to rebalance the global economy or to allow the neoliberal states to manage the ongoing restructuring of accumulation. Their simplicity is symptomatic of the mainstream's superficial understanding of the crisis; they point to a slow and very bumpy recovery, with the emergence of deep financial, fiscal, exchange rate and unemployment crises in one country after another, and over a long period of time.

Most recovery plans bypass the need for an alternative mechanism of social integration, fail to recognise that the manipulation of personal debt will be insufficient to stabilise demand and employment, and ignore the fact that the contraction of credit, wages and pensions and the need for fiscal retrenchment will compromise long term demand growth. Although state spending has plugged the gap during the crisis, this is unsustainable without significant changes in taxation and the distribution of income, but these are not currently on the cards.[23] Recovery plans also presume that contractionary fiscal policies are essential to protect state credit ratings in the short-run and avoid inflation in the long run, and envision that, after the return of 'normal' conditions, the manipulation of interest rates should become once again the most prominent macroeconomic policy tool. That is, the neoliberal camp essentially expects the global system of accumulation to get back to its pre-crisis state (plus or minus some marginal tinkering) after a prolonged and rather costly period of instability.[24]

---

23   'The current economic upheaval demonstrates that access to credit is no replacement for real wage growth and adequate social protection. As such, political interventions to stem the current financial crisis need to address the chronic liquidity and impending solvency problems faced by the household sector ... [due to] the huge stock of unsecured debt that must be serviced at the same time as asset prices are falling ... Moreover, these households may no longer be able to continue funding consumption through debt if consumer credit dries up. What is more, undoubtedly households will be left footing the bill for the US government's multiple [bank] bail-out packages ... Whether through increased income taxes or further reductions in government services, households are expected to face their own adversity while being relied on to jump-start the economy' (Montgomerie 2009, pp.18–19).

24   For the IMF's current views of the road to recovery, see Strauss-Kahn (2010) and Lipsky (2010).

Even more alarmingly, although many proposals to address the crisis and prevent a repeat have been aired, three years after the onset of the crisis and two years after the collapse of Lehman Brothers very little of substance has actually happened. The ideas on the table or being discussed in the world's legislatures include a devaluation of the dollar to help rebalance the US economy, a coordinated set of higher inflation targets to erode public debts while preventing explosive capital movements to low inflation countries (see Leunig 2009, p.11), the taxation of bank assets and financial transactions, a review of supervisory agency responsibilities, the prohibition of certain types of short-selling, regulatory changes requiring the financial institutions to prepare 'living wills' and/or buy insurance against possible failure, and rules to increase capital requirements countercyclically, constrain leveraging and speculation, ban proprietary trading, restrict the hedge funds and cap bonuses. Other suggestions include stricter regulation of the credit rating agencies, increased transparency in derivatives trading (for example, through the creation of centralised exchanges), and stronger consumer protection against predatory lending.[25]

However, no significant macroeconomic adjustments have taken place yet, and the financial institutions have been lobbying ferociously against any attempt to curb their operations. They argue that the US and UK should not deliberately maim a large industry in which they have a comparative advantage, and that taxation or regulation would lead to the mass exodus of banks, hedge funds and traders to Switzerland, Singapore or the Gulf.[26] Their well-funded campaign is only part of the problem.

Macroeconomic adjustments have been hamstrung by a number of major economic challenges that remain in place. A first is the conflicting pressures on the dollar (it must fall to help correct the US current account deficit, but it tends to rise whenever there is uncertainty elsewhere, especially in the systemically important countries or the Eurozone); China's parallel unwillingness to let its currency appreciate is a second. Structural contradictions within the Eurozone are a further difficulty: between surplus and deficit countries; between entrenched monetary conservatism and the need to deploy expansionary policies to address the crisis in the smaller countries; and – more fundamentally – between monetary unification and continuing fiscal fragmentation.

A fourth obstacle is the extraordinarily inflexible monetary policy apparatus that has remained in place to lock in low inflation (see Saad-Filho

---

25   See Blanchard (2009), and Wolf (2010).
26   These threats of mass exit are hollow because the state, in these rival financial centres, does not have the resources to support and, if necessary, bail out the relatively aggressive institutions which might want to be based there.

2007a and Chapter 13). Its rigidities are compounded by significant monetary policy differences between the US, Japan, the UK and the Eurozone. For example, the first two do not have legally binding inflation targets to raise, the UK cannot act in isolation, and the ECB has been built to enforce low inflation, and its governance structure makes it difficult to change course (see Palley 2010). Complications of a different order would arise if inflation rose too fast in certain countries, because governments would be compelled to limit their fiscal stimuli and raise interest rates, potentially stalling the recovery.

Finally, another set of difficulties concerns reaching legislative agreement about how to tax the financial sector, set capital requirements, dismantle institutions that are too big to fail (and, therefore, that have in-built incentives to behave recklessly), and unscramble players' incentives (bonuses are outrageously high in the good times, and absurd when the financial sector refuses to lend even though it is being propped up by the state). These difficulties are especially visible in the debates surrounding the financial market reform bill in the US Congress. In conclusion, the largest economic crisis since 1929 has demonstrated that transferring control of capital to finance fosters speculation and systemic instability and does not improve macroeconomic performance. Yet, the institutional imperatives of reproduction of neoliberalism make it difficult for governments to introduce a new economic policy framework.

5   **Coming Out of Left Field**

Although the left has been severely weakened by the neoliberal onslaught, it should seek to intervene in the current debates offering democratic policy alternatives defending jobs, salaries, pensions and welfare standards, improving the quality of investment, protecting the environment, and seeking to turn the current crisis *in* neoliberalism into a *crisis of neoliberalism*.[27] These proposals can be framed, initially, along two axes.

First, no concessions should be offered on jobs, pensions or welfare. Those who benefitted disproportionately from the good times, and whose greed caused the crisis, should pay for it. Besides, offering concessions to protect individual employers or countries will only intensify the continuing race to the bottom under neoliberalism.

---

27   Pro-poor (democratic) economic policy alternatives to neoliberalism are reviewed in MacEwan (1999) Saad-Filho (2007b).

Second, the left can demand the takeover of the financial system and its transformation into a public utility. This can be justified at two levels. On the one hand, the economic argument for profits is that they encourage capitalists to invest wisely in order to multiply their capital and avoid losses. However, if the financial sector is unproductive and if its losses must be socialised, especially when they are large, there is no justification for profits in this sector. On the other hand, governments have given huge sums of money to the banks, but the banks are refusing to lend. The banks are not interested in low-risk-low-return operations, and they have to rebuild their reserves. This bottleneck is helping to perpetuate the crisis. Such a 'catch-22' is unavoidable given the institutional structure of the financial system, the imperatives of competition, and the constraints imposed by the crisis.

Nationalisation without (further) compensation will cut this Gordian knot. Ideally, it should be supplemented by closing down the hedge funds and other institutions trading only between themselves and performing no productive service for the economy, pegging bankers' compensation to civil servants' salaries, imposing capital controls and centralising currency trading, abolishing the secondary markets for public securities, and creating a democratically accountable management structure for the financial sector. If the state runs the banks according to public policy goals, it will not have to accommodate short-term profitability; the banks will no longer be involved in socially destructive businesses, and society can be more certain that there will be no financial crises or bailouts in the future. At a strategic level, nationalisation is important because the ownership of financial assets is at the core of the reproduction of capitalism today. Paradoxically, this is also the weakest social relation both economically and ideologically now, and a mass campaign to nationalise finance could destabilise the class relations at the core of neoliberalism.

It goes without saying that state ownership of finance does not signal the abolition of capitalism. The state had full ownership or significant control of finance in France and Iceland until a few years ago, and in Brazil and South Korea under their respective military dictatorships. Legal ownership can help, but what really matters are the objectives of government policy and which class and other interests are served by the financial institutions. As opposed to financial system-led systems, state-led co-ordination of economic activity is potentially more advantageous for the working class because the state is the only social institution that is at least potentially democratically accountable and that can influence the pattern of employment, the production and distribution of goods and services and the distribution of income and assets at the level of society as a whole.

In addition to the financial reforms sketched above, a democratic economic strategy can focus on the expansion of two complementary areas: the sectors producing goods and services for the workers and the poor (and where production is, often, relatively labour-intensive, as in construction and non-durable consumer goods), and the sectors that can help to relax the balance of payments constraint in deficit or vulnerable countries. They can be prioritised through the adoption of policies enforcing capital controls, maintaining exchange rates compatible with current account balance, avoiding domestic and external debt, introducing accommodating fiscal and monetary policies and rising tax ratios, and securing investment in public and environmentally sustainable goods. All these goals are compatible with a green investment strategy, which, especially in the large economies, has become imperative in order to avoid global environmental collapse.

Left mobilisation along these lines will not be welcomed by the neoliberal elite. The left should have no illusions that there is an 'antagonistic' relationship between production and finance under neoliberalism simply because financial gains are, by definition, deductions from the surplus value extracted by industrial capital. This principle is too abstract to support a political alliance between the left and the industrial – or the 'national' – bourgeoisie. Industrial capital is *materially* committed to the reproduction of neoliberalism, and the expectation that industrial capitalists will suddenly decide to follow Keynesian, developmentalist or democratic economic policies drastically misunderstands contemporary capitalism.[28]

This essay has argued that neoliberalism is a material form of social reproduction and social rule encompassing the structure of accumulation, international exchanges, the state, ideology and the reproduction of the working class, and which is compatible with a wide variety of policies under a supposedly 'free-market' umbrella. This totality has been destabilised by the crisis, and the neoliberal consensus is attempting to restore the *status quo ante* as much as possible. This goal is grounded in the realities of social reproduction, and supported by the class alliances which structure, and benefit from, neoliberalism.

---

28   See the following defence of the City of London by the director-general of the Confederation of British Industry (CBI): 'The City is a vital part of the UK, not a "bloated excrescence" that unbalances the economy, the CBI director-general said yesterday ... Richard Lambert said the City benefited the nation as a whole ... Mr Lambert said that in a free society "it is not the job of a politician - or, for that matter, of a regulator - to argue that a particular form of activity is or is not of social value"'. See: CBI Chief Defends City as Vital to UK', *Financial Times*, 4 September 2009, p.2.

In sharp contrast with these stabilizing goals, the destabilisation of neoliberalism is a project of the radical left, and the spectrum for alliances at the top is very limited. Conversely, the scope for alliances at the bottom of the world's society is, potentially, unlimited. A left strategy to transcend neoliberalism must be based on mass political movements transforming the state and the processes of socio-economic reproduction and political representation – that is, imposing a new system of accumulation, including a new configuration of the economy and more equal distributions of income, wealth and power.

If the global working class remains passive, the crisis will be resolved through an increase in the rate of exploitation. The default position in capitalism is that the workers are not only penalised disproportionately by crises; they must also compensate the capitalists for their losses.[29] This is partly because of the way in which capitalist economies absorb and process adverse shocks and, partly, because the workers are, by definition, closer to the edge of survival and have much greater difficulty turning changing circumstances to their advantage. This makes it essential to reinforce the distributional aspect of economic policy during the crisis by strengthening the links between economic and social policies in order to protect the vulnerable when they need it most (at a minimum, through the imposition of an extraordinary 'crisis tax' on the rich and on large corporations), while, at the same time, imposing progressive structural changes in the current modality of economic and social reproduction.

In sum, the alternative for the workers is to push the cost of the crisis on to the capitalists through a campaign for the takeover of the financial system and the democratization of finance, which would contribute to the destabilisation of neoliberalism. Large-scale mobilisations depend on the left's ability to imagine an alternative future including the values of democracy, solidarity, satisfaction of basic needs and environmental sustainability. They can draw inspiration from the historical struggles for the limitation of the working day, for public health and education, for citizenship rights, and for the extension of democracy, in which the tireless work of millions of left activists has been essential to bring significant gains for the majority.

---

29   'Over the past three quarters, America has seen national income rise by $200bn ... but profits have increased by $280bn while wages have fallen by $90bn. In Britain, where recovery has been slower, national income has grown by £27bn since the middle of last year; higher profits have accounted for £24bn of the rise. Wages have risen by £2bn' (see Elliott 2010).

References

Aalbers, M and B Christophers (2014) 'Centring Housing in Political Economy, Housing', *Housing, Theory and Society*, 31 (4), pp. 373–394.

Abrahamsen, R. (2000) *Disciplining Democracy: Development Discourse and Good Governance in Africa*. London: Zed Books.

Agénor, P.R. (2001) 'Monetary Policy under Flexible Exchange Rates: An Introduction to Inflation Targeting', Central Bank of Chile Working Paper no.124, https://ideas .repec.org/p/chb/bcchwp/124.html (accessed 24 June 2018).

Aglietta, M. (1979) *A Theory of Capitalist Regulation: The US Experience*. London: Verso.

Aglietta, M. (1980) 'La Dévalorisation du Capital: Etude des Liens entre Accumulation et Inflation', *Economie Appliquée* 33 (2), pp. 387–423.

Ahmad, A. (2004) 'Imperialism of Our Time', in L. Panitch and C. Leys (eds) *Socialist Register*, pp. 43–62.

Akyüz, Y. (2010) Why the IMF and the International Monetary System Need More Than Cosmetic Reform. *South Centre Research Paper*, 32, https://ideas.repec.org/p/tek/ wpaper/2010-11.html (accessed 6 June 2018).

Albo, G. (2008) 'Neoliberalism and the Discontented', in L. Panitch and C. Leys (eds.) *Socialist Register*, London: Merlin Press.

Albo, G. (1997) 'A World Market of Opportunities? Capitalist Obstacles and Left Economic Policy', in L. Panitch and C. Leys (eds.) *Socialist Register*, pp.5–47.

Alesina, A. (1989) 'Politics and Business Cycles in Industrial Democracies', *Economic Policy* 8, pp.58–98.

Alesina, A. and L. Summers (1993) 'Central Bank Independence and Macroeconomic Performance: Some Comparative Evidence', *Journal of Money, Credit, and Banking* 25 (2), pp.151–162.

Allio, R. (1978) *Le Contraddizioni Economiche di Proudhon Nella Critica di Marx*. Bologna: Patron Editore.

Arestis, P. and M. Glickman (2002) 'Financial Crisis in Southeast Asia: Dispelling Illusion the Minskyan Way', *Cambridge Journal of Economics* 26, pp.237–260.

Arestis, P. and P. Howells (1996) 'Theoretical Reflections on Endogenous Money, the Problem of Convenience Lending', *Cambridge Journal of Economics*, 20 (5), pp.539–551.

Arestis, P. and M. Sawyer (1998) 'New Labour, New Monetarism', *Soundings* 9, pp. 24–41, reprinted in *European Labour Forum* 20, Winter 1998–99, pp. 5–10.

Arestis, P. and M. Sawyer (2005) 'Inflation Targeting: A Critical Appraisal', unpublished manuscript.

Arestis, P. and M. Sawyer (2010) 'What Monetary Policy after the Crisis?', *Review of Political Economy*, 22 (4): 499–515.

Argitis, G. and C. Pitelis (2001) 'Monetary Policy and the Distribution of Income: Evidence for the United States and the United Kingdom', *Journal of Post Keynesian Economics* 23 (4): 617–638.

Armstrong, P., A. Glyn and J. Harrison (1991) *Capitalism since 1945*. Oxford: Blackwell.

Arnon, A. (1984) 'Marx's Theory of Money: the Formative Years', *History of Political Economy*, 16 (4), pp.555–575.

Ashman, S and B. Fine (2013) 'Neo-liberalism, Varieties of Capitalism, and the Shifting Contours of South Africa's Financial System', *Transformation*, 81–82, pp.145–178.

Attewell, P.A. (1984) *Radical Political Economy, A Sociology of Knowledge Analysis*, New Brunswick, N.J.: Rutgers University Press.

Ayers, A. (2008) 'We All Know a Democracy When We See One: (Neo)Liberal Orthodoxy in the Democratisation and Good Governance Project', *Policy and Society* 27(1), pp.1–13.

Ayers, A. (2009) 'Imperial Liberties: Democratisation and Governance in the 'New' Imperial Order', *Political Studies* 57(1), pp.1–27.

Ayers, A. (2012) 'An Illusion of the Epoch: Critiquing the Ideology of "Failed States"', *International Politics* 49, pp.568–590.

Ayers, A. and A. Saad-Filho (2015) 'Democracy Against Neoliberalism: Paradoxes, Limitations, Transcendence', *Critical Sociology*, 41 (4–5), 2015, pp.597–618.

Backhaus, H.-G. (1974) 'Dialectique de la Forme Valeur', *Critiques de l'Economie Politique*, 18: 5–33.

Ball, L. and N. Sheridan (2003) *Does Inflation Targeting Matter?* IMF Working Paper No. 03/129.

Banaji, J. (2010) *Theory as History: Essays on Modes of Production and Exploitation.* Leiden and Boston: Brill.

Baran, P. (1973) *The Political Economy of Growth*. Harmondsworth: Penguin.

Baran, P. and P. Sweezy (1966) *Monopoly Capital*. London: Penguin.

Barber, W.J. (1995) 'Chile con Chicago: A Review Essay', *Journal of Economic Literature* 33, pp.1941–1949.

Barker, C. (2001) 'Socialists', in: E. Bircham and J. Charlton (eds.) *Anti-Capitalism: a Guide to the Movement*. London: Bookmarks.

Bauman, Z. (1991) 'Communism: A Post-Mortem', *Praxis International* 10 (3–4), pp.185–192.

Baumol, W. (1982) 'Contestable Markets: an Uprising in the Theory of Industrial Structure', *American Economic Review* 72, pp.1–15.

Bayliss, K and B. Fine (eds.) (2008) *Whither the Privatisation Experiment?: Electricity and Water Sector Reform in Sub-Saharan Africa*. Basingstoke: Palgrave Macmillan.

Bayliss, K, B. Fine and E van Waeyenberge (eds.) (2011) *The Political Economy of Development: The World Bank, Neo-Liberalism and Development Research*, London: Pluto Press.

Bebchuk, L., A. Cohen and H. Spamann (2009) 'The Wages of Failure: Executive Compensation at Bear Stearns and Lehman 2000–2008', http://www.law.harvard.edu/faculty/bebchuk/pdfs/BCS-Wages-of-Failure-Nov09.pdf (accessed 17 June 2018).

Beer, Max (1953) *A History of British Socialism*, 2 Vols. London: G. Allen Unwin.

Bellamy Foster, J. and H. Holleman (2010) 'The Financial Power Elite', *Monthly Review*, May, pp.1–19.

Bellamy Foster, J. and R.W. McChesney (2012) *The Global Stagnation and China*, http://monthlyreview.org/2012/02/01/the-global-stagnation-and-china#en49 (accessed 6 July 2018)

Bellofiore, R. (1989) 'A Monetary Labor Theory of Value', *Review of Radical Political Economics* 21 (1–2), pp.1–26.

Bernanke, B. (2004) *The Great Moderation: Remarks at the meetings of the Eastern Economic Association*, www.federalreserve.gov/BOARDDOCS/SPEECHES/2004/20040220/default.htm (accessed 23 June 2018).

Bernanke, B., T. Laubach, F. Mishkin and A. S. Posen (1999). *Inflation Targeting: Lessons from the International Experience*. Princeton: Princeton University Press.

Bernanke, B. and F. Mishkin (1997) 'Inflation Targeting: A New Framework for Monetary Policy?', *Journal of Economic Perspectives* 11 (2), pp.97–116.

Best, M. (1972) 'Notes on Inflation', *Review of Radical Political Economics*, 4 (4), pp.85–112.

Bibow, J. (2010) *A Post Keynesian Perspective on the Rise of Central Bank Independence: A Dubious Success Story in Monetary Economics*, Levy Institute Working Paper no.625, www.levyinstitute.org/pubs/wp_625.pdf (accessed 23 June 2018).

Birch, K. and V. Mykhnenko (eds.) (2010) 'Introduction: A World Turned Right-Way Up', in *The Rise and Fall of Neoliberalism: The Collapse of an Economic Order?* London: Zed Books, pp.1–20.

Blanchard, O. (2009) *The Crisis: Basic Mechanisms, and Appropriate Policies*, IMF Working Paper 09/80.

Bleaney, M. (1976) *Underconsumption Theories: A History and Critical Analysis*. London: Lawrence and Wishart.

Boddy, R. and J. Crotty (1975) 'Class Conflict and Macro-Policy: the Political Business Cycle', *Review of Radical Political Economics*, 7, pp.1–19.

Boddy, R. and J. Crotty (1976) 'Wage-Push and Working-Class Power: A Reply to Howard Sherman', *Monthly Review* 27 (10), pp.35–43.

Bordo, M.D., R.T. Dittmar and W.T. Gavin (2003) *Gold, Fiat Money, and Price Stability*. NBER Working Paper no. 10171.

Bortkiewicz, L. von (1949) 'On the Correction of Marx's Fundamental Theoretical Construction on the Third Volume of Capital', in P.M. Sweezy (ed.) *Karl Marx and the Close of His System*, Clifton: A.M. Kelley.

Bortkiewicz, L. von (1952) 'Values and Prices in the Marxian System', *International Economic Papers* 2, pp.5–60.

Bourdieu, P. (1998) *Acts of Resistance: Against the New Myths of Our Time*. Cambridge: Polity Press.

Bowles, S. and H. Gintis (2000) 'Walrasian Economics in Retrospect', *Quarterly Journal of Economics* 115 (4), pp. 1411–1439.

Bracking, S. (2009) *Money and Power: Great Predators in the Political Economy of Development*. London: Pluto Press.

Brancaccio, E. and G. Fontana (2013) '"Solvency rule" versus "Taylor rule": An Alternative Interpretation of the Relation Between Monetary Policy and the Economic Crisis', *Cambridge Journal of Economics* 37 (1): 17–33.

Bray, John (1931) *Labour's Wrongs and Labour's Remedy; or, The Age of Might and the Age of Right* (Leeds, 1831). London: LSE Reprints.

Brenner, R. (1998) 'The Economics of Global Turbulence', New Left Review, 229.

Brenner, R. (2009) 'Interview on the Current Crisis', at www.hani.co.kr/arti/society/society_general/335869.html (accessed 16 June 2018).

Bresnahan, R. (2003) 'Chile Since 1990: The Contradictions of Neoliberal Democratization', *Latin American Perspectives* 30 (5), pp.3–15.

Brooker, P. (2009) *Non-Democratic Regimes,* 2nd Edition. Houndmills: Palgrave Macmillan.

Brown, W. (2003) 'Neoliberalism and the End of Liberal Democracy', *Theory and Event*, 7(1), https://muse.jhu.edu/login?auth=0&type=summary&url=/journals/theory_and_event/v007/7.1brown.html (accessed 6 June 2018) at:

Brunhoff, S. de (1973) *La Politique Monétaire, Un Essai d'Intérpretation Marxiste*, Paris: Presses Universitaires de France.

Brunhoff, S. de (1976) *Marx on Money*. New York: Urizen Books.

Brunhoff, S. de (1982) 'Questioning Monetarism', *Cambridge Journal of Economics* 6, pp.285–294.

Brunhoff, S. de and J. Cartelier (1974) 'Une Analyse Marxiste de l'Inflation', *Critique Sociale de France*, 4 (reprinted in S. de Brunhoff, *Les Rapports d'Argent*. Grenoble: Presses Universitaires de Grenoble, 1979.

Brunhoff, S. de and P. Ewenczyk (1979) 'La Pensée Monétaire de K. Marx au XIXe et au XXe Siècles', in: S. de Brunhoff (ed.) *Les Rapports d'Argent*. Grenoble: PUG-F. Maspéro.

Bryan, D and M Rafferty (2014) 'Political Economy and Housing in the Twenty First Century – From Mobile Homes to Liquid Housing', *Housing, Theory and Society* 31 (4), pp.404–412.

Burdekin, R. and P. Burkett (1996) *Distributional Conflict and Inflation: Theoretical and Historical Perspectives*. London: Macmillan.

Burgin, A. (2012) *The Great Persuasion: Reinventing Free Markets since the Depression*. Cambridge, MA: Harvard University Press.

Byres, T.J. (1995) *Capitalism from Above and Capitalism from Below: An Essay in Comparative Political Economy*. London: Macmillan.

Cahill, D. (2013) 'Ideas-Centred Explanations of the Rise of Neoliberalism: A Critique', *Australian Journal of Political Science*, 48 (1), pp.71–84.

Cahill, D. (2014) *The End of Laissez-Faire? On the Durability of Embedded Neoliberalism*. Cheltenham: Edward Elgar.

Cairns, J. and A. Sears (2012) *The Democratic Imagination: Envisioning Popular Power in the 21st Century*. Toronto: University of Toronto Press.

Callinicos, A. (2001) *Against the Third Way*. London: Polity Press.

Callinicos, A. (2014) *Deciphering Capital: Marx's Capital and Its Destiny*. London: Bookmarks.

Cammack, P. (1989) 'Bringing the State Back In?', *British Journal of Political Science* 19 (2), pp.261–290.

Cammack, P. (1997) *Capitalism and Democracy in the Third World: The Doctrine for Political Development*. London: Leicester University Press.

Cammack, P. (2006) *The Politics of Global Competitiveness*, https://papers.ssrn.com/sol3/papers.cfm?abstract_id=981846 (accessed 6 June 2018).

Campbell, A. (2011) 'The Role of Workers in Management: The Case of Mondragón', *Review of Radical Political Economics* 43(3), pp.328–333.

Carare, A. and M.R. Stone (2003) *Inflation Targeting Regimes*. IMF Working Paper No. 03/9.

Carare, A., A. Shaechter, M. Stone and M. Zelmer (2002) *Establishing Initial Conditions in Support of Inflation Targeting*. IMF Working Paper No. 02/102, http://www.imf.org/en/Publications/WP/Issues/2016/12/30/Establishing-Initial-Conditions-in-Support-of-Inflation-Targeting-15876 (accessed 23 June 2018).

Cardoso, E. and R. Dornbusch (1987) 'Brazil's Tropical Plan', *American Economic Review*, May.

Cardoso, F.H. and E. Faletto (1979) *Dependency and Development in Latin America*. Berkeley: University of California Press.

Carlin, W. and D. Soskice (1990) *Macroeconomics and the Wage Bargain: A Modern Approach to Employment, Inflation and the Exchange Rate*. Oxford: Oxford University Press.

Carrier, J. and D. Miller (eds.) (1998) *Virtualism: The New Political Economy*. Oxford: Berg.

Carvalho-Filho, I. (2010) 'Inflation targeting and the crisis: An empirical assessment', *IMF Working Paper no.10/45*, https://www.imf.org/external/pubs/ft/wp/2010/wp1045.pdf (accessed 23 June 2018).

Cassel, E. (2004) *The War on Civil Liberties: How Bush and Ashcroft have Dismantled the Bill of Rights*. Chicago, IL: Lawrence Hill Books.

Castree, N. (2006) 'Commentary', *Environment and Planning A* 38 (1), pp. 1–6.

Cecchetti, S.G. and M. Ehrmann (1999) *Does Inflation Targeting Increase Output Volatility? An International Comparison of Policymakers' Preferences and Outcomes*. NBER Working Paper No. 7426, www.nber.org/papers/w7426 (accessed 23 June 2018).

CGD (Commission on Growth and Development) (2008) *The Growth Report: Strategies for Sustained Growth and Inclusive Development*. Washington, DC: World Bank, http://cgd.s3.amazonaws.com/GrowthReportComplete.pdf (accessed 6 June 2018).

Chang, H.-J. and I. Grabel (2004). *Reclaiming Development: An Alternative Economic Policy Manual*. London: Zed Books.

Chang, H-J (2011) *23 Things They Don't Tell You About Capitalism*, London: Penguin.

Chang, H-J. (ed.) (2003) *Rethinking Development Economics*. London: Anthem Press.

Chang, K-S, B. Fine and L Weiss (eds.) (2012) *Developmental Politics in Transition: The Neoliberal Era and Beyond*, Basingstoke: Palgrave Macmillan.

Chattopadhyay, P. (1994) *The Marxian Concept of Capital and the Soviet Experience: Essay in the Critique of Political Economy*, Westport, Conn.: Praeger.

Chomsky, N. (2010) *The Corporate Takeover of US Democracy*, www.inthesetimes.com/article/5502/the_corporate_takeover_of_u.s._democracy/ (accessed 6 June 2018).

Clarke, S. (1988) *Keynesianism, Monetarism and the Crisis of the State*. Aldershot: Edward Elgar.

Clarke, S. (1994) *Marx's Theory of Crisis*. London: Macmillan.

Cleaver, H. (1989) 'Close the IMF, Abolish Debt and End Development: A Class Analysis of the International Debt Crisis', *Capital and Class* 39, pp.17–50.

Coe, N, P Lai and D Wójcik (2014) 'Integrating Finance into Global Production Networks' *Regional Studies*, 48 (5), pp.761–777.

Collini, S. (2010) 'Blahspeak', *Londres Review of Books*, 8 April.

Connolly, W. (1993) *The Terms of Political Discourse*. Oxford: Blackwell.

Cottrell, A. (1994) 'Post-Keynesian Monetary Economics', *Cambridge Journal of Economics* 18, pp.587–605.

Crouch, C. (2004) *Post-Democracy*. Cambridge: Polity Press.

Crouch, C. (2009) 'Privatised Keynesianism: An Unacknowledged Policy Regime', *British Journal of Politics and International Relations*, 11 (3), pp.382–399.

Cukierman, A.(1982) Central Bank Strategy, Credibility, and Independence: Theory and Evidence. Cambridge, Mass.: MIT Press.

Dahl, R.A. (1972) *Polyarchy: Participation and Opposition*. New Haven, CT: Yale University Press.

Dahl, R.A. (1989) *Democracy and its Critics*. New Haven, CT: Yale University Press.

Dale, G. (2012) 'Double Movements and Pendular Forces: Polanyian Perspectives on the Neoliberal Age', *Current Sociology*, 60 (1), pp.3–27.

Dalziel, P. (1990) 'Market Power, Inflation, and Incomes Policies', *Journal of Post Keynesian Economics* 12, pp.424–438.

Dardot, P. and C. Laval (2013) *The New Way of the World: On Neoliberal Society*. London: Verso.

Davidson, P. (1972a) *Money and the Real World*. London: Macmillan.

Davidson, P. (1972b) 'A Keynesian View of Friedman's Theoretical Framework for Monetary Analysis', *Journal of Political Economy*, reprinted in: *Money and Employment, the Collected Writings of Paul Davidson*. London: Macmillan, 1990.

Davidson, P. (1978) 'Why Money Matters, Lessons from a Half-century of Monetary Theory', *Journal of Post Keynesian Economics* 1 (1), pp.46–70.

Davidson, P. (1982) *International Money and the Real World*. London: Macmillan.

Davidson, P. (1989) 'Keynes and Money', in: R. Hill (ed.) *Keynes, Money and Monetarism*. London: Macmillan.

Davidson, P. (1994) *Post-Keynesian Macroeconomic Theory*. London: Macmillan.

Davies, M. and W. Siew (2009) '45 percent of world's wealth destroyed: Blackstone CEO', www.reuters.com/article/wtUSInvestingNews/idUSTRE52966Z20090310 (accessed 17 June 2018).

Dean, M. (1999) *Governmentality: Power and Rule in Modern Society*. London: Sage.

Debelle, G., P. Masson, M. Savastano and S. Sharma (1998) *Inflation Targeting as a Framework for Monetary Policy*, www.imf.org/external/pubs/ft/issues/issues15/ (accessed 23 June 2018).

Denis, A. (2004) 'Two Rhetorical Strategies for *Laissez-Faire*', *Journal of Economic Methodology* 11 (3), pp. 341–357.

Denis, A. (2006) 'Collective and Individual Rationality: Robert Malthus's Heterodox Theodicy', *History of Economic Ideas*, 14 (2), pp.9–31.

Desai, M. (1989) 'The Transformation Problem', *Journal of Economic Surveys* 2(4), pp.295–333.

Desai, M. (1992) 'The Transformation Problem', in G.A. Caravale (ed.) *Marx and Modern Economic Analysis*, Aldershot: Edward Elgar.

Devine, P. (1974) 'Inflation and Marxist Theory', *Marxism Today*, March, pp. 79–92.

Diamond, L. (2002) 'Thinking about Hybrid Regimes', *Journal of Democracy* 13(2), pp.21–35.

Diamond, L. (2008) *The Spirit of Democracy: The Struggle to Build Free Societies Across the World*. New York, NY: Henry Holt.

Diamond, L., J.J. Linz and S. Lipset (1988–89) *Democracy in Developing Countries,* 4 Volumes. London: Adamantine Press.

Díaz-Alejandro, C. (1985) Good-Bye Financial Repression, Hello Financial Crash. *Journal of Development Economics* 19, pp.1–24.

Dobb, M. (1940) *Political Economy and Capitalism*, London: Routledge and Kegan Paul.

Dobb, M. (1943) 'Review of Theory of Capitalist Development, by Paul M, Sweezy', *Science & Society* 7: 270–275.

Dobb, M. (1967) 'Marx's "Capital" and Its Place in Economic Thought', *Science & Society* 31, 4: 527–540.

Doherty, M. (2011) 'It Must Have Been Love ... But It's over Now: The Crisis and Collapse of Social Partnership in Ireland', *European Review of Labour and Research*, 71 (3), pp.371–385.

Dollars and Sense (1978) 'Monopolies and Inflation', in: URPE (ed.) *US Capitalism in Crisis*. New York: URPE.

Dornbusch, R. and M. Simonsen (eds.) (1983) *Inflation, Debt and Indexation*. Cambridge, Mass: MIT Press.

Dotsey, M. (2006) 'A Review of Inflation Targeting in Developed Countries', https:// core.ac.uk/download/pdf/6648848.pdf (accessed 23 June 2018).

Dow, S. (1984) 'Methodology and the Analysis of a Monetary Economy', *Economies et Sociétés*, 18, pp.7–35.

Dow, S. (1996) 'Horizontalism: A Critique', *Cambridge Journal of Economics*, 20 (4), pp.497–508.

Dowd, D.F. (1976) 'Stagflation and the Political Economy of Decadent Monopoly Capitalism', *Monthly Review* 28 (5), pp.14–29.

Duménil, G. (1980) *De la Valeur aux Prix de Production*. Paris: Economica.

Duménil, G. (1983–84) 'Beyond the Transformation Riddle: A Labor Theory of Value', *Science & Society* 33 (4), pp.427–450.

Duménil, G. (1984) 'The So-Called "Transformation Problem" Revisited: A Brief Comment', *Journal of Economic Theory* 33, pp.340–348.

Duménil, G. and D. Lévy (1991) 'Szumski's Validation of the Labour Theory of Value: A Comment', *Cambridge Journal of Economics* 15 (3), pp.359–364.

Duménil, G. and D. Lévy (1993) *The Economics of the Profit Rate: Competition, Crises and Historical Tendencies in Capitalism*. Aldershot: Edward Elgar.

Duménil, G. and D. Lévy (2000a) 'The Conservation of Value: A Rejoinder to Alan Freeman', *Review of Radical Political Economics* 32 (1), pp. 119–146.

Duménil, G. and D. Lévy (2000b) *Manufacturing and Global Turbulence: Brenner's Misinterpretation of Profit Rate Differentials*. Unpublished paper.

Duménil, G. and D. Lévy (2004) *Capital Resurgent: Roots of the Neoliberal Revolution*. Cambridge, MA.: Harvard University Press.

Duménil, G. and D. Lévy (2011) *The Crisis of Neoliberalism*. Cambridge, MA: Harvard University Press.

Dymski, G. (1990) 'Money and Credit in Radical Political Economy: A Survey of Contemporary Perspectives', *Review of Radical Political Economics* 22 (2–3), pp.38–65.

Dymski, G. and R. Pollin (1994) *New Perspectives in Monetary Macroeconomics: Explorations in the Tradition of Hyman P. Minsky*. Ann Arbor: University of Michigan Press.

ECLAC (2008) *Social Panorama of Latin America*. Santiago: ECLAC.

Ehrbar, H. (1989) 'Mathematics and the Labor Theory of Value', *Review of Radical Political Economics* 21 (3), pp.7–12.

Eichengreen, B. (2002) *Can Emerging Markets Float? Should They Inflation Target?* Banco Central do Brasil Working Paper Series No. 36.

EIU (Economist Intelligence Unit) (2011) *Democracy Index 2011: Democracy under Stress*. London: EIU.

Eldred, M. (1984) 'A Reply to Gleicher', *Capital & Class* 23: 135–137.

Eldred, M. and M. Hanlon (1981) 'Reconstructing Value-Form Analysis', *Capital & Class* 13: 24–60.

Eley, G. (2002) *Forging Democracy: The History of the Left in Europe, 1850–2000*. Oxford: Oxford University Press.

Elliott, L. (2010) 'So Much For The Spring of Discontent', *The Guardian*, 29 March, p.26.

Elson, D. (1979) 'The Value Theory of Labour', in D. Elson (ed.) *Value, The Representation of Labour in Capitalism*, London: CSE Books.

Engels, F. (1981) 'Supplement', in K. Marx, *Capital 3*, Harmondsworth: Penguin.

Engels, F. (1998a) *Anti-Duhring*, CD-Rom, London: Electric Books.

Engels, F. (1998b) *Introduction to The Class Struggles in France, 1848–1850*, http://www.marxists.org/archive/marx/works/1895/03/06.htm (accessed 6 June 2018).

Ernst, J. (1982) 'Simultaneous Valuation Extirpated: a Contribution to the Critique of the Neo-Ricardian Concept of Value', *Review of Radical Political Economics* 14 (2), pp.85–94.

Ewing, K. (2010) *The Bonfire of the Liberties: New Labour, Human Rights and the Rule of Law*. Oxford: Oxford University Press.

Fasenfest, D. (2011) 'Terrorism, Neo-Liberalism and Political Rhetoric', *Critical Sociology* 37(4), pp.379–382.

Ferguson, J. (2007) 'Formalities of Poverty: Thinking about Social Assistance in Neoliberal South Africa', *African Studies Review*, 50 (2), pp.71–86.

Financial, Times (2010) 'Moody's Warns US Over Credit Rating Fears', 4 February, p.17.

Fine, B. (1980) *Economic Theory and Ideology*, London: Edward Arnold.

Fine, B. (1983) 'A Dissenting Note on the Transformation Problem', *Economy & Society* 12, 4: 520–525.

Fine, B. (1985–86) 'Banking Capital and the Theory of Interest', *Science & Society* XLIX (4), Winter, pp.387–413.

Fine, B. (1990) 'On the Composition of Capital, A Comment on Groll and Orzech', *History of Political Economy* 22 (1), pp.149–155.

Fine, B. (1992) 'On the Falling Rate of Profit', in G.A. Caravale (ed.) *Marx and Modern Economic Analysis*, Aldershot: Edward Elgar.

Fine, B. (1997) 'The New Revolution in Economics', *Capital and Class*, 61, pp.143–148.

Fine, B. (1998a) *Labour Market Theory: A Constructive Reassessment*. London: Routledge.

Fine, B. (1998b) *The Political Economy of Diet, Health and Food Policy*. London: Routledge.

Fine, B. (2001a) *Globalisation and Development: The Imperative of Political Economy*, unpublished manuscript.

Fine, B. (2001b) *Social Capital versus Social Theory*, London: Routledge.

Fine, B. (2002) *The World of Consumption: The Cultural and Material Revisited*. London: Routledge.

Fine, B. (2006) 'The Developmental State and the Political Economy of Development', in K.S. Jomo and B. Fine (eds.) *The New Development Economics: After the Washington Consensus*. Delhi: Tulika Books.

Fine, B. (2009a) 'Neo-liberalism as Financialisation', in: A. Saad-Filho and G. Yalman (eds.) *Transitions to Neoliberalism in Middle-Income Countries: Policy Dilemmas, Economic Crises, Mass Resistance*. London: Routledge.

Fine, B. (2009b) 'Development as Zombieconomics in the Age of Neo-Liberalism', *Third World Quarterly* 30 (5), pp.885–904.

Fine, B. (2010a) *Theories of Social Capital: Researchers Behaving Badly*, London: Pluto Press.

Fine, B. (2010b) 'Zombieconomics: The Living Death of the Dismal Science', in K. Birch and V. Mykhnenko (eds.) *The Rise and Fall of Neoliberalism: The Collapse of an Economic Order?* London: Zed Books.

Fine, B. (2010c) 'Locating Financialisation', *Historical Materialism*, 18, (2), pp. 97–116.

Fine, B. (2013) *Towards a Material Culture of Financialisation*, FESSUD Working Paper Series, no 15, http://fessud.eu/wp-content/uploads/2013/04/Towards-a-Material-Culture-of-Financialisation-FESSUD-Working-Paper-15.pdf (accessed 6 July 2018).

Fine, B. (2013–14) 'Financialisation from a Marxist Perspective', *International Journal of Political Economy* 42 (4), pp.47–66.

Fine, B. (2014a) 'Across Developmental State and Social Compacting: The Peculiar Case of South Africa', unpublished manuscript.

Fine, B. (2014b) 'The Continuing Enigmas of Social Policy', prepared for the UNRISD project on Towards Universal Social Security in Emerging Economies, UNRISD Working Paper 2014-10, http://www.unrisd.org/Fine.

Fine, B. (ed.) (1986) *The Value Dimension: Marx versus Ricardo and Sraffa*. London: Routledge and Kegan Paul.

Fine, B. and O. Dimakou (2016) *Macroeconomics: A Critical Companion*. London: Pluto Press.

Fine, B. and D. Hall (2012) 'Terrains of Neoliberalism: Constraints and Opportunities for Alternative Models of Service Delivery', in D.A. McDonald and G. Ruiters (eds.) *Alternatives to Privatisation*. London: Routledge.

Fine, B. and L. Harris (1979) *Rereading Capital*. London: Macmillan.

Fine, B. and L. Harris (1985) *The Peculiarities of the British Economy*. London: Lawrence and Wishart.

Fine, B. and E. Leopold (1993) *The World of Consumption*. London: Routledge.

Fine, B. and D. Milonakis (2009) *From Economics Imperialism to Freakonomics: The Shifting Boundaries Between Economics and Other Social Sciences*. London: Routledge.

Fine, B. and D. Milonakis (2011) '"Useless but True": Economic Crisis and the Peculiarities of Economic Science', *Historical Materialism*, 19 (2), pp.3–31.

Fine, B. and A. Murfin (1984) *Macroeconomics and Monopoly Capitalism*. Brighton: Wheatsheaf.

Fine, B. and Z. Rustomjee (1996) *The Political Economy of South Africa: From Minerals-Energy Complex to Industrialisation*. London: Hurst and Co.

Fine, B. and A. Saad-Filho (2013) *The Elgar Companion to Marxist Economics*. Aldershot: Edward Elgar.

Fine, B. and A. Saad-Filho (2014) 'Politics of Neoliberal Development: Washington Consensus and post-Washington Consensus' in H. Weber (ed.) *Politics of Neoliberalism*. London: Routledge, pp.154–166.

Fine, B. and A. Saad-Filho (2016) *Marx's Capital*, 6th ed. London: Pluto Press.

Fine, B. and C. Stoneman (1996) 'Introduction: State and Development', *Journal of Southern African Studies* 22 (1), pp.5–26.

Fine, B. et al (1996) *Consumption in the Age of Affluence: The World of Food*. London: Routledge.

Fine, B., D. Johnston, A. Santos and E. Van Waeyenberge (2016) 'Nudging or Fudging: The World Development Report 2015', *Development and Change*, 47 (4), pp.640–663.

Fine, B., C. Lapavitsas and D. Milonakis (1999) 'Addressing the World Economy: Two Steps Back', *Capital and Class* 67, pp.47–90.

Fine, B., C. Lapavitsas and J. Pincus (eds.) (2001) *Development Policy in the Twenty-first Century: Beyond the Post-Washington Consensus*. London: Routledge.

Fine, B., C. Lapavitsas and A. Saad-Filho (2004) 'Transforming the Transformation Problem: Why the 'New Interpretation' is a Wrong Turning', *Review of Radical Political Economics* 36 (1), pp.3–19.

Fine, B., J. Saraswati and D. Tavasci (eds.) (2013) *Beyond the Developmental State: Industrial Policy into the 21st Century*. London: Pluto.

Foley, D. (1982) 'The Value of Money, the Value of Labour Power and the Marxian Transformation Problem', *Review of Radical Political Economics* 14, 2: 37–47.

Foley, D. (1983) 'On Marx's Theory of Money', *Social Concept* 1 (1), pp.5–19.

Foley, D. (1986) *Understanding Capital: Marx's Economic Theory*. Cambridge, Mass.: Harvard University Press.

Foley, D. (1994) *Asset Speculation in Marx's Theory of Money*, unpublished manuscript.

Foley, D. (2000) 'Recent Developments in the Labor Theory of Value', *Review of Radical Political Economics* 32 (1), pp.1–39.

Fontana, G. (2006) *The 'New Consensus' View of Monetary Policy*, Levy Institute Working Paper no.476, http://www.levyinstitute.org/publications/the-new-consensus-view-of-monetary-policy (accessed 23 June 2018).

Forder, J. (2003) 'Central Bank Independence: Economic Theory, Evidence and Political Legitimacy', *International Papers in Political Economy* 10 (2): 1–53.

Forder, J. (n.d.) The Theory of Credibility: Confusions, Limitations, and Dangers. Unpublished manuscript.

France, A. (2009) *The Red Lily*, http://www.gutenberg.org/ebooks/3920 (accessed 6 June 2018)

Friedman, M. (2002) *Capitalism and Freedom*. Chicago, IL: University of Chicago Press.

Gallie, W.B. (1956) 'Essentially Contested Concepts', *Aristotelian Society* 56, pp.167–198.

Gamble, A. and P. Walton (1976) *Capitalism in Crisis: Inflation and the State*. London: Macmillan.

German, L. (2001) 'Anticapitalism', in: E. Bircham and J. Charlton (eds.) *Anti-Capitalism: a Guide to the Movement*. London: Bookmarks.

Ghosh, J. (2012) 'The Emerging Left in the "Emerging" World', *Economic and Political Weekly* 47 (24), pp.33–38.

Gill, S. (2002) 'Constitutionalizing Inequality and the Clash of Globalizations', *International Studies Review* 4 (2), pp.47–66.

Gills, B. and J. Rocamora (1992) 'Low Intensity Democracy', *Third World Quarterly* 13 (3), pp.501–523.

Gills, B., J. Rocamora and R. Wilson (eds.) (1993) *Low Intensity Democracy: Political Power in the New World Order*, London: Pluto Press.

Gingrich, J (2015) 'Varying Costs to Change? Institutional Change in the Public Sector', *Governance*, 28 (1), pp.41–60.

Gleicher, D. (1985–86) 'The Ontology of Labour Values', *Science & Society* 49, 4:463–471.

Gleicher, D. (1989) 'Labor Specialization and the Transformation Problem', *Review of Radical Political Economics* 21 (1–2), pp.75–95.

Glick, M. and H. Ehrbar (1986–87) 'The Labour Theory of Value and Its Critics', *Science & Society* 50, 4: 464–478.

Glyn, A. (1995) 'Social Democracy and Full Employment', *New Left Review* 211, pp.33–55.

Glyn, A. and B. Sutcliffe (1972) *Workers, British Capitalism and the Profit Squeeze*. Harmondsworth: Penguin.

Goodhart, C.A.E. (1989) 'Has Moore become Too Horizontal?', *Journal of Post Keynesian Economics*, 12 (1), pp.29–34.

Goodhart, C.A.E. (1991) 'Is the Concept of an Equilibrium Demand for Money Meaningful? A reply to "Has the Demand for Money been Mislaid?"', *Journal of Post Keynesian Economics*, 14 (1), pp.134–136.

Gordon, D.M. (1981) 'Capital-Labor Conflict and the Productivity Slowdown', *American Economic Review* 71 (2), pp.30–35.

Gordon, T. (2006) *Cops, Crime and Capitalism: The Law and Order Agenda in Canada*. Halifax: Fernwood Publishing.

Gowan, P. (1999) *The Global Gamble: Washington's Faustian Bid for World Dominance*. London: Verso.

Graeber, D (2014) 'Anthropology and the Rise of the Professional-Managerial Class', *Journal of Ethnographic Theory*, 4 (3), pp.73–88.

Gray, A. (1947) *The Socialist Tradition: Moses to Lenin*. London: Longmans, Green Co.

Gray, J. (1831) *The Social System*. Edinburgh.

Gray, J. (1848) *Lectures on the Nature and Use of Money*. Edinburgh.

Green, D. (2008) *From Poverty to Power*. London: Oxfam.

Green, F. and B. Sutcliffe (1987) *The Profit System*. Harmondsworth: Penguin.

Greenspan, A. (2008) *Testimony of Dr. Alan Greenspan to the Committee of Government Oversight and Reform*, 23 October, https://www.gpo.gov/fdsys/pkg/CHRG-110hhrg55764/html/CHRG-110hhrg55764.htm (accessed 17 June 2018).

Greenspan, A. (2009) 'Equities Show Us The Way to a Recovery', *Financial Times*, 30 March, p.13.

Grilli, V., D. Masciandaro and G. Tabellini (1991) 'Political and Monetary Institutions and Public Finance Policies in the Industrial Countries', *Economic Policy* 13, pp.341–392.

Groll, S. and Z. Orzech (1987) 'Technological Progress and Values in Marx's Theory of the Decline in the Rate of Profit, an Exegetical Approach', *History of Political Economy* 19 (4), pp.591–613.

Groll, S. and Z. Orzech (1989) 'Stages in the Development of a Marxian Concept, the Composition of Capital', *History of Political Economy* 21 (1), pp.57–76.

Grossman, H. (1977) 'Marx, Classical Political Economy, and the Problem of Dynamics', *Capital & Class* 2, pp.32–55.

Grou, P. (1977) *Monnaie, Crise Économique*. Paris: Maspéro.

Gunn, C. (2011) 'Workers' Participation in Management, Workers' Control of Production: Worlds Apart', *Review of Radical Political Economics*, 43 (3), pp.317–327.

Guttman, R. (1994) *How Credit-Money Shapes the Economy: the United States in a Global System*. Armonk: M.E. Sharpe.

Hammond, G. (2012) *State of the Art of Inflation Targeting*. Centre for Central Banking Studies, Handbook no.29, https://www.bankofengland.co.uk/ccbs/state-of-the-art-of-inflation-targeting (accessed 23 June 2018).

Hands, D. (2010) 'Economics, Psychology and the History of Consumer Choice Theory', *Cambridge Journal of Economics*, 34 (4), pp.633–648.

Hart, G. (2002) *Disabling Globalization: Places of Power in Post-Apartheid South Africa*. Durban: University of Natal Press.

Hart, G. (2008) 'The Provocations of Neoliberalism: Contesting the Nation and Liberation after Apartheid', *Antipode*, 40 (4), pp.678–705.

Harvey, D. (1999) *The Limits to Capital*, London: Verso.

Harvey, D. (2003) *The New Imperialism*. London: Verso.

Harvey, D. (2005) *A Brief History of Neoliberalism*. Oxford: Oxford University Press.

Harvey, D. (2010) *A Companion to Marx's Capital*. London: Verso.

Hayek, F. (1944) *The Road to Serfdom*. Chicago, IL: University of Chicago Press.

Hayek, F. (1960) *The Constitution of Liberty*. Chicago, IL: University of Chicago Press.

HDR (Human Development Report) (2002) *Deepening Democracy in a Fragmented World*. New York, NY: UNDP.

Heller, A. (1976) *The Theory of Need in Marx*. London: Allison & Busby.

Held, D. (1996) *Models of Democracy*. Cambridge: Polity Press.

Henderson, J.P. (1985) 'An English Communist, Mr. Bray [and] His Remarkable Work', *History of Political Economy* 17 (1), pp.73–95.

Herman, S.N. (2011) *Taking Liberties: The War on Terror and the Erosion of American Democracy*. New York, NY: Oxford University Press.

Hertz, N. (2001) *The Silent Takeover: Global Capitalism and the Death of Democracy*. London: William Heinemann.

Hilferding, R. (1981) *Finance Capital*. London: Routledge and Kegan Paul.

Himmelweit, S. and S. Mohun (1978) 'The Anomalies of Capital', *Capital & Class* 6, pp.67–105.

Historical Materialism (1999) 'Symposium: Robert Brenner and the World Crisis, Part 1', summer.

Holloway, J. and S. Picciotto (1978) *State and Capital*. London: Edward Arnold.

Hoover, K. and R. Plant (1989) *Conservative Capitalism in Britain and the United States: A Critical Appraisal*. London: Routledge.

Howard, M. (1983) *Profits in Economic Theory*, London: Macmillan.

Howard, M. and J. King (1990) 'The "Second Slump": Marxian Theories of Crisis after 1973', *Review of Political Economy* 2 (3), pp.267–291.

Hunt, A. (1980) 'Taking Democracy Seriously', in: *Marxism and Democracy*. London: Lawrence and Wishart.

Huntington, S. (1991) *The Third Wave: Democratization in the Late Twentieth Century*. Norman OK: Oklahoma Press.

IMF (2015) *Global Financial Stability Report*. Washington DC: IMF.

Isaac, A.G. (1991) 'Economic Stabilization and Money Supply Endogeneity in a Conflicting Claims Environment', *Journal of Post Keynesian Economics* 14 (1), pp.93–110.

Itoh, M. and C. Lapavitsas (1999) *Political Economy of Money and Finance*. London: Macmillan.

Jacobi, O., J. Bergmann and W. Mueller-Jentsch (1975) 'Problems in Marxist Theories of Inflation', *Kapitalistate* 3, pp.107–125.

Jessop, B. (1991) 'Accumulation Strategies, State Forms and Hegemonic Projects', in: S. Clarke (ed.) *The State Debate*. London: Macmillan, pp.140–162.

Jomo, K.S. (2001) *Growth After the Asian Crisis: What Remains of the East Asian Model?* G24 Discussion Paper Series, https://ideas.repec.org/p/unc/g24pap/10.html (accessed 6 July 2018).

Jomo, K. and B. Fine (eds.) (2006) *The New Development Economics: After the Washington Consensus*. Delhi: Tulika Books.

Kaldor, N. (1970) 'The New Monetarism', *Lloyds Bank Review*, July, pp.1–18.

Kaldor, N. (1982) *The Scourge of Monetarism*. Oxford: Oxford University Press.

Kaldor, N. (1985) 'How Monetarism Failed', *Challenge*, May-June, pp.4–13.

Kalecki, M. (1990a) 'Political Aspects of Full Employment', in: Collected Works, Vol.1. Oxford: Clarendon Press.

Kalecki, M. (1990b) 'The Business Cycle and Inflation', in: Collected Works, Vol.1. Oxford: Clarendon Press.

Kalecki, M. (1990c) 'Essays in the Theory of Economic Fluctuations', in: Collected Works, Vol.1. Oxford: Clarendon Press.

Kalecki, M. (1997) 'Introductory Remarks on Inflationary and Deflationary Processes', in: Collected Works, Vol.7. Oxford: Clarendon Press.

Karliner, J. (2001). 'Where Do We Go From Here? Pondering the Future of Our Movement', *CorpWatch*, 11 October 2001, www.corpwatch.org.

Kay, C. (1989) *Latin American Theories of Development and Underdevelopment*. London: Routledge.

Khor, M. (2010) 'Analysis of the Doha Negotiations and the Functioning of the World Trade Organization', *South Centre Research Paper* 30. https://www.southcentre.int/wp-content/uploads/2013/05/RP30_Analysis-of-the-DOHA-negotiations-and-WTO_EN.pdf.

Kiely, R. (2005) *The Clash of Globalisations: Neo-Liberalism, the Third Way and Anti-Globalisation*. Leiden: Brill.

Kiely, R. (2007) *The New Political Economy of Development: Globalization, Imperialism, Hegemony*. London: Palgrave.

Kimball, J. (1948) *The Economic Doctrines of John Gray*. Catholic University of America, Studies in Economics n.21. Washington, D.C.: Catholic University.

King, J.E. (1983) 'Utopian or Scientific? A Reconsideration of the Ricardian Socialists', *History of Political Economy* 15 (3), pp.345–373.

Klein, N. (2007) *The Shock Doctrine: The Rise of Disaster Capitalism*. Toronto: Alfred A. Knopf.

Kliman, A. and S. Williams (2015) 'Why "Financialisation" Hasn't Depressed US Productive Investment', *Cambridge Journal of Economics*, 39 (1), pp.67–92.

Knei-Paz, B. (1978) *The Social and Political Thought of Leon Trotsky*, Oxford: Clarendon Press.

Knibbe, M. (2015) 'Metrics Meta About a Metametric: The Consumer Price Level as a Flawed Target for Central Bank Policy', *Journal of Economic Issues*, 49 (2): 355–371.

Konings, M. (2018) *Capital and Time: For a New Critique of Neoliberal Reason*. Stanford: Stanford University Press.

Kotz, D. (1982) 'Monopoly, Inflation, and Economic Crisis', *Review of Radical Political Economics* 14 (4), pp.1–17.

Kotz, D. (1987) 'Radical Theories of Inflation', in: URPE (ed.) *The Imperiled Economy*. Book 1: Macroeconomics from a Left Perspective. New York: URPE.

Kotz, D. (2009) 'The Financial and Economic Crisis of 2008', *Review of Radical Political Economics* 41(3), pp.305–317.

Kotz, D. (2015) *The Rise and Fall of Neoliberal Capitalism*. Cambridge, MA: Harvard University Press.

Kotz, D., T. McDonough, and M. Reich (2010) (eds.) *Contemporary Capitalism and Its Crises: Social Structure of Accumulation Theory for the 21st Century*. Cambridge: Cambridge University Press.

Kozul-Wright, R. (2006) 'Globalization Now and Again', in K.S. Jomo (ed.) *Globalization under Hegemony: The Changing World Economy*. Oxford: Oxford University Press.

Krier, D (2005) *Speculative Management: Stock Market Power and Corporate Change*, Albany NY: State University of New York Press.

Krier, D. (2008) 'Critical Institutionalism and Financial Globalization: A Comparative Analysis of American and Continental Finance', *New York Journal of Sociology* 1, pp.130–186.

Krippner, G. (2005) 'The Financialization of the American Economy', *Socio-Economic Review* 3, pp.173–208.

Krippner, G. (2011) *Capitalizing on Crisis: The Political Origins of the Rise of Finance*. Cambridge, MA: Harvard University Press.

Kulish, N. (2011) As Scorn for Vote Grows, Protests Surge Around Globe, *New York Times*, 27 September, http://www.nytimes.com/2011/09/28/world/as-scorn-for-vote-grows-protests-surge-around-globe.html?pagewanted=all (accessed 6 June 2018)

Kurki, M. (2010) 'Democracy and Conceptual Contestability: Reconsidering Conceptions of Democracy in Democracy Promotion', *International Studies Review* 12, pp.362–386.

Labica, G. (2007) 'From Imperialism to Globalisation', in S. Budgen, S. Kouvelakis and S. Žižek (eds.) *Lenin Reloaded: Toward a Politics of Truth*. Durham, N.C.: Duke University Press.

Laibman, D. (1982) 'Technical Change, the Real Wage and the Rate of Exploitation', *Review of Radical Political Economics* 14 (2), pp.95–105.

Lanchester, K. (2010) *Whoops: Why Everyone Owes Everyone and No One Can Pay*. London: Allen Lane.

Landerretche, O., V. Corbo and K. Schmidt-Hebbel (2001) *Does Inflation Targeting Make a Difference?* Central Bank of Chile Working Papers No 106.

Langley, P (2008) *The Everyday Life of Global Finance*. Oxford: Oxford University Press.

Lapavitsas, C. (1991) 'The Theory of Credit Money: A Structural Analysis', *Science and Society* 55 (3), pp.291–322.

Lapavitsas, C. (1996) 'The Classical Adjustment Mechanism of International Balances: Marx's Critique', *Contributions to Political Economy* 15, pp.63–79.

Lapavitsas, C. (1997) 'The Political Economy of Central Banks, Agents of Stability or Source of Instability?', *International Papers in Political Economy* 4 (3), pp.1–52.

Lapavitsas, C. (2000a) 'On Marx's Analysis of Money Hoarding in the Turnover of Capital', *Review of Political Economy* 12 (2), pp.219–235.

Lapavitsas, C. (2000b) 'Money and the Analysis of Capitalism: The Significance of Commodity Money', *Review of Radical Political Economics* 32 (4), pp.631–656.

Lapavitsas, C. and A. Saad-Filho (2000) 'Three Prerequisites for an Alternative Theory of Money and Credit', in: A. Freeman, A. Kliman and J. Wells (eds.) *New Value Theory*. Cheltenham: Edward Elgar.

Larner, W. (2000) 'Neo-liberalism: Politics, Ideology, Governmentality', *Studies in Political Economy* 63, pp.5–25.

Lavoie, D. (1986) 'Marx, the Quantity Theory, and the Theory of Value', *History of Political Economy* 18 (1), pp.155–170.

Lavoie, M. (1992) *Foundations of Post-Keynesian Economic Analysis*. Aldershot: Edward Elgar.

Le Monde Diplomatique (2009) 'Greenspan's View', mondediplo.com/2009/01/18greenspan (accessed 16 June 2018).

Lebowitz, M. (1992) *Beyond Capital: Marx's Political Economy of the Working Class*. London: Macmillan.

Lee, C.-O. (1990) *On the Three Problems of Abstraction, Reduction and Transformation in Marx's Labour Theory of Value*, PhD Thesis, University of London.

Lee, F. and S. Harley (1998) 'Peer Review, the Research Assessment Exercise and the Demise of Non-Mainstream Economics', *Capital and Class* 66, pp.23–52.

Leftwich, A. (1996) 'On the Primacy of Politics in Development', in: *Democracy and Development: Theory and Practice*. Cambridge: Polity Press.

Lemke, T (2001) 'The Birth of Bio-Politics: Michel Foucault's Lecture at the Collège De France on Neo-Liberal Governmentality', *Economy & Society* 30 (2), pp.190–207.

Lemke, T. (2002) 'Foucault, Governmentality and Critique, *Rethinking Marxism* 14 (3), pp.49–64.

Lenin, V.I. (1899) *The Development of Capitalism in Russia*, https://www.marxists.org/archive/lenin/works/1899/devel/ (accessed 6 July 2018).

Lenin, V.I. (1917) *The State and* Revolution, http://www.marxists.org/archive/lenin/works/1917/staterev/ch01.htm (accessed 6 June 2018)

Lenin, V.I. (2001) 'The Proletarian Revolution and the Renegade Kautsky', in: *Democracy and Revolution*. Broadway: Resistance Books.

Leunig, T. (2009) 'Coordinated Inflation Could Bail Us All Out', *Financial Times*, 15 February, https://www.ft.com/content/224ae9f2-fb95-11dd-bcad-000077b07658 (accessed 17 June 2018).

Levacic, R. and A. Rebmann (1982) *Macroeconomics: An Introduction to Keynesian-Neoclassical Controversies*. London: Macmillan.

Levidow, L. and B. Young (1981, 1985) *Science, Technology and the Labour Process, Marxist Studies*, 2 Vols., London: Free Association Books.

Leys, C. (2008) *Total Capitalism: Market Politics, Market State*. London: Merlin Press.

Linz, J.J. and A. Stepan (1978) *The Breakdown of Democratic Regimes*. 4 Volumes. Baltimore MD: Johns Hopkins University Press.

Lipietz, A. (1982) 'The So-Called Transformation Problem Revisited', *Journal of Economic Theory* 26 (1), pp.59–88.

Lipietz, A. (1983) *Le Monde Enchanté: De la Valeur à L'Envol Inflationniste*. Paris: La Découverte.

Lipietz, A. (1984) 'The So-Called "Transformation Problem" Revisited: A Brief Reply to Brief Comments', *Journal of Economic Theory* 33 (2), pp.352–355.

Lipset, S.M. (1994) 'The Social Requisites of Democracy Revisited', *American Sociological Review* 59, pp.1–22.

Lipsky, J. (2010) 'The Road Ahead for Central Banks: Meeting New Challenges to Financial Stability', http://www.imf.org/external/np/speeches/2010/061810.htm (accessed 17 June 2018).

Loranger, J.-G. (1982a) 'Le Rapport entre la Pseudo-Monnaie et la Monnaie: de la Possibilité à la Réalité des Crises', *Critiques de l'Economie Politique* 18, pp.114–132.

Loranger, J.-G. (1982b) 'Pseudo-Validation du Crédit et Etalon Variable de Valeur', *Economie Appliquée* 35 (3), pp.485–499.

MacEwan, A. (1999) *Neo-liberalism or Democracy?* London: Zed Books.

Macpherson, C.B. (1977) *The Life and Times of Liberal Democracy*. Oxford: Oxford University Press.

Madra, Y and F Adaman (2014) 'Neoliberal Reason and Its Forms: De-Politicisation through Economisation', *Antipode*, 46 (3), pp.691–673.

Mage, S. (1963) *The Law of the Falling Tendency of the Rate of Profit, Its Place in the Marxian System and Relevance to the US Economy*, PhD Thesis, Columbia University.

Mair, P. (2009) *Ruling the Void: The Hollowing Out of Western Democracy*. London: Verso.

Mandel, E. (1968) *Marxist Economic Theory*. London: Merlin Press.

Mandel, E. (1975) *Late Capitalism*. London: New Left Books.

Mann, G. (2013) 'The Monetary Exception: Labour, Distribution and Money in Capitalism', *Capital & Class* 37 (2): 197–216.

Marangos, J. (2007) 'Was Shock Therapy Consistent with the Washington Consensus?', *Comparative Economic Studies,* 49 (1), pp.32–58.

Marangos, J. (2008) 'The Evolution of the Anti-Washington Consensus Debate: From Post-Washington Consensus to After the Washington Consensus', *Competition and Change* 12 (3), pp.227–244.

Marazzi, C. (1977) 'Money in the World Crisis: The New Basis of Capitalist Power', *Zerowork* 2, pp.91–111.

Marazzi, C. (2010) *The Violence of Financial Capitalism*, Los Angeles: Semiotext(e).

Marglin, S. (1974) 'What Do Bosses Do?', *Review of Radical Political Economics* 6 (2), pp.60–112.

Marglin, S. and J. Schor (eds.) (1990) *The Golden Age of Capitalism: Reinterpreting the Postwar Experience*. Oxford: Clarendon Press.

Marx, K. (1859) *A Contribution to the Critique of Political Economy*. Collected Works, Vol. 29, pp.257–417. London: Lawrence & Wishart, 1987.

Marx, K. (1974) 'Critique of the Gotha Programme', in *The First International and After*, Harmondsworth: Penguin.

Marx, K. (1976, 1978b, 1981b) *Capital*, 3 Vols., Harmondsworth: Penguin.

Marx, K. (1978, 1969, 1972) *Theories of Surplus Value*, 3 Vols., London: Lawrence and Wishart.

Marx, K. (1981) *Grundrisse*, Harmondsworth: Penguin.

Marx, K. (1983, 1984) *Capital*, Vols. 1 and 3. London: Lawrence & Wishart.

Marx, K. (1987) *A Contribution to the Critique of Political Economy*, Collected Works, Vol. 29. London: Lawrence & Wishart.

Marx, K. (1988a) *Letter to Kugelmann, July 11, 1868*, Collected Works, Vol.43, London: Lawrence and Wishart.

Marx, K. (1988b) *Collected Works*, vol. 30, London: Lawrence and Wishart.

Marx, K. and F. Engels (1998) *The Communist Manifesto*. London: The Electric Book Company, CD-Rom.

Mattick, P. (1978) *Economics, Politics, and the Age of Inflation*. White Plains: M.E. Sharpe.

McNally, D (2014) *Global Slump: The Economics and Politics of Crisis and Resistance*. Oakland: PM Press.

McNally, D. (2006) *Another World Is Possible: Globalization and Anti-Capitalism*, Winnipeg: Arbeiter Ring Publishing.

McNally, D. (2012) 'Unity of the Diverse: Working Class Formations and Popular Uprisings from Cochabamba to Cairo', in: C. Barker, L. Cox, J. Krinsky and A. Nilsen (eds.) *Marxism and Social Movements*. Leiden: Brill, pp.401–424.

Medema, S. (2009) *The Hesitant Hand: Taming Self-Interest in the History of Economic Ideas*. Princeton: Princeton University Press.

Medio, A. (1977) 'Neoclassicals, Neo-Ricardians, and Marx', in J.G. Schwartz (ed.) *The Subtle Anatomy of Capitalism*, Santa Monica: Goodyear.

Meek, R.L. (1956) 'Some Notes on the "Transformation Problem"', *Economic Journal* 66, pp.94–107.

Meek, R.L. (1973) *Studies in the Labour Theory of Value*, London: Lawrence and Wishart.

Menger, A. (1899) *The Right to the Whole Produce of Labour*, with an Introduction by H. S. Foxwell. London: Macmillan.

Merton, R. (1968) *Social theory and Social Structure*, enlarged edition. New York: Free Press.

Messori, M. (1991) 'Financing in Kalecki's Theory', *Cambridge Journal of Economics* 15, pp.301–313.

Mészáros, I. (2006) 'The Structural Crisis of Politics', *Monthly Review* 58 (4), http://monthlyreview.org/2006/09/01/the-structural-crisis-of-politics (accessed 6 June 2018).

Mills, C.W. (1959) *The Sociological Imagination.* Oxford: Oxford University Press.

Milonakis, D and B. Fine (2009) *From Political Economy to Economics: Method, the Social and the Historical in the Evolution of Economic Theory.* London: Routledge.

Minsky, H.P. (1975) *John Maynard Keynes.* New York: Columbia University Press.

Minsky, H.P. (1986) *Stabilizing an Unstable Economy.* New Haven: Yale University Press.

Mirowski, P. (2007) 'Naturalizing the Market on the Road to Revisionism: Bruce Caldwell's *Hayek's Challenge* and the Challenge of Hayek Interpretation', *Journal of Institutional Economics* 3 (3), pp.351–372.

Mirowski, P. (2009) 'Postface: Defining Neoliberalism' in P. Mirowski and D. Plehwe (eds.) *The Road from Mont Pèlerin: The Making of the Neoliberal Thought Collective.* Cambridge, MA: Harvard University Press.

Mirowski, P. and D. Plehwe (eds.) (2009) *The Road from Mont Pèlerin: The Making of the Neoliberal Thought Collective.* Cambridge, MA: Harvard University Press.

Mishkin, F.S. (1999) 'Inflation Experiences with Different Monetary Policy Regimes', *Journal of Monetary Economics* 43, pp.579–605.

Mishkin, F.S. and K. Schmidt-Hebbel (2002) 'A Decade of Inflation Targeting in the World: What do We Know and What do We Need to Know?', in N. Loayza and R. Soto (eds.) *Inflation Targeting: Design, Performance, Challenges.* Santiago: Central Bank of Chile.

Mohun, S. (1991) 'Value', in in T. Bottomore (ed.) *A Dictionary of Marxist Thought*, 2nd ed, Oxford: Blackwell.

Mohun, S. (1994) 'A Re(in)statement of the Labour Theory of Value', *Cambridge Journal of Economics* 18, pp.391–412.

Mohun, S. (2015) 'Class Structure and the US Personal Income Distribution, 1918–2012', *Metroeconomica* 67 (2): 334–363.

Mollo, M.L.R. (1999) 'Money Endogeneity: Post-Keynesian and Marxian Views Compared', *Research in Political Economy* 18, pp.3–26.

Montgomerie, J. (2009) 'The Pursuit of (Past) Happiness? Middle-class Indebtedness and American Financialisation', *New Political Economy*, 14 (1), 2009, pp.1–24.

Moore, B. (1979) 'The Endogenous Money Stock', *Journal of Post Keynesian Economics*, 2 (1), pp.49–70.

Moore, B. (1983) 'Unpacking the Post Keynesian Black Box: Bank Lending and the Money Supply', *Journal of Post Keynesian Economics* 5 (4), pp.537–556.

Moore, B. (1986) 'How Credit Drives the Money Supply, The Significance of Institutional Development', *Journal of Economic Issues* 20 (2), pp.443–452.

Moore, B. (1988) *Horizontalists and Verticalists: The Macroeconomics of Credit Money.* Cambridge: Cambridge University Press.

Moore, B. (1991) 'Has the Demand for Money been Mislaid? A reply to "Has Moore Become Too Horizontal?"', *Journal of Post Keynesian Economics* 14 (1), pp.125–133.

Morishima, M. (1973) *Marx's Economics – A Dual Theory of Value and Growth*, Cambridge: Cambridge University Press.

Morris, J. (1972) 'The Monetary Crisis of World Capitalism', *Monthly Review* 23 (8), pp.17–27.

Morris, J. (1973) 'The Crisis of Inflation', *Monthly Review* 25 (4), pp.1–22.

Morris, J. (1974) 'Stagflation', *Monthly Review* 26 (7), pp.1–10.

Moseley, F. (1999) 'The United States Economy at the Turn of the Century: Entering a New Era of Prosperity?', *Capital and Class* 67, pp.25–46.

Moseley, F. (2000a) 'The "New Solution" to the Transformation Problem: a Sympathetic Critique', *Review of Radical Political Economics* 32, 2: 282–316.

Moseley, F. (2000b) *The Determination of Constant Capital in the Case of a Change in the Value of the Means of Production*, unpublished manuscript.

Munck, R. (2005) 'Neoliberalism and Politics, and the Politics of Neoliberalism', in: A. Saad-Filho and D. Johnston (eds.) *Neoliberalism: A Critical Reader.* London: Pluto Press, pp.60–69.

Naples, M. (1989) 'A Radical Economic Revision of the Transformation Problem', *Review of Radical Political Economics* 21, 1–2: 137–158.

Nell, E.J. (1992) *Transformational Growth and Effective Demand*, New York: New York University Press.

Nell, E.J. and G. Deleplace (eds.) (1996) *Money in Motion: The Circulation and Post-Keynesian Approaches.* London: Macmillan.

Neumann, M.J.M. and J. von Hagen (2002) 'Does Inflation Targeting Matter?', *Federal Reserve Bank of St Louis Review* 84, pp.149–153.

Norfield, T. (2016) *The City.* London: Verso.

O'Connor, J. (1973) *The Fiscal Crisis of the State.* New York: St. Martin's Press.

O'Connor, J. (2010) 'Marxism and the Three Movements of Neoliberalism', *Critical Sociology* 36 (5), pp.691–715.

O'Donnell, G., P. Schmitter and L. Whitehead (1986) *Transitions from Authoritarian Rule: Prospects for Democracy.* 4 Volumes. Baltimore MD: Johns Hopkins University Press.

Okishio, N. (1974) 'Value and Production Price', *Kobe University Economic Review* 20, pp.1–19.

Olshansky, B. (2007) *Democracy Detained.* New York NY: Seven Stories Press.

Orléan, A. (1982) 'Inflation et Souveraineté Monétaire', *Critiques de l'Economie Politique* 18, pp.93–113.

Osborne, D. and T. Gaebler (1992) *Reinventing Government: How the Entrepreneurial Spirit is Transforming the Public Sector.* New York NY: Basic Books.

Osborne, G. and J. Sachs (2010) 'A Frugal Budgetary Policy Is The Better Solution', *Financial Times*, 15 March, p.15.

Ost, D. (2000) '"Illusory Corporatism" in Eastern Europe: Neoliberal Tripartism and Postcommunist Class Identities', *Politics and Society*, 28 (4), pp.503–530.

Ost, D. (2011) 'Illusory Corporatism Ten Years Later', *Warsaw Forum of Economic Sociology*, 2 (1), pp.19–49.

Palley, T. (1996) *Post-Keynesian Economics: Debt, Distribution and the Macro Economy*. London: Macmillan.

Palley, T. (2010) *Europe's Debt Crisis and Keynes' Green Cheese Solution*, http://www .insightweb.it/web/content/europe%E2%80%99s-debt-crisis-and-keynes%E2%80 %99-green-cheese-solution (accessed 17 June 2018).

Palma, G. (1981) 'Dependency and Development: A Critical Overview', in D. Seers (ed.) *Dependency Theory: A Critical Reassessment*. London: Francis Pinter.

Palma, G. (1998) 'Three and a Half Cycles of 'Mania, Panic and [Asymmetric] Crash': East Asia and Latin America Compared', *Cambridge Journal of Economics* 22 (6), pp.789–808.

Palma, G. (2009) 'The Revenge of the Market on the Rentiers', *Cambridge Journal of Economics*, 33 (4), pp.829–869.

Panitch, L. and S. Gindin (2004) 'Global Capitalism and American Empire', in L. Panitch and C. Leys (eds.) *Socialist Register*, pp.1–42.

Panitch, L. and S. Gindin (2005) 'Finance and American Empire' in L. Panitch and C. Leys (eds.) *Socialist Register: The Empire Reloaded*. London: Merlin Press.

Panitch, L. and S. Gindin (2009) 'Finance and American Empire', in L. Panitch and M. Konings (eds.) *American Empire and the Political Economy of Global Finance*. London: Palgrave.

Panitch, L. and S. Gindin (2012) *The Making of Global Capitalism: The Political Economy of American Empire*. London: Verso.

Panitch, L. and M. Konings (eds.) (2008) *American Empire and the Political Economy of Global Finance*. London: Palgrave.

Parenti, M. (2011) *Democracy for the Few*, 9th edition. Stamford CT: Cengage Learning.

Perelman, M. (1996) *The Pathology of the US Economy*. London: Macmillan.

Perelman, M. (1999) 'Marx, Devalorisation, and the Theory of Value', *Cambridge Journal of Economics* 23, 6: 719–728.

Piketty, T. (2014) *Capital in the Twenty-First Century*. Cambridge MA: Harvard University Press.

Plant, R. (2010) *The Neo-Liberal State*. Oxford: Oxford University Press.

Polanyi, K. (2001) *The Great Transformation: The Political and Economic Origins of Our Time*. Boston: Beacon Press.

Polanyi-Levitt, K. (2013) *From the Great Transformation to the Great Financialization*. London: Zed Books.

Pollin, R. (1991) 'Two Theories of Money Supply Endogeneity: Some Empirical Evidence', *Journal of Post Keynesian Economics* 13 (3), pp.366–396.

Pollin, R. (1993) 'Money Supply Endogeneity: What Are the Questions and Why Do They Matter?', in: E. Nell and G. Deleplace (eds.) *Money in Motion: The Circulation and Post Keynesian Approaches*. New York: Macmillan.

Popper, K.R. (1945) *The Open Society and Its Enemies*. London: Routledge.

Proudhon, P.-J. (1923) *Système des Contradictions Economiques ou Philosophie de la Misère* (2 Vols.). Paris: Marcel Rivière.

Radice, H. (2000) 'Responses to Globalisation: a Critique of Progressive Nationalism', *New Political Economy*, 5 (1), pp.5–19.

Reati, A. (1986) 'The Deviation of Prices from Labour Values: Aan Extension to the Non-Competitive Case', *Cambridge Journal of Economics* 10, pp.35–42.

Regan, A (2009) 'The Impact of the Eurozone Crisis on Irish Social Partnership: A Political Economic Analysis', ILO International Training Centre, http://www.ilo.org/ ifpdial/information-resources/publications/WCMS_213211/lang--en/index.htm (accessed 6 June 2018).

Reinhard, C. and K. Rogoff (2010) *This Time is Different*, Princeton: Princeton University Press.

Reuten, G. and M. Williams (1989) *Value-Form and the State, The Tendencies of Accumulation and the Determination of Economic Policy in Capitalist Society*, London: Routledge.

Ricardo, D. (1951) 'Proposals for an Economical and Secure Currency'. *The Works and Correspondence of David Ricardo*, Vol. 4, Cambridge: Cambridge University Press.

Robinson, W.I. (1996) *Promoting Polyarchy: Globalization, US Intervention and Hegemony.* New York NY: Cambridge University Press.

Robinson, W.I. (2006) Promoting Polyarchy in Latin America', in: E. Hershberg and F. Rosen (eds.) *Latin America after Neoliberalism*. New York NY: The New Press, pp.97–119.

Rochon, L.-P. and M. Setterfield (2007) 'Interest Rates, Income Distribution, and Monetary Policy Dominance', *Journal of Post Keynesian Economics* 30 (1): 13–42.

Rodrik, D. (2007) *One Economics, Many Recipes*. Princeton: Princeton University Press.

Roemer, J.E. (1979) 'Continuing Controversy on the Falling Rate of Profit, Fixed Capital and Other Issues', *Cambridge Journal of Economics* 3, pp.379–398.

Roger, S. (2010) 'Inflation Targeting Turns 20', *Finance and Development* 47 (1), http:// www.imf.org/external/pubs/ft/fandd/2010/03/roger.htm (accessed 23 June 2018).

Rooksby, E. (2011) Towards a "Revolutionary Reformist" Strategy: Within, Outside and Against the State', *Critique* 39 (1), pp.27–51.

Roper, B. (2013) *The History of Democracy: A Marxist Interpretation.* London: Pluto Press.

Rosdolsky, R. (1977) *The Making of Marx's 'Capital'*, London: Pluto Press.

Rosenberg, J. (2000) *The Follies of Globalisation Theory*. London: Verso.

Rosenberg, J. (2005) 'Globalization Theory: A Post Mortem', *International Politics* 42, pp.2–74.

Rosenberg, S. and T. Weisskopf (1981) 'A Conflict Theory Approach to Inflation in the Postwar U.S. Economy', *American Economic Review* 71 (2), pp.42–47.

Rostow, W. (1960) *The Stages of Economic Growth: A Non-Communist Manifesto*. Cambridge: Cambridge University Press, third revised edition, 1990.

Rousseas, S. (1986) *Post Keynesian Monetary Economics*. Armonk: M.E. Sharpe.

Rousseas, S. (1989) 'On the Endogeneity of Money Once More', *Journal of Post Keynesian Economics* 11 (3), pp.474–478.

Rowthorn, B. (1980) *Capitalism, Conflict and Inflation*. London: Lawrence and Wishart.

Rubin, I.I. (1975) *Essays on Marx's Theory of Value*, Montréal, Black Rose Books.

Rubin, I.I. (1978) 'Abstract Labour and Value in Marx's System', *Capital & Class* 5: 107–140.

Rude, C. (2005) 'The Role of Financial Discipline in Imperial Strategy', in L. Panitch and C. Leys (eds.) *Socialist Register*, pp.82–107.

Saad-Filho, A. (1993) 'Money, Labour and "Labour-Money": A Review of Marx's Critique of John Gray's Monetary Analysis, *History of Political Economy* 25 (1), pp.65–84.

Saad-Filho, A. (1996) 'The Value of Money, the Value of Labour Power, and the Net Product: An Appraisal of the 'New Approach' to the Transformation Problem', in A. Freeman and G. Carchedi (eds.) *Marx and non-Equilibrium Economics*. Aldershot: Edward Elgar.

Saad-Filho, A. (1997) 'Concrete and Abstract Labour in Marx's Theory of Value', *Review of Political Economy* 9 (4), pp.457–477.

Saad-Filho, A. (2000a) 'Inflation Theory: A Critical Literature Review and a New Research Agenda', *Research in Political Economy* 18, pp.335–362.

Saad-Filho, A. (2000b). '"Vertical" versus "Horizontal" Economics: Systems of Provision, Consumption Norms and Labour Market Structures', *Capital and Class* 72, pp.209–214.

Saad-Filho, A. (2002) *The Value of Marx: Political Economy for Contemporary Capitalism*, London: Routledge.

Saad-Filho, A. (2003) 'Introduction', in: *Anti-Capitalism: A Marxist Introduction*, London: Pluto Press.

Saad-Filho, A. (2005) 'The Rise and Decline of Latin American Structuralism and Dependency Theory', in K.S. Jomo and E.S. Reinert (eds.) *The Origins of Development Economics: How Schools of Economic Thought Have Addressed Development*. London: Zed Books and New Delhi: Tulika Books.

Saad-Filho, A. (2007a) 'Monetary Policy in the Neoliberal Transition', in R. Albritton, B. Jessop and R. Westra (eds.) *Political Economy and Global Capitalism*, London, Anthem Press.

Saad-Filho, A. (2007b) 'There is Life beyond the Washington Consensus: An Intro-duction to Pro-Poor Macroeconomic Policies', *Review of Political Economy*, 19 (4), pp.513–37.

Saad-Filho, A. (2008) 'Marxian and Keynesian Critiques of Neoliberalism', in L. Pa-nitch, C. Leys, G. Albo and V. Chibber (eds.) *Socialist Register*. London: Merlin Press, pp.337–345.

Saad-Filho, A. (2011) 'Crisis *in* Neoliberalism or Crisis *of* Neoliberalism?', in L. Panitch, G. Albo and V. Chibber (eds.) *Socialist Register*. London: Merlin Press: 242–259.

Saad-Filho, A. (2014) 'The "Rise of the South"', in L. Pradella and T. Marois (eds.) *Polar-izing Development*. London: Pluto Press.

Saad-Filho, A. and D. Johnston (2005) *Neoliberalism: A Critical Reader*. London: Pluto Press.

Saad-Filho, A. and M.L.R. Mollo (2002) Inflation and Stabilization in Brazil: a Political Economy Analysis. *Review of Radical Political Economics* 34 (2), pp.109–135.

Saad-Filho, A. and G. Yalman (eds.) (2010) *Neoliberalism in Middle Income Countries: Policy Dilemmas, Economic Crises, Forms of Resistance*. London: Routledge.

Sachs, J. (2000) Interview for *Commanding Heights: The Battle for the World Economy*, 15 June, http://www.pbs.org/wgbh/commandingheights/shared/minitext/int_jef freysachs.html (accessed 6 June 2018)

Santos, A.C. (2014), 'Financial Literacy, Financialisation and Neo-liberalism', FESSUD Working Paper Series, no 11, https://ideas.repec.org/p/fes/wpaper/wpaper11.html (accessed 6 June 2018).

Sawyer, M.C. (1985) *The Economics of Michal Kalecki*. Macmillan, London.

Sawyer, M.C. (1989) *The Challenge of Radical Political Economy*. Aldershot, Edward Elgar.

Schumpeter, J. (1976) *Capitalism, Socialism and Democracy*. London: Allen and Unwin.

Seton, F. (1957) 'The "Transformation Problem"', *Review of Economic Studies* 24, pp.149–160.

Shaikh, A. (1973). *Theories of Value and Theories of Distribution*, PhD Thesis, Columbia University.

Shaikh, A. (1977) 'Marx's Theory of Value and the "Transformation Problem"', in J.G. Schwartz (ed.) *The Subtle Anatomy of Capitalism*, Santa Monica: Goodyear.

Shaikh, A. (1981) 'The Poverty of Algebra', in I. Steedman (ed.) *The Value Controversy*, London: Verso.

Shaikh, A. (1982) 'Neo-Ricardian Economics, A Wealth of Algebra, a Poverty of Theory', *Review of Radical Political Economics* 14, 2: 67–83.

Shaikh, A. (1984) 'The Transformation from Marx to Sraffa', in E. Mandel and A. Free-man (eds.) *Ricardo, Marx, Sraffa*, London: Verso.

Sherman, H. (1972) 'Inflation, Profits and the New Economic Policy', *Review of Radical Political Economics* 4 (4), pp.113–121.

Sherman, H. (1976a) *Stagflation: A Radical Theory of Unemployment and Inflation*. New York: Harper and Row.

Sherman, H. (1976b) 'Inflation, Unemployment, and Monopoly Capital', *Monthly Review* 27 (10), pp.25–35.

Slater, P. (ed.) (1980) *Outlines of a Critique of Technology*, Atlantic Highlands: Humanities Press.

Smith, A (2009) *An Inquiry into the Nature and Causes of the Wealth of Nations*, http://www.gutenberg.org/files/3300/3300-h/3300-h.htm (accessed 6 June 2018).

Smith, H. (2000) 'Introduction', in: *Democracy and International Relations: Critical Theories, Problematic Practices*. Basingstoke: Macmillan.

Smith, M. (1994) *Invisible Leviathan: The Marxist Critique of Market Despotism beyond Postmodernism*, Toronto: University of Toronto Press.

Spero, N. (1969) 'Notes on the Current Inflation', *Monthly Review* 21 (2), pp.29–32.

Ste. Croix, G. de (1984) 'Class in Marx's Conception of History', *New Left Review* 146, pp.94–111.

Stedman Jones, D. (2012) *Masters of the Universe: Hayek, Friedman, and the Birth of Neoliberal Politics*. Princeton: Princeton University Press.

Steindl, J. (1952) *Maturity and Stagnation in American Capitalism*. Oxford: Blackwell.

Stiglitz, J. (1998) "More Instruments and Broader Goals: Moving toward the Post-Washington Consensus", *WIDER Annual Lecture* 2, https://www.wider.unu.edu/publication/more-instruments-and-broader-goals-0.

Stiglitz, J. (2010a) *Freefall: America, Free Markets, and the Sinking of the World Economy*, London: Allen Lane.

Stiglitz, J. (2010b) 'The Non-Existent Hand', *London Review of Books*, 22 April, https://www.lrb.co.uk/v32/n08/joseph-stiglitz/the-non-existent-hand (accessed 17 June 2018).

Strauss-Kahn, D. (2010) 'World Can Grow Faster With Right Policies', http://www.imf.org/external/pubs/ft/survey/so/2010/NEW060510A.htm (accessed 17 June 2018).

Svensson, L.E.O. (1997a) 'Optimal Inflation Targets, "Conservative" Central Banks, and Linear Inflation Contracts', *American Economic Review* 87 (1): 98–114.

Svensson, L.E.O. (1997b) 'Inflation Forecast Targeting: Implementing and Monitoring Inflation Targets', *European Economic Review* 41: 1111–1146.

Sweezy, P. (1968) *The Theory of Capitalist Development*, New York: Monthly Review Press.

Sweezy, P. (1974) 'Baran and the Danger of Inflation', *Monthly Review* 27 (7), pp.11–14.

Sweezy, P. and H. Magdoff (1970) 'Notes on Inflation and the Dollar', *Monthly Review* 21 (10), pp.1–13.

Sweezy, P. and H. Magdoff (1979) 'Inflation without End?', *Monthly Review* 31 (6), pp.1–10.

Sweezy, P. and H. Magdoff (1983) 'Supply-side Theory and Capital investment', *Monthly Review* 34, pp.1–9.

Szumski, J. (1989) 'The Transformation Problem Solved?' *Cambridge Journal of Economics* 13, pp.431–452.

Szumski, J. (1991) 'On Duménil and Lévy's Denial of the Existence of the So-Called Transformation Problem: A Reply', *Cambridge Journal of Economics* 15 (3), pp.365–371.

Szymanski, A. (1984) 'Productivity Growth and Capitalist Stagnation', *Science and Society* 48 (3), pp.295–322.

Tamás, G.M. (2011) *The Failure of Liberal Democracy*, http://www.socialistproject.ca/leftstreamed/ls115.php (accessed 6 June 2018)

Tcherneva, P. (2015) 'When a Rising Tide Sinks Most Boats: Trends in US Income Inequality', *Levy Economics Institute of Bard College, Policy Note 2015/4*, http://www.levyinstitute.org/publications/when-a-rising-tide-sinks-most-boats-trends-in-us-income-inequality (accessed 23 June 2018).

Tett, G. (2009a) *Fool's Gold: How Unrestrained Greed Corrupted a Dream*. London: Little, Brown & Co.

Tett, G. (2009b) 'Lost Through Destructive Creation', https://www.ft.com/content/0d55351a-0ce4-11de-a555-0000779fd2ac, 9 March 2009 (accessed 17 June 2018).

The Economist (2008) 'Capitalism at Bay', 16 October 2008.

Therborn, G. (1977) 'The Rule Of Capital and the Rise of Democracy', *New Left Review* 103, pp.3–41.

Thompson, E.P. (1978) *The Poverty of Theory*. London: Merlin Press.

Thornton, H. (1802) *An Enquiry into the Nature and Effects of the Paper Credit of Great Britain*. London: George Allen and Unwin, 1939.

Trilateral Commission (1975) *The Crisis of Democracy: Report on the Governability of Democracies to the Trilateral Commission*. New York NY: New York University Press.

Tully, J. (2006) *Understanding Imperialism Today: From Colonial Imperialism, Through Decolonization to Post-Colonial Imperialism*. Cambridge: Cambridge University Press.

Tully, J. (2008) 'On Law, Democracy and Imperialism', in: E. Christodoulidis and S. Tierney (eds.) *Political Theory and Public Law*. London: Ashgate, pp.69–102.

UNCTAD (2012) *Trade and Development Report: Policies for Inclusive and Balanced Growth*, http://unctad.org/en/PublicationsLibrary/tdr2012_en.pdf (accessed 23 June 2018).

Van der Pijl, K. (2011) 'Arab Revolts and Nation-State Crisis', *New Left Review* 70, pp.27–49.

Van Waeyenberge, E. (2007) *Exploring the Emergence of a New Aid Regime: Selectivity, Knowledge and the World Bank*, PhD thesis, University of London.

Volcker, P.A. (2008) *The Economic Club of New York*, 101st Year, 395th Meeting, http://classic-web.archive.org/web/20081031090245/http://econclubny.org/files/Transcript_Volcker_April_2008.pdf (accessed 23 June 2018).

Vroey, M. de (1981) 'Value, Production and Exchange', in I. Steedman (ed.) *The Value Controversy*, London: Verso.

Vroey, M. de (1982) 'On the Obsolescence of the Marxian Theory of Value: A Critical Review', *Capital & Class* 17, pp.34–59.

Vroey, M. de (1984) 'Inflation: A Non-Monetarist Monetary Interpretation', *Cambridge Journal of Economics* 8, pp.381–399.

Vroey, M. de (1985). 'La Theorie Marxiste de la Valeur, Version Travail Abstrait: Un Bilan Critique', in G. Dostaler and M. Lagueux (eds.) *Un Echiquier Centenaire: Théorie de la Valeur et Formation des Prix.* Paris: La Découverte.

Wacquant, L (2009) *The Neoliberal Government of Social Insecurity.* Durham, NC: Duke University Press.

Wade, R (2013) 'How High Inequality plus Neoliberal Governance Weakens Democracy', *Challenge*, 56 (6), pp.5–37.

Watkins, S. (2010) 'Shifting Sands', *New Left Review* 61, pp.5–27.

WDM [World Development Movement] (2000) *States of Unrest: Resistance to IMF Policies in Poor Countries.* London: World Development Movement.

Weber, M. (1972) 'Politics as a Vocation', in: H.H. Gerth and C.W. Mills (eds.) *From Max Weber.* New York NY: Oxford University Press, pp.77–128.

Weber, M. (1978) *Economy and Society,* 2 Volumes. Berkeley: University of California Press.

Webster, E, K Joynt and A Metcalfe (2013) *Repositioning Peak-Level Social Dialogue in South Africa: NEDLAC into the Future.* Johannesburg: NEDLAC.

Weeks, J. (1977) 'The Sphere of Production and the Analysis of Crisis in Capitalism', *Science and Society* 41 (3), pp.281–302.

Weeks, J. (1979) 'The Process of Accumulation and the Profit Squeeze Hypothesis', *Science and Society* 43 (3), pp.259–280.

Weeks, J. (1981) *Capital and Exploitation.* London: Edward Arnold.

Weeks, J. (1982) 'A Note on Underconsumptionist Theory and the Labour Theory of Value', *Science and Society* 46 (1), pp.60–76.

Weeks, J. (1983) 'On the Issue of Capitalist Circulation and the Concepts Appropriate to Its Analysis', *Science & Society* 48, 2: 214–225.

Weeks, J. (2010) *Capital, Exploitation and Crises.* London: Routledge.

Weintraub, S. (1981) 'An Eclectic Theory of Income Shares', *Journal of Post Keynesian Economics* 4(1), pp.10–24.

Weisskopf, T., S. Bowles and D. Gordon (1985) 'Two Views of Capitalist Stagnation: Underconsumption and Challenges to Capitalist Control', *Science and Society* 49 (3), pp.259–286.

Weller, C.E. (2001) 'Financial Crises after Financial Liberalisation: Exceptional Circumstances or Structural Weakness?', *Journal of Development Studies* 38 (1), pp.98–127.

Wells, D. (1992) 'Consumerism and the Value of Labour Power', *Review of Radical Political Economics* 24 (2), pp.26–33.

Williamson, J. (1993) Democracy and the "Washington consensus"', *World Development* 21 (8), pp.1329–1336.

Williamson, J. (2007) 'Shock Therapy and the Washington Consensus: A Comment', *Comparative Economic Studies* 49 (1), pp.59–60.

Winternitz, J. (1948) 'Values and Prices, A Solution to the So-Called Transformation Problem', *Economic Journal* 58, 2: 276–280.

Witztum, A (2013) *Behavioural Economics, Game Theory and Das Adam Smith Problem*, http://www.eshet.net/conference/paper_view.php?id=1012&p=38 (accessed 6 June 2018).

Wolf, M. (2009a) 'Is America the New Russia?', *Financial Times*, 14 April, https://www .ft.com/content/09f8c996-2930-11de-bc5e-00144feabdc0 (accessed 16 June 2018).

Wolf, M. (2009b) *Seeds of Its Own Destruction*, https://www.ft.com/content/c6c5bd36 -0c0c-11de-b87d-0000779fd2ac *Financial Times* 8 March 2009 (accessed 17 June 2018).

Wolf, M. (2010) 'Why Cautious Reform Of Finance Is The Risky Option', *Financial Times*, 28 April, p.13.

Wolin, S. (2008) *Democracy Inc.* Princeton NJ: Princeton University Press.

Wood, E.M. (1981) 'The Separation of the Economic and the Political in Capitalism', *New Left Review* 127, pp.66–95.

Wood, E.M. (1988) 'Capitalism and Human Emancipation', *New Left Review* 167, pp.3–20.

Wood, E.M. (1995) *Democracy against Capitalism: Renewing Historical Materialism.* Cambridge: Cambridge University Press.

Wood, E.M. (2002) 'Global Capital, National States', in M. Rupert and H. Smith (eds.) *Now More Than Ever: Historical Materialism and Globalisation.* London: Routledge.

Wood, E.M. (2008) *Citizens to Lords: A Social History of Western Political Thought from Antiquity to the Middle Ages.* London: Verso.

World Bank (1993) *The East Asian Miracle: Economic Growth and Public Policy, A World Bank Policy Research Report.* Oxford: Oxford University Press.

Worrell, M.P. (2011) *Why Nations Go to War: A Sociology of Military Conflict.* New York NY: Routledge.

Worrell, M.P. (2013) *Terror: Social, Political, and Economic Perspectives.* New York NY: Routledge.

Wray, L.R. (2014) *Central Bank Independence: Myth and Misunderstanding*, Levy Institute Working Paper no.791, www.levyinstitute.org/pubs/wp_791.pdf (accessed 23 June 2018).

Wray, R. (1990) *Money and Credit in Capitalist Economies.* Aldershot: Edward Elgar.

Wright, E.O. (1977) 'Alternative Perspectives in Marxist Theory of Accumulation and Crisis', in J.G. Schwartz (ed.) *The Subtle Anatomy of Capitalism*, Santa Monica: Goodyear.

Zacharia, F. (1997) 'The Rise of Illiberal Democracy', http://www.foreignaffairs.com/articles/53577/fareed-zakaria/the-rise-of-illiberal-democracy (accessed 6 June 2018).

Zacharia, F. (2004) *The Future of Freedom: Illiberal Democracy at Home and Abroad.* London: WW Norton.

Zarifian, P. (1975) *Inflation et Crise Monétaire.* Paris: Editions Sociales.

Zysman, J (1983) *Governments, Markets and Growth.* London: Cornell University Press.

Index

www.ingramcontent.com/pod-product-compliance
Lightning Source LLC
Chambersburg PA
CBHW070901030426
42336CB00014BA/2287